CONTENTS

<u>ANSWER KEY</u>

1.1. – RATE OF CHANGE

In the world that surrounds us things change: the temperature, the direction and strength of the wind, the prices of products, the velocity of objects, population size, our height, weight etc.

Example 1: Oil prices, represented as a function of time P(t):
1. As you can see there have been periods of time in history in which the prices

Price of oil

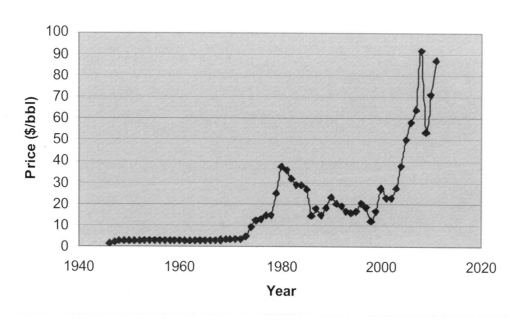

have changed slowly, Identify one of them: _____

2. In other periods the prices have been changing very quickly, identify one

    positive change: _____ and one negative change: _____

3. In this graph what are the <u>units</u> of the <u>change</u> of price: _____

4. Find the <u>average rate of change</u> in oil prices between 1970 and 1985. Is this average similar to the real change in prices? Explain your answer.

5. Find the average rate of change between 1945 and 2005, how can this change be represented graphically?

Example 2: Population of 20 – 29 year olds in southern Europe for example, represented as a function of time P(t):

Spain´s Birth Rate

6. During what period of time the fastest change occurs? _____

7. In this graph what are the <u>units</u> of the <u>change</u> of birth:_____

8. Find the <u>average rate of change</u> between 1960 and 2000. Is this average similar to the real change in births? Explain your answer.

9. Find the average rate of change between 2000 and 2010, how can this change be represented graphically?

1.2. – DEFINITION OF DERIVATIVE

1. The derivative is the _____

2. Given the function, sketch the tangent in each one of the points:

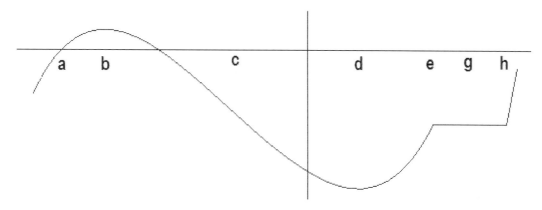

Fill the table with: Positive, negative, zero or doesn't exist.

	x = a	x = b	x = c	x = d	x = e	x = g	x = h
f(x)							
f'(x)							

3. Given the function, sketch the tangent in each one of the points:

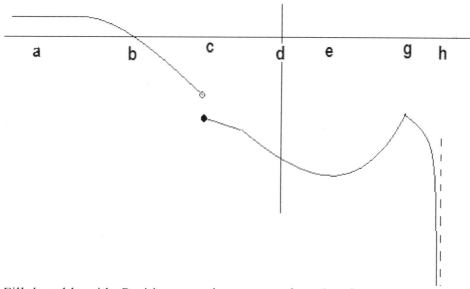

Fill the table with: Positive, negative, zero or doesn't exist.

	x = a	x = b	x = c	x = d	x = e	x = g	x = h
f(x)							
f'(x)							

4. Given the function $f(x) = -x^2$. f represents the temperature as the function of height x given in km:

5. Fill the blanks and indicate the corresponding points on the graph:

   f(1) = ___   f(1.4) = ___

   Draw the line that connects the points and find its slope

   m = ___

6. Fill the blanks and indicate the corresponding points on the graph:

   f(1) = ___   f(1.2) = ___

   Draw the line that connects the points and find its slope

   m = ___

(Graph shown at right: y-axis labeled with values 0.7, 0.4, 0.1, −0.5, −0.8, −1.1, −1.4, −1.7, −2, −2.3, −2.6, −2.9, −3.2, −3.5, −3.8, −4.1, −4.4, −4.7; x-axis labeled −0.2, 0.2, 0.4, 0.6, 0.8, 1, 1.2, 1.4, 1.6, 1.8, with the downward-opening parabola of f(x) = −x².)

7. Fill the blanks and indicate the corresponding points on the graph:

   f(1) = ___   f(1.1) = ___ .

   Draw the line that connects the points and find its slope

   m = ___

8. What do you think the slope of the tangent at the point where x = 1 is? _____

9. Looking at the process to find the slope at the point where x = 1, can you think how to find the slope of the tangent in general?

10. What does the slope **between 2 points** represent? Make reference to height and temperature and give units.

11. What does the slope of the tangent to the function **at a certain point** (the derivative) represent? Make reference to height and temperature and give units.

12. The slope between 2 points is _____

13. The slope at a certain point is _____

8

FORMAL DEFINITION OF DERIVATIVE

Definition: Let y = f(x) be a function. The derivative of f is the function whose value at x is the limit:

$$f'(x) = \lim_{h \to 0} \frac{f(x+h) - f(x)}{h}$$

Provided this limit exists. If this limit exists for each x in an open interval (a, b), then we say that f is differentiable on [a, b].

Differentiate the following functions, use the definition ONLY:

1. $f(x) = mx + b$

$$\frac{df}{dx} = f'(x) = \lim_{h \to 0} \frac{f(x+h) - f(x)}{h} = \lim_{h \to 0} \frac{\underline{\quad\quad\quad} - \underline{\quad\quad\quad}}{h} =$$

2. $f(x) = x^2 + k$

$$\frac{df}{dx} = f'(x) = \lim_{h \to 0} \frac{f(x+h) - f(x)}{h} = \lim_{h \to 0} \frac{\underline{\quad\quad\quad} - \underline{\quad\quad\quad}}{h} =$$

3. $f(x) = x^3 + k$

$$\frac{df}{dx} = f'(x) = \lim_{h \to 0} \frac{f(x+h) - f(x)}{h} = \lim_{h \to 0} \frac{\underline{\quad\quad\quad} - \underline{\quad\quad\quad}}{h} =$$

4. $f(x) = 4x - 3x^2$

$$\frac{df}{dx} = f'(x) = \lim_{h \to 0} \frac{f(x+h) - f(x)}{h} = \lim_{h \to 0} \frac{\underline{\quad\quad\quad} - \underline{\quad\quad\quad}}{h} =$$

5. $f(x) = \sqrt{x+1}$

$$\frac{df}{dx} = f'(x) = \lim_{h \to 0} \frac{f(x+h) - f(x)}{h} = \lim_{h \to 0} \frac{\underline{\qquad} - \underline{\qquad}}{h} =$$

6. $f(x) = \dfrac{1}{2x+1}$

$$\frac{df}{dx} = f'(x) = \lim_{h \to 0} \frac{f(x+h) - f(x)}{h} = \lim_{h \to 0} \frac{\underline{\qquad} - \underline{\qquad}}{h} =$$

7. $f(x) = \dfrac{-3}{-x+2}$

$$\frac{df}{dx} = f'(x) = \lim_{h \to 0} \frac{f(x+h) - f(x)}{h} = \lim_{h \to 0} \frac{\underline{\qquad} - \underline{\qquad}}{h} =$$

8. $f(x) = \sqrt{2x} + 1$

$$\frac{df}{dx} = f'(x) = \lim_{h \to 0} \frac{f(x+h) - f(x)}{h} = \lim_{h \to 0} \frac{\underline{\qquad} - \underline{\qquad}}{h} =$$

9. $f(x) = \sqrt{3x-5} + 1$

$$\frac{df}{dx} = f'(x) = \lim_{h \to 0} \frac{f(x+h) - f(x)}{h} = \lim_{h \to 0} \frac{ - }{h} =$$

10. $f(x) = \dfrac{4}{5x+1} + 2$

$$\frac{df}{dx} = f'(x) = \lim_{h \to 0} \frac{f(x+h) - f(x)}{h} = \lim_{h \to 0} \frac{ - }{h} =$$

11. $f(x) = \sqrt{2x-3}$

$$\frac{df}{dx} = f'(x) = \lim_{h \to 0} \frac{f(x+h) - f(x)}{h} = \lim_{h \to 0} \frac{ - }{h} =$$

12. $f(x) = \dfrac{1}{3x-4}$

$$\frac{df}{dx} = f'(x) = \lim_{h \to 0} \frac{f(x+h) - f(x)}{h} = \lim_{h \to 0} \frac{ - }{h} =$$

13. Given the following function:

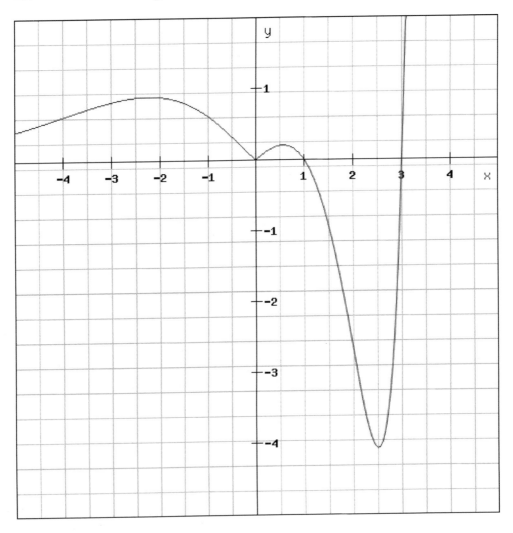

Find:

a. $f(-4) =$ ___ $f'(-4) =$ ___

b. $f(-3) =$ ___ $f'(-3) =$ ___

c. $f(-2.3) =$ ___ $f'(-2.3) =$ ___

d. $f(-1) =$ ___ $f'(-1) =$ ___

e. $f(0) =$ ___ $f'(0) =$ ___

f. $f(0.2) =$ ___ $f'(0.2) =$ ___

g. $f(0.6) =$ ___ $f'(0.6) =$ ___

h. $f(2) =$ ___ $f'(2) =$ ___

i. $f(2.5) =$ ___ $f'(2.5) =$ ___

j. $f(3) =$ ___ $f'(3) =$ ___

Use the information obtained to sketch the derivative on the same graph.

14. When the derivative is positive it means that the function is _____.

15. When the derivative is _____ it means that the function is _____.

16. When the derivative is zero it means that the function has_____.

1.3. – GRAPHING THE DERIVATIVE (GRADIENT FUNCTION)

Draw the graph of the derivative of the following functions on the graph below:

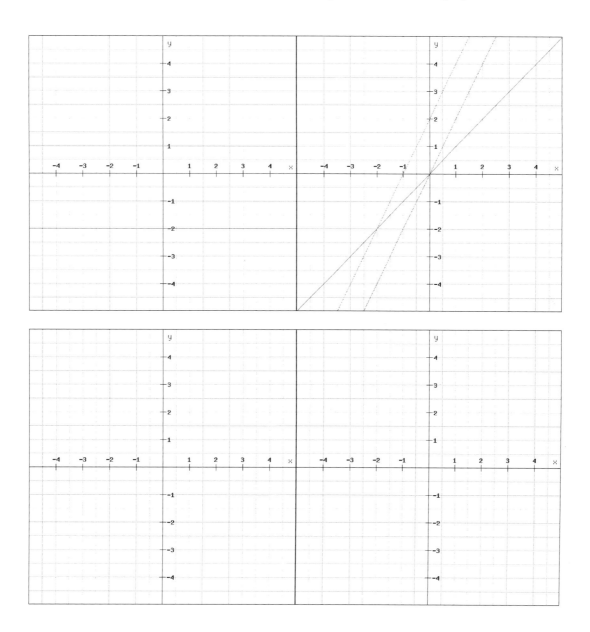

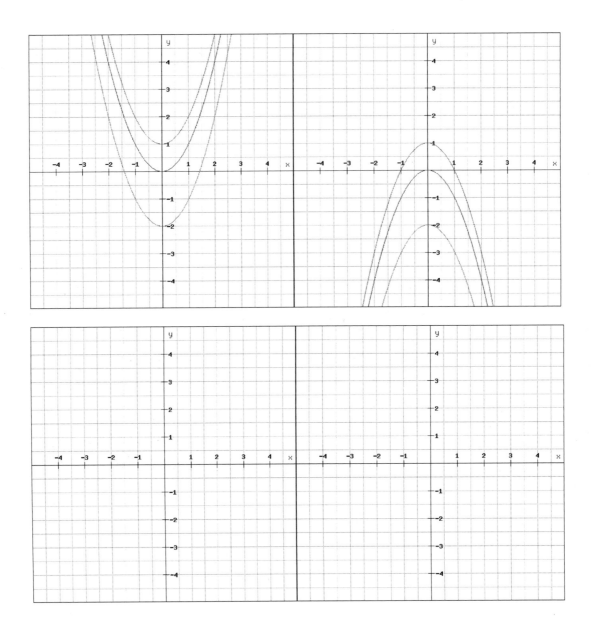

14

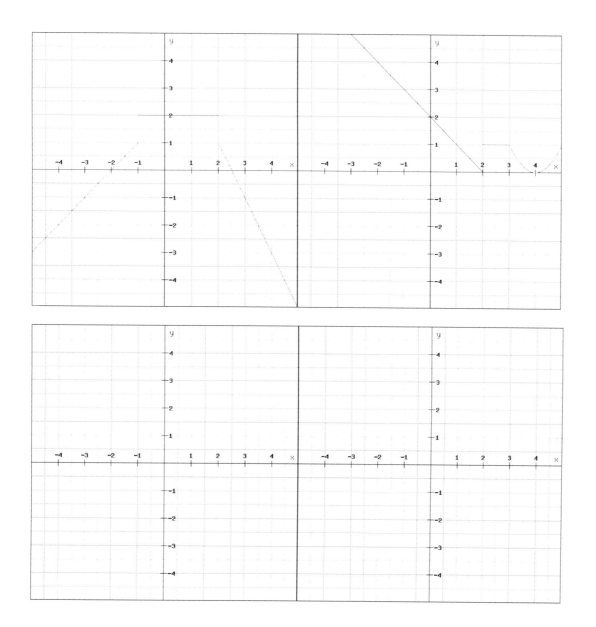

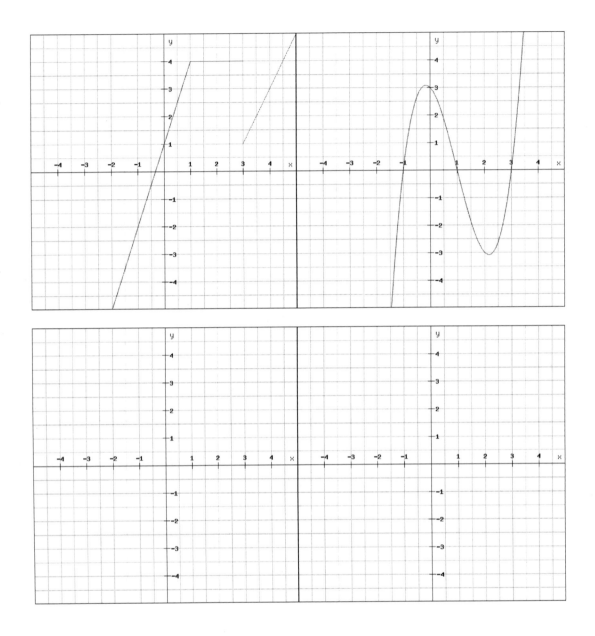

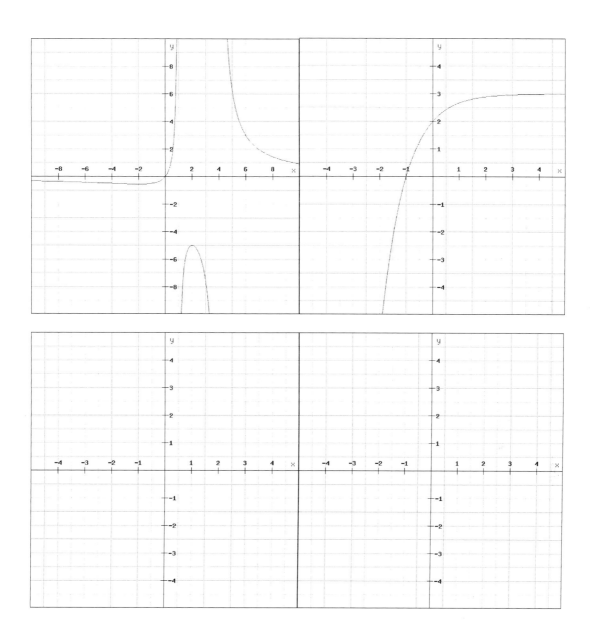

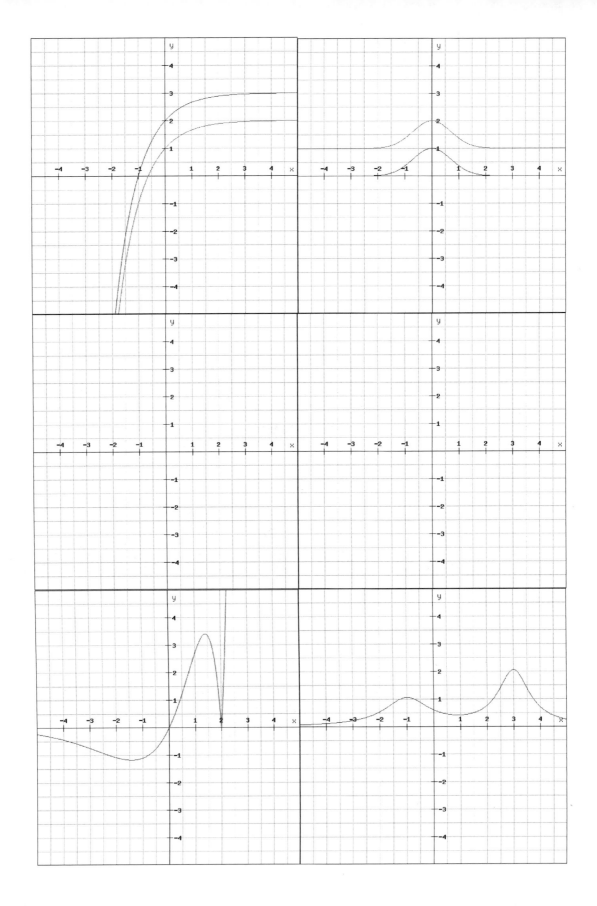

1.4. – GRAPHING THE ANTIDERIVATIVE

Draw the graph of the derivative of the following functions on the graph below:

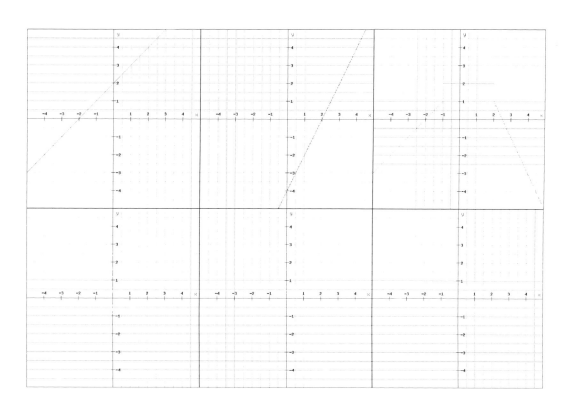

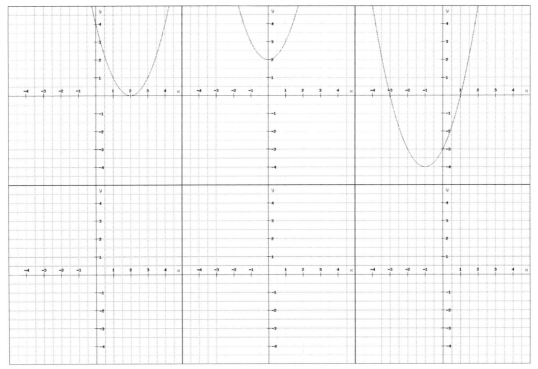

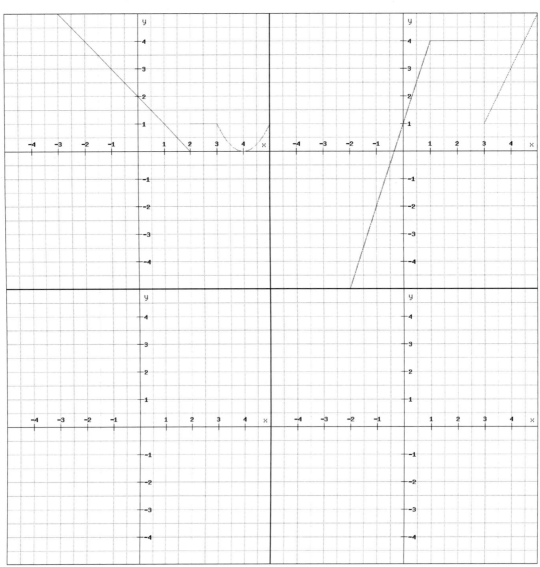

20

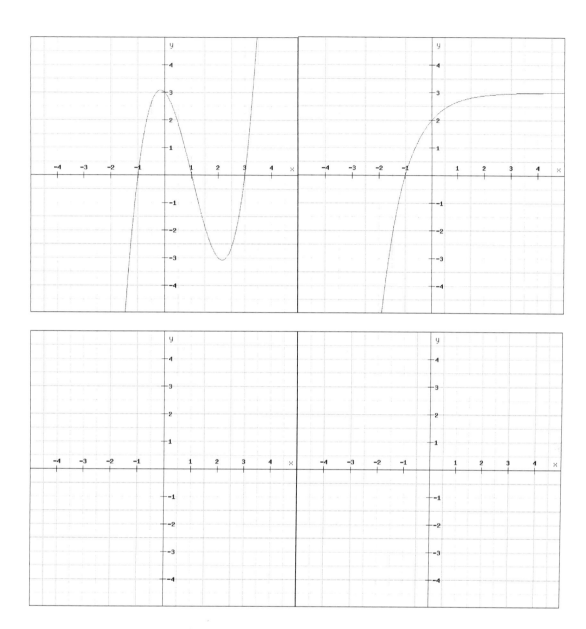

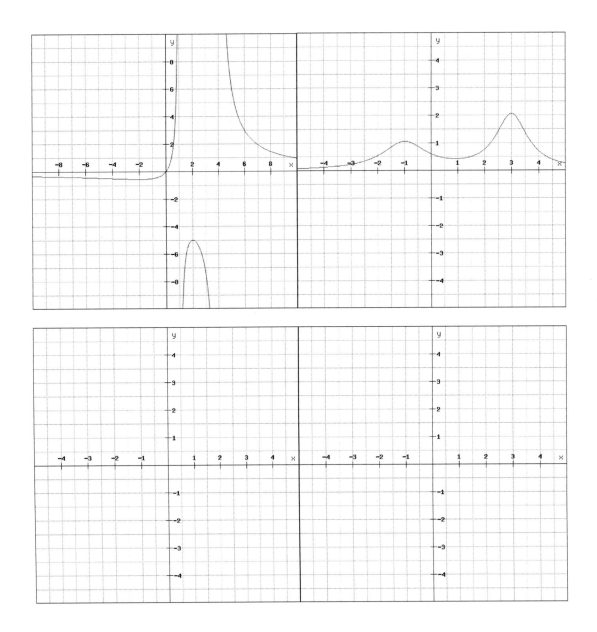

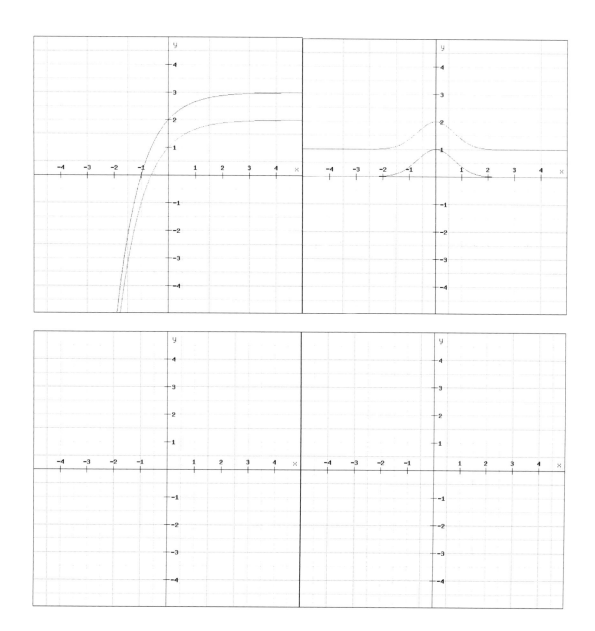

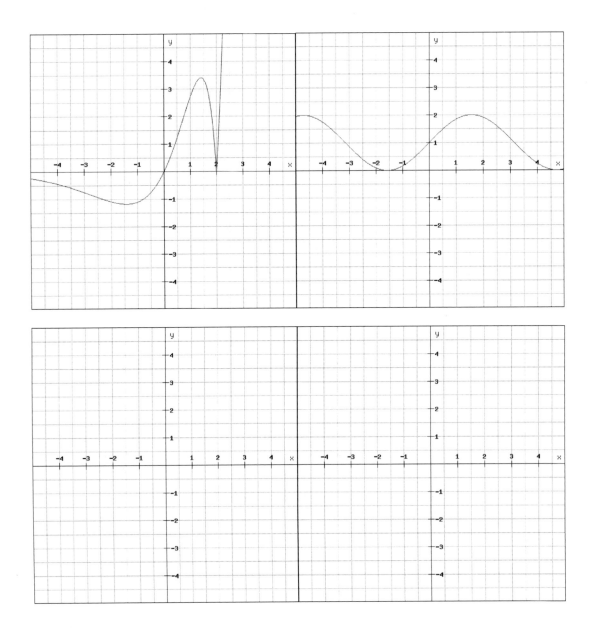

1.5. – TANGENTS AND NORMALS TO FUNCTIONS

1. Given the function $f(x) = 2x^2$. Sketch it.

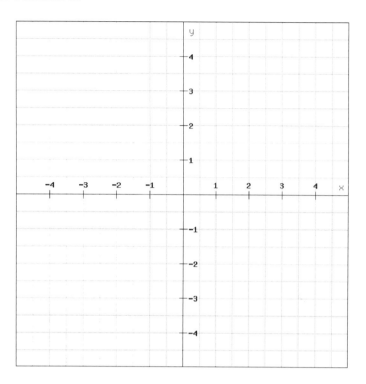

a. Find its derivative (use the definition).

$$f'(x) = \lim_{h \to 0} \frac{f(x+h) - f(x)}{h} = \lim_{h \to 0} \frac{\overline{\qquad} - \overline{\qquad}}{h} =$$

b. Find the slope of the tangent to the function at the point with x = 1. Show the slope found on the graph.

c. Find the slope of the tangent to the function at the point with x = 0. Show the slope found on the graph.

d. Find the point in which the slope of the tangent to the function is 3. Show the point and slope on the graph.

e. Find the point in which the slope of the tangent to the function is –4. Show the point and slope on the graph.

f. Find the point in which the tangent to the function is parallel to the line y = 2x + 3. Show the point, the tangent and the line on the graph.

g. Find the point in which the tangent to the function is parallel to the line y = –5x + 3. Show the point, the tangent and the line on the graph.

h. Find the equation of the tangent to the function at the point with x = 1. Sketch the tangent on graph.

i. Find the equation of the tangent and normal to the function at the point with x = 0. Sketch the tangent and normal on graph.

j. Find the equation of the tangent and normal to the function at the point with x = –2. Sketch the tangent and normal on the graph.

2. Given the function $f(x) = -\dfrac{2}{x} + 1$. Sketch it.

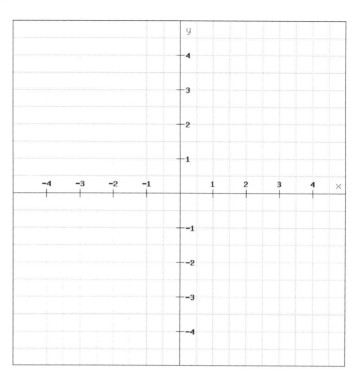

a. Find its derivative (use the definition).

$$f'(x) = \lim_{h \to 0} \frac{f(x+h) - f(x)}{h} = \lim_{h \to 0} \frac{\underline{\hspace{3cm}} - \underline{\hspace{3cm}}}{h} =$$

b. Find the slope of the tangent to the function at the point with x = 1. Show the slope found on the graph.

c. Find the slope of the tangent to the function at the point with x = 0. Show the slope found on the graph.

d. Find the slope of the tangent to the function at the point with $x = \dfrac{1}{2}$.

Show the slope found on the graph.

e. Find the point in which the slope of the tangent to the function is –3. Show the point and slope on the graph.

f. Find the point in which the slope of the tangent to the function is $\frac{1}{2}$. Show the point and slope on the graph.

g. Find the point in which the tangent to the function is parallel to the line $y = -\frac{5}{3}x + 3$. Show the point, the tangent and the line on the graph.

h. Find that point in which the tangent to the function is parallel to the line $y = 6x + 3$. Show the point, the tangent and the line on the graph.

i. Find the equation of the tangent to the function at the point with $x = 1$. Sketch the tangent on graph.

j. Find the equation of the tangent and normal to the function at the point with $x = 0$. Sketch the tangent and normal on graph.

k. Find the equation of the tangent and normal to the function at the point with $x = \frac{1}{2}$. Sketch the tangent and normal on graph.

3. Given the function $f(x) = -x^2 - x$. Sketch it.

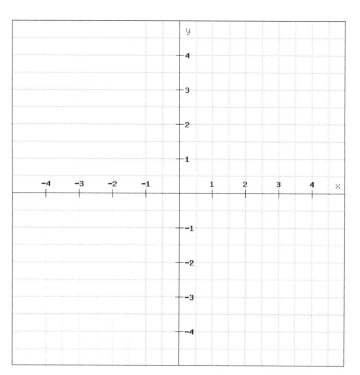

    a. Find its derivative (use the definition).

$$f'(x) = \lim_{h \to 0} \frac{f(x+h) - f(x)}{h} = \lim_{h \to 0} \frac{\underline{} - \underline{}}{h} =$$

    b. Find the slope of the tangent to the function at the point with $x = -1$.
        Show the slope found on the graph.

    c. Find the slope of the tangent to the function at the point with $x = 2$.
        Show the slope found on the graph.

    d. Find the slope of the tangent to the function at the point with $x = -4$.
        Show the slope found on the graph.

    e. Find the point in which the slope of the tangent to the function is 2.
        Show the point and slope on the graph.

f. Find the point in which the slope of the tangent to the function is –2.3. Show the point and slope on the graph.

g. Find the point in which the tangent to the function is parallel to the line $y = 3x + 1$. Show the point, the tangent and the line on the graph.

h. Find the point in which the tangent to the function is parallel to the line $y = -5x + 3$. Show the point, the tangent and the line on the graph.

i. Find the equation of the tangent to the function at the point with $x = -1$. Sketch the tangent on graph.

j. Find the equation of the tangent and normal to the function at the point with $x = 2$. Sketch the tangent and normal on graph.

k. Find the equation of the tangent and normal to the function at the point with $x = -4$. Sketch the tangent and normal on graph.

4. Given the function $f(x) = -3x^2 + 1$. Sketch it.

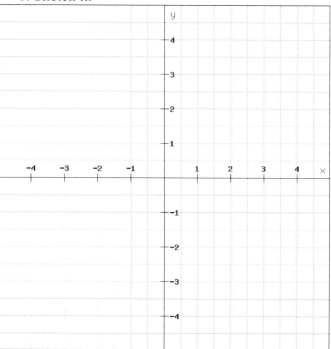

a. Find its derivative (use the definition).

$$f'(x) = \lim_{h \to 0} \frac{f(x+h) - f(x)}{h} = \lim_{h \to 0} \frac{\underline{\hspace{1cm}} - \underline{\hspace{1cm}}}{h} =$$

b. Find $f'(1) = \underline{\hspace{1cm}}$. Show it on the graph.

c. Find $f'(0) = \underline{\hspace{1cm}}$. Show it on the graph.

d. Find $f'(2) = \underline{\hspace{1cm}}$. Show it on the graph.

e. Given that $f'(x) = 3$, find x. Show it on the graph.

f. Given that $f'(x) = -4$, find x. Show it on the graph.

g. Find the point in which the tangent to the function is parallel to the line $y = -5x + 3$. Show the point and tangent on the graph.

h. Find the equation of the tangent and normal to the function at the point with x = 0. Sketch the tangent and normal on graph.

5. Given the function f(x) = $\dfrac{3}{x-2}$. Sketch it.

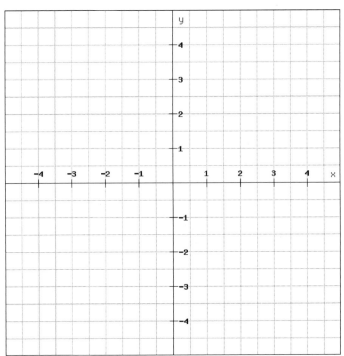

a. Find its derivative (use the definition).

$$f'(x) = \lim_{h \to 0} \frac{f(x+h) - f(x)}{h} = \lim_{h \to 0} \frac{\underline{\qquad} - \underline{\qquad}}{h} = $$

b. Find $f'(1) = $ _____. Show it on the graph.

c. Find $f'(2) = $ _____. Show it on the graph.

d. Find $f'(\frac{1}{2}) = $ _____. Show it on the graph.

e. Given that $f'(x) = -3$, find x. Show it on the graph.

f. Given that $f'(x) = \dfrac{1}{2}$, find x. Show it on the graph.

g. Find the point in which the tangent to the function is parallel to the line $y = -\frac{5}{3}x + 3$. Show the point, the line and the tangent on the graph.

h. Find the equation of the tangent to the function at the point with $x = 1$. Sketch the tangent on graph.

i. Find the equation of the tangent and normal to the function at the point with $x = 2$. Sketch the tangent and normal on graph.

j. Find the equation of the tangent and normal to the function at the point with $x = \frac{1}{2}$. Sketch the tangent and normal on graph.

1.6. – DERIVATIVES

Polynomial Functions Differentiate the following functions:

$$f(x) = x^n$$

$$f'(x) = nx^{n-1}$$

1. $f(x) = 5$

2. $f(x) = 3$

3. $f(x) = x$

4. $f(x) = 5x$

5. $f(x) = 5kx+1$

6. $f(x) = -2x$

7. $f(x) = -2x - 3$

8. $f(x) = -2x + 3$

9. $f(x) = x^2 + 3x - 10$

10. $f(x) = x^2 + 7x - 1$

11. $f(x) = bx^6 + 2x + 7$

12. $f(x) = x^{22} + x - 1$

13. $f(x) = x^4 + 2x + 1$

14. $f(x) = x^5 + x$

15. $f(x) = x^{22} - \dfrac{1}{x}$

16. $f(x) = x^2 - 2x + \dfrac{1}{x^2}$

17. $f(x) = a\,x^5 - 2x^4 - \dfrac{5}{x^2} + \dfrac{1}{x^3}$

18. $f(x) = 5x^2 - 10x + \dfrac{1}{x^{\frac{2}{3}}} + \dfrac{1}{x^{-2}}$

19. $f(x) = -5x^{20} - \dfrac{1}{x^{-2}}$

20. $f(x) = -x^3 + 6x^2 - 8 - \sqrt{x} - \sqrt[3]{x}$

21. $f(x) = -x^5 - 6x^2 + 2x + \sqrt{x^6} - \sqrt[3]{x^4}$

22. $f(x) = -x^7 + x^2 - 5x - x\sqrt{x} - x\sqrt[3]{x} - \sqrt[3]{x^{-2}}$

23. $f(x) = -bx^4 - 4x^2 - 4$

24. $f(x) = -x^{-2} + 3x$

25. $f(x) = -15x^{-2} - 3x^{-5}$

26. $f(x) = \dfrac{5}{2}x^{-3} - b6x$

27. $f(x) = \dfrac{1}{6}x^3 - 3 + \dfrac{\sqrt{x}+3}{3} - \dfrac{1+x\sqrt{2}}{7}$

28. $f(x) = \dfrac{2}{3}x^{\frac{2}{3}} - 3x^{\frac{1}{2}} + 2e^2 - x\log(3)$

29. $f(x) = 3x^2 + \dfrac{2}{3}x^{\frac{4}{9}} - 5x^{\frac{2}{5}}$

30. $f(x) = x^2 + 3x + 4 + 3x^2 + b\dfrac{7}{6}x^{-\frac{4}{9}} - 5x^{\frac{3}{2}}$

31. $f(x) = -12x - 13 + 3bx + 4 + 3x^{-3} + \dfrac{7}{6}x^{-\frac{1}{9}} - 5x^{\frac{-7}{2}}$

32. $f(x) = -x^3 + 6x^2 - 8 - x\sqrt{x} - \sqrt[3]{x} + \cos(4)x^{-1}$

33. $f(x) = x^2 + 9x - 4 + 3x^2 + \dfrac{7}{6}x^{-\frac{4}{9}} - 5x^{\frac{3}{2}} + \ln(2)x^2$

34. $f(x) = 8x - x\sqrt{x} - \sqrt[3]{2x}$

35. $f(x) = -x^3 + 6x^{22} - 8 - x\sqrt{x} - \sqrt[3]{x}x^2$

Exponential functions:

36. $f(x) = 8x - e^x$

37. $f(x) = 2e^x - x$

38. $f(x) = 5e^x - \sqrt{x} - \sqrt[3]{2x}$

39. $f(x) = -3e^x - x\sqrt{x} - \sqrt[5]{x^2}$

$$\boxed{\begin{array}{l} f(x) = e^x \\[4pt] f'(x) = e^x \end{array}}$$

Logarithmic functions:

40. $f(x) = 2\ln(x) - \sqrt{x\sqrt{x}}$

41. $f(x) = \dfrac{1}{\sqrt[5]{x}} - \dfrac{\sqrt{x}}{2x} - \dfrac{\sqrt[5]{x^2}}{\sqrt{x}} - \ln(x)$

42. $f(x) = \dfrac{\sqrt{x}+3}{3} - \dfrac{1+x\sqrt{2}}{7} - \dfrac{2}{3x} + \log(x)$

$$\boxed{\begin{array}{l} f(x) = \ln(x) \\[6pt] f'(x) = \dfrac{1}{x} \\[10pt] \text{Change of base:} \\[4pt] f(x) = \log_b(x) = \dfrac{\ln(x)}{\ln(b)} \\[10pt] f'(x) = \dfrac{1}{\ln(b)x} \end{array}}$$

43. $f(x) = 2e^x - \dfrac{\ln(5)}{\sqrt{2x}} - \log_2(x)$

44. $f(x) = \ln(7) - \dfrac{\cos(1)+\sqrt{2}}{7}e^x - x\sqrt{\dfrac{1}{2x}} - 2\log_e(x)$

45. $f(x) = \cos(5) - \ln(7) - \dfrac{x\ln(11)+\sqrt{2}}{\cos(7)} - \dfrac{\sin(1)}{3+\sqrt{2}}x + \log_9(x)$

Trigonometric functions:

46. $f(x) = \ln(8) - 2e^x + \cos(x)$

47. $f(x) = \cos(2)x^2 - 23.7e^x - \sin(x)$

48. $f(x) = x^{-\frac{13}{9}} - 33^{\sqrt{2}} - 2\cos(x)$

$f(x) = \sin(x)$
$f'(x) = \cos(x)$
$f(x) = \cos(x)$
$f'(x) = -\sin(x)$

49. $f(x) = (1 + 2^{\sqrt{2}})x - e^x + 5\cos(x)$

50. $f(x) = 2\sin(x) + \sin(8)\ln(6)x - e^x$

51. $f(x) = \cos(x) + \dfrac{5\sqrt{x}}{3x} - e^x$

PRODUCT RULE $(fg)' = f'g + fg'$

52. $f(x) = (x + 2)(x + 3)$

53. $f(x) = (x^2 - 2)(x^2 + 3)$

54. $f(x) = (2x + 2)(5x^2 - 3 + e^x)$

55. $f(x) = (-x + 2 - \cos(x))(5x^8 - 3x)$

56. $f(x) = (-x^9 + 2 + \sin(x))(x + 3x^2)$

57. $f(x) = (2\ln(x) + 3x^2 + \frac{7}{6}x^{-\frac{4}{9}} - 5x^{\frac{3}{2}})(x^2 - 1 - \cos(x))$

58. $f(x) = (2\log(x) - \frac{7}{6}\frac{2}{x^{\frac{2}{3}}} - 5\frac{2}{x})(x^2 - 1) + \sin(x)$

59. $f(x) = \left(\log_3(x) + \dfrac{7}{6}\dfrac{2}{x^{\frac{2}{3}}} - 5\dfrac{2}{x}\right)(x^2 - 1 + e^x - \sin(x)) - e^x + \log_2(x)$

60. $f(x) = \left(\dfrac{1}{6}\dfrac{1}{x^{-\frac{2}{3}}} - \dfrac{2}{x^5}\right)(x^2 - \sqrt{x}) + \cos(x)$

61. $f(x) = \left(\dfrac{1}{6}x - \dfrac{2}{x^{\frac{1}{2}}}\right)\left(x^2 - \dfrac{1}{\sqrt[3]{x}} - \sin(x) + \cos(x) + e^x\right) + e^x + \cos(x)$

QUOTIENT RULE $\left(\dfrac{f}{g}\right)' = \dfrac{f'g - fg'}{g^2}$

62. $f(x) = \dfrac{x+1}{2x^2}$

63. $f(x) = \dfrac{2x^2 + x}{x^2}$

64. $f(x) = \dfrac{x^2 + \sqrt{x} + 1}{-x^4}$

65. $f(x) = \dfrac{x^{\frac{2}{3}} - x}{2x^2 + x}$

66. $f(x) = -4\dfrac{\sin(x) + x}{3x}$

67. $f(x) = \dfrac{x - \log(x)}{\log(x) + 1}$

68. $f(x) = \tan(x)$

69. $f(x) = 2\dfrac{x + e^x}{\cos(x)}$

70. $f(x) = \sec(x)$

71. $f(x) = \cos ec(x)$

72. $f(x) = \dfrac{\sin(x) + \ln(x)}{x^4}$

73. $f(x) = \dfrac{x^{-\frac{2}{5}} + \sin(x) + \ln(x)}{2x^{3.2} + 1}$

74. $f(x) = \dfrac{\sin(x)(x + 1)}{2x^2}$

75. $f(x) = \dfrac{(3x + 1)(2x + 2)}{e^x}$

76. $f(x) = \dfrac{e^x}{2x}$

CHAIN RULE $\qquad (f(g))' = f'(g)g'$

77. $f(x) = \sin(3x)$

78. $f(x) = -3\tan(-2x)$

79. $f(x) = 2\cos(6x^2)$

80. $f(x) = -(4x + 5)^2$

81. $f(x) = -3(6x - 1)^{-10}$

82. $f(x) = 2(3x^2 + 3)^{80}$

83. $f(x) = e^{4x} + 2^{2x}$

84. $f(x) = 5e^{4x} - 3^{4x}$

85. $f(x) = e^{\sin(x)}$

86. $f(x) = (5 - 3x^{2.3})^{-6}$

87. $f(x) = 5^x$

88. $f(x) = 5^{\sin(x)}$

89. $f(x) = 5^{\cos(2x)}$

90. $f(x) = (7 - x)^{-2}$

91. $f(x) = x\sin(2x)$

92. $f(x) = 4xe^{3x}$

93. $f(x) = 3x^2\cos(5x^2)$

94. $f(x) = e^x - 4^x$

95. $f(x) = -2^x + x$

96. $f(x) = 7^x - x^{10}$

97. $f(x) = 5e^x + 3^x$

98. $f(x) = \left(\dfrac{2}{3}\right)^x$

99. $f(x) = \left(\dfrac{1}{4}\right)^{x+1}$

100. $f(x) = -3x\log_2(3x + 2)$

101. $f(x) = 4x^5\log_4(5x^2 + x)$

102. $f(x) = (2 - 3x)(4 + 5x)^{-3}$

103. $f(x) = (5 - \ln(x))e^{\sin(x)}$

104. $f(x) = (\sin(3x))^3$

105. $f(x) = (4x^2 + 3x + 2 - e^x)^{\frac{5}{4}}$

106. $f(x) = \sqrt{(\sin(3x) + 2x)}$

107. $f(x) = \dfrac{3}{\sqrt{(\ln(x))}}$

108. $f(x) = x^2(\sin(3x^2 - 5x + 3) + 2x)$

109. $f(x) = \sqrt{\dfrac{2x+1}{2^x}}$

110. $f(x) = 3^{\sqrt{x}}$

111. $f(x) = 3^{\sqrt[3]{x}} + x$

112. $f(x) = (\ln(3x^2 + x))^{-2}$

113. $f(x) = \sin(\ln(x^2))$

114. $f(x) = 2^{\cos(x^2)}$

115. $f(x) = \ln(x + \cos(\sqrt{x}))$

116. $f(x) = \dfrac{\sin(3x^2) - \ln(2x-1)}{e^{2x} + 4x}$

117. $f(x) = \dfrac{Ln(\sin(3x+1)^{-2})}{\left(\dfrac{1}{\cos(2x)}\right)}$

Derivative of inverse trigonometric functions

$f(x) = y = \arcsin(x)$

That means:

$x = \sin(y)$

From here:

$\dfrac{dx}{dy} = \cos(y)$

$\dfrac{dx}{dy} = \sqrt{1 - (\sin(y))^2}$

$\dfrac{dy}{dx} = \dfrac{1}{\sqrt{1 - (\sin(y))^2}}$

And Finally:

$\dfrac{dy}{dx} = \dfrac{1}{\sqrt{1 - x^2}}$

1. Find the derivative of $f(x) = y = \arccos(x)$

2. Find the derivative of $f(x) = y = \arctan(x)$

Find the derivative:

3. $f(x) = \arccos(2x)$

4. $f(x) = \arcsin(\frac{x}{3})$

5. $f(x) = \arccos(\frac{2-x}{3})$

6. $f(x) = \arctan(\frac{x-2}{3})$

7. $f(x) = \arccos(-5x)$

8. $f(x) = \arcsin(\frac{1}{x})$

9. $f(x) = \arctan(\frac{1}{\sqrt[4]{x}})$

10. $f(x) = \arccos(\sin(x))$

11. $f(x) = \arccos(e^x)$

12. $f(x) = \dfrac{2}{\arctan(2x)}$

13. $f(x) = \dfrac{\arccos(x^2)}{2x}$

14. $f(x) = 4^{\arcsin(x)}$

15. $f(x) = \sin(2x)\arcsin(x^2 - 5x)$

IMPLICIT DIFFERENTIATION

Find $\dfrac{dy}{dx}$:

1. $y^2 + x = y$

2. $y^2 + 3xy = y^3$

3. $5xy^2 + x + 2 = y$

4. $y^2 - 2x = y - 3x$

5. $4y^2 + 2x^4 = e^y$

6. $2y^4 + x = y + x$

7. $y^2 - x = yx - x$

8. $y + yx + y^2x^2 = 2 - x$

9. $xy^2 + \ln(yx) = x$

10. $x\sin(xy) = y$

11. Given the relation $y^3 + 2x^3 = 1$

    a. Find $\dfrac{dy}{dx}$ (use implicit differentiation).

    b. From the original relation make y a function of x (Isolate y)

    c. Differentiate the function found in b with respect to x.

    d. Show that the derivative obtained in a is identical to the one obtained in c (should substitute y obtained in b)

    e. (5%) Find the tangent to the curve at $x = 1$

    f. (4%) Find the normal to the curve at $x = -1$

12. Given the relation $x + \sin(y) = 1$

    a. Find $\dfrac{dy}{dx}$ (use implicit differentiation).

    b. Find the equation of the <u>tangent</u> and <u>normal</u> to the function at $y = \dfrac{\pi}{6}$.

13. Given the relation $x + \ln(y) = 1$

    a. Find $\dfrac{dy}{dx}$ (use implicit differentiation).

    b. Find the equation of the <u>tangent</u> and <u>normal</u> to the function at $x = 1$.

14. Given the function $f(x) = (x+1)^2 \cos(\ln(x))$

    a. Obtain its derivative.

    b. Find the equation of the <u>tangent</u> and <u>normal</u> to the function at x = 1.

15. Given the function $f(x) = \cos(2^x - 2) + x^{\frac{3}{2}}$

    a. Obtain its derivative.

    b. Find the equation of the <u>tangent</u> and <u>normal</u> to the function at x = 1.

HIGHER DERIVATIVES

Given the function f in the derivative indicated, $\dfrac{d^n f}{dx^n} = f^n(x)$ means the nth derivative.

1. $f(x) = x^2$

   $\dfrac{df}{dx} = f'(x) =$

   $\dfrac{d^2 f}{dx^2} = f''(x) =$

2. $f(x) = \ln(x)$

   $\dfrac{df}{dx} = f'(x) =$

   $\dfrac{d^2 f}{dx^2} = f''(x) =$

3. $f(x) = \sin(x)$

   $\dfrac{df}{dx} = f'(x) =$

   $\dfrac{d^2 f}{dx^2} = f''(x) =$

4. $f(x) = e^{2x}$

   $\dfrac{df}{dx} = f'(x) =$

   $\dfrac{d^2 f}{dx^2} = f''(x) =$

   $\dfrac{d^3 f}{dx^3} = f'''(x) =$

   $\dfrac{d^n f}{dx^n} = f^{(n)}(x) =$

5. $f(x) = xe^x$

$$\frac{df}{dx} = f'(x) =$$

$$\frac{d^2 f}{dx^2} = f''(x) =$$

$$\frac{d^3 f}{dx^3} = f'''(x) =$$

$$\frac{d^n f}{dx^n} = f^{(n)}(x) =$$

6. $f(x) = \sin(e^x)$

$$\frac{df}{dx} = f'(x) =$$

$$\frac{d^2 f}{dx^2} = f''(x) =$$

$$\frac{d^3 f}{dx^3} = f'''(x) =$$

$$\frac{d^n f}{dx^n} = f^{(n)}(x) =$$

7. $f(x) = \ln(2x)$

$$\frac{df}{dx} = f'(x) =$$

$$\frac{d^2 f}{dx^2} = f''(x) =$$

$$\frac{d^3 f}{dx^3} = f'''(x) =$$

$$\frac{d^n f}{dx^n} = f^{(n)}(x) =$$

1.7. – STATIONARY (OR CRITICAL) POINTS

Functions may describe level of production, benefit, position, sugar level, efficiency of an engine, wind resistance or any other physical or other variable. Usually it is out interest to maximize benefit, efficiency or minimize lost. As a result we are usually interested in the maximum or minimum points of a function.

1. In a maximum or minimum point of a "smooth" function the slope of the tangent to the function is _____. Sketch an example:

2. There is one more situation in which the slope of the tangent to the function is _____ , such point is called: _____. Sketch an example:

3. In order to find a stationary points′ x coordinate we equal the _____ to ____.
   For example the function $f(x) = 2x^2 + 2x$, $f'(x) = $ _____ , $x = $

4. To find the stationary points′ y coordinate we _____.
   In the last example $f(__) = $

5. Once we found the stationary point we have to decide if it's a _____ , _____ or _____ .

6. We will discuss 3 methods to check if a function has minimum, maximum or horizontal inflection point at a certain point.

The 3 methods are:

1. Check the **value of the function** on both "sides" of the point and close to it. If both sides' values are higher the point is _____, if both sides are lower the point is _____ and if one side is higher and the other lower we have _____. Example: $f(x) = 2x^2 + 2x$

2. Build a diagram including all the zeros in the first derivative and all the places it is not defined, indicating **the sign of the derivative**. Example: $f(x) = 2x^4 + x^2$

3. Use the 2nd derivative. As you could see if the 2nd derivative, at the point in which the 1st derivative is 0, is positive the function is _____ and the point would be a _____, if the 2nd derivative, at the point in which the 1st derivative is 0, is negative the function is _____ and the point would be a _____, if the 2nd derivative is also 0 this test is _____.
   Example: $f(x) = 2x^3 + x^2$

   Example: $f(x) = x^4$

SECOND DERIVATIVE

1. The 1st derivative of a function gives the _____.

2. In case $f(x) = x^2$, the first derivative is _____ and the 2nd derivative is _____. As

    you can see the second derivative is always _____ and that means that

    the function is always _____.

3. In case $f(x) = x^3 - 3x^2$:

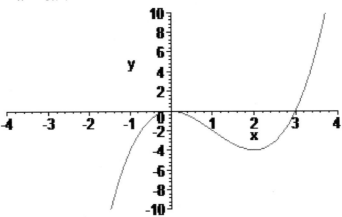

    The first derivative is _____ and the 2nd derivative is _____. As you can see

    the second derivative is positive for _____ , negative for _____

    and exactly 0 for _____. That means that when the 2nd derivative is

    positive the function is_____ when the 2nd derivative is negative

    the function is_____ and when the 2nd derivative is 0 the function

    might have _____.

4. In case $f(x) = x^4$

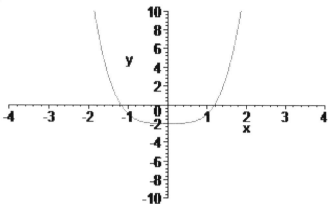

The first derivative is _____ and the 2nd derivative is _____. As you can see

the second derivative is positive for _____ , negative for _____

and exactly 0 for _____. That means that when the 2nd derivative is

positive the function is_____ when the 2nd derivative is negative

the function is_____ and when the 2nd derivative is 0 the function

might have _____ but in this case it has a _____.

5. If $f'(a) = 0$ it means the function has a _____ at a.

6. If f'$(a) < 0$ it means the function is_____ at a.

7. If $f'(a) \neq$ and $f''(a) = 0$ it means the function has a _____ at a.

8. If possible, fill the following table with a sketch of the function around the point
   where $x = a$.

	$f''(a) = 0$	$f''(a) > 0$	$f''(a) < 0$
$f'(a)=0$			
$f'(a) > 0$			
$f'(a) < 0$			

4. A certain function satisfies the conditions:

$$f(a) = 2 \qquad f'(a) = 1 \qquad f''(a) < 0$$

Sketch a function that satisfies these conditions around a

5. A certain function satisfies the conditions:

$$f(a) = -2 \qquad f'(a) = -2 \qquad f''(a) < 0$$

Sketch a function that satisfies these conditions around a

6. A certain function satisfies the conditions:

$$f(a) = 0 \qquad f'(a) = -2 \qquad f''(a) = 0$$

Sketch a function that satisfies these conditions around a

7. A certain function satisfies the conditions:

$$f(a) = 3 \qquad f'(a) = 3 \qquad f''(a) = 0$$

Sketch a function that satisfies these conditions around a

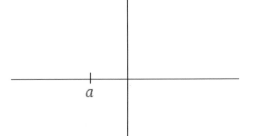

8. Sketch the graph of a function which has all the following properties:

a. $\lim\limits_{x \to \infty} f(x) = -\infty$

b. $\lim\limits_{x \to -\infty} f(x) = 1$

c. $f(1) = 2, f(3) = 1$

d. $f'(x) > 0$ if $x < 2$

e. $f'(x) > 0$ if $x > 2$

f. $f'(2) = 0$

g. $f''(x) > 0$ if $x < -1$

h. $f''(x) < 0$ if $-1 < x$

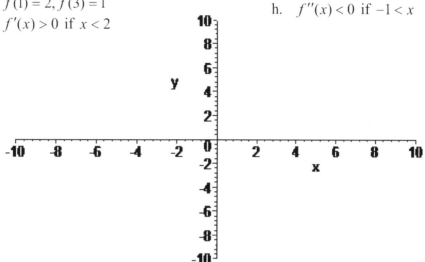

9. Sketch the graph of a function which has all the following properties:

a. $\lim\limits_{x \to 2^-} f(x) = -\infty$

b. $\lim\limits_{x \to 2^+} f(x) = \infty$

c. $\lim\limits_{x \to -\infty} f(x) = 0$

d. $f(-2) = 2, f(5) = 1, f(0) = 0$

e. $f'(x) > 0$ if $x < -2$ or $x > 5$

f. $f'(x) > 0$ if $-2 < x < 2, 2 < x < 5$

g. $f'(5) = 0, f'(-2) = 0$

h. $f''(x) > 0$ if $x < -3$ or $x > 2$

i. $f''(x) < 0$ if $-3 < x < 2$

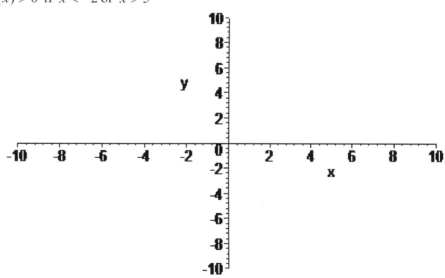

10. Sketch the graph of a function which has all the following properties:

a. g has domain
   $(-\infty, -2) \cup (-2, \infty)$
b. g has range $(-5, \infty)$
c. The graph of g has a vertical asymptote at x = -2
d. $\lim\limits_{x \to -\infty} f(x) = 2$
e. $\lim\limits_{x \to \infty} f(x) = -5$

f. $\lim\limits_{x \to 3} f(x) = 2$
g. G is discontinuous at x = 3
h. $g'(x) > 0$ at $(-\infty, -2)$
i. $g'(x) < 0$ at $(-2, 3)$
j. $g'(4)$ does not exist. But g is continuous at 4.

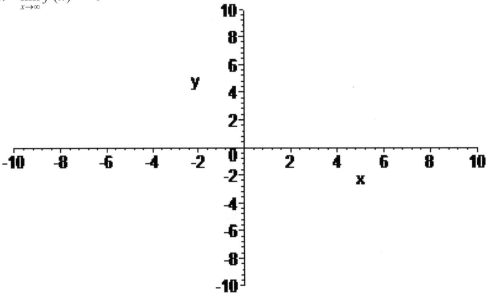

11. Given the function $f(x) = ax^2 + bx + c$. It is known the function has a maximum at the point (1, 1). It is also known that the line y = -2x is tangent to the function at the point with x = 2. Find a, b and c.

12. Given the function $f(x) = x^3 + ax^2 + bx + c$. It is known the function has a

   minimum at x = 1, passes throught the point (0, -1) and has an inflection point at

   the point where x = 2/3. Find a, b and c.

13. Given the function $f(x) = ax^3 + bx^2 + cx$. It is known the function has a critical

   point at (0, 0) and that the point (2, -16) is an inflection point. Find a, b and c.

14. Given the function $f(x) = \dfrac{a}{x} + bx^2$ find a and b knowing it has an extrema at (1, 3)

1.8. – FUNCTION ANALYSIS

Function analysis is an important idea in math. The steps indicated should be made in the analysis of the following functions. Order of the steps might change.

The steps are:

1. Find the domain.

2. Find the _____ asymptotes (in case they exist) and the corresponding limits.

3. Find the horizontal/slant asymptotes (in case they exist) and the corresponding limits.

4. Find __ intercept.

5. Find __ intercept(s).

6. Find extrema of the function (_____, minimum, _____ points) using the 1st and/or 2nd derivatives.

7. Sketch the function.

8. Discuss the concavity of the function

9. Dicuss the continuity of the function.

10. Indicate the range of the function.

11. Indicate the intervals of increase and decrease of the function.

The functions are classified in the following types:

a. **Polynomial functions with natural powers.**

b. **Polynomial functions with rational powers.**

c. **Rational functions.**

d. **General functions.**

A. POLYNOMIALS WITH NATURAL POWER

1. Graph the following functions. Obtain and indicate all x and y intercepts maximum, minimum and inflection points on the graph (include their coordinates)

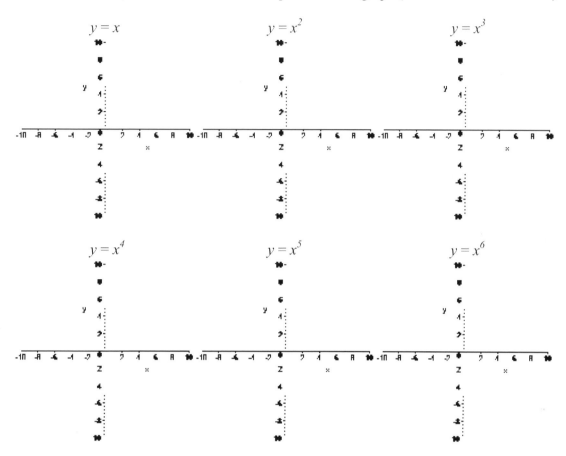

State at least one conclusion

2. Graph the following functions. Obtain and indicate all x and y intercepts maximum, minimum and inflection points on the graph (include their coordinates)

$$y = (x+2)^2 + 1 \qquad\qquad y = (x-2)^3 - 3 \qquad\qquad y = (x+3)^4 - 6$$

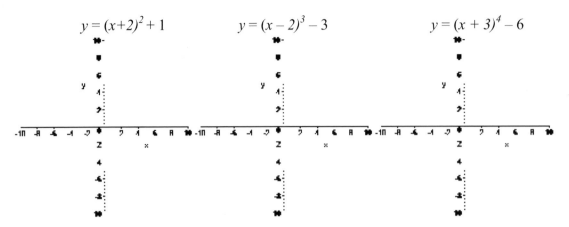

State at least one conclusión in relation to the previous part.

3. Graph the following functions. Obtain and indicate all x and y intercepts maximum, minimum and inflection points on the graph (include their coordinates)

$$y = -(x+2)^2 + 1 \qquad\qquad y = -(x-2)^3 - 3 \qquad\qquad y = -(x+3)^4 - 6$$

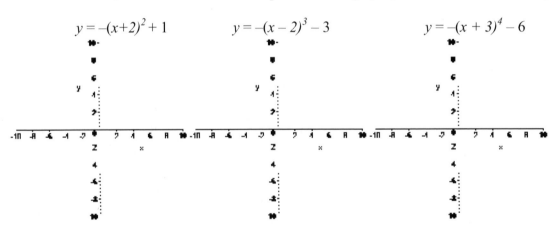

State at least one conclusión in relation to the previous part.

4. Graph the following functions. Obtain and indicate all x and y intercepts:

$y = x(x^2+1) =$ $y = x(x+1)(x+1)$ $y = x(x+1)(x-1)$

$y = -x(x+2)(x-3)$ $y = x(x^3+1)$ $y = x(x^3-1)$

$y = x^2(x+1)(x+1)$ $y = x^2(x+1)(x-2)$ $y = -x^2(x+1)(x-2)$

$y = (x-0)(x-1)(x-2)(x-3)$ $y = 2(x-0)(x-1)(x-2)(x-3)$ $y = -4(x-0)(x-1)(x-2)(x-3)$

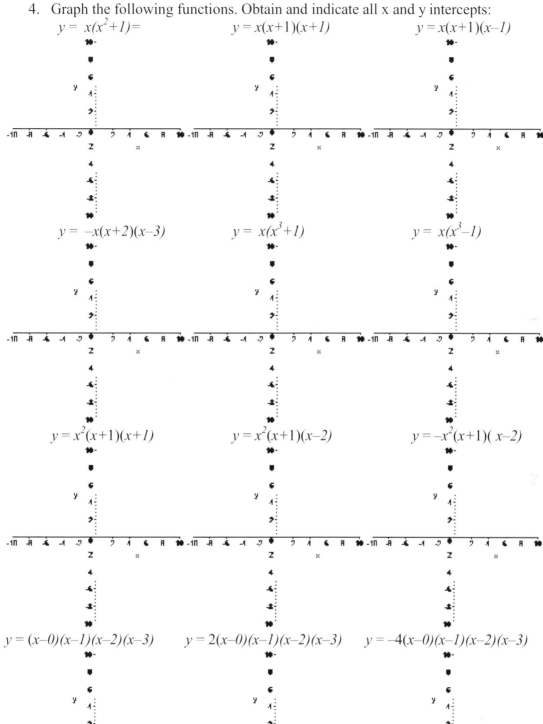

67

5. Fill the blanks (expand)

       a) $y = x^3$

       b) $y = x(x^2+1) = \underline{\hspace{3cm}}$

       c) $y = x(x+1)(x+1) = \underline{\hspace{3cm}}$

       d) $y = x(x+1)(x-1) = \underline{\hspace{3cm}}$

       e) $y = -x(x+2)(x-3) = \underline{\hspace{3cm}}$

       f) $y = -(x-1)^3 = \underline{\hspace{3cm}}$

All the functions in this section are of the _____ degree. They all have an

_____ . They all have at least 1 _____. Sometimes they have

_____ . If at one end the function tends to _____

then on the other end it will tend to _____.

6. Fill the blanks (expand)

       a) $y = x^4$

       b) $y = x(x^3+1) = \underline{\hspace{3cm}}$

       c) $y = x(x^3-1) = \underline{\hspace{3cm}}$

       d) $y = x^2(x+1)(x+1) = \underline{\hspace{3cm}}$

       e) $y = x^2(x+1)(x-1) = \underline{\hspace{3cm}}$

       f) $y = x^2(x+1)(x-2) = \underline{\hspace{3cm}}$

       e) $y = -x^2(x+1)(x-2) = \underline{\hspace{3cm}}$

       f) $y = -(x-2)^4$

All the functions in this section are of the _____ degree. They all have at

least one _____ point. Sometimes they have two _____ and one _____ or

two _____ and one _____ . If on one end the function tends to _____

then on the other end it will tend to _____ as well.

7. Given the functions:

       a) $y = (x-1)(x-2)(x-3)(x-4)$ b) $y = 2(x-1)(x-2)(x-3)(x-4)$

       c) $y = 3(x-1)(x-2)(x-3)(x-4)$ d) $y = -4(x-1)(x-2)(x-3)(x-4)$

All the functions in this section are of the _____ degree. On multiplying a

function by a number, the _____ stays the same. The _____

intercept changes. The general aspect of the function is similar/very different

(circle the right answer)

8. Graph the following functions

$y = -(x-1)(x-2)^2(x-4)^3$ $y = -(x-2)^3(x-4)^4$ $y = (x-2)(x^2-1)(x^2+1)$

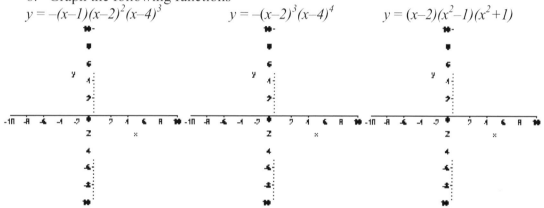

In case a factor is of 1st degree on the graph it will correspond an _____

In case a factor is of even degree on the graph it will correspond a _____ or _____

In case a factor is of odd (> 1) degree on the graph it will correspond an _____

9. Graph the following functions. Obtain and indicate all x and y intercepts on the graph (include their coordinates). <u>Sketch a dashed line</u> (use a pen or pencil) to indicate horizontal and/or vertical asymptotes.

a) $y = \dfrac{2x}{x-1}$

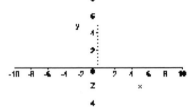

Vertical asymptote(s): _____

Horizontal asymptote(s): _____

b) $y = \dfrac{1}{(x+1)(x-2)}$

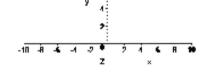

Vertical asymptote(s): _____

Horizontal asymptote(s): _____

c) $y = \dfrac{3x^2}{(x+1)(x-4)}$

Vertical asymptote(s): _____

Horizontal asymptote(s): _____

d) $y = xe^x$

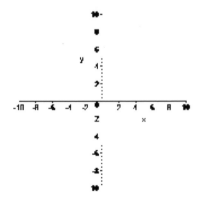

Vertical asymptote(s): _____

Horizontal asymptote(s): _____

10. Given the following function:

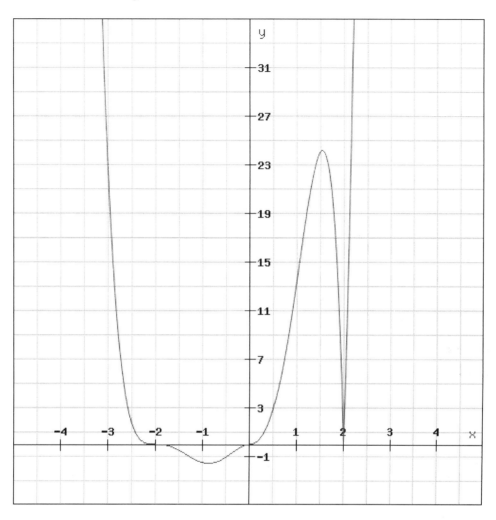

Fill the table:

x = a	x = –3	x = –2	x = – 1	x = –0.6	x = 0	x =1	x = 1.5	x = 2
f(x)								
f'(x)								
f''(x)								

Conclusions:

a. In a "smooth" maximum or minimum the _____.

b. In a horizontal inflection point _____.

c. In a non–horizontal inflection point _____.

11. Use GDC to sketch the functions $f(x) = x^3$ and $g(x) = 4^x + 2^{-x} - 8$

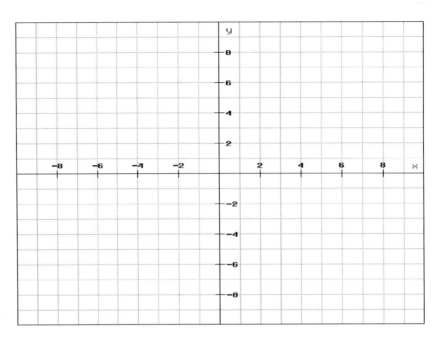

Find the values of x for which f(x) > g(x)

12. Use GDC to sketch the functions $f(x) = x^2$ and $g(x) = \ln(x)$

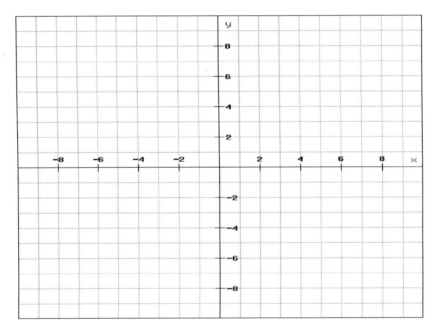

Find the values of x for which f(x) > g(x)

13. $f(x) = x^4, x \in [-1, 2]$

Domain: _____

Vertical asymptotes: _____

Horizontal asymptotes: _____

Slant Asymptotes: _____

y intercept: _____

x intercept(s): _____

Extrema (using the 1st and if needed 2nd derivatives)

Range of the function: _____

Function Increases: _____

Function decreases: _____

Concave up: _____

Concave down: _____

Inflection point(s)_____

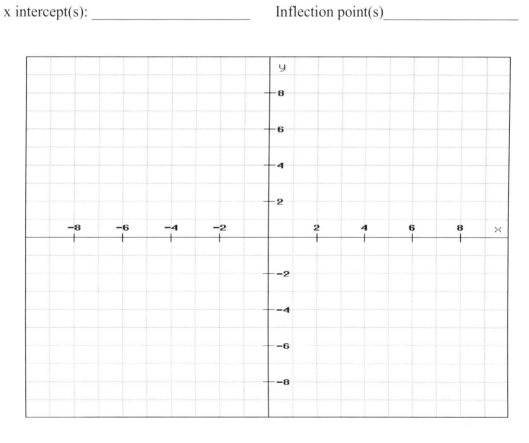

14. $f(x) = -x^6 + 6, x \in \mathbb{R}$

Domain: _____

Vertical asymptotes: _____

Horizontal asymptotes: _____

Slant Asymptotes: _____

y intercept: _____

x intercept(s): _____

Extrema (using the 1st and if needed 2nd derivatives)

Range of the function: _____

Function Increases: _____

Function decreases: _____

Concave up: _____

Concave down: _____

Inflection point(s)_____

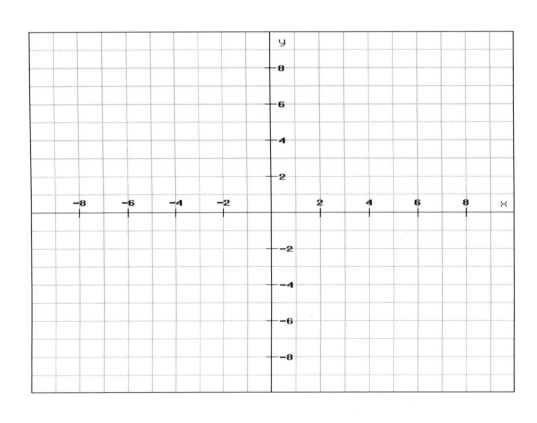

74

15. $f(x) = x^2(x+2), x \in [-\frac{3}{2}, \frac{1}{2}]$

Domain: _____

Extrema (using the 1st and if needed 2nd derivatives)

Vertical asymptotes: _____

Horizontal asymptotes: _____

Range of the function: _____

Slant Asymptotes: _____

Function Increases: _____

Function decreases: _____

Concave up: _____

y intercept: _____

Concave down: _____

x intercept(s): _____

Inflection point(s)_____

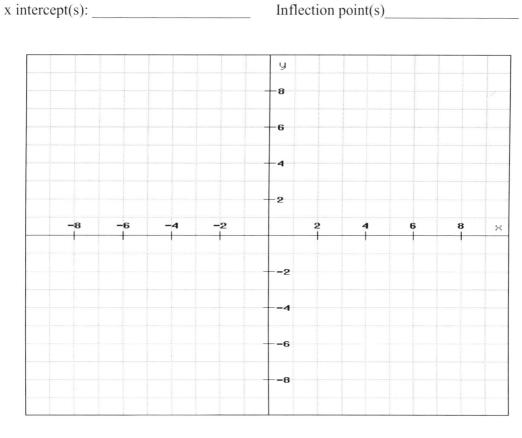

16. $f(x) = x(x+2)(x-1), x \in \mathbb{R}$

Domain: _____

Vertical asymptotes: _____

Horizontal asymptotes: _____

Slant Asymptotes: _____

y intercept: _____

x intercept(s): _____

Extrema (using the 1st and if needed 2nd derivatives)

Range of the function: _____

Function Increases: _____

Function decreases: _____

Concave up: _____

Concave down: _____

Inflection point(s)_____

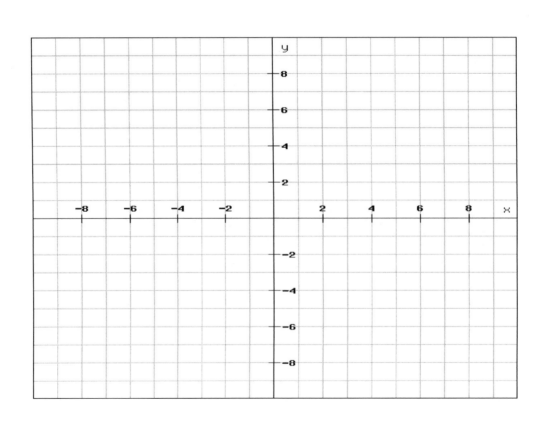

17. $f(x) = 2x^3 + 11x^2 + 10x - 8, x \in \mathbb{R}$

Domain: _____

Extrema (using the 1st and if needed 2nd derivatives)

Vertical asymptotes: _____

Horizontal asymptotes: _____

Range of the function: _____

Slant Asymptotes: _____

Function Increases: _____

Function decreases: _____

Concave up: _____

y intercept: _____

Concave down: _____

x intercept(s): _____

Inflection point(s)_____

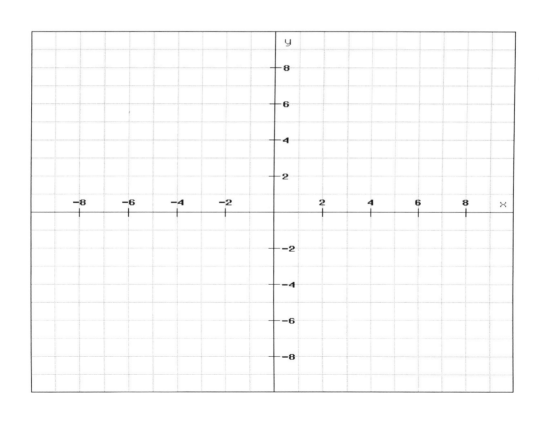

18. $f(x) = x^3 - x^2, x \in [0,2]$

Domain: _____

Vertical asymptotes: _____

Horizontal asymptotes: _____

Slant Asymptotes: _____

y intercept: _____

x intercept(s): _____

Extrema (using the 1st and if needed 2nd derivatives)

Range of the function: _____

Function Increases: _____

Function decreases: _____

Concave up: _____

Concave down: _____

Inflection point(s)_____

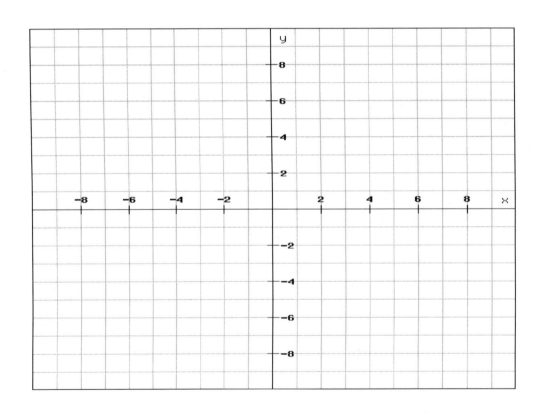

19. $f(x) = 2x^4 - 4x^2, x \in \mathbb{R}$

Domain: _____

Vertical asymptotes: _____

Horizontal asymptotes: _____

Slant Asymptotes: _____

y intercept: _____

x intercept(s): _____

Extrema (using the 1st and if needed 2nd derivatives)

Range of the function: _____

Function Increases: _____

Function decreases: _____

Concave up: _____

Concave down: _____

Inflection point(s)_____

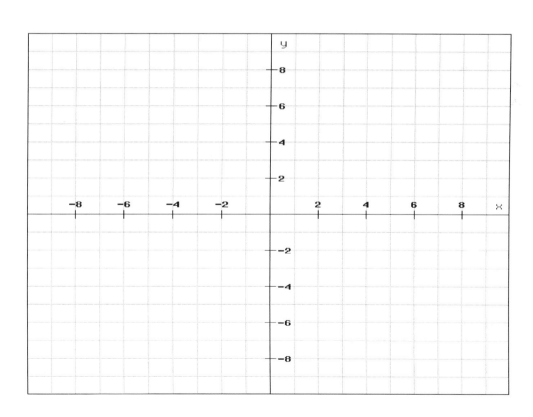

20. $f(x) = x^4 - 2x^3, x \in \mathbb{R}$

Domain: _____

Vertical asymptotes: _____

Horizontal asymptotes: _____

Slant Asymptotes: _____

y intercept: _____

x intercept(s): _____

Extrema (using the 1st and if needed 2nd derivatives)

Range of the function: _____

Function Increases: _____

Function decreases: _____

Concave up: _____

Concave down: _____

Inflection point(s)_____

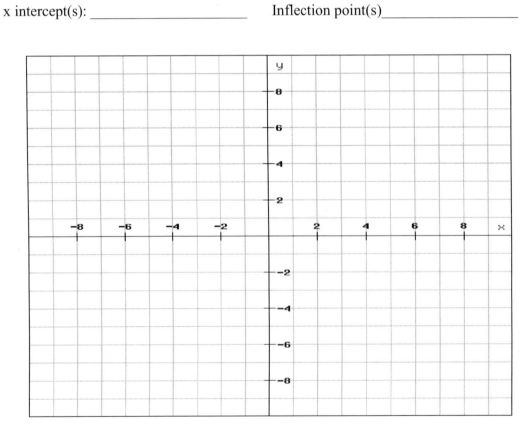

21. Write a possible expression of a function of the 3rd degree that intercepts the x axis at (2, 0), (−3, 0) and (−0.5, 0). Is it possible to make this function have a y intercepts (0, 10)? If yes, find the expression, if no explain why.

22. Write a possible expression of a function of the 4th degree that intercepts the x axis at (1, 0), (2, 0), (5, 0) and (−1, 0). Is it possible to make this function have a y intercepts (0, 5)? If yes, find the expression, if no explain why.

23. Write the expression of the function $f(x) = x^3$ shifted 2 positions to the right and 3 positions down.

24. Write the expression of the function $f(x) = x^4$ shifted 4 positions to the left and 6 positions up.

25. In case the first derivative of a function is 0 at a certain point, this point can be a

_____ or a _____ or a _____ .

26. In case the 1st derivative is 0 and the 2nd derivative is positive at a certain point,

the point must be a _____ .

27. In case the 1st derivative is 0 and the 2nd derivative is negative at a certain point,

the point must be a _____ .

28. In case the 1st derivative is 0 and the 2nd derivative is also 0 at a certain point, the

point _____ .

29. In the parts where $f'(x) > 0$ the function is _____ .

30. In the parts where $f''(x) > 0$ the function is _____ .

B. POLYNOMIALS WITH RATIONAL POWER

31. $f(x) = x^{\frac{2}{3}}, x \in \mathbb{R}$

Domain: _____

Vertical asymptotes: _____

Horizontal asymptotes: _____

Slant Asymptotes: _____

y intercept: _____

x intercept(s): _____

Extrema (using the 1st and if needed 2nd derivatives)

Range of the function: _____

Function Increases: _____

Function decreases: _____

Concave up: _____

Concave down: _____

Inflection point(s)_____

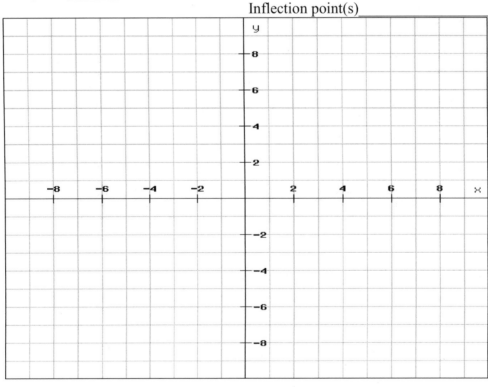

32. $f(x) = x^{\frac{4}{3}}, x \in \mathbb{R}$

Domain: _____

Vertical asymptotes: _____

Horizontal asymptotes: _____

Slant Asymptotes: _____

y intercept: _____

x intercept(s): _____

Extrema (using the 1st and if needed 2nd derivatives)

Range of the function: _____

Function Increases: _____

Function decreases: _____

Concave up: _____

Concave down: _____

Inflection point(s)_____

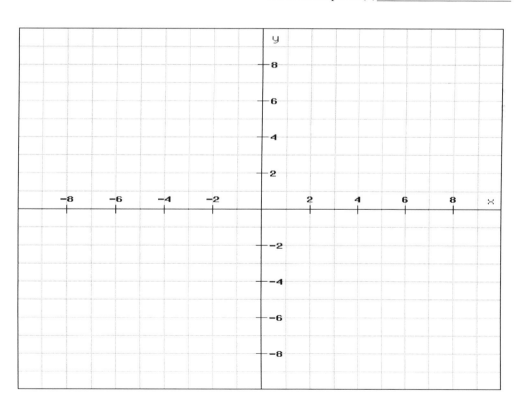

33. $f(x) = 2x^{-\frac{4}{3}}, x \in \mathbb{R}$

Domain: _____

Vertical asymptotes: _____

Horizontal asymptotes: _____

Slant Asymptotes: _____

y intercept: _____

x intercept(s): _____

Extrema (using the 1st and if needed 2nd derivatives)

Range of the function: _____

Function Increases: _____

Function decreases: _____

Concave up: _____

Concave down: _____

Inflection point(s)_____

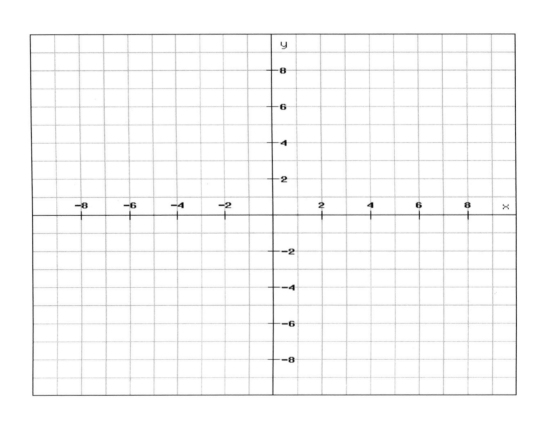

34. $f(x) = x - x^{\frac{2}{3}}, x \in \mathbb{R}$

Domain: _____

Vertical asymptotes: _____

Horizontal asymptotes: _____

Slant Asymptotes: _____

y intercept: _____

x intercept(s): _____

Extrema (using the 1st and if needed 2nd derivatives)

Range of the function: _____

Function Increases: _____

Function decreases: _____

Concave up: _____

Concave down: _____

Inflection point(s)_____

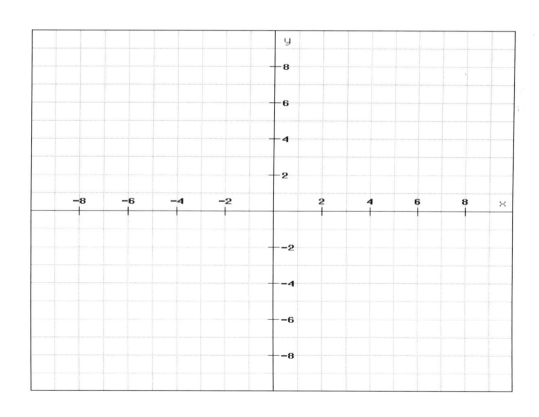

85

35. $f(x) = x + x^{-\frac{2}{3}}, x \in \mathbb{R}$

Domain: _____

Vertical asymptotes: _____

Horizontal asymptotes: _____

Slant Asymptotes: _____

y intercept: _____

x intercept(s): _____

Extrema (using the 1st and if needed 2nd derivatives)

Range of the function: _____

Function Increases: _____

Function decreases: _____

Concave up: _____

Concave down: _____

Inflection point(s)_____

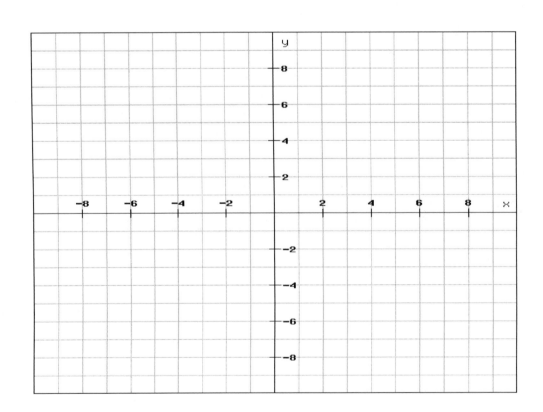

C. RATIONAL FUNCTIONS

36. $f(x) = \dfrac{3(x+2)}{(x-5)(x+2)} + 4, x \in \mathbb{R}$

Domain: _____

Vertical asymptotes: _____

Continuity: _____

Horizontal asymptotes: _____

y intercept: _____

x intercept(s): _____

Extrema (using the 1st and if needed 2nd derivatives)

Range of the function: _____

Function Increases: _____

Function decreases: _____

Concave up: _____

Concave down: _____

Inflection point(s)_____

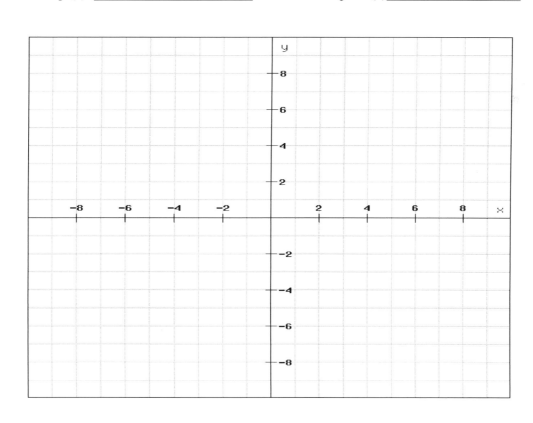

37. $f(x) = \dfrac{2x}{x+1}, x \in \mathbb{R}$

Domain: _____

Extrema (using the 1st and if needed 2nd derivatives)

Vertical asymptotes: _____

Horizontal asymptotes: _____

Range of the function: _____

Function Increases: _____

Continuity: _____

Function decreases: _____

y intercept: _____

Concave up: _____

Concave down: _____

x intercept(s): _____

Inflection point(s)_____

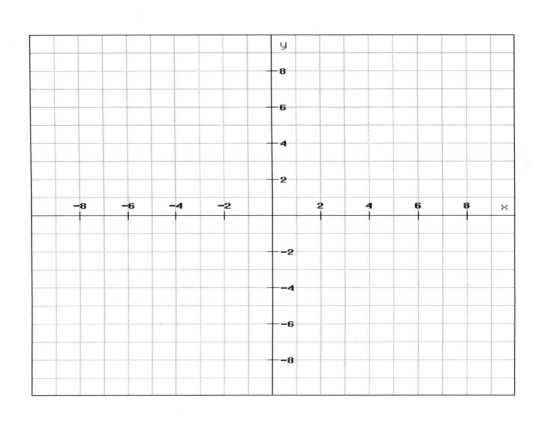

38. $f(x) = \dfrac{1}{x^2}, x \in \mathbb{R}$

Domain: _____

Vertical asymptotes: _____

Horizontal asymptotes: _____

Continuity: _____

y intercept: _____

x intercept(s): _____

Extrema (using the 1st and if needed 2nd derivatives)

Range of the function: _____

Function Increases: _____

Function decreases: _____

Concave up: _____

Concave down: _____

Inflection point(s) _____

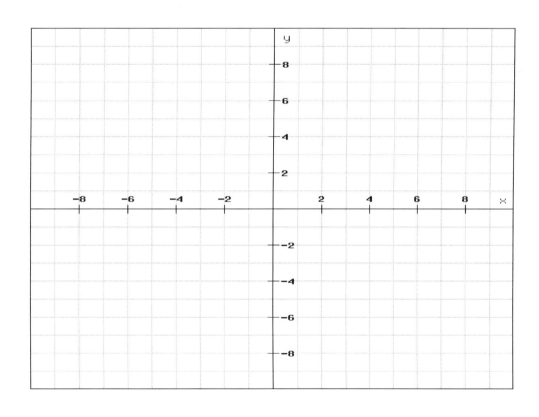

39. $f(x) = \dfrac{2}{(x-3)^2} - 4, x \in \mathbb{R}$

Domain: _____

Vertical asymptotes: _____

Horizontal asymptotes: _____

Continuity: _____

y intercept: _____

x intercept(s): _____

Extrema (using the 1st and if needed 2nd derivatives)

Range of the function: _____

Function Increases: _____

Function decreases: _____

Concave up: _____

Concave down: _____

Inflection point(s)_____

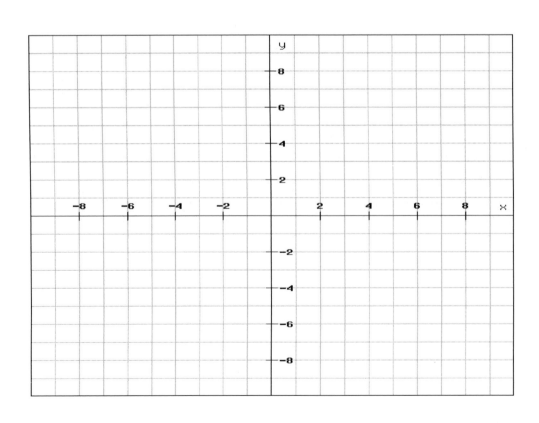

40. $f(x) = \dfrac{1}{x^2 + 1}, x \in \mathbb{R}$

Domain: _____

Vertical asymptotes: _____

Horizontal asymptotes: _____

Continuity: _____

y intercept: _____

x intercept(s): _____

Extrema (using the 1st and if needed 2nd derivatives)

Range of the function: _____

Function Increases: _____

Function decreases: _____

Concave up: _____

Concave down: _____

Inflection point(s)_____

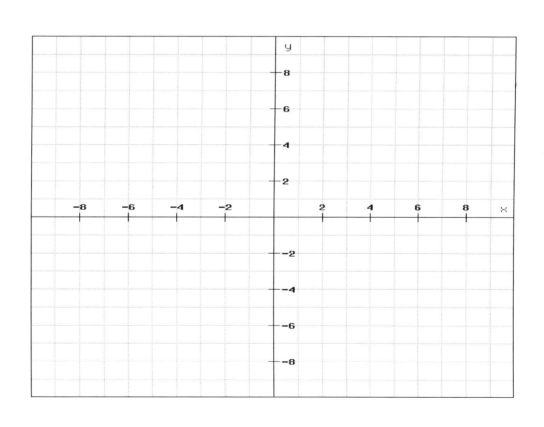

41. $f(x) = \dfrac{x}{x^2 + 2}, x \in \mathbb{R}$

Domain: _____

Vertical asymptotes: _____

Horizontal asymptotes: _____

Continuity: _____

y intercept: _____

x intercept(s): _____

Extrema (using the 1st and if needed 2nd derivatives)

Range of the function: _____

Function Increases: _____

Function decreases: _____

Concave up: _____

Concave down: _____

Inflection point(s) _____

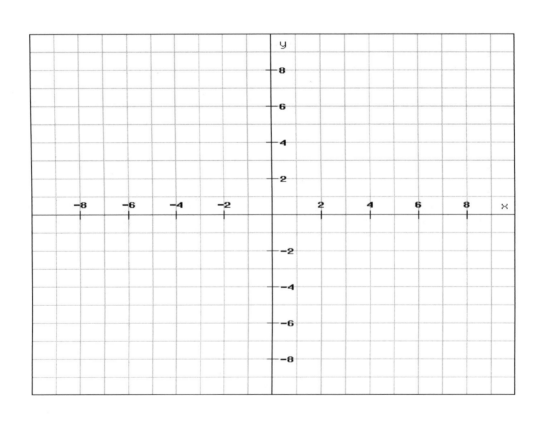

42. $f(x) = \dfrac{2}{(x-2)(x+3)}, x \in \mathbb{R}$

Domain: _____

Vertical asymptotes: _____

Horizontal asymptotes: _____

Continuity: _____

y intercept: _____

x intercept(s): _____

Extrema (using the 1st and if needed 2nd derivatives)

Range of the function: _____

Function Increases: _____

Function decreases: _____

Concave up: _____

Concave down: _____

Inflection point(s)_____

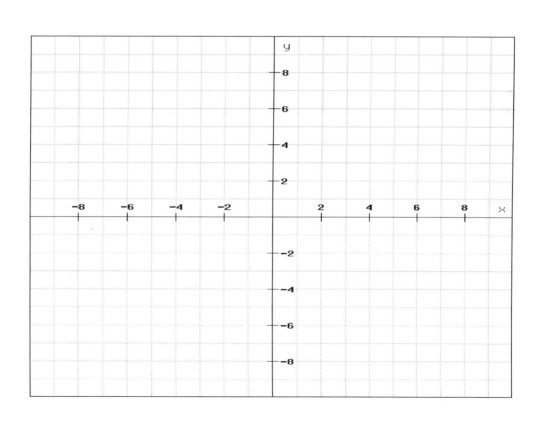

43. $f(x) = \dfrac{-3}{x^2 - 5x - 6}, x \in \mathbb{R}$

Domain: _____

Vertical asymptotes: _____

Horizontal asymptotes: _____

Continuity: _____

y intercept: _____

x intercept(s): _____

Extrema (using the 1st and if needed 2nd derivatives)

Range of the function: _____

Function Increases: _____

Function decreases: _____

Concave up: _____

Concave down: _____

Inflection point(s)_____

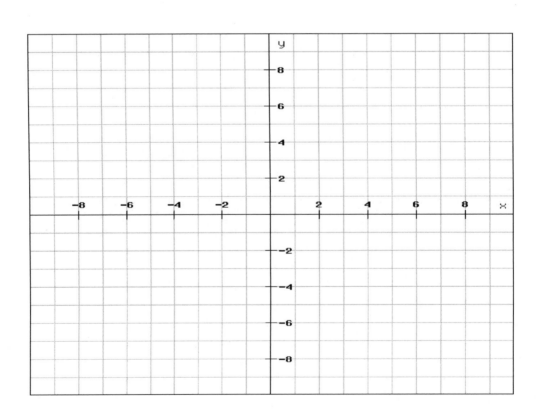

94

44. $f(x) = \dfrac{x^2}{x-1}, x \in \mathbb{R}$

Domain: _____

Vertical asymptotes: _____

Horizontal asymptotes: _____

Slant Asymptotes: _____

y intercept: _____

x intercept(s): _____

Extrema (using the 1st and if needed 2nd derivatives)

Range of the function: _____

Function Increases: _____

Function decreases: _____

Concave up: _____

Concave down: _____

Inflection point(s)_____

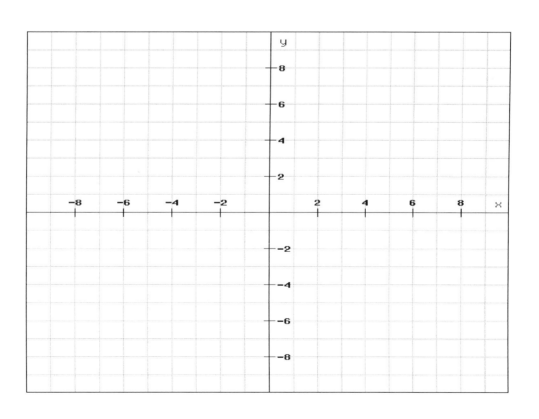

45. $f(x) = \dfrac{2x^2}{(x+3)(x-1)}, x \in \mathbb{R}$

Domain: _____

Extrema (using the 1st and if needed 2nd derivatives)

Vertical asymptotes: _____

Horizontal asymptotes: _____

Range of the function: _____

Slant Asymptotes: _____

Function Increases: _____

Function decreases: _____

y intercept: _____

Concave up: _____

Concave down: _____

x intercept(s): _____

Inflection point(s)_____

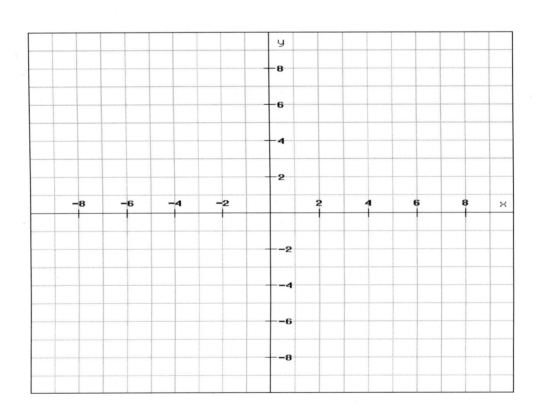

46. $f(x) = \dfrac{x^2 + 3}{x - 1}, x \in \mathbb{R}$

Domain: _____

Vertical asymptotes: _____

Horizontal asymptotes: _____

Slant Asymptotes: _____

y intercept: _____

x intercept(s): _____

Extrema (using the 1st and if needed 2nd derivatives)

Range of the function: _____

Function Increases: _____

Function decreases: _____

Concave up: _____

Concave down: _____

Inflection point(s)_____

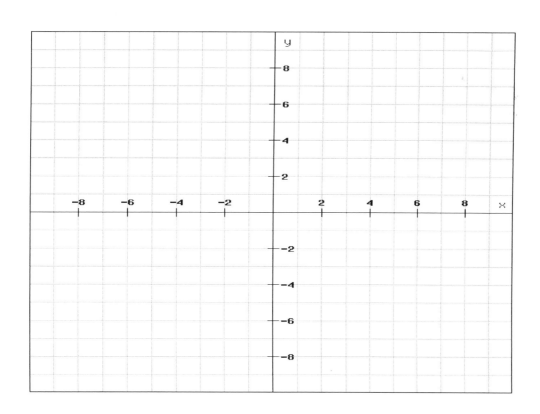

47. $f(x) = \dfrac{-1}{x^2 - x}, x \in \mathbb{R}$

Domain: _____

Vertical asymptotes: _____

Horizontal asymptotes: _____

Slant Asymptotes: _____

y intercept: _____

x intercept(s): _____

Extrema (using the 1st and if needed 2nd derivatives)

Range of the function: _____

Function Increases: _____

Function decreases: _____

Concave up: _____

Concave down: _____

Inflection point(s) _____

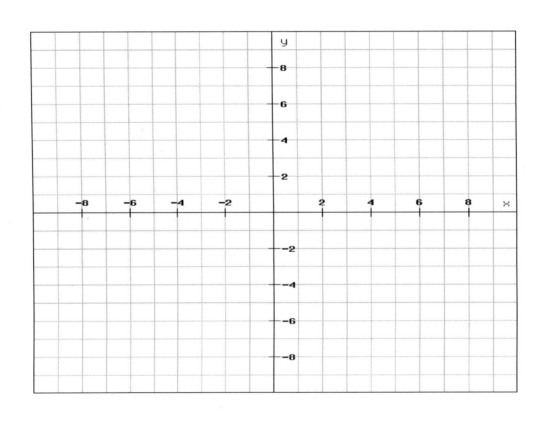

48. $f(x) = \dfrac{3x+1}{x^2 - x}, x \in \mathbb{R}$

Domain: _____

Vertical asymptotes: _____

Horizontal asymptotes: _____

Slant Asymptotes: _____

y intercept: _____

x intercept(s): _____

Extrema (using the 1st and if needed 2nd derivatives)

Range of the function: _____

Function Increases: _____

Function decreases: _____

Concave up: _____

Concave down: _____

Inflection point(s)_____

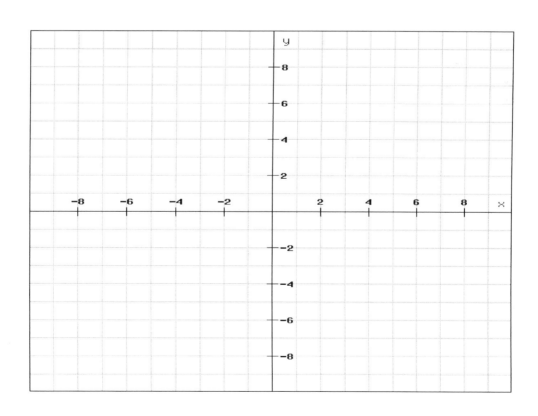

49. Sketch the following function $f(x) = 2x + 3$, on the 2nd graph, sketch the following: $f(x) = \dfrac{(2x+3)(x+1)}{(x+1)}$

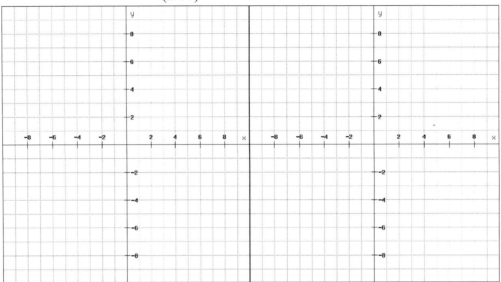

50. Determine the equations of all the asymptotes of the following functions and discuss their continuity:

a. $f(x) = \dfrac{2x^3 + 3x + 1}{x^3 - x}$

b. $f(x) = \dfrac{x^3 - x^2}{x^2 - 3x + 2}$

c. $f(x) = \dfrac{5x^3 + 3x^2 + 1}{x^2 - 2}$

d. $f(x) = \dfrac{x - 2x^2}{3x^2 - 9x + 6}$

51. Vertical asymptotes are of the form _____. Their origin is a function in which a certain value of _____ makes the denominator of the function _____ and the numerator _____.

52. Horizontal asymptotes are of the form _____. Their meaning is significant for _____ and _____ of x. Sometimes a function can have a certain horizontal asymptote for _____ and a different horizontal asymptote for _____. In a rational function which is of the form _____, when _____ the function will have a horizontal asymptote of the form _____.

53. Slant (or oblique) asymptotes are of the form _____. Their meaning is significant for _____ and _____ of x. Sometimes a function can have a certain horizontal asymptote for _____ and a different horizontal asymptote for _____. In a rational function which is of the form _____, when _____ the function will have a slant asymptote.

54. (T/F) All functions must have at least one vertical asymptote.

55. (T/F) All functions must have at least one horizontal asymptote.

56. (T/F) All functions must have at least one slant asymptote.

57. (T/F) A function that has two vertical asymptotes cannot have a slant asymptote.

58. (T/F) A function that has two slant asymptotes cannot have a horizontal asymptote.

D. GENERAL FUNCTIONS

59. $f(x) = e^x - x, x \in \mathbb{R}$

Domain: _____

Vertical asymptotes: _____

Horizontal asymptotes: _____

Slant Asymptotes: _____

y intercept: _____

x intercept(s): _____

Extrema (using the 1ˢᵗ and if needed 2ⁿᵈ derivatives)

Range of the function: _____

Function Increases: _____

Function decreases: _____

Concave up: _____

Concave down: _____

Inflection point(s)_____

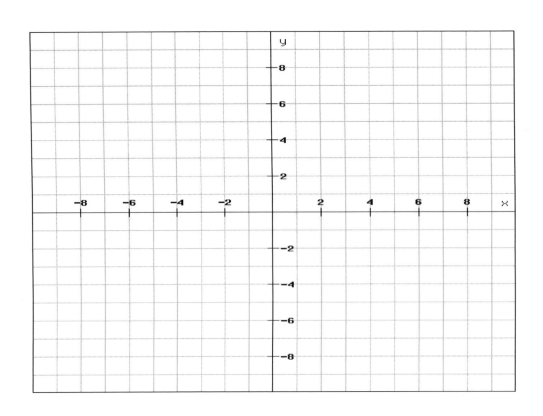

60. $f(x) = e^x + x, x \in \mathbb{R}$

Domain: _____

Vertical asymptotes: _____

Horizontal asymptotes: _____

Slant Asymptotes: _____

y intercept: _____

x intercept(s): _____

Extrema (using the 1st and if needed 2nd derivatives)

Range of the function: _____

Function Increases: _____

Function decreases: _____

Concave up: _____

Concave down: _____

Inflection point(s)_____

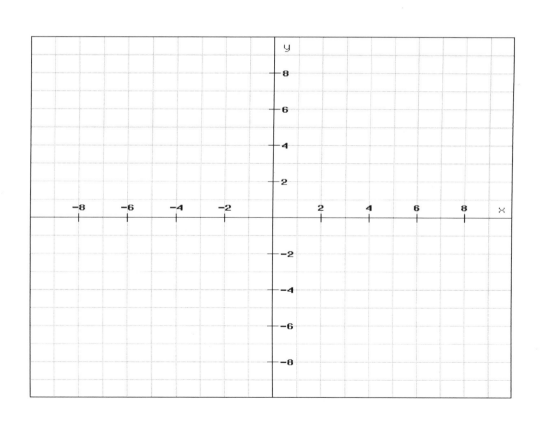

61. $f(x) = \dfrac{2}{1+e^x}$

Domain: _____

Vertical asymptotes: _____

Horizontal asymptotes: _____

Slant Asymptotes: _____

y intercept: _____

x intercept(s): _____

Extrema (using the 1st and if needed 2nd derivatives)

Range of the function: _____

Function Increases: _____

Function decreases: _____

Concave up: _____

Concave down: _____

Inflection point(s) _____

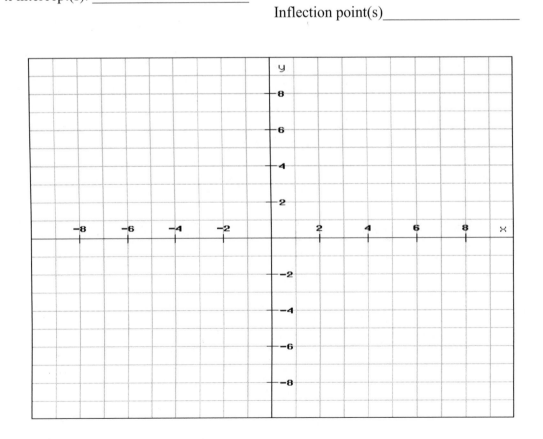

62. $f(x) = \dfrac{2}{2 - e^x}$

Domain: _____

Vertical asymptotes: _____

Horizontal asymptotes: _____

Slant Asymptotes: _____

y intercept: _____

x intercept(s): _____

Extrema (using the 1st and if needed 2nd derivatives)

Range of the function: _____

Function Increases: _____

Function decreases: _____

Concave up: _____

Concave down: _____

Inflection point(s)_____

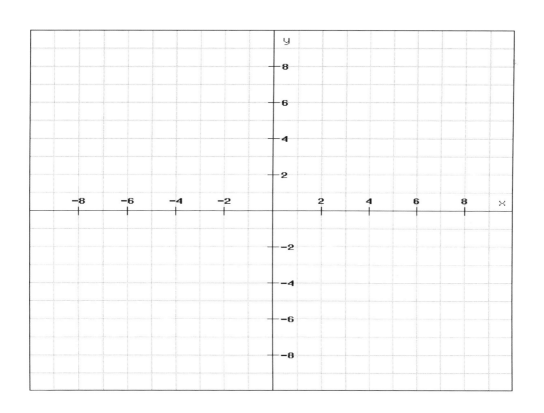

63. $f(x) = x\ln(x), x \in \mathbb{R}$

Domain: _____

Vertical asymptotes: _____

Horizontal asymptotes: _____

Slant Asymptotes: _____

y intercept: _____

x intercept(s): _____

Extrema (using the 1st and if needed 2nd derivatives)

Range of the function: _____

Function Increases: _____

Function decreases: _____

Concave up: _____

Concave down: _____

Inflection point(s)_____

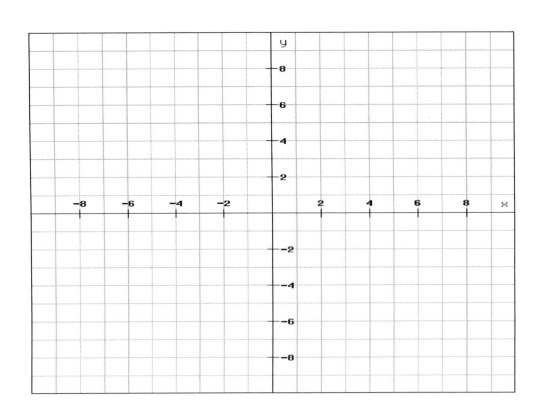

64. $f(x) = x \ln(x^2), x \in \mathbb{R}$

Domain: _____

Vertical asymptotes: _____

Horizontal asymptotes: _____

Slant Asymptotes: _____

y intercept: _____

x intercept(s): _____

Extrema (using the 1st and if needed 2nd derivatives)

Range of the function: _____

Function Increases: _____

Function decreases: _____

Concave up: _____

Concave down: _____

Inflection point(s)_____

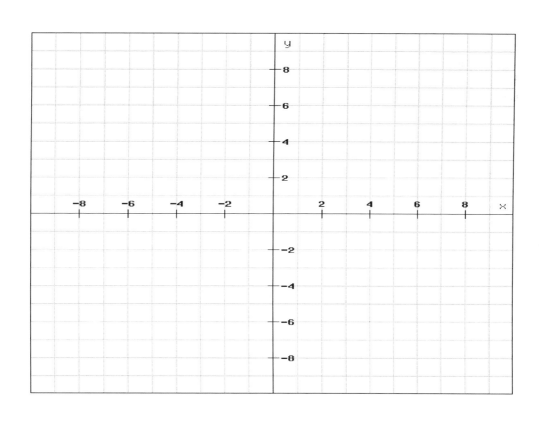

65. $f(x) = x^2 \ln(x), x \in \mathbb{R}$

Domain: _____

Extrema (using the 1st and if needed 2nd derivatives)

Vertical asymptotes: _____

Horizontal asymptotes: _____

Range of the function: _____

Slant Asymptotes: _____

Function Increases: _____

Function decreases: _____

y intercept: _____

Concave up: _____

Concave down: _____

x intercept(s): _____

Inflection point(s)_____

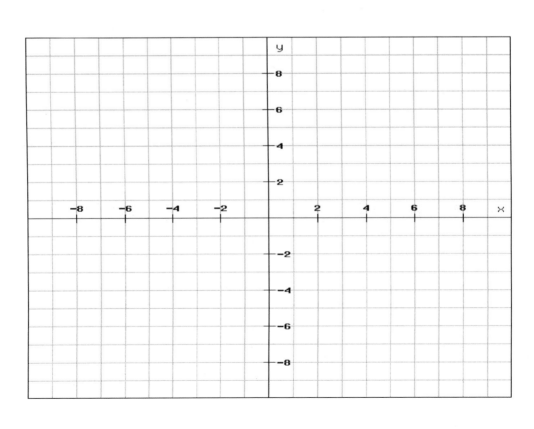

66. $f(x) = x(\ln(x))^2, x \in \mathbb{R}$

Domain: _____

Vertical asymptotes: _____

Horizontal asymptotes: _____

Slant Asymptotes: _____

y intercept: _____

x intercept(s): _____

Extrema (using the 1st and if needed 2nd derivatives)

Range of the function: _____

Function Increases: _____

Function decreases: _____

Concave up: _____

Concave down: _____

Inflection point(s)_____

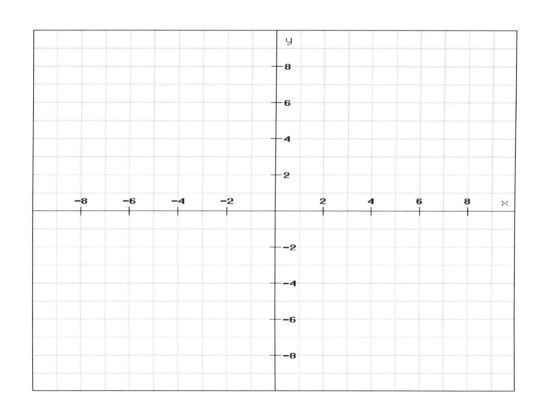

109

67. $f(x) = \dfrac{\ln(x)}{x}, x \in \mathbb{R}$

Domain: _____

Vertical asymptotes: _____

Horizontal asymptotes: _____

Slant Asymptotes: _____

y intercept: _____

x intercept(s): _____

Extrema (using the 1st and if needed 2nd derivatives)

Range of the function: _____

Function Increases: _____

Function decreases: _____

Concave up: _____

Concave down: _____

Inflection point(s) _____

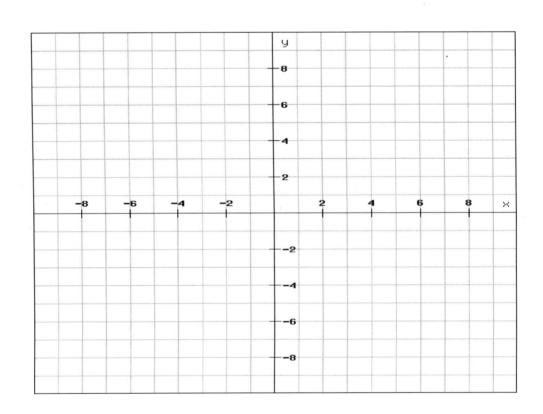

68. $f(x) = \sqrt{x} - x, x \in \mathbb{R}$

Domain: _____

Extrema (using the 1st and if needed 2nd derivatives)

Vertical asymptotes: _____

Horizontal asymptotes: _____

Range of the function: _____

Slant Asymptotes: _____

Function Increases: _____

Function decreases: _____

y intercept: _____

Concave up: _____

Concave down: _____

x intercept(s): _____

Inflection point(s)_____

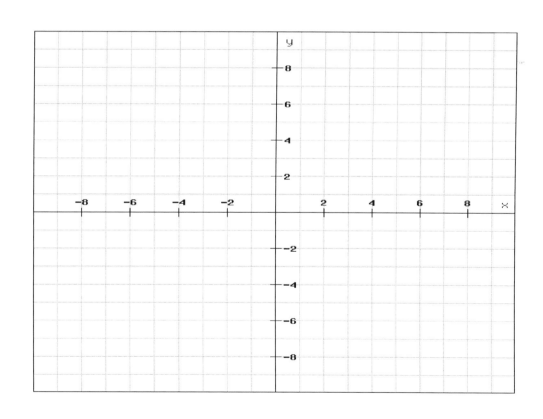

69. $f(x) = x^2 - \dfrac{1}{x}, x \in \mathbb{R}$

Domain: _____

Vertical asymptotes: _____

Horizontal asymptotes: _____

Slant Asymptotes: _____

y intercept: _____

x intercept(s): _____

Extrema (using the 1st and if needed 2nd derivatives)

Range of the function: _____

Function Increases: _____

Function decreases: _____

Concave up: _____

Concave down: _____

Inflection point(s)_____

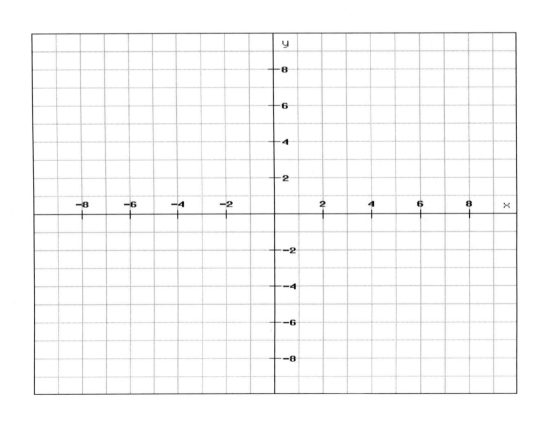

70. $f(x) = x^2 + \dfrac{2}{x}, x \in \mathbb{R}$

Domain: _____

Vertical asymptotes: _____

Horizontal asymptotes: _____

Slant Asymptotes: _____

y intercept: _____

x intercept(s): _____

Extrema (using the 1st and if needed 2nd derivatives)

Range of the function: _____

Function Increases: _____

Function decreases: _____

Concave up: _____

Concave down: _____

Inflection point(s)_____

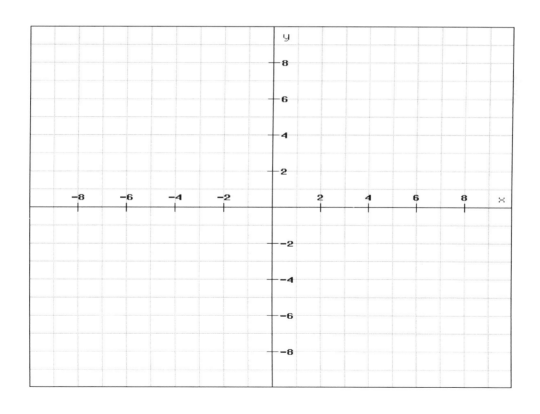

71. $f(x) = \sin(x^2), x \in \mathbb{R}$

Domain: _____

Vertical asymptotes: _____

Horizontal asymptotes: _____

Slant Asymptotes: _____

y intercept: _____

x intercept(s): _____

Extrema (using the 1st and if needed 2nd derivatives)

Range of the function: _____

Function Increases: _____

Function decreases: _____

Concave up: _____

Concave down: _____

Inflection point(s)_____

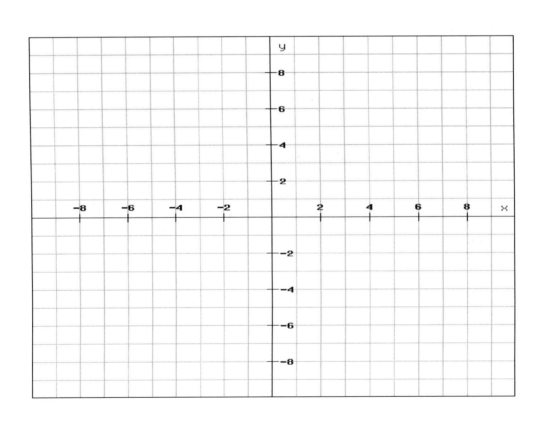

114

72. $f(x) = \sin(x) + x, x \in \mathbb{R}$

Domain: _____

Vertical asymptotes: _____

Horizontal asymptotes: _____

Slant Asymptotes: _____

y intercept: _____

x intercept(s): _____

Extrema (using the 1st and if needed 2nd derivatives)

Range of the function: _____

Function Increases: _____

Function decreases: _____

Concave up: _____

Concave down: _____

Inflection point(s)_____

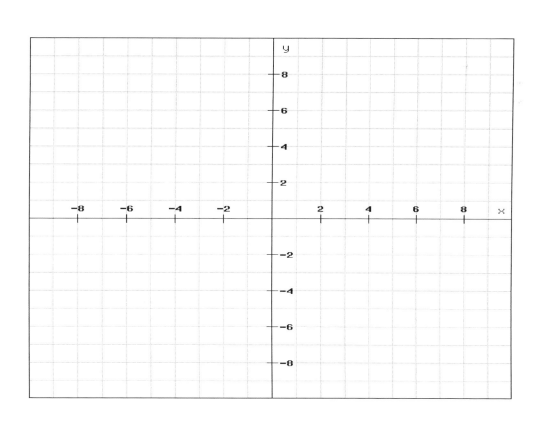

73. $f(x) = x(1 - \ln(x^2)), x \in \mathbb{R}$

Domain: _____

Vertical asymptotes: _____

Horizontal asymptotes: _____

Slant Asymptotes: _____

y intercept: _____

x intercept(s): _____

Extrema (using the 1st and if needed 2nd derivatives)

Range of the function: _____

Function Increases: _____

Function decreases: _____

Concave up: _____

Concave down: _____

Inflection point(s) _____

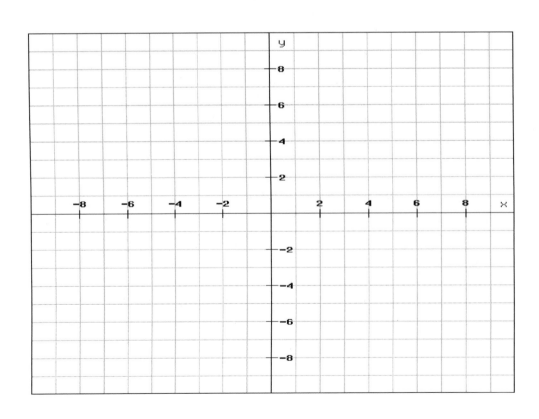

74. $f(x) = e^{x-x^2}, x \in \mathbb{R}$

Domain: _____

Vertical asymptotes: _____

Horizontal asymptotes: _____

Slant Asymptotes: _____

y intercept: _____

x intercept(s): _____

Extrema (using the 1st and if needed 2nd derivatives)

Range of the function: _____

Function Increases: _____

Function decreases: _____

Concave up: _____

Concave down: _____

Inflection point(s) _____

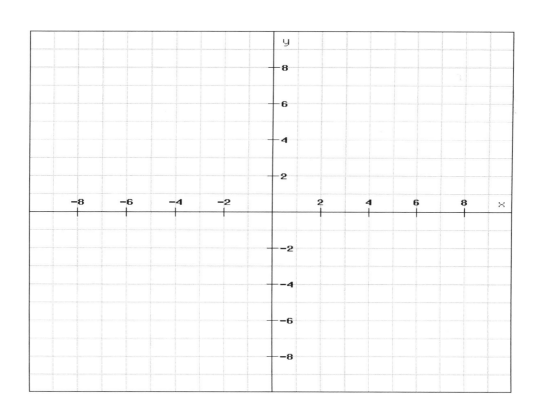

117

75. $f(x) = x^3(1 - \ln(x^2)), x \in \mathbb{R}$

Domain: _____

Vertical asymptotes: _____

Horizontal asymptotes: _____

Slant Asymptotes: _____

y intercept: _____

x intercept(s): _____

Extrema (using the 1st and if needed 2nd derivatives)

Range of the function: _____

Function Increases: _____

Function decreases: _____

Concave up: _____

Concave down: _____

Inflection point(s) _____

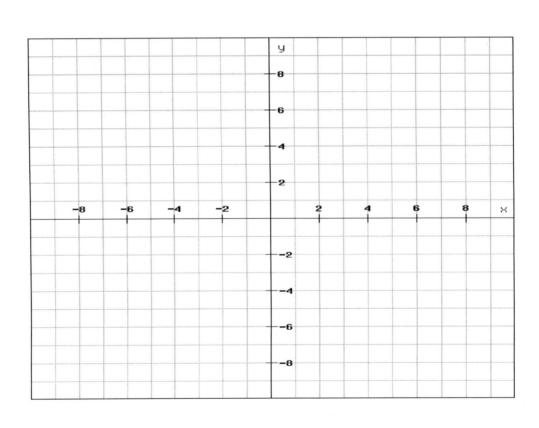

76. $f(x) = e^{x^3 - x^2}, x \in \mathbb{R}$

Domain: _____

Vertical asymptotes: _____

Horizontal asymptotes: _____

Slant Asymptotes: _____

y intercept: _____

x intercept(s): _____

Extrema (using the 1st and if needed 2nd derivatives)

Range of the function: _____

Function Increases: _____

Function decreases: _____

Concave up: _____

Concave down: _____

Inflection point(s)_____

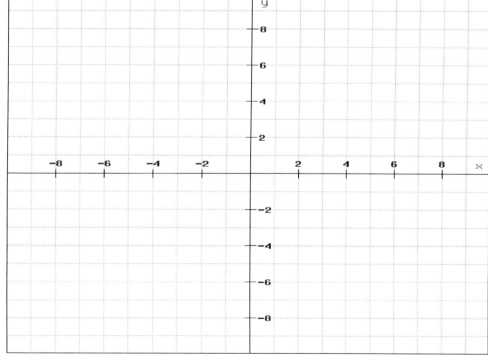

119

77. $f(x) = \ln(x^2 - 1), x \in \mathbb{R}$

Domain: _____

Vertical asymptotes: _____

Horizontal asymptotes: _____

Slant Asymptotes: _____

y intercept: _____

x intercept(s): _____

Extrema (using the 1st and if needed 2nd derivatives)

Range of the function: _____

Function Increases: _____

Function decreases: _____

Concave up: _____

Concave down: _____

Inflection point(s)_____

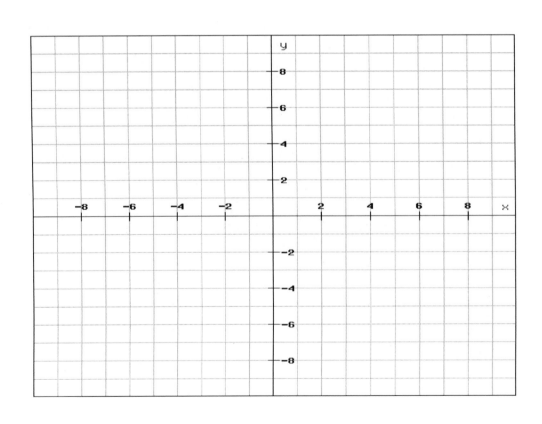

120

78. $f(x) = \ln(4 - x^2), x \in \mathbb{R}$

Domain: _____

Vertical asymptotes: _____

Horizontal asymptotes: _____

Slant Asymptotes: _____

y intercept: _____

x intercept(s): _____

Extrema (using the 1st and if needed 2nd derivatives)

Range of the function: _____

Function Increases: _____

Function decreases: _____

Concave up: _____

Concave down: _____

Inflection point(s) _____

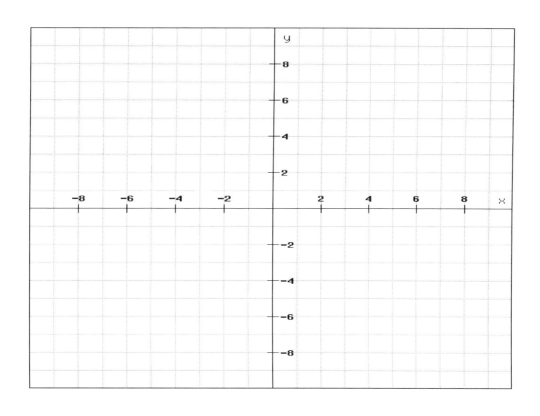

121

79. $f(x) = \sqrt{3x - x^2}$

Domain: _____

Vertical asymptotes: _____

Horizontal asymptotes: _____

Slant Asymptotes: _____

y intercept: _____

x intercept(s): _____

Extrema (using the 1st and if needed 2nd derivatives)

Range of the function: _____

Function Increases: _____

Function decreases: _____

Concave up: _____

Concave down: _____

Inflection point(s)_____

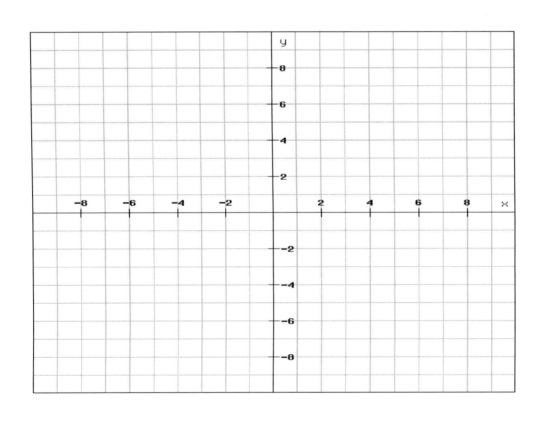

80. $f(x) = \dfrac{1}{\sqrt{3x - x^2}}$

Domain: _____

Vertical asymptotes: _____

Horizontal asymptotes: _____

Slant Asymptotes: _____

y intercept: _____

x intercept(s): _____

Extrema (using the 1st and if needed 2nd derivatives)

Range of the function: _____

Function Increases: _____

Function decreases: _____

Concave up: _____

Concave down: _____

Inflection point(s)_____

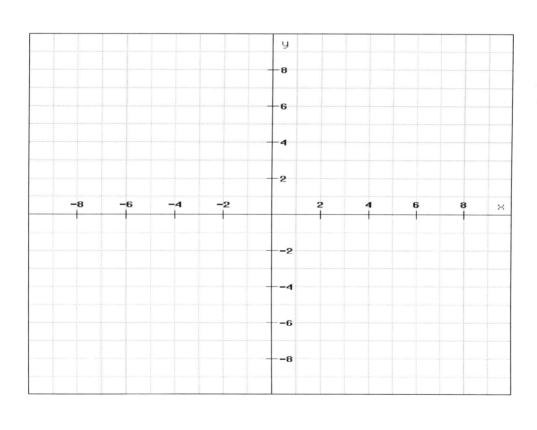

81. $f(x) = \dfrac{1}{\sin(x)+1}, x \in \mathbb{R}$

Domain: _____

Extrema (using the 1st and if needed 2nd derivatives)

Vertical asymptotes: _____

Horizontal asymptotes: _____

Range of the function: _____

Slant Asymptotes: _____

Function Increases: _____

Function decreases: _____

y intercept: _____

Concave up: _____

Concave down: _____

x intercept(s): _____

Inflection point(s)_____

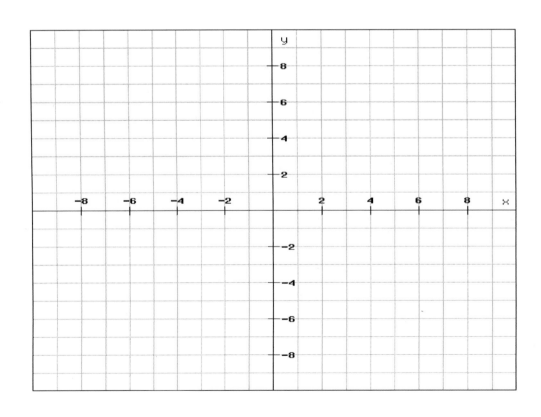

1.9. – INDEFINITE INTEGRATION

Integration is the inverse operation to differentiation. Its origin was the necessity to calculate areas and volumes of shapes that are not formed by straight lines (spheres, ellipsoids etc.)

Notation:

$\frac{dy}{dx} = f'(x) \rightarrow y = f(x) + c, c \in \mathbb{R}$, y is the underivative of f'(x)

The set of all antiderivatives is called the indefinite integral $\int f(x)dx$, f(x) is the integrand, x is the variable of integration, usually we write:

$$\int f(x)dx = F(x) + c$$

Example:

If $f(x) = x^2 + C$ then $f'(x) = 2x$

Therefore

$\int (2x)dx = x^2 + C$

Exercises:

1. $\int x^{75} - 12x + 2dx =$

2. $\int \frac{1}{x^3} - 3x^{\frac{2}{3}} + 31xdx =$

3. $\int \sqrt[4]{\frac{1}{x^3}} - x + 1 + \pi + \cos(1) + edx =$

4. $\int \frac{1}{x^3} - 3x + 3dx =$

5. $\int \frac{1}{x^2} - \frac{3}{\sqrt{2x^3}} dx =$

6. $\int \frac{4}{x^5} - \frac{3}{2x^2} dx =$

7. $\int \frac{-5}{x^{55}} - \frac{5}{7x^{211}} dx =$

8. $\int \frac{2}{x} - \frac{5}{x} dx =$

> **Important: The "primitive function" means the integral.**

$$\int x^n \, dx = \frac{x^{(n+1)}}{n+1} + C \quad n \neq -1$$

$$\int \frac{1}{x} \, dx = \ln(x) + C$$

125

9. $\int \dfrac{2}{x^3} + \dfrac{5}{3x^{10}} - \dfrac{2}{x}\, dx =$

10. $\int \dfrac{15}{x} - x^{12}\, dx =$

11. $\int \dfrac{2}{x^3} + \dfrac{5}{3x^{10}} - \dfrac{2}{x}\, dx =$

12. $\int \sqrt{\dfrac{a}{x}} + \dfrac{a}{x} + \dfrac{x}{a} - ae^x + \dfrac{1}{a} + x^a\, dx =$

13. $\int 0.1x - 0.2e^x\, dx =$

14. $\int \dfrac{1}{x} - 15e^x + 0.2\, dx =$

15. $\int \sqrt{\dfrac{2}{x}} + \dfrac{2}{3} - e^x\, dx =$

16. $\int \dfrac{2}{x^{40}} + \dfrac{2}{7x^{12}} - 5e^x\, dx =$

17. $\int 7\cos(x) + 12x\, dx =$

18. $\int -\cos(x) - \sin(x) - \dfrac{2}{x} + \dfrac{2}{x^2} - e^x\, dx =$

19. $\int \cos(4) + 7e^x + \dfrac{3}{x^{12}}\, dx =$

20. $\int \cos(x) + \sin(x) + \dfrac{3}{x}\, dx =$

21. $\int \cos(4) + \sin(x) + \dfrac{3}{\sqrt{x^7}}\, dx =$

22. $\int 7 - \dfrac{a}{x} + \dfrac{b}{2x^5} + 4\, dx =$

23. $\int \dfrac{1}{3}\cos(x) + \dfrac{1}{2} - \sqrt{3}e^x + \sqrt{3} + \sqrt{2}x - \dfrac{2}{x} + \dfrac{1}{2x} + 1 + x\, dx =$

24. $\int \dfrac{1}{3}\sin(x) + \dfrac{5}{2} - \sqrt{3}e^x + \sqrt{7} + \sqrt{2}x - \dfrac{a}{x} + \dfrac{1}{bx} + 1 + x\, dx =$

$$\boxed{\int e^x\, dx = e^x + C}$$

$$\int \sin(x)\, dx = -\cos(x) + C$$

$$\int \cos(x)\, dx = \sin(x) + C$$

Since integration is the inverse process to differentiation the following integrals are immediate:

(See that if you differentiate right side you obtain the left side)

$$\int (ax+b)^n \, dx = \frac{(ax+b)^{(n+1)}}{a(n+1)} + C \quad n \neq -1$$

$$\int \frac{1}{ax+b} \, dx = \frac{\ln(ax+b)}{a} + C$$

$$\int e^{(ax+b)} \, dx = \frac{e^{(ax+b)}}{a} + C$$

$$\int \cos(ax+b) \, dx = \frac{\sin(ax+b)}{a} + C$$

$$\int \sin(ax+b) \, dx = -\frac{\cos(ax+b)}{a} + C$$

More in general:

$$\int (g(x))^n \, g'(x)dx = \frac{g(x)^{n+1}}{n+1} + C, n \neq -1$$

Example: $\int (3x^2 + 5x)^{-4} (6x+5)dx = \frac{(3x^2+5x)^{-3}}{-3} + C, n \neq -1$

See that if you differentiate right side you obtain the left side.

$$\int (g(x))^{-1} g'(x)dx = Ln(|g(x)|) + C$$

Example: $\int (3x^2 + 5x)^{-1} (6x+5)dx = Ln(|3x^2 + 5x|) + C$

See that if you differentiate right side you obtain the left side.

$$\int e^{g(x)} g'(x)dx = e^{g(x)} + C$$

Example: $\int e^{(3x^2+5x)}(6x+5)dx = e^{(3x^2+5x)} + C$

See that if you differentiate right side you obtain the left side.

$$\int \cos(g(x)) g'(x)dx = \sin(g(x)) + C$$

Example: $\int \cos(3x^2 + 5x)(6x+5)dx = \sin(3x^2 + 5x) + C$

See that if you differentiate right side you obtain the left side.

$$\int \sin(g(x)) g'(x)dx = -\cos(g(x)) + C$$

Example: $\int \sin(3x^2 + 5x)(6x+5)dx = -\cos(3x^2 + 5x) + C$

See that if you differentiate right side you obtain the left side.

And in general:

$$\int (f(g(x))g'(x)dx = F(g(x)) + C$$

Exercises:

25. $\displaystyle\int 2x \cos(x^2)dx =$

26. $\displaystyle\int -2\sin(-x^3)x^2 dx =$

27. $\displaystyle\int xe^{x^2+3} dx =$

28. $\displaystyle\int \cos(x^3+1)x^2 dx =$

29. $\displaystyle\int \frac{4x}{x^2+2} dx =$

30. $\displaystyle\int x^3 \sin(x^4+5)dx =$

31. $\displaystyle\int \frac{4}{(3x+5)^7} dx =$

32. $\displaystyle\int e^{\frac{x}{2}} dx =$

33. $\displaystyle\int 2x \sin(3x^2+52)dx =$

34. $\displaystyle\int 5\cos(3x+5)dx =$

35. $\displaystyle\int \frac{20x+2}{5x^2+x} dx =$

36. $\displaystyle\int \frac{2}{5}\cos(\frac{x}{2}+5)dx =$

37. $\displaystyle\int \frac{x^2}{x^3+3} dx =$

38. $\displaystyle\int (3x^2-4)e^{x^3-4x} dx =$

39. $\displaystyle\int 5x(x^2-4)^{-6} dx =$

40. $\displaystyle\int 15(e^x-4)^{11} e^x dx =$

41. $\displaystyle\int x^2 e^{4x^3+17} dx =$

129

42. $\displaystyle \int e^{-5x+7}\, dx =$

43. $\displaystyle \int \frac{2x+3}{x^2+3x}\, dx =$

44. $\displaystyle \int \frac{4x+2}{2x^2+2x+7}\, dx =$

45. $\displaystyle \int \frac{4}{7}\cos(-7x+11)\, dx =$

46. $\displaystyle \int \frac{4x}{3}\cos(3x^2+15)\, dx =$

47. $\displaystyle \int \frac{4}{7}\sin(3x+5)\, dx =$

48. $\displaystyle \int \frac{4x}{3(x^2-5)^4}\, dx =$

49. $\displaystyle \int \frac{2x-5}{(x^2-5x)^5}\, dx =$

50. $\displaystyle \int -\frac{2x^3}{(x^4-3)^5}\, dx =$

51. $\displaystyle \int -\frac{2x}{3(x^2-3)}\, dx =$

52. $\displaystyle \int \frac{3x^2+5x}{x}\, dx =$

53. $\displaystyle \int \frac{x^3+x^2-2\sqrt{x}+1}{\sqrt[3]{x}}\, dx =$

54. $\displaystyle \int \frac{\sqrt{x}}{x^4}\, dx =$

55. $\displaystyle \int \left(\sqrt{x}+\sqrt{\frac{1}{x}}\right)dx =$

56. $\displaystyle \int \frac{\sqrt{x}+\sqrt[3]{x^2}}{\sqrt[6]{x^5}}\, dx =$

57. $\displaystyle \int \frac{x^2+\sqrt[3]{x^2}}{\sqrt{x}}\, dx =$

58. $\displaystyle \int \frac{dx}{x^2\,\sqrt[5]{x^2}} =$

59. $\int (3x + 5)dx =$

60. $\int (5x - 7)^{-3} \, dx =$

61. $\int (15x - 7)^{-\frac{1}{2}} \, dx =$

62. $\int (12x + 3)^{\frac{4}{7}} \, dx =$

63. $\int (12x + 3)^{-\frac{1}{12}} \, dx =$

64. $\int 6x(3x^2 + 5)^2 \, dx =$

65. $\int 18x(6x^3 + 5)^{-1} dx =$

66. $\int (60x^3 - 7)(15x^4 - 7x)^{-3} \, dx =$

67. $\int (\frac{1}{x} + 1)(\ln(x) + x)^{-\frac{1}{2}} \, dx =$

68. $\int 3x^4 (2x^5 + 3)^{\frac{4}{7}} \, dx =$

69. $\int (\frac{1}{\sqrt{x}} + 2)(\sqrt{x} + x)^{\frac{2}{5}} \, dx =$

70. $\int x^{-1} dx =$

71. $\int x^{-2} dx =$

72. $\int e^{2x} (e^{2x} + 2)^{-\frac{21}{4}} \, dx =$

73. $\int \frac{2}{x + 1} dx =$

74. $\int \dfrac{1}{5x+1}\,dx =$

75. $\int \dfrac{x}{3x^2+5}\,dx =$

76. $\int \dfrac{2x}{x^2+1}\,dx =$

77. $\int \dfrac{x^2}{x^3-5}\,dx =$

78. $\int \dfrac{2x^3}{3x^4-5}\,dx =$

79. $\int \dfrac{x^{-\frac{1}{2}}-2}{x^{\frac{1}{2}}-x}\,dx =$

80. $\int \dfrac{3x^2+1}{x^3+x}\,dx =$

81. $\int \dfrac{3x^7}{2x^8+1}\,dx =$

82. $\int \dfrac{5x^{\frac{3}{2}}-4x}{x^{\frac{5}{2}}-x^2}\,dx =$

83. $\int \dfrac{-5e^x}{e^x-4}\,dx =$

84. $\int \dfrac{2e^{3x+1}}{e^{3x+1}-3}\,dx =$

85. $\int \dfrac{14e^{7x+2}-2}{e^{7x+2}-x}\,dx =$

86. $\int \dfrac{4x+1}{8x^2+4x+4}\,dx =$

87. $\int \dfrac{(\tan(x)+3)^{-2}}{(\cos(x))^2}\,dx =$

88. $\int \dfrac{\sin(x)}{\cos(x)}\,dx =$

89. $\int \dfrac{1-\sin(x)}{x+\cos(x)}\,dx =$

90. $\int \dfrac{1}{x\ln(x)}\,dx =$

91. $\int \dfrac{1}{x\ln(2x)}\,dx =$

92. $\int \dfrac{1}{(3x+1)\ln(3x+1)}\,dx =$

93. $\int \dfrac{3x^2+5x-1}{x}\,dx =$

94. $\int \dfrac{x^3+x^2-2\sqrt{x}+1}{\sqrt[3]{x}}\,dx =$

95. $\int \dfrac{\sqrt{x}}{x^4}\,dx =$

96. $\int \left(\sqrt{x}+\dfrac{1}{x}\right)dx =$

97. $\int \dfrac{\sqrt{x}+\sqrt[3]{x^2}}{\sqrt[6]{x^5}}\,dx =$

98. $\int \dfrac{x^2+\sqrt[3]{x^2}}{\sqrt{x}}\,dx =$

99. $\int \dfrac{dx}{x^2\sqrt[5]{x^2}} =$

100. $\int \left(\dfrac{1}{x^2}-\dfrac{1}{x+1}\right)dx =$

101. $\int \left(\sqrt{x}+\dfrac{1}{\sqrt{x}}\right)^2 dx =$

102. $\int \left(x^2+\dfrac{1}{x}\right)^3 dx =$

103. $\int \left(\dfrac{1}{x^2}+\dfrac{1}{1+x^2}\right)dx =$

104. $\int \left(\sqrt{x} + \dfrac{1}{x}\right)^2 dx =$

105. $\int (nx)^{\frac{1-n}{n}} dx =$

106. $\int (a^{2/3} - x^{2/3})^3 dx =$

107. $\int (\sqrt{x} + 1)(x - \sqrt{x} + 1)\, dx =$

108. $\int \dfrac{(x^2 + 1)(x^2 - 2)}{\sqrt[3]{x^2}}\, dx =$

109. $\int \sqrt{\dfrac{5}{x^3}}\, dx =$

110. $\int (x + \sqrt{x})^2 dx =$

111. $\int \dfrac{5}{x + 4}\, dx =$

112. $\int (x + \dfrac{1}{x^2})^3 dx =$

113. $\int \dfrac{2}{2x + 3}\, dx =$

114. $\int \dfrac{e^x}{e^x + 4}\, dx =$

115. $\int \dfrac{x^2}{x^3 + 8}\, dx =$

116. $\int \dfrac{a\, dx}{a - x} =$

117. $\int \dfrac{e^{2x}}{e^{2x} + 2}\, dx =$

118. $\int \dfrac{\operatorname{sen} x}{2 + \cos x}\, dx =$

119. $\displaystyle\int \frac{sen(Ln(x))}{x}dx =$

120. $\displaystyle\int \frac{dx}{tg\frac{x}{5}} =$

121. $\displaystyle\int \frac{tg\sqrt{x}}{\sqrt{x}}\,dx =$

122. $\displaystyle\int x\cot g(x^2 + 1)\,dx =$

123. $\displaystyle\int \frac{Ln^3(x)}{x}dx =$

124. $\displaystyle\int \frac{e^x}{e^x - 1}\,dx =$

125. $\displaystyle\int \frac{\sqrt{x} + Ln(x)x}{x}dx =$

126. $\displaystyle\int \frac{x}{\sqrt{x^2 + 1}}\,dx =$

127. $\displaystyle\int \sqrt{2 - 5x}\,\,dx =$

128. $\displaystyle\int \sqrt{5x^2 - 4x + 3}\,\,(10x - 4)\,dx =$

129. $\displaystyle\int \frac{x^2}{\sqrt{x^3 + 2}}dx =$

130. $\displaystyle\int \frac{3x^2}{\sqrt{1 - 2x^3}}\,dx =$

131. $\displaystyle\int 3x\sqrt{1 - 2x^2}\,\,dx =$

132. $\displaystyle\int \frac{x + 3}{\sqrt{x^2 + 6x + 4}}dx =$

133. $\displaystyle\int \frac{dx}{\sqrt{x + 3} - \sqrt{x + 2}} =$

134. $\displaystyle\int \frac{\sqrt{x^2+4}+x}{\sqrt{x^2+4}}\,dx =$

135. $\displaystyle\int \frac{dx}{\sqrt{x}\sqrt{1+\sqrt{x}}} =$

136. $\displaystyle\int \frac{e^x}{\sqrt{1+e^x}}\,dx =$

137. $\displaystyle\int (\cos x - \operatorname{sen} x)\,dx =$

138. $\displaystyle\int \frac{2-2\operatorname{sen}^2 x + 3\cos x}{\cos x}\,dx =$

139. $\displaystyle\int \operatorname{sen} x \cdot \cos x\,dx =$

140. $\displaystyle\int \frac{\operatorname{sen}^2 x - 1 + 5\operatorname{sen}^3 x}{2\operatorname{sen}^2 x}\,dx =$

141. $\displaystyle\int 4^x\,dx =$

142. $\displaystyle\int 7^x\,dx =$

143. $\displaystyle\int 5^{2x}\,dx =$

144. $\displaystyle\int x \cdot 6^{x^2}\,dx =$

145. $\displaystyle\int (\cos 3x)2^{\sin 3x}\,dx =$

146. $\displaystyle\int e^x \cdot 9^{e^x}\,dx =$

147. $\displaystyle\int x^2 \cdot 6^{4x^3+1}\,dx =$

148. $\displaystyle\int \frac{4^{\sqrt{x}}}{\sqrt{x}}\,dx =$

149. $\int e^{3x} dx =$

150. $\int x e^{3x^2} dx =$

151. $\int \dfrac{e^x + e^{-x}}{\left(e^x - e^{-x}\right)^2} dx =$

152. $\int \dfrac{e^{3x} + e^x + 2}{e^x} dx =$

153. $\int e^x \left(e^x + 2\right)^2 dx =$

154. $\int \cos x \cdot e^{\sin x} dx =$

155. $\int \dfrac{e^{\frac{1}{x}}}{x^2} dx =$

156. $\int e^x \sqrt{1 - e^x} \, dx =$

157. $\int \left(x^2 - 2\right) e^{x^3 - 6x + 5} dx =$

158. $\int \left(e^x - e^{-x}\right)\left(e^x + e^{-x}\right)^4 dx =$

159. $\int \dfrac{1}{2x + 3} dx =$

160. $\int \dfrac{1}{2 - 3x} dx =$

161. $\int \dfrac{x^2 + 2x + 3}{x} dx =$

162. $\int \dfrac{e^x}{1 + e^x} dx =$

163. $\int \dfrac{(\ln x)^3}{x} dx =$

164. $\int \dfrac{x+2}{x-1} dx =$

165. $\int \dfrac{x^2+2x+3}{x+1} dx =$

166. $\int (e^x - e^{-x})^2 dx =$

167. $\int \dfrac{\cos x}{\sin x} dx =$

168. $\int \dfrac{\ln(x)}{x} dx =$

169. $\int \dfrac{x\,dx}{x+1} =$

170. $\int x^2 e^{x^3} dx =$

171. $\int \dfrac{x-2}{x+1} dx =$

172. $\int \dfrac{2x-3}{x+1} dx =$

INTEGRATION BY PARTS

$$\int f'(x)g(x) = f(x)g(x) - \int f(x)g'(x)$$

173. $\quad \int \ln(x)dx =$

174. $\quad \int \dfrac{L n(x)}{x^2} dx =$

175. $\quad \int x \ln(x)dx =$

176. $\quad \int x^2 \ln(x)dx =$

177. $\quad \int x \sin(x)dx =$

178. $\quad \int x^2 \sin(2x)dx =$

179. $\int \mathrm{tg}^2\, x\, dx =$

180. $\int (x^2 + x)e^{-3x}\, dx =$

181. $\int (2 - x^2)\cos(-3x)\, dx =$

182. $\int e^x \cos(x)\, dx =$

183. $\int e^{2x} \sin(3x) dx =$

184. $\int \left(\ln(x) \right)^2 dx =$

INTEGRALS ARCSIN, ARCOS, ARCTAN TYPE

185. $\int \dfrac{2}{x^2+1} \cdot dx =$

186. $\int \dfrac{2x}{x^2+1} \cdot dx =$

187. $\int \dfrac{-11}{x^2+4} \, dx =$

188. $\int \dfrac{7}{2x^2+3} \, dx =$

189. $\int \dfrac{1}{x^2+2x+2} \, dx =$

190. $\displaystyle\int \frac{-15}{x^2 + 4x + 10}\, dx =$

191. $\displaystyle\int \frac{2}{x^2 - 6x + 10}\, dx =$

192. $\displaystyle\int \frac{1}{\sqrt{1 - 4x^2}}\, dx =$

193. $\displaystyle\int \frac{1}{1 + 9x^2}\, dx =$

194. $\displaystyle\int \frac{x}{\sqrt{1 - x^4}}\, dx =$

195. $\displaystyle\int \frac{e^x}{1+e^{2x}}\,dx =$

196. $\displaystyle\int \frac{x^2}{1+x^6}\,dx =$

197. $\displaystyle\int \frac{1}{\sqrt{1-\frac{x^2}{4}}}\,dx =$

198. $\displaystyle\int \frac{1}{1+\frac{x^2}{9}}\,dx =$

INTEGRATION USING A CHANGE OF VARIABLE

199. $\int \dfrac{e^x}{e^x + 1}\, dx =$

200. $\int \dfrac{1}{x\sqrt{x-1}} \cdot dx =$

201. $\int \dfrac{x^5}{(1 + x^2)^4} \cdot dx =$

202. $\int x.\sqrt{x-1} \cdot dx =$

203. $\int \dfrac{x}{(x-2)^3} \cdot dx =$

204. $\int \sqrt{4-x^2}\, dx$ (use x = 2sin(t))

205. $\int \cos \sqrt{x}\,dx$ (use $x = t^2$)

ORDER OF OPERATIONS:

1.   Is it an immediate integral?   If not:

2.   Is it possible to rewrite the integrand (factorize, divide, add, subtract, divide numerator and denominator etc.) and make it an immediate integral? If not:

3.   Is it possible to use integration by parts? (Usually if there is a product. A single expression can always be multiplied by 1)

4.   A change of variable?

PRACTICE

206. $\int x \, sen(1-x^2) \, dx =$

207. $\int \dfrac{1}{1+x^2} \, dx =$

208. $\int (tgx + \cot gx)^2 \, dx =$

209. $\int \dfrac{dx}{senx} =$

210. $\int \dfrac{dx}{senx \cdot \cos x} =$

211. $\int \dfrac{e^x}{\sqrt{1-e^{2x}}}dx=$

212. $\int \dfrac{dx}{e^x\sqrt{1-e^{-2x}}}=$

213. $\int \dfrac{dx}{x(Ln^2(x)+1)}=$

214. $\int \dfrac{e^{\sqrt{x}}+x}{\sqrt{x}}dx=$

215. $\int \dfrac{x-\sqrt{arctg\,2x}}{1+4x^2}dx=$

216. $\int \dfrac{x^2}{\sqrt{1-x^6}}\, dx =$

217. $\int \dfrac{dx}{\sqrt{4-x^2}} =$

218. $\int \dfrac{dx}{9+x^2} =$

219. $\int \dfrac{dx}{\sqrt{25-x^2}} =$

220. $\int \dfrac{dx}{16+x^2} =$

221. $\displaystyle\int \frac{dx}{\sqrt{1-9x^2}} =$

222. $\displaystyle\int \frac{dx}{1+16x^2} =$

223. $\displaystyle\int \frac{e^{2x}}{\sqrt{1-e^{4x}}}\,dx =$

224. $\displaystyle\int \frac{x}{4+x^4}\,dx =$

225. $\displaystyle\int \frac{x^2}{\sqrt{100-x^6}}\,dx =$

226. $\displaystyle\int \frac{x^3}{1+x^8}\,dx =$

227. $\displaystyle\int \frac{\sin(\theta)}{1+\cos^2(\theta)}\,d\theta =$

228. $\displaystyle\int \sqrt{\frac{arcsen(x)}{1-x^2}}\,dx =$

229. $\displaystyle\int \frac{a^x}{1+a^{2x}}\,dx =$

230. $\displaystyle\int \frac{x}{\cos^2 x^2}\,dx =$

231. $\displaystyle\int \frac{e^t}{\sqrt{1-e^{2t}}}\, dt =$

232. $\displaystyle\int \frac{dx}{x^2\left(1+\left(\frac{1}{x}\right)^2\right)} =$

233. $\displaystyle\int \frac{dx}{x^2+7} =$

234. $\displaystyle\int \frac{dx}{\sqrt{4-x^2}} =$

235. $\displaystyle\int \frac{\sqrt{2+x^2}}{\sqrt{4-x^4}}\, dx =$

236. $\int \dfrac{dx}{x\sqrt{x^2-2}} =$

237. $\int \dfrac{x}{a^4+x^4}\,dx =$

238. $\int \dfrac{1+2x}{1+x^2}\,dx =$

239. $\int \dfrac{dx}{3x^2+5} =$

240. $\int \dfrac{2x+3}{2x+1}\,dx =$

241. $\displaystyle\int \frac{2x-5}{3x^2+2}\,dx =$

242. $\displaystyle\int \frac{x^3}{\sqrt{a^4-x^4}}\,dx =$

243. $\displaystyle\int \frac{dx}{\sqrt{9-16x^2}} =$

244. $\displaystyle\int \frac{x}{(x+1)^2}\,dx =$

245. $\displaystyle\int 3^{2+x}\,dx =$

246. $\displaystyle\int \frac{3^x + 4^{x+1}}{5^x}\,dx =$

247. $\displaystyle\int 3^x e^x\,dx =$

248. $\displaystyle\int a^{5x^2} 10x\,dx =$

249. $\displaystyle\int x 7^{x^2}\,dx =$

250. $\displaystyle\int e^x \sqrt{a - be^x}\,dx =$

251. $\int \dfrac{dx}{\sqrt{a-bx}} =$

252. $\int x^{n-1} \cdot \sqrt{a+bx^n}\, dx =$

253. $\int \dfrac{e^x}{e^{2x}+1}\, dx =$

254. $\int \dfrac{x}{\sqrt{3x^2-3}}\, dx =$

255. $\int \dfrac{2+\sqrt[6]{x-1}}{\sqrt[3]{(x-1)^2}-\sqrt{x-1}}\,dx$ (use $x-1=t^6$)

256. $\int \dfrac{x-\sqrt{x-1}}{x+\sqrt{x-1}}\,dx$ (use $x-1=t^2$)

257. $\int \dfrac{x\ln(2x^2+2)}{x^2+1}\,dx =$

158

258. $\int \dfrac{2x}{x-4} dx =$

259. $\int \dfrac{e^x}{1+e^x} dx =$

260. $\int \dfrac{5x}{(x-4)^3} dx =$

261. $\int (-2x+5)^{3/2} dx =$

262. $\int xe^{-2x} dx =$

263. $\displaystyle\int \frac{\ln(x)}{x}\,dx =$

264. $\displaystyle\int x^2 e^{-2x}\,dx =$

265. $\displaystyle\int \frac{t}{t^4+16}\,dt =$

266. $\displaystyle\int \frac{e^x}{\sqrt{1-e^{2x}}}\,dx =$

267. $\displaystyle\int \frac{dx}{x^2+6x+13}\,dx =$

268. $\displaystyle\int \frac{\cos(x)}{\sqrt{4-\sin^2(x)}}\,dx =$

1.10. – DEFINITE INTEGRTION

The result of indefinite integration is a: _____ $= F(x) = \int f(x)dx$

The result of definite integration is _____ $= \int_{a}^{b} f(x)dx = F(b) - F(a)$

Definite integration represents the "**area under the graph**".

1. Above the x axis definite integrals have a _____ .

2. Below the x axis definite integrals have a _____ .

3. $\int_{2}^{3} \dfrac{1}{x} + 2x\,dx =$

4. $\int_{\pi}^{\frac{3\pi}{2}} \cos(x) + x\,dx =$

5. $\int_{1}^{e} (\ln(x))dx =$

6. $\displaystyle\int_{2}^{6} x^2 + 1\,dx =$

7. $\displaystyle\int_{0}^{2} 3^x\,dx =$

8. $\displaystyle\int_{1}^{\sqrt{2}} x\cdot 2^{-x^2}\,dx =$

9. $\displaystyle\int_{0}^{\frac{\pi}{6}} (\cos\theta)4^{-\sin\theta}\,d\theta =$

10. $\displaystyle\int_{-3}^{-1} 10^{-x}\,dx =$

11. $\displaystyle\int_{0}^{\frac{1}{2}} \frac{1}{\sqrt{1-x^2}}\,dx =$

12. $\displaystyle\int_{\sqrt{2}}^{2} \frac{1}{x\sqrt{x^2-1}}\,dx$

13. $\int_{-1}^{1} \frac{1}{1+x^2} dx$

14. $\int_{0}^{3} e^{3-x} dx$

15. $\int_{0}^{1} \frac{x^3}{x^4+1} dx$

16. $\int_{\frac{\pi}{6}}^{\frac{\pi}{2}} \frac{\cos(x)}{\sin(x)} dx$

17. $\int_{0}^{\frac{1}{6}} \frac{1}{\sqrt{1-9x^2}} dx$

18. $\int_{\sqrt{3}}^{3} \frac{1}{9+x^2} dx$

19. $\int_{1}^{e^2} \frac{3}{x} dx$

BOUNDARY CONDITION

20. Given that $\int \dfrac{1}{x} dx = F(x) + C$ and that $F(1) = 2$ find C.

21. Given that $\int \sin(2x) dx = F(x) + C$ and that $F(\pi) = 1$ find C.

22. Given that $\int e^{2x} + (x-1)^6 dx = F(x) + C$ and that $F(0) = 1$ find C.

23. Given that $\int \sqrt{x} + x dx = F(x) + C$ and that $F(1) = 1$ find C.

24. Find the area enclosed between the functions $f(x) = x^2 - x$ and the x axis. Make a sketch to show the mentioned area.

25. Find the area enclosed between the function $f(x) = x^3 - 6x^2 + 8x$ and the x axis. Make a sketch to show the mentioned area.

26. Find the area enclosed between the function $f(x) = -x^3 + 3x^2 - 4$ and the x axis
    Make a sketch to show the mentioned area.

27. Find the area enclosed between the functions $f(x) = x^2 + x$ and $g(x) = x + 2$.
    Make a sketch to show the mentioned area.

28. Find the area enclosed between the functions $f(x) = x^2 + 2$ and $g(x) = -x^2 + 3$. Make a sketch to show the mentioned area.

29. Find the area enclosed between the functions $f(x) = x^4 - 2x + 1$ and $g(x) = -x^2 + 1$. Make a sketch to show the mentioned area.

30. Find the area enclosed between the functions $f(x) = 2 - x^2$ and $g(x) = |x|$. Make a sketch to show the mentioned area.

31. Find the area enclosed between the function $f(x) = x^2 + 2x + 2$, the tangent to $f(x)$ at its extrema and the tangent to $f(x)$ with a slope 6. Make a sketch to show the mentioned area.

32. Find the area enclosed between the functions $f(x) = 5 - x^2 + 4x$ and $g(x) = 5$. Make a sketch to show the mentioned area.

33. Find the area enclosed between the functions $f(x) = x^2 - 2x$ and $g(x) = x$. Make a sketch to show the mentioned area.

34. The area enclosed between the curve $y = a(1 - (x - 2)^2)$ with $a > 0$ and the x axis is 12. Find a. Make a sketch to show the mentioned area.

35. Given the function $f(x) = ae^{\frac{x}{3}} + \dfrac{1}{x^2}, x \neq 0$, find:

    a. $\displaystyle\int_{1}^{2} f(x)dx$ in terms of a.

    b. If F(x) is a primitive of f(x) find a knowing that $F(1) = 0$ and $F(2) = \dfrac{1}{2}$

36. Find the area bounded by: $y = e^{-x}$; $x = 0$; $y = 0$ and $x = 1$. Make a sketch to show the mentioned area.

37. Find the area enclosed between the function $f(x) = 1 - e^{-x}$, the tangent to $f(x)$ at the point where x = 0 and the line x = 2. Make a sketch to show the mentioned area.

VOLUMES OF REVOLUTION

One possible way to create a Volume of Revolution is by spinning a certain area around the x axis or y axis.

For example, the volume of revolution formed by spinning the function $f(x) = x^2$ around the x axis between 0 and 2 is the following:

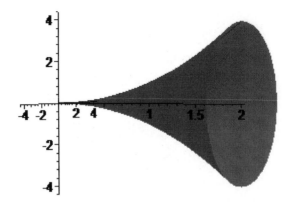

Since a volume o f revolution can be seen as the sum of the areas of infinite circles with changing sizes and can be calculated by (in this case):

$$V = \int_0^2 \pi x^2 \, dx = \left[\pi \frac{x^3}{3} \right]_0^2 = \frac{8\pi}{3}$$

In general it is given by:

$$V = \int_a^b \pi \left(f(x) \right)^2 dx \text{ (spinning around the x axis)}$$

$$V = \int_c^d \pi \left(f(y) \right)^2 dy \text{ (spinning around the x axis)}$$

1. Find the volume of revolution formed by the function $f(x) = x + 1, x \in [0,5]$
   a. Around the x axis.
   b. Around the y axis.

2. Find the volume of revolution formed by the function $f(x) = e^x, x \in [0,1]$

    a. Around the x axis.
    b. Around the y axis.

3. Find the volume of revolution formed by the function

    $f(x) = \sqrt{\sin(2x)}, x \in [0, \frac{\pi}{6}]$ Around the x axis.

4. Find the volume of revolution formed by the function $f(x) = \sqrt{x-1}, x \in [2,3]$

    a. Around the x axis.
    b. Around the y axis.

1.11. – KINEMATICS

1. The displacement of an object is measure in _____.

2. The velocity of an object is the _____ and it is

   measured in _____. Mathematically it is the _____ of the

   displacement.

3. The acceleration of an object is the _____ and it is

   measured in _____. Mathematically it is the _____ of the

   velocity or the _____ of the displacement.

4. An object accelerates from rest with a = 2 m/s^2 during 4 seconds, write down

   its velocity: _____.

5. An object moves at 12 m/s and accelerates with a = –3 m/s^2 during 2 seconds,

   write down its final velocity: _____.

6. If the distance run by an object after t seconds is given by $d(t) = 2t^2 + 3t + 5$,
   find:

   a. Its initial position.

   b. Its position after 2 seconds.

   c. Its velocity after 2 seconds.

   d. Its acceleration after 2 seconds.

7. The velocity of an object after t seconds is given by $v(t) = 2\sin(3t)$, find:

    a. Its initial velocity.

    b. Its initial acceleration.

    c. The period of its motion.

8. The velocity of an object after t seconds is given by $v(t) = e^{-\frac{x}{a}}$, find:

    a. Its initial velocity.

    b. Given that its initial acceleration is -3 m/s^2, find a.

    c. Given that the initial displacement of the object is 2m, find its displacement after 3 seconds.

9. The acceleration of an object is given by $a(t) = \dfrac{1}{(t+1)^2}$, find:

    a. Given that v(0) = 0, find its velocity as a function time.

    b. Given that d(0) = 0, find its displacement as a function time.

    c. Write the acceleration and the velocity of the object after a long period

10. The acceleration of an object is given by $a(t) = 3\cos(2t)$, find:

    a. Given that v(0) = 0, find its velocity as a function time.

    b. Given that d(0) = 0, find its displacement as a function time.

2.1. – VECTORS

Physical magnitudes in nature are classified in different ways. One of the classifications is to scalars and vectors.

From a physical point of view:

Scalars are magnitudes the have only "size", for example mass, temperature, speed, volume, time etc. **Vectors** on the other hand are the magnitudes that have a "size" (the magnitude) and a "direction", for example: position, velocity, acceleration, force, electric field etc.

From a mathematical point of view:

A vector is a "collection of numbers or symbols" in a certain order. A scalar would be a "Collection" of a single number.

Vectors:

In case it is a collection of n objects, it is called a n–dimensional vector. So the vector $\vec{A}$ given by

$$\vec{A} = \begin{bmatrix} A_1 \\ A_2 \\ .. \\ .. \\ A_n \end{bmatrix}$$

is a n–dimensional column vector with n components, $A_1, A_2, ..., A_n$. A row vector is of the form $\vec{B} = [B_1, B_2, ..., B_n]$ where $\vec{B}$ is a n–dimensional row vector with n components $B_1, B_2, ..., B_n$.

Transposing a vector means changing _____ to _____ or _____ to _____.

What is a null vector?

A null vector is a vector with all the components of the vector equal to _____.

Exercises

1. Give an example of a 3–dimensional column vector:

2. Give an example of a 4–dimensional row null vector:

3. Give an example of a 1–dimensional _____ vector (and fill the blank):

4. Sketch the vectors: (1, 3), (–3, 1), (–3, –4). (5, –2) on the following diagram:

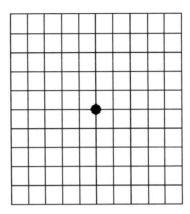

5. Circle the points: (1, 3), (–3, 1), (–3, –4). (5, –2) on the previous system.

   Assume that the origin is the blackened dot. The notation of vectors is identical

   to the notation of _____ when they are written in _____. However on

   sketching a free vector there is an _____ number of possibilities while

   on sketching a point only _____ possibility that makes reference to a

   chosen _____.

6. The vectors from exercises 4 are _____ dimensional (they have __ dimensions).

7. A vector starts at the point (2, –7) and ends at the point (1, 3), the vector is

   (__,__)

8. A vector starts at the point (12, 3, 0) and ends at the point (11, –3. –2), the vector

   is (___,___,___)

Magnitude of a vector

The magnitude is the "size", the length of the arrow. **It is denoted by** $\left|\vec{A}\right|$

9. Find the magnitude of the vectors: (1, 3), (–3, 1), (–3, –4). (0, –2).

As you could observe in general the magnitude of a vector is given by:

$$\left|\vec{A}\right| = \sqrt{a_1{}^2 + a_2{}^2 + \ldots + a_n{}^2}$$

10. The magnitude of a vector is always _____.

11. Find the magnitude of the vectors:

$\vec{A} = (1, 0, -3, -4)$

$\vec{B} = (-3, -2, -4)$

$\vec{C} = (1, 2)$

$\vec{D} = (3, 4)$

$\vec{E} = (1, 2, -3)$

$\vec{F} = (0, 0, 0, -12, 0, 0, 0, 0, 0)$

The direction of a vector means: "where does it point"

12. In 1D how many possible directions exist? In 2D how many possible directions exist?

13. Given the vector $\vec{a} = (1, 1)$. Its magnitude is ____. Sketch it on the following diagram (Assume is "starts" at the centre).

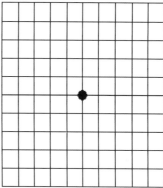

14. Given the vector (–4, 3). Its magnitude is _____. Sketch it on the following

diagram (Assume is "starts" at the centre). It forms an angle of _____ with the

_____, therefore its direction is _____ and an angle of _____ with the _____ there

for its direction can also be written as _____. The form (–4, 3) of the vector is

called **Algebraic notation**. The vector can also be written as: _____

that is the **geometrical notation**.

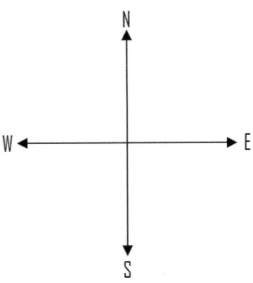

When are two vectors equal?

Two vectors $\vec{A}$ and $\vec{B}$ are equal if they are of the <u>same dimension</u> and if their <u>corresponding components are equal</u>.

15. Given $\vec{A} = \begin{bmatrix} 2 \\ a_2 \\ -4 \\ 1 \end{bmatrix}$ $\vec{B} = \begin{bmatrix} b_1 \\ 3 \\ 4 \\ b_4 \end{bmatrix}$ and $\vec{A} = \vec{B}$. Find all the missing components.

16. Which of the following vectors are equal:

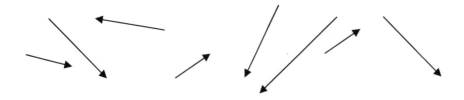

How can two vectors be added?

Analytically:

Two vectors can be added only if they are of the same dimension and the addition is given by

$$\vec{A} + \vec{B} = \begin{bmatrix} a_1 \\ a_2 \\ \vdots \\ a_n \end{bmatrix} + \begin{bmatrix} b_1 \\ b_2 \\ \vdots \\ b_n \end{bmatrix} = \begin{bmatrix} a_1 + b_1 \\ a_2 + b_2 \\ \vdots \\ a_n + b_n \end{bmatrix}$$

17. Given that $\vec{A} = \begin{bmatrix} 2 \\ 3 \\ 4 \\ 1 \end{bmatrix}, \vec{B} = \begin{bmatrix} 5 \\ -2 \\ 3 \\ 7 \end{bmatrix}$ Find $\vec{A} + \vec{B} =$

Graphically:

18. Sketch the vector $\vec{a} = (3.\,4)$ on the following diagram (start at point A):

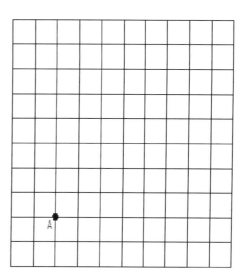

19. Where it ends (denote the point as B), sketch the vector $(2, -5)$, where it ends

denote the point as C. Sketch the vector that connects the points A and C, that

vector is _____.

20. Sum the vectors $(3, 4)$ and $(2, -5)$ analytically. What is your conclusion?

21. Another conclusion is that the vectors $\overrightarrow{AB} + \overrightarrow{BC} = $ _____

22. Consider

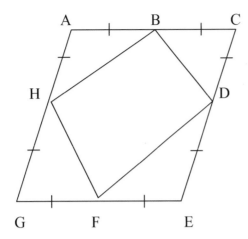

Determine each vector sum:

a) $\overrightarrow{AH} + \overrightarrow{HG} = $

b) $\overrightarrow{HB} + \overrightarrow{BD} = $

c) $\overrightarrow{GF} + \overrightarrow{BC} = $

d) $\overrightarrow{GF} + \overrightarrow{CB} = $

e) $\overrightarrow{FD} + \overrightarrow{DE} = $

f) $\overrightarrow{GH} - \overrightarrow{AH} = $

g) $\overrightarrow{HF} - \overrightarrow{DF} = $

h) $\overrightarrow{GF} + \overrightarrow{FD} + \overrightarrow{DH} + \overrightarrow{HE} = $

i) $\overrightarrow{GF} - \overrightarrow{FD} + \overrightarrow{FD} + \overrightarrow{FB} = $

23. Sum the vectors (1,–2), (3, 1), (2, 5) analytically and graphically. Did you obtain the same result?

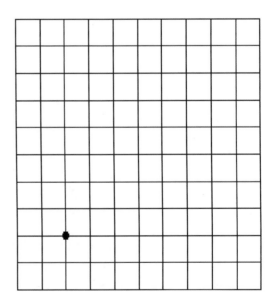

24. Vectors start at a _____ and end in a different _____.

25. The only situation in which the coordinates of a vector are identical to the coordinates of the point it ends at is the case in which the vector starts at the

_____

26. Given the vectors $\vec{A} = (10,0)$ and $\vec{B}$. $\left|\vec{B}\right| = 5$ and the angle between the vectors is $60°$.

    a. Draw the 2 vectors on a plane.
    b. Sum the 2 vectors **graphically**.
    c. Sum the 2 vectors **analytically.**

How can 2 vectors be subtracted?

Analytically:

Two vectors can be subtracted only if they are of the same dimension, given by

$$\vec{A} - \vec{B} = \begin{bmatrix} a_1 \\ a_2 \\ \vdots \\ a_n \end{bmatrix} - \begin{bmatrix} b_1 \\ b_2 \\ \vdots \\ b_n \end{bmatrix} = \begin{bmatrix} a_1 - b_1 \\ a_2 - b_2 \\ \vdots \\ a_n - b_n \end{bmatrix}$$

27. Given the two vectors $\vec{A} = \begin{bmatrix} 2 \\ 3 \\ 4 \\ 1 \end{bmatrix}, \vec{B} = \begin{bmatrix} 5 \\ -2 \\ 3 \\ 7 \end{bmatrix}$ Find $\vec{A} - \vec{B} =$

Graphically:

28. Given the vectors $\vec{a} = (3. 4)$ and $\vec{b} = (2, -1)$. Find $\vec{a} - \vec{b}$ using the graphical method. On the following diagram (start at point A) sketch the vector $\vec{a}$:

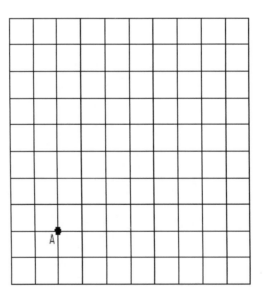

29. Where it ends (denote the point as B), sketch the vector $-\vec{b}$, where it ends

    denote the point as C. Sketch the vector that connects the points A and C, that

    vector is $\vec{a} - \vec{b}$, its coordinates are (___ , ___).

30. Consequently we can say that subtraction of the vector $\vec{d}$ is done by adding the

    vector _____

How can a vector be multiplied by a scalar?

If k is a scalar and $\vec{A}$ is a n–dimensional vector, then $k\vec{A} = k\begin{bmatrix} a_1 \\ a_2 \\ \vdots \\ a_n \end{bmatrix} = \begin{bmatrix} ka_1 \\ ka_2 \\ \vdots \\ ka_n \end{bmatrix}$

31. Given the row vectors $\vec{A} = \begin{bmatrix} 25 & 20 & 5 \end{bmatrix}$ and $\vec{B} = \begin{bmatrix} 7 & 5 & -3 \end{bmatrix}$ Find:

    a. $2\vec{A} =$

    b. $-\vec{A} =$

    c. $3\vec{A} - 2\vec{B} =$

    d. $-\vec{A} + 4\vec{B} =$

What is a unit vector?

A unit vector $\vec{U}$ is defined as $\vec{U} = \begin{bmatrix} u_1 \\ u_2 \\ \vdots \\ u_n \end{bmatrix}$ where $\sqrt{u_1^2 + u_2^2 + u_3^2 + \ldots + u_n^2} = 1$

32. The magnitude of a unit vector is _____.

33. Given the vector $\vec{U} = k(2, -3)$. Find k so that $\vec{U}$ would be a unit vector.

34. Given the vector $\vec{U} = k(1, -4, 6)$. Find k so that $\vec{U}$ would be a unit vector.

35. Draw a conclusion of the last 2 exercises, what is the value of k in general?
Given the vector $\vec{A}$, find the unit vector that has the same direction.

36. Given the vector $\vec{a} = (\dfrac{1}{\sqrt{3}}, \dfrac{\sqrt{5}}{3}, \dfrac{1}{3})$. Is it a unit vector?

37. Given the vector $\vec{a} = (1, 0, \dfrac{1}{10})$. Is it a unit vector? If not, find a unit vector that has the same direction.

38. Given the vector $\vec{a} = (1, 1, 1)$. Is it a unit vector? If not, find a unit vector that has the same direction.

39. Write 2 examples of bidmensional unit vectors.

40. Write 2 examples of tridmensional unit vectors.

41. Given the vector $\vec{A} = (a, \dfrac{-1}{3}, \dfrac{1}{3})$.

    a. Find a so $\vec{A}$ is a unit vector.

    b. In case a = 1, find a vector with magnitude 5 that has the same direction.

    c. In case a = 2, find a vector with magnitude 4 that with opposite direction.

42. Given the points A = (1, 2, 5), B = (–2, 4, 4), C = (1, –1, –3)

Assuming these points form a parallelogram, find the 4th vertex of this parallelogram.

43. An object is located at point A = (1, 2, 5) in front of a mirror whose nearest point to A is B = (3, 4, 6). Sketch a diagram of the situation and find the point in which the reflection of the object isobserved.

44. A lost airplane was detected at 10pm on radar located at the point A = (–30, 22, 13) (in km) with velocity (12, 120, 22) (in km/h). Assuming the airplane continued with the same velocity for 30 more minutes find its last known location.

45. Given the point A = (10, 12, 5). Find a point distanced 2 units from this point in the direction (1, 1, 1).

What is meant by vectors being linearly independent?

A set of vectors $\vec{A}_1, \vec{A}_2, \ldots, \vec{A}_m$ are considered to be linearly independent if

$k_1\vec{A}_1 + k_2\vec{A}_2 + \ldots\ldots + k_m\vec{A}_m = \vec{0}$ has only one solution of $k_1 = k_2 = \ldots\ldots = k_m = 0$

46. Given the vectors $\vec{A} = \begin{bmatrix} 5 \\ 2 \end{bmatrix}$ and $\vec{B} = \begin{bmatrix} 3 \\ 0 \end{bmatrix}$ are they linearly independent?

47. Given the vectors $\vec{A} = \begin{bmatrix} 12 \\ 3 \end{bmatrix}$ and $\vec{B} = \begin{bmatrix} 4 \\ 1 \end{bmatrix}$ are they linearly independent?

48. Given the vectors $\vec{A} = \begin{bmatrix} 1 \\ 0 \\ 2 \end{bmatrix}$ and $\vec{B} = \begin{bmatrix} 1 \\ 3 \\ 0 \end{bmatrix}$ are they linearly independent?

49. Given the vectors $\vec{A} = \begin{bmatrix} -4 \\ 2 \\ 6 \end{bmatrix}$ and $\vec{B} = \begin{bmatrix} -6 \\ 3 \\ 9 \end{bmatrix}$ are they linearly independent?

50. Given the vectors $\vec{A} = \begin{bmatrix} 1 \\ 3 \end{bmatrix}$, $\vec{B} = \begin{bmatrix} 4 \\ 1 \end{bmatrix}$ and $\vec{C} = \begin{bmatrix} 12 \\ -25 \end{bmatrix}$ are they linearly independent?

51. Given the vectors $\vec{A} = \begin{bmatrix} -1 \\ 9 \end{bmatrix}$, $\vec{B} = \begin{bmatrix} 5 \\ -3 \end{bmatrix}$ and $\vec{C} = \begin{bmatrix} -4 \\ -2 \end{bmatrix}$ are they linearly independent?

52. Given the vectors $\vec{A} = \begin{bmatrix} 2 \\ 4 \end{bmatrix}$, $\vec{B} = \begin{bmatrix} 6 \\ 12 \end{bmatrix}$ and $\vec{C} = \begin{bmatrix} -9 \\ -18 \end{bmatrix}$ are they linearly independent?

53. Given the vectors $\vec{A}_1 = \begin{bmatrix} 25 \\ 64 \\ 144 \end{bmatrix}$, $\vec{A}_2 = \begin{bmatrix} 5 \\ 8 \\ 12 \end{bmatrix}$, $\vec{A}_3 = \begin{bmatrix} 1 \\ 1 \\ 1 \end{bmatrix}$ are they linearly independent?

54. Given the vectors $\vec{A}_1 = \begin{bmatrix} 1 \\ 2 \\ 5 \end{bmatrix}$, $\vec{A}_2 = \begin{bmatrix} 2 \\ 5 \\ 7 \end{bmatrix}$, $A_3 = \begin{bmatrix} 6 \\ 14 \\ 24 \end{bmatrix}$ are they linearly independent?

55. Given the vectors $\vec{A}_1 = \begin{bmatrix} 25 \\ 64 \\ 89 \end{bmatrix}$, $\vec{A}_2 = \begin{bmatrix} 5 \\ 8 \\ 13 \end{bmatrix}$, $\vec{A}_3 = \begin{bmatrix} 1 \\ 1 \\ 2 \end{bmatrix}$ are they linearly independent?

56. **Important note:** n linearly independent vectors in an n–dimensional vector

space form a _____

57. In 2D space _____ vectors are needed to form a **base**.

58. In 3D space _____ vectors are needed to form a **base**.

59. Given the vectors $\vec{A} = \begin{bmatrix} 2 \\ 4 \end{bmatrix}$, $\vec{B} = \begin{bmatrix} 6 \\ 12 \end{bmatrix}$,do they form a base in 2D?

60. Given the vectors $\vec{A} = \begin{bmatrix} 2 \\ 3 \\ -1 \end{bmatrix}$, $\vec{B} = \begin{bmatrix} 2 \\ -4 \\ 5 \end{bmatrix}$, $\vec{C} = \begin{bmatrix} 4 \\ 20 \\ -14 \end{bmatrix}$, do they form a base in 3D?

Cartesian Notation:

In 2D:

1. The vector $\vec{a} = (2, -3)$ can be written as the sum of the vectors $\vec{i} = (1, 0)$ and $\vec{j} = (0, 1)$ in the following way:

$$\vec{a} = (2, -3) = \_\vec{i} + \_\vec{j} = \_(1, 0) + \_(0, 1) = (\_, 0) + (0, \_) = (\_, \_)$$

2. Given the following diagram:

ABC is equilateral,
AB = 2cm, AE = 1cm

Express the following vectors in terms of $\vec{i}$ and $\vec{j}$

$\overrightarrow{AB} =$

$\overrightarrow{AC} =$

$\overrightarrow{AD} =$

$\overrightarrow{AE} =$

$\overrightarrow{EB} =$

$\overrightarrow{EC} =$

$\overrightarrow{ED} =$

$\overrightarrow{BD} =$

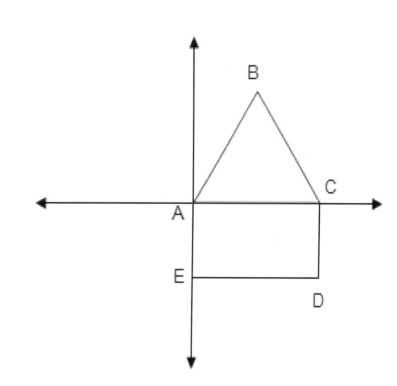

In 3D:

3. The vector $\vec{a} = (2, -3, 5)$ can be written as the sum of the vectors $\vec{i} = (1, 0, 0)$, $\vec{j} = (0, 1, 0)$ and $\vec{k} = (0, 0, 1)$ in the following way:

$$\vec{a} = (2, -3, 5) = \_\vec{i} + \_\vec{j} + \_\vec{k} = \_(1, 0, 0) + \_(0, 1, 0) + \_(0, 0, 1) = (\_, 0, 0) + (0, \_, 0) + \_(0, 0, \_)$$

4. Write the following vectors in the Cartesian notation:

(6, 7, −8) =

(−3, 4, 7) =

(−1, 0, 1) =

(0, 0, 7) =

Some algebraic properties of vectors:

If **u**, **v** and **w** are vectors, α and β are two scalars and **0** is the zero vector:

(i)   **u** + **v** = **v** + **u**   Example:_____

(ii)   **u** + (**v** + **w**) = (**u** + **v**) + **w**   Example:_____

(iii)   **v** + (−**v**) = **0**   Example:_____

(iv) $(\alpha\beta\mathbf{v}) = \alpha(\beta\mathbf{v})$ Example:_____

(v) $(\alpha+\beta)\mathbf{v} = \alpha\mathbf{v} + \beta\mathbf{v}$ Example:_____

(vi) $\alpha(\mathbf{u} + \mathbf{v}) = \alpha\mathbf{u} + \alpha\mathbf{v}$ Example:_____

(vii) $|\alpha\mathbf{v}| = \alpha|\mathbf{v}|$ Example:_____

2.2. – THE SCALAR OR DOT OR INNER PRODUCT

The scalar product is a way of interaction between two vectors to get a scalar quantity
(Classical example would be Work = Force • Displacement)

The scalar product of $\vec{a} = (a_1, a_2, ..., a_n)$ and $\vec{b} = (b_1, b_2, ...a_n)$ is defined by:

$$\vec{a} \bullet \vec{b} = \left|\vec{a}\right|\left|\vec{b}\right|\cos(\theta) = a_1 b_1 + a_2 b_2 + ... a_n b_n$$

θ is the angle between vectors **a** and **b**.

Exercises

1. If the angle between two vectors is _____ their dot product is 0.

2. If the angle between two vectors $\vec{a}$ and $\vec{b}$ is _____ their dot product is $\left|\vec{a}\right|\left|\vec{b}\right|$

3. If the angle between two vectors $\vec{a}$ and $\vec{b}$ is _____ their dot product is $-\left|\vec{a}\right|\left|\vec{b}\right|$

4. Calculate:

    $\vec{i} \cdot \vec{i} =$ $\vec{i} \cdot \vec{j} =$

5. Given that $\vec{A} = A_x \vec{i} + A_y \vec{j} + A_z \vec{k}$ and $\vec{B} = B_x \vec{i} + B_y \vec{j} + B_z \vec{k}$ find

    $\vec{A} \cdot \vec{B} =$

6. Given the vectors: $\vec{a} = (-1, 5, 3)$, $\vec{b} = (-1, 2, -4)$, $\vec{c} = (5, -4)$, $\vec{d} = (1, -8)$,
    $\vec{g} = (-5, -1, 7)$. Find:

    a. $\vec{a} \cdot \vec{b} =$

    b. $\vec{b} \cdot \vec{a} =$

    c. $\vec{a} \cdot \vec{c} =$

    d. $\vec{d} \cdot \vec{c} =$

    e. $\vec{a} \cdot \vec{g} =$

    f. $\vec{g} \cdot \vec{g} =$

    g. $\vec{g} \cdot \vec{b} =$

7. Given the vectors: $\vec{a} = (-1, 1, 1)$, $\vec{b} = (-1, 2, -4)$, find the angle between them.

8. Given the vectors: $\vec{a} = (-1, 6)$, $\vec{b} = (-1, -4)$, find the angle between them.

9. Given the vectors: $\vec{a} = (-1, 5, 3)$, $\vec{b} = (2, -10, -6)$, find the angle between them.

10. Given the vectors: $\vec{a} = (-1, 5, 3)$, $\vec{b} = (5, -2, 5)$, find the angle between them.

11. Given the vectors: $\vec{a} = (t, -h, 0)$, $\vec{b} = (-t, h, 0)$, find the angle between them.

12. Given the vector: $\vec{a} = (1, 4, -3)$, Write down a vector that is perpendicular to it. Write down a vector that is parallel to it.

13. Given the vector: $\vec{a} = (a, a, a)$, Write down a vector that is perpendicular to it. Write down a vector that is parallel to it (in terms of a).

14. Given the vector: $\vec{a} = (7,-3)$, Write down a vector that is perpendicular to it.
Write down a vector that is parallel to it.

15. Given the vector: $\vec{a} = (t,h,m)$, Write down a vector that is perpendicular to it.
Write down a vector that is parallel to it (in terms of t, h and m).

16. Given the vectors: $\vec{a} = (-1,1,1)$, $\vec{b} = (-1,2,-4)$. Find

$\vec{a} \cdot \vec{a} =$

$\vec{b} \cdot \vec{b} =$

Conclusion: The dot product of a vector with itself is equal to _____

17. Given the vectors $\vec{a} = (1,5,k)$ and $\vec{b} = (-1,2,4)$

    a. Find their dot product if k = 1.

    b. Find the angle between them in case k = 2.

    c. Find the value of k to make these 2 vectors perpendicular.

    d. Find the value of k to make these 2 vectors parallel.

18. Given the vectors $\vec{a} = (7, 2, -4)$ and $\vec{b} = (-1, b, a)$

    a. Calculate their dot product if a = 1, b = 2

    b. Calculate the angle between them in the same case.

    c. Calculate what value of a will make these 2 vectors perpendicular in case a = b.

    d. Calculate what values of a and b will make these 2 vectors parallel.

19. Given the vectors $\vec{a} = (3, -1)$ and $\vec{b} = (5, b)$

    a. Calculate their dot product if b = 15

    b. Calculate the angle between them in the same case.

    c. Calculate what value of b will make these 2 vectors parallel.

.

Some Properties of Dot Product
For some vectors **u**, **v** and **w**,

    (i) $\mathbf{u} \cdot \mathbf{v} = \mathbf{v} \cdot \mathbf{u}$ Example: _____

    (ii) $(\mathbf{u} + \mathbf{v}) \cdot \mathbf{w} = \mathbf{u} \cdot \mathbf{w} + \mathbf{v} \cdot \mathbf{w}$ Example: _____

    (iii) $(\alpha\mathbf{u}) \cdot \mathbf{v} = \alpha(\mathbf{u} \cdot \mathbf{v})$, α is scalar   Example: _____

    (iv) $\mathbf{u} \cdot \mathbf{u} \geq 0$ and $\mathbf{u} \cdot \mathbf{u} = 0$ if $\mathbf{u} = \mathbf{0}$ Example: _____

    (v) $|\mathbf{u}|^2 = \mathbf{u} \cdot \mathbf{u}$ Example: _____

2.3. – THE VECTOR OR CROSS PRODUCT

The vector product is a way of interaction between two vectors to get a vector quantity (Classical example would be **Angular Momentum** = **r** × **p**)

In **3D** the vector product of $\vec{a} = (a_1, a_2, a_3)$ and $\vec{b} = (b_1, b_2, b_3)$ is defined by:

> **The vector $\vec{c}$ that has a <u>magnitude</u> $= \left| \vec{a} \times \vec{b} \right| = \left| \vec{a} \right| \left| \vec{b} \right| \sin(\theta)$ and <u>direction</u> perpendicular to both $\vec{a}$ and $\vec{b}$ (following the "right hand rule"). θ is the angle between vectors $\vec{a}$ and $\vec{b}$.**

$\vec{c}$ can be calculated in general in the following way:

$$\vec{c} = \vec{a} \times \vec{b} = \begin{vmatrix} \vec{i} & \vec{j} & \vec{k} \\ a_1 & a_2 & a_3 \\ b_1 & b_2 & b_3 \end{vmatrix}$$

Exercises

1. The cross product between 2 vectors is a _____.

2. The cross product between 2 parallel vectors is: _____.

3. Given the vectors $\vec{a} = (4, 2, -1)$, $\vec{b} = (-8, -4, 2)$, find:

   a. $\vec{a} \times \vec{b} =$

   b. $\vec{a} \times \vec{a} =$

4. Given the vectors $\vec{a} = (1,5,0)$, $\vec{b} = (1,0,1)$, $\vec{c} = (1,1,1)$, find:

a. $\vec{a} \times \vec{c} =$

b. $\vec{c} \times \vec{a} =$

c. $2\vec{b} \times \vec{c} =$

d. $\vec{a} \times (\vec{b} \times \vec{c})$

5. Given the vectors $\vec{a} = (1,5,0)$, $\vec{b} = (1,0,1)$, $\vec{c} = (1,1,1)$. State whether the following expressions are vectors, scalars or meaningless. Calculate the values of the expressions that are not meaningless:

a. $\vec{a} \bullet (\vec{b} \times \vec{c}) =$

b. $3\vec{a} \times (\vec{b} \times \vec{c}) =$

c. $\vec{a} \times (\vec{b} + 2\vec{c}) =$

d. $(\vec{a} \times \vec{c}) \times (\vec{b} + \vec{c}) =$

e. $4\vec{a} + (\vec{b} \bullet \vec{c}) =$

f. $\vec{a} \times (\vec{a} \bullet \vec{a}) =$

g. $(\vec{b} \times (\vec{b} + \vec{b})) \bullet \vec{b} =$

h. $(\vec{a} \bullet \vec{a})^{\vec{b} \bullet \vec{c}} =$

6. Find a vector perpendicular to the vector (1, 2, –1)

7. Find a vector that will be perpendicular to <u>both</u> (1, 2, –1) and the vector you found in 6)

8. Find a **<u>unity</u>** vector parallel to the vector you found in 6.

9. If **u** and **v** are parallel, then $\quad$ **u** × **v** = _____

10. For any **u**: $\quad$ (**u** × **u**) = _____

11. For any **u, v**: $\quad$ |**u** × (**u** × **v**)| = _____

12. Given the vectors $\vec{a} = (1, -5, -2)$ and $\vec{b} = (7, 7, 1)$, find a vector perpendicular to both of them.

13. Given the points A = (0, 1, 1), B = (–2, 1, 2) and C = (1, 1, –3). Find a vector perpendicular to the plane formed by these points.

Graphical interpretation of cross product

$\left|\vec{a} \times \vec{b}\right| = \left|\vec{a}\right|\left|\vec{b}\right|\sin(\theta)$ = **The area of the parallelogram formed by the vectors** $\vec{a}$ **and** $\vec{b}$

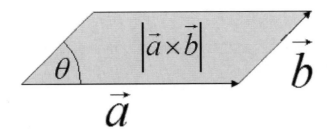

14. Find the area of the triangle with the vertices: A = (0, 1, 1), B = (−2, 1, 2) and C = (1, 1, −3)

15. Find the area of the quadrilateral with the vertices A = (2, 1, 3), B = (-5, −1, 2), C = (1, 1, −3) and D = (-2, -5, -6)

16. Find the area of the triangle with the vertices A = (5, 1, 1), B = (0, −1, 2) and C = (1, 1, −3)

200

17. Find the area of the quadrilateral with the vertices A = (1, 1, 1), B = (2,2, 2), C = (-1, -1, 1) and D = (-2, -2, 2)

Some properties of cross product:

(i) $\mathbf{u} \times \mathbf{v} = -(\mathbf{v} \times \mathbf{u})$ Example: _____

(ii) $(\alpha\mathbf{u}) \times \mathbf{v} = \alpha(\mathbf{u} \times \mathbf{v})$ Example: _____

(iii) $\mathbf{u} \times (\mathbf{v} + \mathbf{w}) = (\mathbf{u} \times \mathbf{v}) + (\mathbf{u} \times \mathbf{w})$ Example: _____

(iv) $(\mathbf{u} \times \mathbf{v}) \cdot \mathbf{w} = \mathbf{u} \cdot (\mathbf{v} \times \mathbf{w})$ (mixed product)

2.4. – LINES

Lines in 2D and 3D

The <u>Vector equation</u> of a line in 2D. 3D or more is:

$$\vec{r} = \vec{a} + t\vec{d}$$

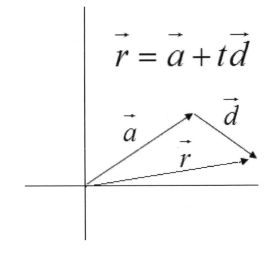

Where $\vec{r}$ is the <u>position</u> vector from to the origin to any point on the line, $\vec{d}$ is the direction vector of the line, it can be any vector parallel to the line, $\vec{a}$ is a <u>constant</u> vector from the origin to any point on the line and t is any real number.

Can also be written in the form:

$$(x, y, z) = (a_1, a_2, a_3) + t(d_1, d_2, d_3)$$

Or in the <u>parametric form</u>:

$$x = a_1 + td_1$$
$$y = a_2 + td_2$$
$$z = a_3 + td_3$$

Or in the <u>Cartesian or symmetric or continuous</u> form (just <u>isolate t and equal</u>)

$$\frac{x - a_1}{d_1} = \frac{y - a_2}{d_2} = \frac{z - a_3}{d_3}$$

Exercises

1. Given the vector $\vec{a} = (1,3)$ and $\vec{d} = (1,-2)$. Find following vectors, sketch them on the diagram, start at the origin. Connect the end points of all the vectors.

    a. $\vec{r_1} = \vec{a} + \vec{d}$

    b. $\vec{r_2} = \vec{a} + 2\vec{d}$

    c. $\vec{r_3} = \vec{a} + 3\vec{d}$

    d. $\vec{r_4} = \vec{a} - \vec{d}$

    e. $\vec{r_5} = \vec{a} - 2\vec{d}$

    f. $\vec{r_6} = \vec{a} - 3\vec{d}$

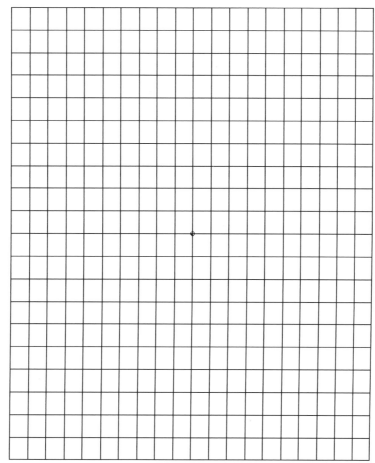

    g. What is your conclusion?

    h. Write down the equation of the line.

    i. Repeat the process with $\vec{a} = (2,1)$ and $\vec{d} = (-2,4)$, what is your conclusion?

2. A line in 2D or 3D using the vector form can be written in _____ number

of ways. The reason is that: _____

3. To describe a certain line, if we choose the direction vector to be a unity vector

we have _____ possibilities for our choice.

4. Find the vector equations, parametric equations and the symmetric equations for the line passing through the points P = (2, −1, 6) and Q = (3, 1, −2).

5. Write the equation of the straight line that passing through the points (1,2), (2, 8)

    a. In the vector form
    b. In the parametric form
    c. In the symmetric (continuous) form

6. Find the parametric equation and the symmetric equations for the line L passing through (1, −2, 4) and parallel to $\mathbf{v} = \mathbf{i} + \mathbf{j} - \mathbf{k}$

7. Which one of the following points lies on the given line (show your answer)

$x = 3t,$
$y = 2t - 5$
$z = -t + 1$

A. $(1, -3, 1)$
B. $(30, 15, 9)$
C. $(-6, -1, 3)$
D. $(-12, -13, 5)$

8. Find the equation of a line perpendicular to the line passing thorough the points $A = (1, 1, 1)$ and $B = (7, 2, 2)$. Find the equation of a line perpendicular to both of the lines.

9. Write the equation of a line parallel to the z axis in the vector form in 3 different ways.

10. Write the equation of a line parallel to the xy plane in the vector form in 3 different ways.

11. Find the angle between the lines $\dfrac{x-1}{4} = \dfrac{y+5}{-4} = \dfrac{2z-3}{2}$ and

$\dfrac{2x-1}{4} = \dfrac{2y+5}{-1} = \dfrac{z-3}{2}$

12. Find the angle between the lines $(x, y, z) = (0, 0, 1) + t(1, 1, 1)$ and
$(x, y, z) = (1, -1, 1) + t(-1, 2, 1)$

13. Given that the lines $(x, y, z) = (0, 0, 1) + t(a, 0, -1)$ and
$(x, y, z) = (1, -1, 1) + t(3, 4, 0)$ form an angle of 60°, find a.

14. The position of a car in reference to its last known destination is given by the equation $(x, y, z) = (10, -4) + t(-1, 3)$. Position in km, velocity in km/h, t in hours.

    a. Find the initial position of the car.

    b. Find the initial distance between the car and its last destination.

    c. Find the position of the car 2 hours later and its distance from the destination.

    d. Find the speed of the car in km/h.

    e. Sketch a diagram of the situation for the 2 hours mentioned:

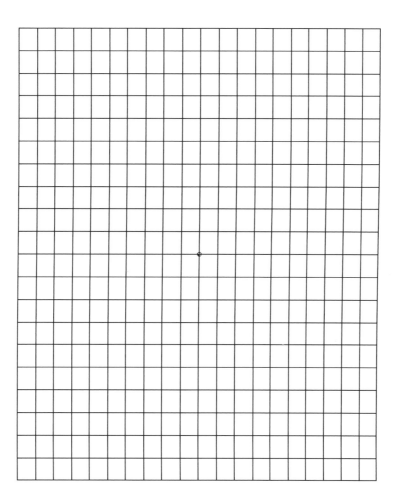

15. An airplane is located at position $\vec{p} = (200, 150, 10)$ km from the control tower. It is moving with velocity vector $\vec{v} = (-160, -120, -8)$ km/h. The x coordinate is oriented east/west and the y coordinate north/south. The z coordinate is the vertical coordinate.

   a. Sketch a diagram that includes the control tower and the location of the airplane.

   b. Assuming the airplane flies with constant velocity, find the position of the airplane 6 minutes later.

   c. Find the air distance between the airplane and the tower.

   d. Find the ground distance between the airplane and the tower (the distance between the shadow of the airplane and the tower).

   e. Find the air speed of the airplane.

   f. Find the ground speed of the airplane (the speed of the shadow of the airplane on the ground).

   g. In case the airplane does not change its velocity, how long will it take it to reach the airport?

   h. What will be the height of the airplane at that moment? Is that the appropriate height for landing?

2.5. – RELATIVE POSITON BETWEEN LINES

TWO DIMENSIONS

1. Two lines can_____, _____ or _____. In order to find the relative position of the lines the system of equations needs to be solved.

2. If the system has _____ solutions the lines are _____. $\vec{d_1} \cdot \vec{d_2} =$ ___.

   Direction vectors are _____.

3. If the system has _____ solutions the lines are _____. $\vec{d_1} \cdot \vec{d_2} =$ ___

   Direction vectors are _____.

4. If the system has _____ solutions the lines are _____. $\vec{d_1} \cdot \vec{d_2} =$ ___

   Direction vectors are _____.

Given the following lines, write them in all possible forms, find their relative position. In case they intersect find their point of intersection and the angle between them.

5. $(x, y) = (1, -2) + k\,(3, -2)$ and $(x, y) = (-3, -2) + s\,(-6, 4)$

6. $(x, y) = (0, 3) + k\,(-1, 2)$ and $(x, y) = (-1, 2) + s\,(-1, 4)$

7. $(x, y) = (0, 0) + k(-1, -3)$ and $(x, y) = (2, 2) + s(3, -1)$

8. $(x, y) = (2, -5) + k(-3, -4)$ and $(x, y) = (8, 3) + s(6, 8)$

9. $3x + 2y = 5$ and $-2x + y = 1$

THREE DIMENSIONS

10. Two lines can_____, _____, _____ or _____. In order to find the relative position of the lines the system of equations needs to be solved by equaling the x, y and z coordinates of the lines and solving for s and t.

11. If the system has _____ solutions the lines are _____. $\vec{d_1} \cdot \vec{d_2} = $ ___.

    Direction vectors are _____.

12. If the system has _____ solutions the lines are _____. $\vec{d_1} \cdot \vec{d_2} = $ ___.

    Direction vectors are _____.

13. If the system has _____ solutions the lines are _____. $\vec{d_1} \cdot \vec{d_2} = $ ___.

    Direction vectors are _____.

14. If the system has _____ solutions the lines are _____. $\vec{d_1} \cdot \vec{d_2} = $ ___.

    Direction vectors are _____.

Given the following pairs of equations, determine whether they represent the same line, parallel lines, intersecting lines or none of the above. If the lines have an intersection, calculate it.

15. $\vec{r} = (1,3,2) + s(-1,2,3)$ and $\vec{c} = (1,3,2) + t(5,-10,1)$

16. $\vec{r} = (2,1,0) + s(2,2,1)$ and $\vec{c} = (-4,-5,-3) + t(10,10,5)$

17. $\dfrac{x-1}{-1} = \dfrac{y}{2}$ and $\dfrac{2x-1}{-1} = \dfrac{y-1}{3}$

18. $(x, y, z) = (1, -2, 0) + k\,(3, -2, 1)$ and $(x, y, z) = (-3, -2, 1) + s\,(-6, 4, 0)$

19. $(x, y, z) = (1, 0, 1) + k (1, -2, 1)$ and $(x, y, z) = (1, -5, 3) + s (1, 3, -1)$

20. $\dfrac{x-1}{-1} = \dfrac{y}{2} = \dfrac{3z+2}{3}$ and $\dfrac{2x-1}{-1} = \dfrac{y}{2} = \dfrac{z-1}{2}$

21. $\dfrac{x-2}{3} = \dfrac{y-1}{-1} = \dfrac{z+1}{2}$ and $\dfrac{x-1}{-6} = \dfrac{y+1}{2} = \dfrac{z+2}{-4}$

22. Write the equation of 2 lines in 3D such that:

     a.   The lines will be coincident.

     b.   The lines will be parallel.

     c.   The lines will be intersecting

     d.   The lines will be skew

     e.   The lines will intersect with an angle of 60°

     f.   The lines will intersect with an angle of 90° (perpendicular)

23. Write the equations of 3 lines that intersect at a point.

24. Write the equations of 3 parallel lines

25. Write the equations of 3 lines, 2 parallel and a 3rd line that intersects both of them with an angle of 30°.

2.6. – PLANES IN 3D

The <u>Vector equation</u> of a plane in 3D is: $\quad\vec{r} = \vec{P} + t\vec{v} + s\vec{w}$

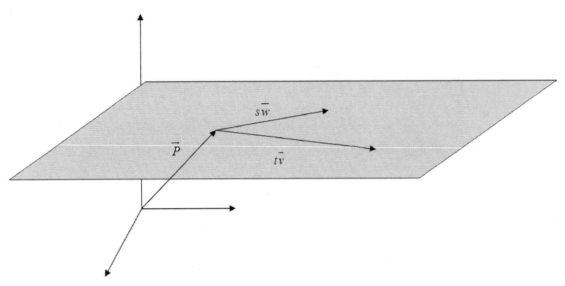

Where

$\vec{r}$ is the <u>position</u> vector from to the origin to any point on the plane (sketch it on the diagram)

$\vec{v}, \vec{w}$ are the "direction vectors" of the plane, they can be any 2 vectors that are not parallel to each other and parallel to the plane.

$\vec{P}$ is a <u>constant</u> vector from the origin to any point on the plane

t and s are real numbers.

Can also be written in the form:

$$(x, y, z) = (P_1, P_2, P_3) + t(v_1, v_2, v_3) + s(w_1, w_2, w_3)$$

Or in the <u>parametric form</u>:

$$x = P_1 + tv_1 + sw_1$$
$$y = P_2 + tv_2 + sw_2$$
$$z = P_3 + tv_3 + sw_3$$

Or in the <u>Cartesian form</u> (just <u>isolate t and s and substitute</u>)

$$Ax + By + Cz + D = 0$$

Exercises

1. A plane in 3D using the <u>vector form</u> can be written in _____ number of ways. The reason is that: _____

2. To describe a certain plane, if we choose the "direction vectors" to be unity vectors, we have _____ possibilities for our choice.

3. To describe a plane using points, we need 3 points that are not on the same ___.

4. Find the equation of the plane that contains the three points: F(1, 2, 1), G(−2, 0, 2) and H(−1, 4, 3) and wrote it in the vector form and parametric form in 2 different ways.

5. Find an equation of the plane passing through the point D = (2, 5, 1) and normal to the vector **n** = **i** − 2**j** + 3**k**. Use the fact as seen in the following diagram that

$$\overrightarrow{AD} \cdot \vec{n} = 0$$

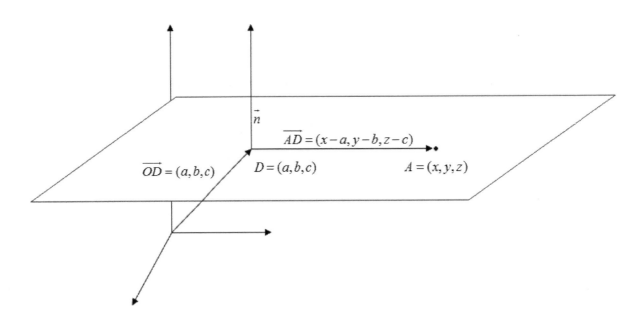

6. In order to write the Cartesian equation of the plane we need to know the _____ vector to the plane and a _____.

7. Find an equation of the plane passing through the points P = (1, 2, 1), Q = (−2, 3, −1) and R = (1, 0, 4) in the Cartesian form.

8. Write an equation of a plane parallel to the z axis in the vector, parametric and Cartesian form.

9. Write an equation of a plane parallel to the xy plane in the vector, parametric and Cartesian form.

10. Write an equation of a plane parallel to the zy plane in the vector, parametric and Cartesian form.

11. Find the equation of the plane containing the lines and write it in all possible forms:

$$\vec{r} = (1,3,2) + s(-1,2,3) \text{ and } \vec{c} = (-5,5,6) + t(-2,4,6)$$

2.7. – RELATIVE POSITIONS BETWEEN LINES AND PLANES

Exercises:

1. In 2D, a line and a plane can be _____.

2. In 3D, a line and a plane can be _____, _____ or _____.In order to find the relative position of the line and plane the system of equations needs to be solved by plugging the parametric equations of the line into the plane..

3. If the system has _____ solutions the line and plane are _____. $\vec{n} \cdot \vec{d} =$ __.

4. If the system has _____ solutions the line and plane are _____. $\vec{n} \cdot \vec{d} =$ __.

5. If the system has _____ solutions the line and plane are _____. $\vec{n} \cdot \vec{d} =$ __.

Given the following lines and planes, find their relative position. If possible find their point of intersection and/or angle between them.

6. $\dfrac{x-1}{-1} = \dfrac{y}{2} = \dfrac{3z+2}{3}$ and $2x - y + 2z = 1$

7. $(x, y, z) = (1, -2, 0) + k\,(3, -9, 1)$ and $3x + y = 2$

8. $(x, y, z) = (3, 2, 2) + s(-3, -2, 0)$ and $-2x + 3y + z = 2$

9. $(x, y, z) = (1, 0, 1) + k(1, -2, 1)$ and $2x - 4y + 2z = 4$

10. $\dfrac{x-1}{-1} = \dfrac{y}{-2} = \dfrac{z-1}{4}$ and $2x + y + z = 5$

11. $\dfrac{x-2}{3} = \dfrac{y-1}{-1} = \dfrac{z+1}{2}$ and $z = -1$

12. $\dfrac{x-1}{-6} = \dfrac{y+1}{2} = \dfrac{z+2}{-4}$ and $3x - y + 2z = 0$

13. Write the equation of a line and a plane in 3D such that:

    a. The line will intersect the plane.

    b. The line will be parallel to the plane

    c. The line will be contained in the plane

    d. The line will intersect the plane with an angle of $60°$

    e. The line will intersect the plane with an angle

14. Summarizing, in case of a line and a plane if the system has _____ there is no

intersection and the line is _____ to the _____, if the system has 1 solution

the line _____ and if the system has _____ the line is _____.

222

2.8. – SYSTEMS OF EQUATIONS

TWO DIMENSIONAL SYSTEMS

1. One equation with 2 variables has _____ number of solution(s).

   Each solution graphically is represented by a _____ .

2. In a system of 2 equations with 2 variables each equation represents a _____ .

3. The possible situations between 2 lines are _____ , _____ and _____ .

4. In case the lines are parallel and we try to solve the system we will get

   _____ solution(s).

5. In case the lines are intersecting and we try to solve the system we will get

   _____ solution(s).

6. In case the lines are _____ and we try to solve the system we will get

   _____ solution(s).

7. In case we have 3 lines the only situation in which the system will have a
   solution is _____ .

8. Given the system :
   x + y = 1
   x + y = 2
   In this case the lines are _____ and the system has _____
   Solution(s)

9. Given the system :
   x + y = 1
   2x + 2y = 2
   In this case the lines are _____ and the system has _____
   solution(s)

10. Given the system :
    x + y = 1
    x + 2y = 2
    In this case the lines are _____ and the system has _____
    solution(s)

1. Given the following system

$$4x - 2y = 3$$
$$x - y = 1$$

Solve or express solution properly, indicate the number of solutions.

2. Given the following system

$$-3x - 2y = 2$$
$$9x + 6y = 5$$

Solve or express solution properly, indicate the number of solutions.

3. Given the following system

$$-3x - 2y = 2$$
$$9x + 6y = 6$$

Solve or express solution properly, indicate the number of solutions.

THREE DIMENSIONAL SYSTEMS

1. Each equation represents a: _____

2. Can you think about the different relative positions of 2 planes?

   _____ , _____ , _____

3. When a system of 2 equations, each with 3 variables, is given the possible number of solutions is:

   a. _____ solutions, that means the planes intersect in a line.

   b. _____ solutions, means the planes intersect in a plane.

   c. _____ solutions, that means the planes are parallel.

4. Can you think about the different relative positions of 3 planes?

5. Given the system, use normal vectors to check the relative position of the planes. Solve or express solution properly.

   $x - 4y + 8z = -2$
   $3x + 3y + z = 1$

6. Given the system, use normal vectors to check the relative position of the planes. Solve or express solution properly.

   $2x - y + z = -2$
   $4x - 2y + 2z = 3$

7. Given the system, use normal vectors to check the relative position of the planes. Solve or express solution properly.

   $7x - y + 2z = -5$
   $-21x + 3y - 6z = -9$

8. Given the system, find a,b, and c so that the planes are coincident. find a,b, and c so that the planes are parallel.

   $ax - by + 2z = 1$
   $18x + 6y - cz = 3$

9. Given the planes $3x + 2y - z = 5$ and $-6x + 3y + z = 2$, find their relative position. In case they intersect, find the line of intersection.

10. Given the planes $7x + 2y - 3z = 2$ and $-14x + 4y - 6z = 2$, find their relative position. In case they intersect, find the line of intersection.

11. Given the planes $7x + 2y - 3z = 2$ and $-14x + 4y - 6z = 4$, find their relative position. In case they intersect, find the line of intersection.

12. A plane parallel to the plane $x + 2y - z = 2$ would be _____ , an

    identical plane would be_____ an intersecting plane would

    be_____

13. Given the plane $\vec{r} = (1,3,2) + w(-1,2,3) + t(0,2,2)$ Find, using vector notation:

    a. A parallel plane.
    b. An identical plane using different vectors and different point.
    c. An intersecting plane.
    d. A plane that intersects this plane with an angle of 30°.

14. Given the planes: $\vec{r} = (1,0,-2) + s(1,4,1) + t(1,-2,5)$ and
$\vec{r} = (-1,-1,2) + s(3,1,1) + t(-1,1,2)$. Find their relative position.

15. There are 8 different possibilities for the previous question, these possibilities are grouped to 3 groups:

0 solutions Planes do not have a common point	**1 solution** Planes have 1 point in common	**Infinite solutions** Planes have infinite points in common
3 parallel planes.		3 planes intersect in a line.
2 identical planes and a 3rd parallel plane.	3 planes intersect at a point.	2 identical planes and 1 that intersects them.
2 parallel planes and a 3rd plane intersecting them.		
3 planes that form a "triangle".		3 identical planes

<u>**Gauss's Method**</u>: Consists in creating a matrix with a triangle of zeros under the diagonal (upper triangular matrix).

<u>**Example 1: System with unique solution**</u>

$$x + 2y + 4z = 5$$
$$x + 4y + 8z = 9$$
$$x + 3y + \ z = 2$$

The system can be written in the following way:

$$\begin{pmatrix} 2 & -3 & 4 \\ 1 & 4 & 8 \\ 3 & 1 & 12 \end{pmatrix}\begin{pmatrix} 5 \\ 9 \\ 14 \end{pmatrix}$$

NewRow3 = Row3 – Row1 gives:

$$\begin{pmatrix} 1 & 2 & 4 \\ 1 & 4 & 8 \\ 0 & 1 & -3 \end{pmatrix}\begin{pmatrix} 5 \\ 9 \\ -3 \end{pmatrix}$$

NewRow2 = Row2 – Row1 gives:

$$\begin{pmatrix} 1 & 2 & 4 \\ 0 & 2 & 4 \\ 0 & 1 & -3 \end{pmatrix}\begin{pmatrix} 5 \\ 4 \\ -3 \end{pmatrix}$$

NewRow3 = Row3 – 0.5 Row1 gives:

$$\begin{pmatrix} 1 & 2 & 4 \\ 0 & 2 & 4 \\ 0 & 0 & -5 \end{pmatrix}\begin{pmatrix} 5 \\ 4 \\ -5 \end{pmatrix}$$

The objective was to obtain a triangle of _____ From here, multiplying we see that $-5z = -5$ so z = _____. We also see $2y + 4z = 4$ so y = _____. From here x is easily obtained, x = _____

So the solution for the system is: (___ , _____ , _____)

Example 2: System infinite solutions (intersection of the planes is a line)

$$2x - 3y + 4z = 5$$
$$x + 4y + 8z = 9 \quad \text{can be written as:}$$
$$3x + y + 12z = 14$$

The system can be written in the following way:

$$\begin{pmatrix} 2 & -3 & 4 \\ 1 & 4 & 8 \\ 3 & 1 & 12 \end{pmatrix} \begin{pmatrix} 5 \\ 9 \\ 14 \end{pmatrix}$$

NewRow3 = Row3 – 3Row2 gives:

$$\begin{pmatrix} 2 & -3 & 4 \\ 1 & 4 & 8 \\ 0 & -11 & -12 \end{pmatrix} \begin{pmatrix} 5 \\ 9 \\ -13 \end{pmatrix}$$

NewRow2 = 2Row2 – Row1 gives:

$$\begin{pmatrix} 2 & -3 & 4 \\ 0 & 11 & 12 \\ 0 & -11 & -12 \end{pmatrix} \begin{pmatrix} 5 \\ 13 \\ -13 \end{pmatrix}$$

NewRow3 = Row3 + Row2 gives:

$$\begin{pmatrix} 1 & 2 & 4 \\ 0 & 11 & 12 \\ 0 & 0 & 0 \end{pmatrix} \begin{pmatrix} 5 \\ 13 \\ 0 \end{pmatrix}$$

The objective was to obtain a triangle of _____ , as can be observed that is not possible and a row of zeros was obtained, that means only 2 equations are independent and third one was a linear combination of those 2. The system will have _____ solutions.

The equations remaining can be written as:

$x + 2y + 4z = 5$

$11y + 12z = 13$

Making $z = \lambda$, $\quad y = \dfrac{13 - \lambda}{11} \quad x = 5 - 2\dfrac{(13 - \lambda)}{11} - \lambda = \dfrac{29}{11} - \dfrac{46}{11}\lambda$

So the solution is the line given by:

$$\left(\frac{29}{11} - \frac{46}{11}\lambda, \frac{13 - \lambda}{11}, \lambda \right)$$

Example 3: System with no solutions

$2x - 3y + 4z = 5$
$x + 4y + 8z = 9$ can be written as:
$3x + y + 12z = 10$

The corresponding matrix A* in which we operate is:

$$\begin{pmatrix} 2 & -3 & 4 \\ 1 & 4 & 8 \\ 3 & 1 & 12 \end{pmatrix} \begin{pmatrix} 5 \\ 9 \\ 10 \end{pmatrix}$$

NewRow3 = Row3 – 3Row2 gives:

$$\begin{pmatrix} 2 & -3 & 4 \\ 1 & 4 & 8 \\ 0 & -11 & -12 \end{pmatrix} \begin{pmatrix} 5 \\ 9 \\ -17 \end{pmatrix}$$

NewRow2 = 2Row2 – Row1 gives:

$$\begin{pmatrix} 2 & -3 & 4 \\ 0 & 11 & 12 \\ 0 & -11 & -12 \end{pmatrix} \begin{pmatrix} 5 \\ 13 \\ -17 \end{pmatrix}$$

NewRow3 = Row3 + Row2 gives:

$$\begin{pmatrix} 1 & 2 & 4 \\ 0 & 11 & 12 \\ 0 & 0 & 0 \end{pmatrix} \begin{pmatrix} 5 \\ 13 \\ -4 \end{pmatrix}$$

The result in the 3rd row means $0 = -4$ which means this system has no solution.

4. Given the system:

$$2x + 2y + 4z = 4$$
$$x + 4y + 8z = 5$$
$$x + 3y + z = 4$$

Solve or express solution properly, indicate the number of solutions.

5. Given the system:

$$2x + 2y + 4z = 4$$
$$x - 4y + 8z = -2$$
$$3x + 3y + z = 1$$

Solve or express solution properly

6. Given the system:

$x + y + z = 1$
$x + 2y + z = 3$
$x + y + z = 2$

Solve or express solution properly, indicate the number of solutions.

7. Given the system:

$x + z = 1$
$x + 2y + z = 3$
$x + y + z = 2$

Solve or express solution properly, indicate the number of solutions.

8. Given the system:

$$x + z = 1$$
$$x + 2y + z = 3$$
$$x + 2z = 2$$

Solve or express solution properly, indicate the number of solutions.

9. Given the system:

$$x + z = 1$$
$$x + 2y + z = 2$$
$$-x + z = 2$$

Solve or express solution properly, indicate the number of solutions.

10. Given the system:

$$x + z = 1$$
$$-2x + 3y + 7z = 2$$
$$-x + y + 2z = 2$$

Solve or express solution properly, indicate the number of solutions.

11. Given the system:

$$x + z = 0$$
$$-2x + 3y + 7z = 0$$
$$-x + y + 2z = 0$$

Solve or express solution properly, indicate the number of solutions.

12. Given the system;

$$x + z = 0$$
$$-2x + 3y + 7z = 0$$
$$-x + y - 2z = 0$$

Solve or express solution properly, indicate the number of solutions.

3.1. – INTRODUCTION TO STATISTICS

In Statistics we try to obtain some conclusions by observing and/or analyzing data.

1. The set of objects that we are trying to study is called _____, the number of elements in the population can be _____ or_____.

2. Usually the _____ is too big and therefore we obtain a _____. This process is called _____.

3. We use the _____ to obtain conclusions about the _____.

Types of DATA

1. _____ data.

2. _____ data that can be divided to _____ or _____.

3. _____ can be counted while _____ data can be _____.

4. Give 5 examples of _____ data:

5. Give 3 examples of _____ _____ data:

6. Give 3 examples of _____ _____ data:

3.2. – FREQUENCY DIAGRAMS

1. In a certain math class the following grades were obtained:

   68, 79, 75, 89, 54, 81, 88, 62, 67, 75, 64, 85, 97, 77, 79, 90, 75, 89, 76, 68

   a. State the number of elements in the set: _____

   b. What kind of data is this? _____

   c. Fill the table:

Grade	Mid – Grade (Mi)	Frequency (fi)	fi x Mi	Cumulative Frequency (Fi)	Fi (%)
51 – 60					
61 – 70					
71 – 80					
81 – 90					
91 – 100					
Total					

   d. Is this the only possible choice for the left column of the table? Why? Discuss the advantages and disadvantages of organizing information in such a way.

   e. Design a new table with a different _____

Grade	Mid – Grade (Mi)	Frequency (fi)	Fi x Mi	Cumulative Frequency (Fi)	Fi (%)

f. Obtain the mean in both cases:

g. State a formula for the mean:

h. The mean of the <u>population</u> is denoted with the Greek letter mu: _____

    and typically it is _____. The mean of the <u>sample</u> is denoted by

    _____

i. State the mode of the set: _____

j. Find the modal interval in both cases:

k. Find the Median using the original data: _____

l. Find the median using the tables, discuss your answer.

m. In general this method of organizing information is called _____

n. The 1st column is called _____ with upper interval boundary and

    _____ interval boundary.

o. The 2nd column is called _____

p. On the following grid paper sketch the corresponding points.

Cumulative frequency

Variable: _____

q. This graph is called cumulative frequency curve or _____

r. Find the median using the graph: _____

s. Find the first quartile (Q_1) using the graph: Q_1 = _____

t. Find the first quartile (Q_1) using the original data: Q_1 = _____

u. Find the third quartile (Q_3) using the graph: Q_3 = _____

v. Find the first quartile (Q_3) using the original data: Q_3 = _____

w. Find P_{30} using the graph: _____Find P_{65} using the graph: _____

x. The <u>Inter Quartile Range</u> is in general _____ in this case it is_____

y. Find the answers to all the different parts using your GDC.

240

2. In a certain class the following heights (in m) of students were collected:

1.77, 1.60, 1.89, 1.54, 1.77, 1.65, 1.86, 1.51, 1.67, 1.94, 1.73, 1.70, 1.66

    a. State the number of elements in the set: _____

    b. What kind of data is this? _____

    c. Fill the table:

Grade	Mid – Grade (Mi)	Frequency (fi)	fi x Mi	Cumulative Frequency (Fi)	Fi (%)
[1.50 – 1.60)					
[1.60 – 1.70)					
[1.70– 1.80)					
[1.80 – 1.90)					
[1.90 – 2.00)					
Total					

    d. Obtain the mean: _____

    e. State the mode of the set: _____

    f. Find the modal interval: _____

    g. Find the Median using the original data: _____

    h. Find the median using the table, discuss your answer.

    i. On the following grid paper sketch the corresponding points.

Cumulative frequency

Variable: _____

j. This graph is called cumulative frequency curve or _____

k. Find the median using the graph: _____

l. Find the first quartile (Q_1) using the graph: Q_1 = _____

m. Find the first quartile (Q_1) using the original data: Q_1 = _____

n. Find the third quartile (Q_3) using the graph: Q_3 = _____

o. Find the first quartile (Q_3) using the original data: Q_3 = _____

p. Find P_{20} using the graph: _____Find P_{80} using the graph: _____

q. The <u>Inter Quartile Range</u> is in general _____ in this case it is_____

r. Find the answers to all the different parts using your GDC.

3. In a certain class students eye color was collected:

   Brown, Black, Brown, Blue, Brown, Blue, Green, Brown, Black, Green

   a. State the number of elements in the set: _____

   b. What kind of data is this? _____
   c. Fill the table:

Eye Color	Mid – Color (Mi)	Frequency (fi)	fi x Mi	Cumulative Frequency (Fi)	Fi (%)
Brown					
Blue					
Green					
Black					
Total					

   d. Obtain the mean: _____

   e. State the mode of the set: _____

   f. Find the modal interval: _____

   g. Find the Median using the original data: _____

   h. Find the median using the table, discuss your answer.

   i. Find the answers to all the different parts using your GDC.

   j. Represent the information in a histogram:

3.3. – MEASURES OF DISPERSION

1. In a certain Biology test the following results were obtained: 80, 80, 80, 80,

    a. Obtain the mean: μ = _____

    b. Represent the results using a histogram:

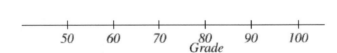

    c. The standard deviation of a set of numbers is defined by:

$$\sigma = \sqrt{\sum_i f_i(x_i - \mu)^2} = \sqrt{f_1(x_1 - \mu)^2 + f_2(x_2 - \mu)^2 + \ldots}$$

    In this case $\sigma =$ _____

    d. How spread is this group of grades?

2. In a certain Physics test the following results were obtained: 70, 80, 80, 90

   a. Obtain the mean: μ = _____

   b. Represent the results using a histogram:

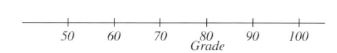

   c. The standard deviation of a set of numbers is defined by:

$$\sigma = \sqrt{\sum_i f_i(x_i - \mu)^2} = \sqrt{f_1(x_1 - \mu)^2 + f_2(x_2 - \mu)^2 + ...}$$

   In this case σ = _____

   d. How spread is this group of grades? Is it more spread than the previous one?

3. The weights in kg of 6 different classes (A, B, C, D, E, F) was collected and represented in the following histograms:

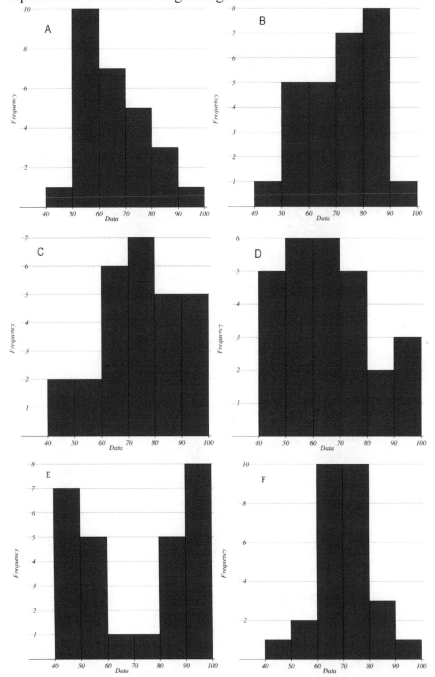

The mean $\bar{x}$ and the S.D. σ are given in the table:

	1	2	3	4	5	6
$\bar{x}$	74.6	65.7	70	72.0	65.7	70.6
σ	14.5	15.6	20.6	12.7	12.1	10.3

a. Find the number of students in the sample: _____

b. Which distribution will the highest SD: _____

c. Which distribution will the lowest SD: _____

d. Match between the histograms and the numerical results. Use the table:

$\bar{x}$ and σ	Class
1	
2	
3	
4	
5	
6	

246

4. In a certain math class the following grades were obtained:

68, 79, 75, 89, 54, 81, 88, 62, 67, 75, 64, 85, 97, 77, 79, 90, 75, 89, 76, 68

    a.   State the number of elements in the set: _____

    b.   What kind of data is this? _____

    c.   Fill the table:

Grade	Mid – Grade (Mi)	Frequency (fi)	fi x Mi	$(Mi - \mu)^2$	$fi(Mi - \mu)^2$
50 – 60					
61 – 70					
71 – 80					
81 – 90					
91 – 100					
Total					

    d.   Obtain the mean: μ = _____

    e.   The numbers in the 6th column give us an idea about the _____

of each _____ to the spread of the data.

    f.   The sum of the numbers in the 6th column gives us an idea about the

_____ of the data. In case this number is 0 it means that

_____ for example:

    g.   Find the Variance:_____Find the Standard Deviation S.D: _____

    h.   Write down the formula for the Variance of a population (σ^2):

    i.   Write down the formula for the Standard Deviation of a population (σ):

    j.   Find the Variance (assuming sample): _____

    k.   Find the Standard Deviation S.D. (assuming sample): _____

    l.   Find the answers to all the different parts using your GDC.

5. In a certain class the following heights (in m) of students were collected:

1.77, 1.60, 1.89, 1.54, 1.77, 1.65, 1.86, 1.51, 1.67, 1.94, 1.73, 1.70, 1.66

    a. State the number of elements in the set: _____

    b. What kind of data is this? _____

    c. Fill the table:

Height	Mid – Height (Mi)	Frequency (fi)	Fi x Mi	$(Mi - \mu)^2$	$fi(Mi - \mu)^2$
[1.50 – 1.60)					
[1.60 – 1.70)					
[1.70– 1.80)					
[1.80 – 1.90)					
[1.90 – 2.00)					
Total					

    d. Obtain the mean: μ = _____

    e. The numbers in the 6th column give us an idea about the _____

    of each _____ to the spread of the data.

    f. The sum of the numbers in the 6th column gives us an idea about the

    _____ of the data. In case this number is 0 it means that

    _____ for example:

    g. Find the Variance (assuming population): _____

    h. Find the Standard Deviation S.D. (assuming population): _____

    i. Find the Variance (assuming sample): _____

    j. Find the Standard Deviation S.D. (assuming sample): _____

    k. The estimate of the variance is called _____ estimate of the population's variance.

    l. Find the answers to all the different parts using your GDC.

6. In a certain class students eye color was collected:

   Brown, Black, Brown, Blue, Brown, Blue, Green, Brown, Black, Green

   a. State the number of elements in the set: _____

   b. What kind of data is this? _____

   c. Fill the table:

Eye Color	Mid – Color (Mi)	Frequency (fi)	Fi x Mi
Brown			
Blue			
Green			
Black			
Total			

   d. What can you say about the measures of spread in this case?

7. The sum of the grades of a group of 3 students is 240. Given that the grades for an arithmetic sequence and that its standard deviation is $\sqrt{128}$:

   a. The mean grade.
   b. The grades of the students.

8. The time it takes a battery to charge was measured by using a sample of 80 battries and the following results were obtained

Time (hours)	Number of batteries
$3 \leq t \leq 4$	1
$4 < t \leq 5$	2
$5 < t \leq 6$	3
$6 < t \leq 7$	9
$7 < t \leq 8$	12
$8 < t \leq 9$	13
$9 < t \leq 10$	4
Total	

Find
   a. The mean.
   b. The standard deviation.
   c. Later it was discovered that one more battery was tested. If the standard deviation has not changed by adding it to the sample, find out how much time it took to charge this battery.

9. A group of students obtained the following grades: 60, x, y, 50, 80. The mean of the sample is 68 and its variance is 136. Find x and y.

3.4. – PERMUTATIONS AND COMBINATIONS

1. Permutations represent a counting process where _____ must be taken into account. For example if we have the 2 elements A, B these 2 elements can be arranged in _____ ways: _____ .

2. Sometimes the word _____ is used instead of permutation.

Multiplication principles

3. n different, mutually exclusive and exhaustive events, k trials. Number of possible outcomes is n^k. For example if a die is rolled 2 times the number of possible results is _____

4. if n changes in every trial. Number of possible outcomes is $n_1 \times n_2 \times n_3 \ldots$ For example in case you roll a die twice and a coin 3 times the number of possible results is _____

5. The total number of ways in which n different objects can be arranged in order is $n! = n \times (n-1) \times (n-2) \ldots\ldots 3 \times 2 \times 1$. For example if we have 5 books we want to order on a shelf the number of possible orders is _____

6. The total number of ways of <u>arranging</u> n objects, taking r at a time is given by

$$^nP_r = \frac{n!}{(n-r)!}$$

For example if we have 5 books in a bag out of which we pick 3 and order those 3 on a shelf. How many possible orders exist?

7. The number of permutations of n objects of which n_1 are identical, n_2 are identical...is

$$\frac{n!}{n_1 \times n_2 \times n_3....}$$

For example if we want to order 5 books on a shelf out of which 2 are identical and the other 3 are identical. How many possible orders exist?

8. The total number of ways of <u>selecting</u> n objects, taking r at a time is given by

$$^nC_r = \binom{n}{r} = \frac{n!}{(n-r)!r!}$$

For example if we have 5 books in a bag out of which we want to select 3 (<u>without ordering them on the shelf</u>, just maybe putting them in a different bag so that order doesn't matter). How many possible orders exist?

3.5. – PROBABILITY

Probability is the science of chance or likelihood of an event happening

If a random experiment is repeated _____ times in such a way that each of the trials is identical and independent, where n(A) is the _____ event A occurred, then:

$$\text{Relative frequency of event A} = P(A) = \frac{n(A)}{N} \quad (N \to \infty)$$

Exercises

1. In an unbiased coin what is P(head) ?

   This probability is called _____.

2. Explain the difference between theoretical probability and "regular" probability.

3. Throw a drawing pin and fill the table:

	Fell pointing upwards	Fell on its side	Total number of throws
Number of events			
Probability			

4. The definition of probability ("*Laplace law*")is:

$$P(A) = \frac{Number \rule{5cm}{0.4pt}}{Total \rule{5cm}{0.4pt}}$$

Properties of probability

1. $0 \leq P(A) \leq 1$

2. $P(U) = 1$

Venn diagrams

Event	Set Language	Venn diagram	Probability result
Complementary event (A')	Not A		$P(A') =$
The _____ of A and B ($A \cap B$)	Set of elements that belongs to A _____ B		$P(A \cup B) =$
The _____ of A and B ($A \cup B$)	Set of elements that belongs to A _____ B _____ both		
If $(A \cap B) = \varnothing$ A and B are said to be: _____	The sets A and B are _____		$P(A \cup B) =$ $P(A \cap B) =$

Exercises

1. The events A and B are such $P(A) = 0.2$, $P(B) = 0.4$ and $P(A \cup B) = 0.5$. Find:

   a. $P(A \cap B)$
   b. $P(B')$
   c. Sketch the corresponding Venn diagram.
   d. $P(A' \cap B)$
   e. $P(A' \cap B')$
   f. Are the events A and B Independent? Explain.

2. The events A and B are such $P(A) = 0.15$, $P(B) = 0.3$ and $P(A \cup B) = 0.4$, Find:

    a. $P(A \cap B)$
    b. $P(B')$
    c. Sketch the corresponding Venn diagram.
    d. $P(A' \cap B)$
    e. $P(A' \cap B')$
    f. Are the events A and B Independent? Explain.

3. The events A and B are such $P(A) = 0.3$, $P(B) = 0.6$ and $P(A \cup B) = 0.9$, Find:

    a. $P(A \cap B)$
    b. $P(B')$
    c. Sketch the corresponding Venn diagram.
    d. $P(A' \cap B)$
    e. $P(A' \cap B')$
    f. Are the events A and B Independent? Explain.

4. The events A and B are such $P(A) = 0.2$, $P(B) = 0.9$ and $P(A \cap B) = 0.1$, Find:

    a. $P(A \cup B)$
    b. $P(B')$
    c. Sketch the corresponding Venn diagram.
    d. $P(A' \cap B)$
    e. $P(A' \cap B')$
    f. Are the events A and B Independent? Explain.

5. 20% of certain city census consume alcohol regularly, 40% do sport regularly and 10% do both.

    a. Represent the information in a diagram.
    b. Calculate the probability that someone chosen at random only drinks alcohol regularly.
    c. Calculate the probability that someone chosen at random only drink alcohol regularly or only practices sport regularly (but not both).
    d. Calculate the probability that someone picked at random does not drink alcohol nor practices sport regularly.

6. P(A) = 0.46, P(B) = 0.33, P(A∩B) = 0.15.

    a. Represent the information in a diagram.
    b. Find the probability that an event is not A nor B.

7. Given the Venn diagram. Shade A∩B

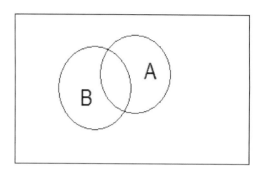

8. Given the Venn diagram. Shade A∩B'

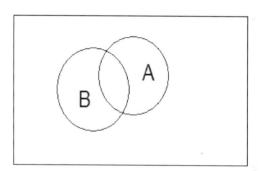

9. Given the Venn diagram. Shade B'

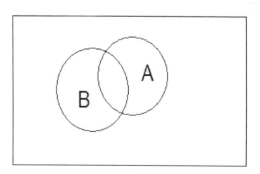

10. Given the Venn diagram. Shade A'∩B'

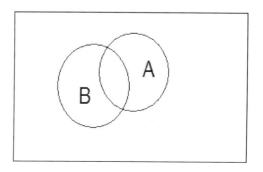

11. Given the Venn diagram. Shade A $\cup$ B

12. Given the Venn diagram. Shade A' $\cup$ B

13. Given the Venn diagram. Shade A' $\cup$ B'

14. Given the Venn diagram. Shade A $\cup$ B

15. Given the Venn diagram. Shade A $\cup$ B'

16. Given the Venn diagram. Shade $A \cap B'$

17. Given the Venn diagram. Shade $A \cap B$

18. Given the Venn diagram. Shade $A \cap B \cap C$

19. Given the Venn diagram. Shade $(A \cup B) \cap C$

20. Given the Venn diagram. Shade $(A' \cup B) \cap C$

21. Given the Venn diagram. Shade (A $\cup$ B) $\cap$ C'

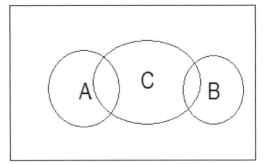

22. Given the Venn diagram. Shade A $\cap$ B $\cap$ C

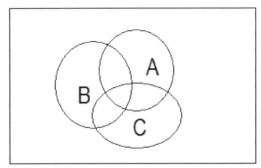

23. Given the Venn diagram. Shade (A $\cap$ B) $\cap$ C'

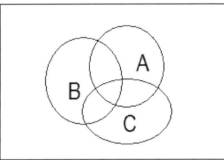

24. Given the Venn diagram. Shade (A' $\cap$ B) $\cap$ C

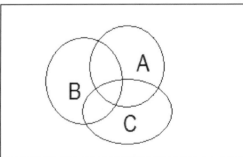

25. Given the Venn diagram. Shade (A $\cap$ B') $\cap$ C

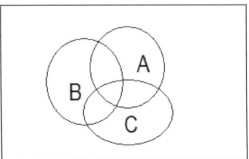

INDEPENDENT EVENTS

Informal definition: P(B) is not influenced by P(A).

Formal definition : $P(A \cap B) = P(A)P(B)$

Exercises

1. What is the difference between independent events and mutually exclusive events?

2. Give an example of independent events.

3. In a certain town the probability of a rainy day is 0.58 and the probability of strong wind is 0.76. If these are independent events, find the probability of:

   a. A rainy windy day.
   b. A dry windy day.
   c. A dry and not windy day.
   d. 2 consecutive rainy days.
   e. 2 consecutive windy rainy days.

CONDITIONAL PROBABILITY

Informal definition: **Knowing** that B has happened, what is the probability that A will happen (Written as P(A|B))

Formal definition: The probability of and event A given event B is:

$$P(A|B) = \frac{P(A \cap B)}{P(B)}, P(B) \neq 0$$

4. Two dice numbered one to six are rolled onto a table.

   a. Sketch a **lattice** diagram to show this information.
   b. Find the probability that the sum is 7.
   c. Find the probability that the sum is more than 7.
   d. Find the probability that the sum is less than 4.
   e. Find the probability that the sum is even.
   f. Find the probability of obtaining a sum of five given that the sum is seven or less.
   g. Find the probability of obtaining a sum of 4 given that the sum is even.

5. A regular and special dice rolled on a table. The special is a 4 sided pyramid numbered with the numbers 1,3,5,7.

    a. Sketch a corresponding diagram.
    b. Find the probability that the sum of the dice will be odd.
    c. Find the probability that the sum of the dice will be 8.
    d. Find the probability that the sum of the dice will be less than 9.
    e. Find the probability of obtaining a sum of 10 knowing that the sum was more or equal to 6.

TOTAL PROBABILITY

Solved Example

It is known that:

    i.   1% of women aged 40 have breast cancer
    ii.   A mammography test has 80% success rate.
    iii.   A mammography test has 10% false alarm rate

A woman receives a positive mammography test, what is the probability she really has cancer?

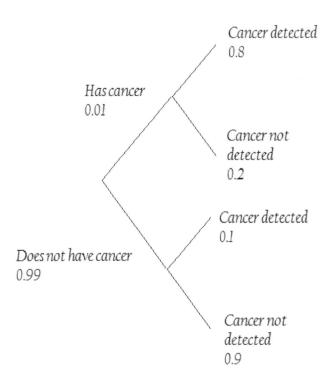

$$P \text{ (True yes| (All Yeses)} = \frac{0.01 \cdot 0.8}{0.01 \cdot 0.8 + 0.99 \cdot 0.1} \approx 0.0748$$

The woman has 7.5% probability to have cancer.

Formal definition: P(A) = P(B)P(A|B) + P(B')P(A|B')

Bayes Theorem:

$$p(B \mid A) = \frac{p(B) \times p(A \mid B)}{p(B) \times p(A \mid B) + p(B') \times p(A \mid B')}$$

Lattice diagrams

2. Two dice numbered one to six are rolled onto a table.

    a. Sketch a corresponding diagram.
    b. Find the probability that the sum is 7.
    c. Find the probability that the sum is more than 7.
    d. Find the probability that the sum is less than 4.
    e. Find the probability that the sum is even.
    f. Find the probability of obtaining a sum of five given that the sum is seven or less.
    g. Find the probability of obtaining a sum of 4 given that the sum is even.

3. A die and coin are rolled on a table.

    a. Sketch a corresponding diagram.
    b. Find the probability of getting Tail and an even number.
    c. Find the probability of getting Tail and a 4.

TREE DIAGRAMS

6. If the probability of tail is 0.53, find the probability of at least one tail in 2 throws.

7. An urn contains 8 cubes of which 5 are black and the rest are white.

    a. What is the probability to draw a white cube?
    b. Draw a tree diagram in case a 1st cube is drawn, it is **NOT replaced** and then another cube is drawn. Indicate all the probabilities on the tree diagram.
    c. Calculate the probability to draw 2 consecutive black cubes.
    d. Calculate the probability to draw **at least** 1 black cube.
    e. Given that the first cube drawn was white, calculate the probability that the 2nd is black.

8. A bag contains 3 red balls, 4 blue balls and 5 green balls. A ball is chosen at random from the bag and is not replaced. A second ball is chosen. Find the probability of choosing one green ball and one blue ball in any order.

9. Given that events A and B are independent with $P(A \cap B) = 0.4$ and $P(A \cap B') = 0$. Find $P(A \cup B)$.

10. Given that P(A) = 0.4, P(B) = 0.7 and P(A $\cup$ B) = 0.8. Find:

    a. P($A \cap B$)
    b. P(A | B)
    c. Determine if A and B are independent events.

11. Given that P(A) = 0.4, P(B) = 0.6 and P(A $\cup$ B) = 0.76.

    a. Find P($A \cap B$)
    b. Are events A and B mutually exclusive? Explain.
    c. Are events A and B independent?

12. The events A and B are independent, where A is the event "it will rain today"
    and B is the event "We will go out for pizza". It is known that

$$P(B) = 0.3, P(A \mid B) = 0.6, P(A \mid B') = 0.5.$$

   a. Complete the following tree diagram.

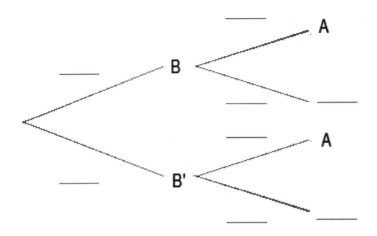

   b. Calculate the probability that it rains knowing we went out for
       pizza.

USING PERMUTATIONS AND COMBINATION IN PROBABILITY

1. 2 oranges and 3 apples are put together in a row. Find the probability that:

    a. The oranges are next to each other.

    b. The oranges are not next to each other.

    c. The apples are next to each other.

    d. The apples are not next to each other.

    e. There are oranges on the sides.

    f. There are no oranges on the sides.

    g. There are apples on the sides.

    h. There are no apples on the sides.

    i. Oranges and apples alternate.

2. A committee of 4 is to be selected out from 7 men and 6 women. Find the probability that:

   a. There are 2 women on the committee.

   b. There are 3 women on the committee.

   c. There are 2 women and 2 men on the committee.

   d. There is at least one men on the committee.

   e. There is at least one of each sex on the committee.

3.6. – DISCRETE RANDOM VARIABLES

1. A _____ takes exactly n numerical values and each of these values corresponds to a single event in the sample space.

2. For example in rolling a die the possible values of X are: {_____}

3. A discrete random variable is one in which we can produce a _____ number of events.

4. If we roll 2 dice the possible values of X are: {_____}

    a. Fill the following table:

x											
P(X = x)											

    b. Represent the information in the table graphically:

    c. $\sum_{i=1}^{i=n} P(X = x_i) = P(X = x_1) + P(X = x_2) + ... + P(X = x_n) = $ _____

    d. Show that the last statement is satisfied in the problem mentioned:

Mean value or Expected of value

    e. Find the mean value of the distribution $E(X) = \mu$.

    f. Deduce the general expression for the mean $E(X)$ discrete probability distribution:

    g. This mean is usually called "the _____ of X".

    h. This number, $E(X)$ can be interpreted in 2 ways:

        A _____ Average.

        A _____ Average.

5. The number of customers entering a shop during 1 hour follows the following table:

x	0	1	3	4	5
P(X = x)	$\dfrac{1}{6}$	$\dfrac{1}{12}$	$\dfrac{5}{12}$	$\dfrac{1}{6}$	

a. Fill the blank in the table.

b. Represent the information in the table graphically:

c. $\displaystyle\sum_{i=1}^{i=n} P(X = x_i) = P(X = x_1) + P(X = x_2) + ... + P(X = x_n) = $ _____

d. Show that the last statement is satisfied in the problem mentioned:

e. Find the mean value of the distribution E(X).

6. Fill the blanks:

    a. $E(a) = $ _____ (a is a constant). Give an example:

    b. $E(aX) = $ _____ .

    c. $E(f(X)) = \sum_{i=i}^{i=n} f(x_i) \times P(X = x_i)$. An example would be:

        $E(aX + b) = $ _____ .

7. Given the following probability distribution

x	2	3	5	6	10
P(X = x)	$\dfrac{1}{6}$	$\dfrac{1}{12}$	$\dfrac{5}{12}$	0	

    a.   Fill the blank.

    b. $E(X) = $ _____

    c. $E(2X) = $ _____

    d. $E(4X) = $ _____

    e. $2E(X) = $ _____

    f. $4E(X) = $ _____

    g. $(E(X))^2 = $ _____

    h. $E(X^2) = $ _____

    i. $E(X^3) = $ _____

    j. $E(\sqrt{X}) = $ _____

    k.   Repeat the process using your GDC.

    l.   In general is $(E(X))^2 = E(X^2)$? _____ Is it possible in a specific case? _____

Variance and standard deviation

a. The Variance measures the _____.

b. Variance is defined as:

$$Var(X) = E((X - \mu)^2) = \sum_{i=i}^{i=n} (x - \mu)^2 P(X = x)$$

Or

$$Var(X) = E(X^2) - (E(X))^2 = E(X^2) - \mu^2$$

Use the data from exercise 7 to find:

Find Var(X) = _____

c. Standard deviation is defined as Sd(X) = _____.

d. In this case Sd(X) = _____. We use the Sd(X) and not the

variance because Sd has _____ as the original

distribution.

e. Calculate Var(2X) = _____. How is it

related to Var(X)?

f. Var(aX) = _____.

g. Var(a) = _____ (a is a constant)

Given 2 distributions:

x	1	2	3	4
P(X = x)	$\dfrac{1}{6}$	$\dfrac{2}{6}$	$\dfrac{1}{6}$	$\dfrac{2}{6}$

x	7	8	9	10
P(X = x)	$\dfrac{1}{6}$	$\dfrac{2}{6}$	$\dfrac{1}{6}$	$\dfrac{2}{6}$

Find for both of them

h. Represent them both on the same graph:

i. The 2nd distribution is _____ as the 1st one only _____

j. E(X) = _____

k. E(X) = _____

l. $E(X^2)$ = _____

m. $E(X^2)$ = _____

n. Var(X) = _____

o. Var(X) = _____

Your conclusions:

p. Var(X + b) = _____

q. Var(a(X + b)) = _____

r. Var(aX + c) = _____

3.7. – PROBABILITY DENSITY FUNCTIONS

1. In occasions, a random variable, does not take exactly n numerical values but an infinite number of values, for example the speed of an object is usually of this nature. This kind of variable is called <u>continuous random variable</u>.

2. For example The probability for a velocity of an object (in m/s) is given by P(x) as a function of its mass x can be given by:

$$P(x) = \begin{cases} \dfrac{4-x}{8} & 0 \le x \le 4 \\ 0 & otherwise \end{cases}$$

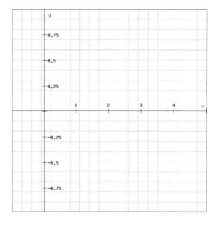

a. Sketch this function.

b. Calculate the area enclosed between the function and the axes. Explain its significance.

c. Write down the most probable velocity of an object (the mode) _____.

d. Write down P(3) = _____ explain the meaning.

e. The expected value E(x) is given by: $\displaystyle\int_{-\infty}^{\infty} P(x)x\,dx$, find it.

f. The median value M is given by: $\displaystyle\int_{x_i}^{M} P(x)\,dx = 0.5$, find it.

g. Calculate $\displaystyle\int_{0}^{1} P(x)x\,dx$, explain its meaning.

3. The probability to have a car accident as a function of age is given by P(x):

$$P(x) = \begin{cases} \dfrac{a}{x-17} & 18 \leq x \leq 100 \\ 0 & otherwise \end{cases}$$

a. Find the value of a, sketch the function.

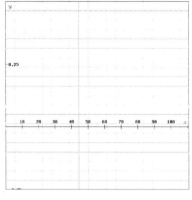

b. Write down the age with highest probability to have an accident (the mode).

h. Write down P(3) = _____ explain the meaning.

i. Write down P(47) = _____ explain the meaning.

j. The expected value E(x) is given by: $\int\limits_{-\infty}^{\infty} P(x)x\,dx$, find it.

k. The median value M is given by: $\int\limits_{x_i}^{M} P(x)\,dx = 0.5$, find it.

l. Calculate $\int\limits_{20}^{30} P(x)x\,dx$, explain its meaning.

4. The probability to succeed in a game as a function of the age in which a young person starts to practice is given by:

$$P(x) = \begin{cases} -b(x^2 - 24x + 108) & 6 \le x \le 18 \\ 0 & otherwise \end{cases}$$

a. Find the value of b, sketch the function.

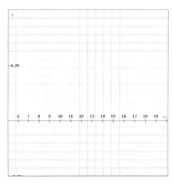

b. Find the age with highest probability to succeed (the mode).

c. Write down P(12) = _____ explain the meaning.

d. Write down P(3) = _____ explain the meaning.

e. The expected value E(x) is given by: $\int_{-\infty}^{\infty} P(x)x\,dx$, find it.

f. The median value M is given by: $\int_{x_i}^{M} P(x)\,dx = 0.5$, find it.

g. Calculate $\int_{4}^{10} P(x)x\,dx$, explain its meaning.

5. The probability density function of a certain continuous random variable is given by P(x).

$$P(x) = \begin{cases} ae^{-x} & 0 \le x \le 1 \\ 0 & otherwise \end{cases}$$

a. Find the probability that the random variable X has a value that lies between 0 and $\frac{1}{2}$? Give your answer in terms of e.

b. Find the expected value and the variance of the distribution. Give your answers exactly, in terms of e.

3.8. – THE BINOMIAL DISTRIBUTION

1. Dichotomous Experiment – An experiment with _____ possible results:

   heads or _____, male or _____, adult or child etc.

2. The probabilities of the results are P(A) and P(A') = _____

3. The variable X is discrete. It is called a Binomial Distribution to B(n, p). n

   is _____ p is _____ and q is _____.

4. The probability that X would have the value k is given by:

$$P(X = k) = \binom{n}{k} p^k q^{n-k}, k = 0, 1, 2...n$$

$$E(x) = \mu = np$$
$$Var(X) = \sigma^2 = npq$$
$$Sd(X) = \sigma = \sqrt{npq}$$

   The mode of X is the value of x with the largest probability.

5. If $B(1, \dfrac{1}{2})$ find:

   a. P(X = 0) = _____

   b. P(X = 1) = _____

   c. P(X = 2) = _____

   d. Mode of X is _____

   e. E(X) = _____ Var(X) = _____ Sd(X) = _____

   f. Write down the probability of the expected value: _____

6. If B(3, $\frac{1}{2}$) find:

    a. P(X = 0) = _____

    b. P(X = 1) = _____

    c. P(X = 2) = _____

    d. P(X = 3) = _____

    e. P(X = 2) = _____ means that _____

    f. Mode of X is _____

    g. P(X < 2) = _____

    h. P(X ≥ 2) = _____

    i. E(X) = _____ Var(X) = _____ Sd(X) = _____

    j. Write down the probability of the expected value: _____

7. If B(3, $\frac{1}{6}$) find:

    a. P(X = 0) = _____

    b. P(X = 1) = _____

    c. P(X = 2) = _____

    d. P(X = 3) = _____

    e. P(X = 2) = _____ means that _____

    f. Mode of X is _____

    g. P(X < 2) = _____

    h. P(X ≥ 2) = _____

    i. E(X) = _____ Var(X) = _____ Sd(X) = _____

    j. Write down the probability of the expected value: _____

8. If B(20, $\frac{1}{2}$) Using GDC binompdf(n,p,x), binompdf(n,p,(x_1,x_n)),

   binomcdf(n,p,x) for P(X ≤ x)

    a. P(X = 5) = _____

    b. P(X = 10) = _____

    c. P(X = 18) = _____

    d. P(X < 8) = _____

    e. P(X ≤ 8) = _____

    f. P(X ≥ 13) = _____

    g. P(X > 13) = _____

    h. E(X) = _____ Var(X) = _____ Sd(X) = _____

    i. Write down the probability of the expected value: _____

9. If B(70, 0.2) Using GDC binompdf(n,p,x), binompdf(n,p,(x_1,x_n)),

   binomcdf(n,p,x) for P(X ≤ x)

    a. P(X = 17) = _____

    b. P(X = 36) = _____

    c. P(X = 28) = _____

    d. P(X < 50) = _____

    e. P(X ≤ 70) = _____

    f. P(X ≥ 38) = _____

    g. P(X > 10) = _____

    h. E(X) = _____ Var(X) = _____ Sd(X) = _____

    i. Write down the probability of the expected value: _____

10. A machine that makes products has a probability of 0.03 to build a defective product. The machine produces 500 products.

    a. Find the most probable number of defective products. Fin its probability.

    b. Find the probability that the machine produced 10 defective products.

    c. Find the probability that the machine produced less than 12 defective products

    d. Find the probability that the machine produced more than 18 defective products

11. A die it thrown 50 times.

    a. Find the probability that exactly 5 "ones" were obtained.

    b. Find the probability that exactly 20 results were even.

    c. Find the probability that less than 12 "ones" were obtained.

    d. Find the probability that more than 17 times a "six" or "five" were obtained.

3.9. – THE POISSON DISTRIBUTION

1. Sometimes presented as "the distribution of the probability of the number of events that will happen in a certain time in a random process". Examples:

- If we study the number of cars crossing a bridge in a given time, a possible event can be: "Number of red cars crossing the bridge in 2 hours".

- If we study the number of rabbits in a given area a possible event can be:

   "_____"

- If we study the number of particles emitted by a radioactive source a possible event can be:

   "_____"

2. In case an event takes place in a given moment, place, volume etc. it is

   _____ of when (or where) other events took place.

3. The longer the time or the bigger the area is etc. the _____ the expected number of events is.

4. The distribution is given by

$$P(X = x) = \frac{e^{-\mu}\mu^{x}}{x!}, x = 0, 1, 2...$$

   $x(t)$ is the number of events in a time t.
   λ is the rate of events per unit of time.

$$m = \lambda t$$

$E(x) = \mu$

$Var(X) = \sigma^2 = \mu$

$Sd(X) = \sigma = \sqrt{\mu}$

   GDC: poissonpdf(m ,x), poissoncdf(m ,x) = P(X > x)

5. Lets observe the Poisson distribution for $\mu = 1$, that means 1 event per hour during 1 hour.

$$P(X = x) = \frac{e^{-1}}{x!}, x = 0, 1, 2, 3, 4, 5, 6$$

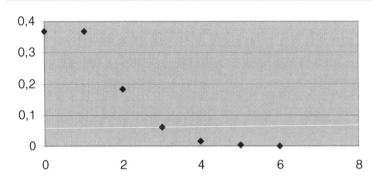

6. Lets observe the Poisson distribution for $\mu = 2$, that means 2 event per hour during 1 hour.

$$P(X = x) = \frac{e^{-2} 2^x}{x!}, x = 0, 1, 2, 3, 4, 5, 6$$

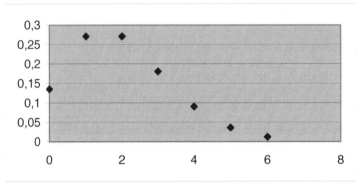

7. Lets observe the Poisson distribution for $\mu = 3$, that means 3 event per hour during 1 hour.

$$P(X = x) = \frac{e^{-3} 3^x}{x!}, x = 0, 1, 2, 3, 4, 5, 6, 7, 8$$

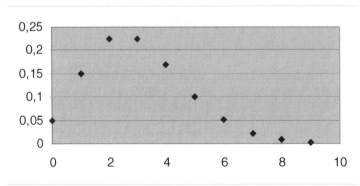

8. In a certain webpage the number of visitors is 200 per hour. Given that the number of visitors was observed during 2 hours, answer:

   a. Write down the probability distribution:

   b. Make a qualitative sketch of the distribution:

   c. m = 200 True / False

   d. λ = 400 True / False

   e. P(X = 400) > P(X = 200) True / False

   f. P(X = 800) > P(X = 400) True / False

9. In a certain ski site the number of visitors is 300 per day. Given that the number of visitors was observed during 3 days, answer:

   a. Write down the probability distribution:

   b. Make a qualitative sketch of the distribution:

c. $m = 900$ True / False

d. $\lambda = 900$ True / False

e. $P(X = 900) > P(X \neq 900)$ True / False

f. $P(X = 820) > P(X = 821)$ True / False

10. Find average number of visitors in a museum is x per hour given that the most probable value of visitors in 3 hours is 180.

11. Given that an atom emits 1 particle in 2 hours, find the probability that in 3 hours the following events will happen.

a. λ = _____

b. m = _____

c. $x(t)$ is the _____

d. P(X = x) = _____

e. P(X = 0) = _____

f.   P(X = 1) = _____

g. P(X = 2) = _____

h. P(X = 3) = _____

i. P(X < 2) = _____

j. E(X) = _____ Var(X) = _____ Sd(X) = _____

k. P(X $\geq$ 2) = _____

l. P(X $\geq$ 3) = _____

m. P(X > 3) = _____

12. Given that average number of customers in a store is 10 per hour. Find the probability that in 4 hours:

a. E(X) = _____ Var(X) = _____ Sd(X) = _____

b. Exactly 40 customers will visit the store.

c. Exactly 45 customers will visit the store.

d. Less than 38 customers will visit the store.

e. More than 43 customers will visit the store.

13. Given that average number of defects in 5 meters of road is 2. Find the probability that in 1 km of road:

a. E(X) = _____ Var(X) = _____ Sd(X) = _____

b. There are exactly 350 defects.

c. There are exactly 450 defects.

d. Less than 370 defects.

e. More than 300 defects.

3.10. – NORMAL DISTRIBUTION

Given the following information about a Group of people:

Weight	[40, 50)	[50, 60)	[60, 70)	[70, 80)	[80, 90)	[90, 100)	[100, 110)
Number of people	4	8	12	11	10	6	2

The histogram that represents this information is:

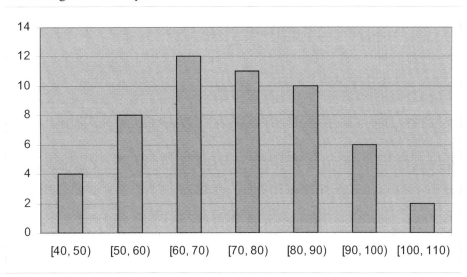

A bigger sample was taken to and the following information was obtained:

Weight	[40, 45)	[45, 50)	[50, 55)	[55, 60)	[60, 65)	[65, 70)	[70, 75)
Number of people	7	12	20	22	30	36	34

Weight	[75, 80)	[80, 85)	[85, 90)	[90, 95)	[95, 100)	[100, 105)	[105, 110)
Number of people	26	16	12	5	3	2	1

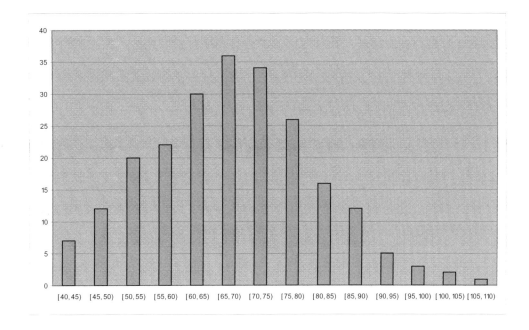

What do you observe? Can you guess how would a bigger sample look like?

As you can see in the second case, the histogram can be approximated by the drawn curve. That curve is called the **normal distribution**. The variables are distributed as for example: height, weight, shoe size and many other variables, specifically biological variables.

The function that describes the normal distribution is:

$$f(z) = \frac{1}{\sqrt{2\pi}} e^{\left(-\frac{z^2}{2}\right)}, \; -\infty < z < \infty$$

1. The normal distribution is characterized by two numbers: The _____ μ and

    the _____ σ

2. Fill the missing data for the following distributions:

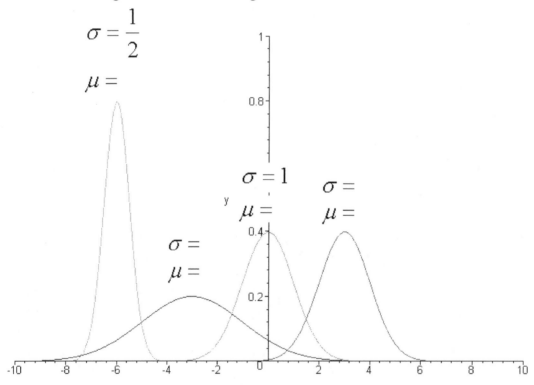

$$\sigma = \frac{1}{2}$$

$$\mu =$$

$$\sigma = 1$$

$$\mu =$$

$$\sigma =$$

$$\mu =$$

$$\sigma =$$

$$\mu =$$

3. **The standard normal distribution** is the one with $\mu =$ __ y $\sigma =$ __ (Green)

4. The mean μ is located at the _____ of the distribution.

5. The standard deviation σ represents the distance between the mean and the

    _____

Properties of the normal distribution

6. The _____ under the curve or the probability from negative infinity to plus infinity is ____

7. The normal distribution is symmetrical that means that the area under the graph on each side of the mean is _____

8. The shape and position of a normal distribution depend on the parameters therefore there is an _____ number of normal distributions.

   The distribution gets will narrower and taller as_____

9. In general the area under the curve in the interval $\mu \pm 1\sigma$ is _____

10. In general the area under the curve in the interval $\mu \pm 2\sigma$ is _____

11. In general the area under the curve in the interval $\mu \pm 3\sigma$ is _____

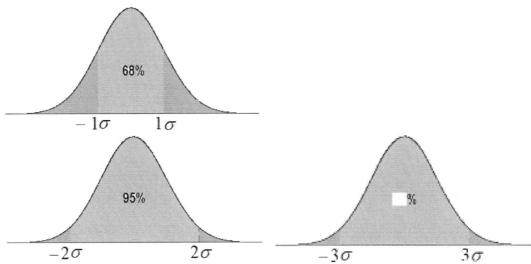

12. σ (the _____) gives us an idea about the _____

13. μ (the _____) indicates the _____

14. Normally the normal distribution is written as N(μ, σ^2), that means that a distribution N(28, 4) will have a mean of _____ and a SD of _____.

FINDING PROBABILIT OF a < Z < b

Shade and calculate use **GDC**: ShadeNorm(a, b) or ShadeNorm(a, b, μ, σ)
(Use large numbers for ∞ or $-\infty$)

15.

a. $P(Z \geq 0) =$ _____

b. $P(Z = 1) =$ _____

c. $P(Z < 1) =$ _____

d. $P(Z \geq 2) =$ _____

e. $P(Z \geq 2.23) =$ _____

f. $P(Z \geq 1.57) =$ _____

g. $P(Z \leq 1.86) =$ _____

h. $P(Z \leq -2) =$ _____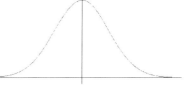

i. $P(Z \leq -2.1) =$ _____

j. $P(Z \geq -3.11) =$ _____

k. $P(Z \geq -2) =$ _____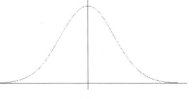

l. $P(Z \geq -0.58) =$ _____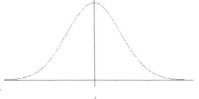

m. $P(Z \leq -2.7) =$ _____

n. $P(-\infty \leq Z \leq -2.7) =$ _____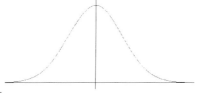

o. $P(3 \leq Z \leq -2.7) =$ _____

p. P$(1 \leq Z \leq 2)$ = _____

q. P$(-1.25 \leq Z \leq 0)$ = _____

r. P$(-2.12 \leq Z \leq 1.65)$ = _____

s. P$(-1.02 \leq Z \leq -0.25)$ = _____

t. P$(0.97 \leq Z \leq 1.76)$ = _____

u. P$(1.54 \leq Z \leq \infty)$ = _____

v. P$(1.31 \leq Z \leq 3.06)$ = _____

FINDING PROBABILIT FOR $a < X < b$

The amount of time to produce a product follows a normal distribution with mean of 40 minutes and S. D. of 8 minutes.

16. Find the probability that the product is produced between 35 and 50 minutes. Shade the corresponding area on the following diagram.
Use **GDC** to find your answer: normalcdf(35, 50, 40, 8)

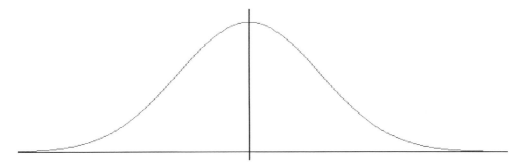

17. Find the probability that the product is produced in more than 38 minutes. Shade the corresponding area on the following diagram.
Use GDC to find your answer: normalcdf(38, 1000, 40, 8)

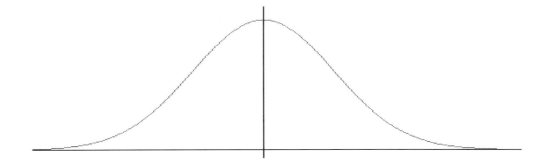

18. Find the probability that the product is produced in less than 34 minutes. Shade the corresponding area on the following diagram.
Use GDC to find your answer: normalcdf(−1000, 34, 40, 8)

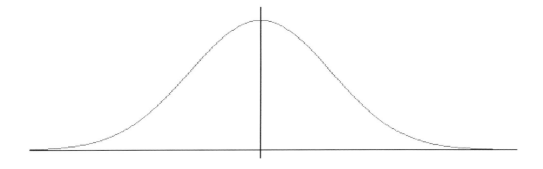

Exercises

19. In a normal distribution N(24, 6) Find and shade:

a. P(X = 25) = _____

b. P(X ≥ 25) = _____

c. P(X ≤ 25) = _____

d. P(X ≥ 15) = _____

e. P(14 ≤ X ≤ 20) = _____

f. (19 ≤ X ≤ 31) = _____

20. In a lake there are 3000 fish distributed according to a normal distribution with a mean of 26cm and a standard deviation of 7cm.

a. Find and shade on the graph the interval in which 68% of the fish lengths are. How many fish in this case?

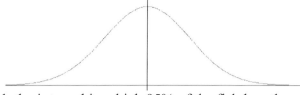

b. Find and shade on the graph the interval in which 95% of the fish lengths are. How many fish in this case?

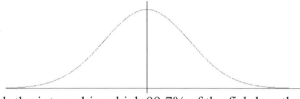

c. Find and shade on the graph the interval in which 99.7% of the fish lengths are. How many fish in this case?

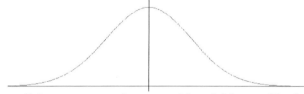

d. Find and the probability for a fish to measure between 23 and 28 cm. Shade on graph. How many fish in this would you expect in this case to be in this interval?

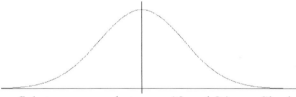

e. Find and the probability for a fish to measure between 12 and 24 cm. Shade on graph. How many fish in this would you expect in this case to be in this interval?

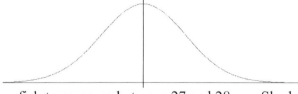

f. Find and the probability for a fish to measure between 27 and 28 cm. Shade on graph. How many fish in this would you expect in this case to be in this interval?

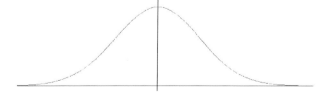

g. Find and shade on graph the probability for a fish to measure more than 26 cm. How many fish in this case?

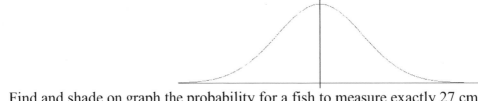

h. Find and shade on graph the probability for a fish to measure exactly 27 cm.

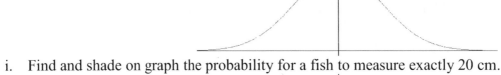

i. Find and shade on graph the probability for a fish to measure exactly 20 cm.

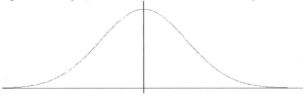

STANDARDIZATION OF THE NORMAL DISTRIBUTION

21. As we already know there is an _____ number of normal distributions,

depending on _____ and _____. The standard distribution is one of them, the

distribution in which the _____ is _____ and the SD is _____

22. Usually in a problem the distribution is not the standard therefore _____ is not

_____ and _____ is not _____. The way to transform any normal

distribution to the standard one is the following:

$$Z = \frac{X - \mu}{\sigma}$$

23. In reality what this expression means is rescaling the variable. And Z is the

number of _____ away from the mean.

Example The personnel manager of a large company requires applicants for a post take a certain test and achieve a score of 515. If test scores are normally distributed with mean 485 and standard deviation 30 what percentage of applicants pass the test?

Calculating the value of Z we get:

$$Z = \frac{X - \mu}{\sigma} = \frac{515 - 485}{30} = 1$$

$P(X \geq 500) = P(Z \geq 1) = 0.1587$, 15.87% of participants would pass the test. This result also means 515 is 1 standard deviation away from the mean.

24. Given a distribution N(22, 5), find the standard variable Z, shade and calculate:

a. $P(X \geq 0) = P(Z \geq 0) =$_____

b. $P(X = 27) = P(Z = 1) =$_____

c. P(X < 20) = P(Z < __) = _____

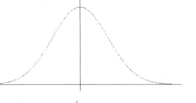

d. P(X ≥ 25) = _____

e. P(X ≥ 15) = _____

f. P(X ≥ 0) = _____

g. P(X ≤ 18) = _____

h. P(−∞ ≤ X ≤ 27) = _____

i. P(20 ≤ X ≤ 25) = _____

j. P(12 ≤ X ≤ 18) = _____

FINDING INVERSE NORMAL PROBABILITIES

25. The amount of time (X) to produce a product follows a normal distribution with mean of 40 minutes and S. D. of 8 minutes.

   a. Find the value of a, if 6% of the value of X are less than a. Shade the corresponding area on the following diagram. Use GDC to find your answer: invNorm(0.06, 40, 8)

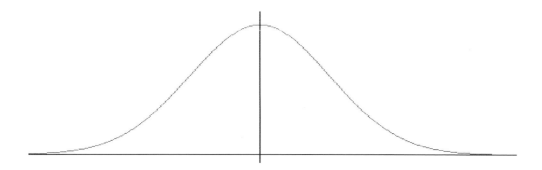

   b. Find the value of a, if 13% of the value of X are more than a. Shade the corresponding area on the following diagram. Use GDC to find your answer: invNorm(0.87, 40, 8)

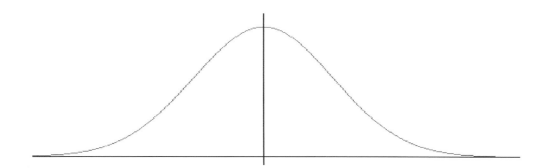

   c. Find the value of a and b if the middle 50% of value of X are between a and b. Shade the corresponding area on the following diagram. Use GDC to find your answer: , invNorm(0.25, 40, 8), invNorm(0.75, 40, 8)

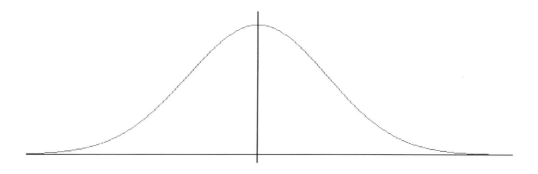

26. In a lake there are 2000 fish distributed according to a normal distribution with a mean of 26cm and a standard deviation of 7cm.

a. Find and shade the length interval for 80% of the fish. How many fish are expected to be in the interval in this case?

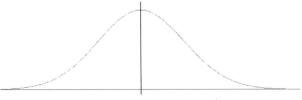

b. Find and shade the length interval for 90% of the fish. How many fish are expected to be in the interval in this case?

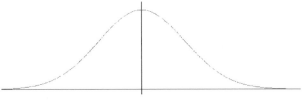

c. Find and shade the length interval for 75% of the fish. How many fish are expected to be in the interval in this case?

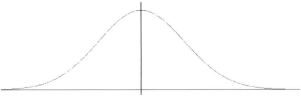

d. There is a probability of 0.2 that a fish's length is more than q, find q. How many fish are expected to be in the interval in this case?

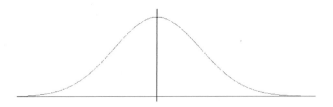

e. There is a probability of 0.32 that a fish's length is less than w, find w. How many fish are expected to be in the interval in this case?

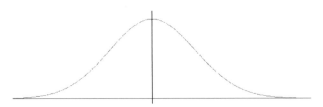

f. There is a probability of 0.4 that a fish's length is between a and b, find a and b. How many fish are expected to be in the interval in this case?

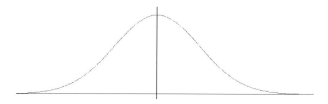

g. There is a probability of 0.6 that a fish's length is between a and b, find a and b. How many fish are expected to be in the interval in this case?

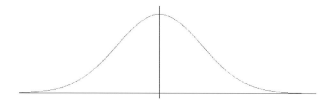

h. There is a probability of 0.1 that a fish's length is less than t, find t. How many fish are expected to be in the interval in this case?

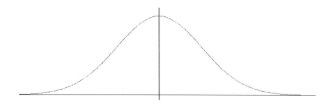

i. Find and shade the interval in which 65% of the fish measure. How many fish are expected to be in the interval in this case?

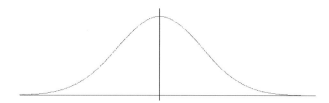

25. Calculate k if P(X ≤ k) = 0.6103 and X is a normal distribution N(15, 4)

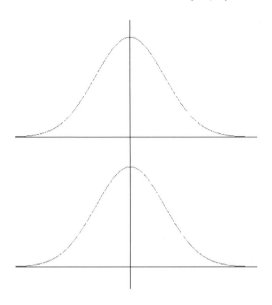

26. It is known that P(X ≤ 7) = 0.9147 and P(X ≤ 6.5) = 0.7517. Calculate
    a. μ and σ
    b.   k so that P(X ≥ k) = 0.3

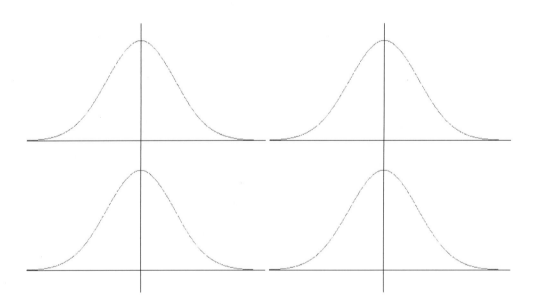

27. 500 high school students' grades are distributed normally with a mean of 72 and a standard deviation of 6.

    a. Find the interval mean plus/minus 2 standard deviations.

    b. What percentage of scores are between scores 60 and 70? How many students in this group?

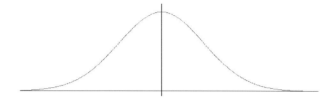

    c. What percentage of scores are more than 88? How many students in this group?

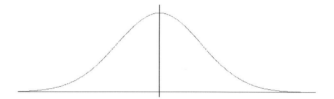

    d. What percentage of scores are less than 60? How many students in this group?

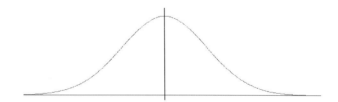

    e. Can students' grades distribute normally? Explain.

28. The time it takes to complete a certain journey is normally distributed with a mean of 50 days and a standard deviation of 4 days.

  a. The probability that the length of the journey lies between 53 and 60 days hours is represented by the shaded area in the following diagram.

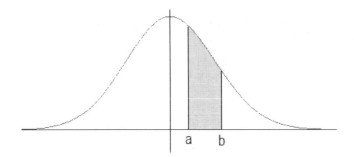

  Write down the values of *a* and *b*.

  b. Find the probability that the length of the journey is more than 57 days.

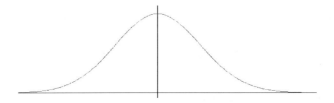

  c. Find the probability that the length of the journey is between 56 and 61 days.

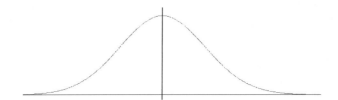

  d. 80% of the travellers complete the journey after x hours. Find x.

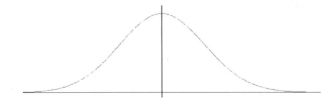

29. The weight of a certain animal is normally distributed with mean of 150 kg and standard deviation of 12 kg. We classify the animals in the following way:

Small   weight < 130
Medium $130 \leq$ weight < 170
Big $170 \leq$ weight

Add these boundaries to your diagram.

a. Find the probability for each one the cases described.

P(weight < 130) = _____

P(130 < weight < 170) = _____

P(weight > 170) = _____

b. There is a probability of 0.2 for an animal to have a weight bigger than q. Find q.

P(weight > q) = 0.2   q = _____

c. In a jungle with 3000 animals how many are expected to have a weight bigger than q?

1.1. – RATE OF CHANGE

Example 1: Oil prices, represented as a function of time P(t):

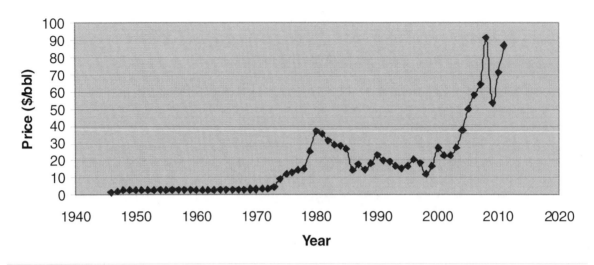

1. As you can see there have been periods of time in history in which the prices have changed slowly, Identify one of them: $t \in (1950, 1970)$

2. In other periods the prices have been changing very quickly, identify one positive change: $t \in (2003, 2005)$ and one negative change: $t \in (2008, 2009)$

3. In this graph what are the <u>units</u> of the <u>change</u> of price: $\left[\dfrac{\$}{bbl \cdot year} \right]$

4. Find the <u>average rate of change</u> in oil prices between 1970 and 1985. Is this average similar to the real change in prices? Explain your answer.

   $Av_{1970-1985} = \dfrac{24}{15} = 1.6 \; \frac{\$}{bbl \cdot year}$ <u>It is not similar to real change as the prices went up</u>

   <u>and down during that period of time.</u>

5. Find the average rate of change between 1945 and 2005, how can this change be represented graphically?

   $Av_{1945-2005} = \dfrac{48}{60} = 0.8 \; \frac{\$}{bbl \cdot year}$ <u>The average rate of change is the slope of the line the</u>

   <u>connects the two points.</u>

Example 2: Population of 20 – 29 year olds in southern Europe for example, represented as a function of time P(t):

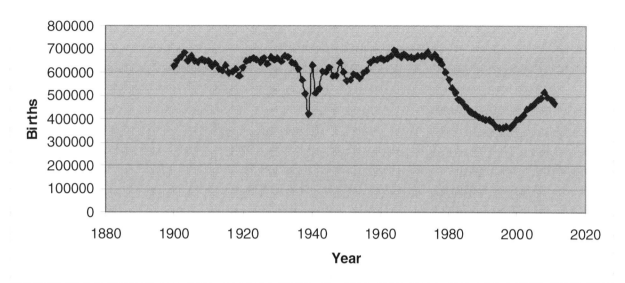

Spain´s Birth Rate

6. During what period of time the fastest change occurs? $t \in (1939, 1940)$

7. In this graph what are the <u>units</u> of the <u>change</u> of birth: $\left[\dfrac{Births}{year}\right]$

8. Find the <u>average rate of change</u> between 1960 and 2000. Is this average similar to the real change in births? Explain your answer.

$$Av_{1960-2000} = -\frac{260000}{40} = -6500 \, {}_{\frac{Births}{year}}$$ <u>It shows some similarity to the real tendency.</u>

9. Find the average rate of change between 2000 and 2010, how can this change be represented graphically?

$$Av_{2000-2010} = \frac{100000}{10} = 10000 \, {}_{\frac{Births}{year}}$$ <u>The average rate of change is the slope of the</u>

<u>line the connects the two points.</u>

1.2. – DEFINITION OF DERIVATIVE

1. The derivative is <u>the slope of the tangent to the function at a certain point.</u>
2. Given the function, sketch the tangent in each one of the points:

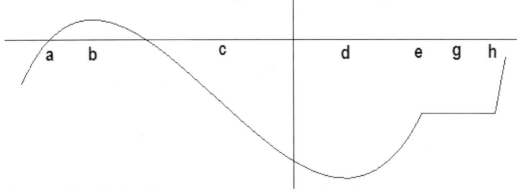

Fill the table with: Positive, negative, zero or doesn't exist.

	x = a	x = b	x = c	x = d	x = e	x = g	x = h
f(x)	Zero	Positive	Negative	Negative	Negative	Negative	Negative
f'(x)	Positive	Zero	Negative	Zero	D.E.	Zero	D.E

3. Given the function, sketch the tangent in each one of the points:

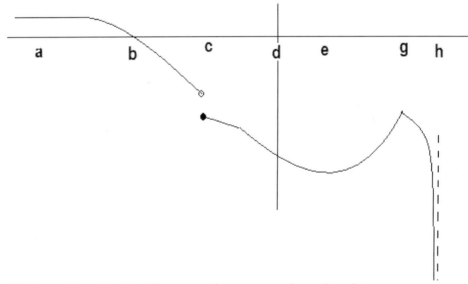

Fill the table with: Positive, negative, zero or doesn't exist.

	x = a	x = b	x = c	x = d	x = e	x = g	x = h
f(x)	Positive	Zero	Negative	Negative	Negative	Negative	D.E.
f'(x)	Zero	Negative	D.E.	Negative	Zero	D.E.	D.E.

4. Given the function $f(x) = -x^2$. f represents the temperature as the function of height x given in km:

5. Fill the blanks and indicate the corresponding points on the graph:
   $f(1) = \underline{-1}$ $f(1.4) = \underline{-1.96}$
   Draw the line that connects the points and find its slope
   $$m = \frac{-1.96-(-1)}{1.4-1} = -2.4$$

6. Fill the blanks and indicate the corresponding points on the graph:
   $f(1) = \underline{-1}$ $f(1.2) = \underline{-1.44}$
   Draw the line that connects the points and find its slope
   $$m = \frac{-1.21-(-1)}{1.2-1} = -2.2$$

7. Fill the blanks and indicate the corresponding points on the graph:
   $f(1) = \underline{-1}$ $f(1.1) = \underline{-1.21}$
   Draw the line that connects the points and find its slope
   $$m = \frac{-1.21-(-1)}{1.1-1} = -2.1$$

8. What do you think the slope of the tangent at the point where x = 1 is? 2

9. Looking at the process to find the slope at the point where x = 1, can you think how to find the slope of the tangent in general? <u>Choose a point very (!, in reality infinitely close) close to it on its left or right and find the slope between those points.</u>

10. What does the slope **between 2 points** represent? Make reference to height and temperature and give units. <u>It represents the **mean** rate of change of temperature with height, its units are degrees/km</u>

11. What does the slope of the tangent to the function **at a certain point** (the derivative) represent? Make reference to height and temperature and give units. <u>It represents the **instantaneous** rate of change of temperature with height, its units are degrees/km</u>

12. The slope between 2 points is <u>the **mean** rate of change</u>

13. The slope at a certain point is <u>the **instantaneous** rate of change</u>

FORMAL DEFINITION OF DERIVATIVE
<u>Differentiate the following functions, use the definition ONLY:</u>

1. $f(x) = mx + b$

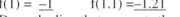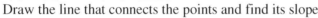

$$\frac{df}{dx} = f'(x) = \lim_{h\to 0}\frac{f(x+h)-f(x)}{h} = \lim_{h\to 0}\frac{m(x+h)+b-mx+b}{h} = m$$

2. $f(x) = x^2 + k$

$$\frac{df}{dx} = f'(x) = \lim_{h\to 0}\frac{f(x+h)-f(x)}{h} = \lim_{h\to 0}\frac{(x+h)^2+k-(x^2+k)}{h} =$$

$$\lim_{h\to 0}\frac{2xh+h^2}{h} = \lim_{h\to 0}\frac{h(2x+h)}{h} = \lim_{h\to 0}\left(2x+h\right) = 2x$$

315

3. $f(x) = x^3 + k$

$$\frac{df}{dx} = f'(x) = \lim_{h \to 0} \frac{f(x+h) - f(x)}{h} = \lim_{h \to 0} \frac{(x+h)^3 + k - (x^3 + k)}{h} =$$

$$\lim_{h \to 0} \frac{3x^2 h + 3xh^2 + h^3}{h} = \lim_{h \to 0} \frac{h(3x^2 + 3xh + h^2)}{h} = \lim_{h \to 0} \left(3x^2 + 3xh + h^2\right) = 3x^2$$

4. $f(x) = 4x - 3x^2$

$$\frac{df}{dx} = f'(x) = \lim_{h \to 0} \frac{f(x+h) - f(x)}{h} = \lim_{h \to 0} \frac{4(x+h) - 3(x+h)^2 - (4x - 3x^2)}{h} = 4 - 6x$$

5. $f(x) = \sqrt{x+1}$

$$\frac{df}{dx} = f'(x) = \lim_{h \to 0} \frac{f(x+h) - f(x)}{h} = \lim_{h \to 0} \frac{\sqrt{x+h+1} - \sqrt{x+1}}{h} =$$

$$\lim_{h \to 0} \frac{\sqrt{x+h+1} - \sqrt{x+1}}{h} \cdot \frac{(\sqrt{x+h+1} + \sqrt{x+1})}{(\sqrt{x+h+1} + \sqrt{x+1})} = \lim_{h \to 0} \frac{(x+h+1) - (x+1)}{h} \cdot \frac{1}{(\sqrt{x+h+1} + \sqrt{x+1})} =$$

$$\lim_{h \to 0} \frac{h}{h} \cdot \frac{1}{(\sqrt{x+h+1} + \sqrt{x+1})} = \frac{1}{2\sqrt{x+1}}$$

6. $f(x) = \dfrac{1}{2x+1}$

$$\frac{df}{dx} = f'(x) = \lim_{h \to 0} \frac{f(x+h) - f(x)}{h} = \lim_{h \to 0} \frac{\dfrac{1}{2(x+h)+1} - \dfrac{1}{2x+1}}{h} =$$

$$\lim_{h \to 0} \frac{(2x+1) - (2(x+h)+1)}{h(2(x+h)+1)(2x+1)} = \lim_{h \to 0} \frac{-2h}{h(2(x+h)+1)(2x+1)} = \frac{-2}{(2x+1)^2}$$

7. $f(x) = \dfrac{-3}{-x+2}$

$$\frac{df}{dx} = f'(x) = \lim_{h \to 0} \frac{f(x+h) - f(x)}{h} = \lim_{h \to 0} \frac{\dfrac{-3}{(-(x+h))+2} - \dfrac{-3}{-x+2}}{h} =$$

$$\lim_{h \to 0} \frac{(3x-6) + 3(-(x+h)+2)}{h(-(x+h)+2)(-x+2)} = \lim_{h \to 0} \frac{-3h}{h(-(x+h)+2)(-x+2)} = \frac{-3}{(-x+2)^2}$$

8. $f(x) = \sqrt{2x} + 1$

$$\frac{df}{dx} = f'(x) = \lim_{h \to 0} \frac{f(x+h) - f(x)}{h} = \lim_{h \to 0} \frac{\rule{2cm}{0.4pt} - \rule{1.5cm}{0.4pt}}{h} =$$

9. $f(x) = \sqrt{3x-5} + 1$

$$\frac{df}{dx} = f'(x) = \lim_{h \to 0} \frac{f(x+h)-f(x)}{h} = \lim_{h \to 0} \frac{\sqrt{3(x+h)-5}+1-(\sqrt{3x-5}+1)}{h} =$$

$$\lim_{h \to 0} \frac{\sqrt{3(x+h)-5}-\sqrt{3x-5}}{h} \cdot \frac{(\sqrt{3(x+h)-5}+\sqrt{3x-5})}{(\sqrt{3(x+h)-5}+\sqrt{3x-5})} =$$

$$\lim_{h \to 0} \cdot \frac{3(x+h)-5-(3x-5)}{h(\sqrt{3(x+h)-5}+\sqrt{3x-5})} = \frac{3}{2\sqrt{3x-5}}$$

10. $f(x) = \dfrac{4}{5x+1} + 2$

$$\frac{df}{dx} = f'(x) = \lim_{h \to 0} \frac{f(x+h)-f(x)}{h} = \lim_{h \to 0} \frac{\dfrac{4}{5(x+h)+1} - \dfrac{4}{5x+1}}{h} =$$

$$\lim_{h \to 0} \frac{(20x+4)-4(5(x+h)+1)}{h(5(x+h)+1)(5x+1)} = \lim_{h \to 0} \frac{-20h}{h(5(x+h)+1)(5x+1)} = \frac{-20}{(5x+1)^2}$$

11. $f(x) = \sqrt{2x-3}$

$$\frac{df}{dx} = f'(x) = \lim_{h \to 0} \frac{f(x+h)-f(x)}{h} = \ldots = \frac{2}{2\sqrt{2x+3}} = \frac{1}{\sqrt{2x+3}}$$

12. $f(x) = \dfrac{1}{3x-4}$

$$\frac{df}{dx} = f'(x) = \lim_{h \to 0} \frac{f(x+h)-f(x)}{h} = \ldots = \frac{-3}{(3x-4)^2}$$

13. Given the following function, find:

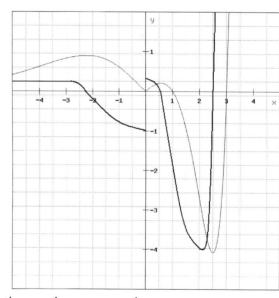

a. $f(-4) \approx 0.6 \quad f'(-4) \approx \dfrac{1}{3}$

b. $f(-3) \approx 0.8 \quad f'(-3) \approx \dfrac{1}{3}$

c. $f(-2.3) \approx 0.9 \quad f'(-2.3) = 0$

d. $f(-1) \approx 0.6 \quad f'(-1) \approx -1$

e. $f(0) = 0 \quad\quad f'(0) = D.E$

f. $f(0.2) \approx 0.2 \quad f'(0.2) \approx 0.3$

g. $f(0.6) \approx 0.2 \quad f'(0.6) \approx 0$

h. $f(2) \approx -2.5 \quad f'(2) \approx -4.5$

i. $f(2.5) = -4 \quad f'(2.5) = 0$

j. $f(3) = 0 \quad\quad f'(3) \approx 10$

Use the information obtained to sketch the derivative on the same graph.

14. When the derivative is positive it means that the function is <u>increasing</u>

15. When the derivative is <u>negative</u> it means that the function is <u>decreasing</u>

16. When the derivative is zero it means that the function has <u>a stationary point (the tangent is horizontal)</u>

1.3. – GRAPHING THE DERIVATIVE (GRADIENT FUNCTION)

Draw the graph of the derivative of the following functions on the graph below:

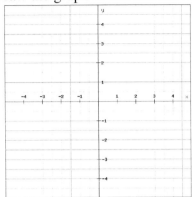 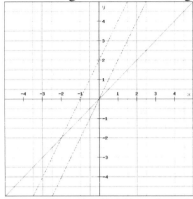

Both same derivative f'(x) = 0

The parallel lines have the same
derivative f'(x) = 2, the other f'(x) = 1

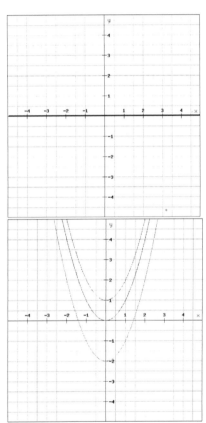 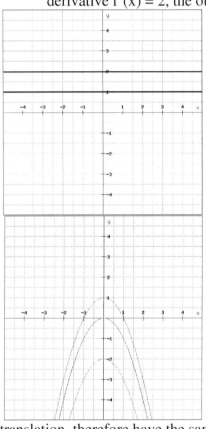

The parabolas only differ in vertical translation, therefore have the same derivative.

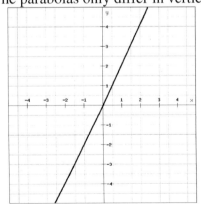 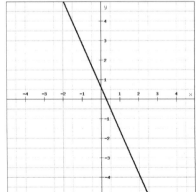

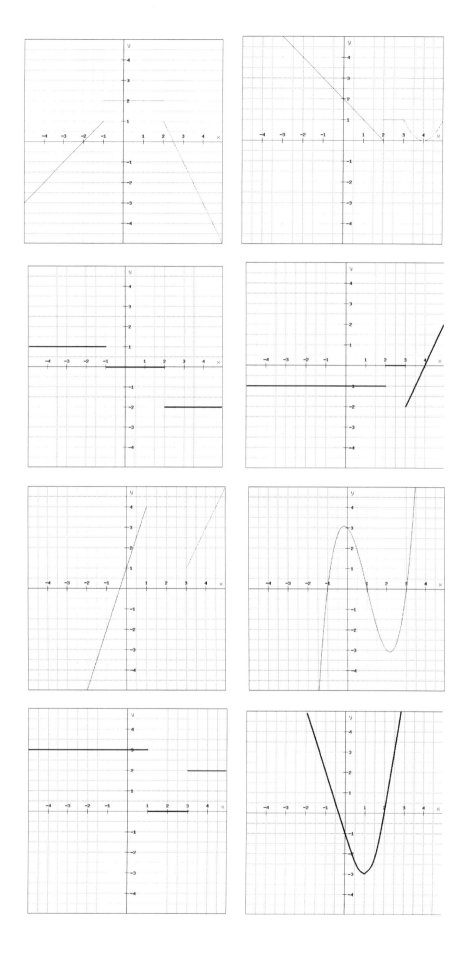

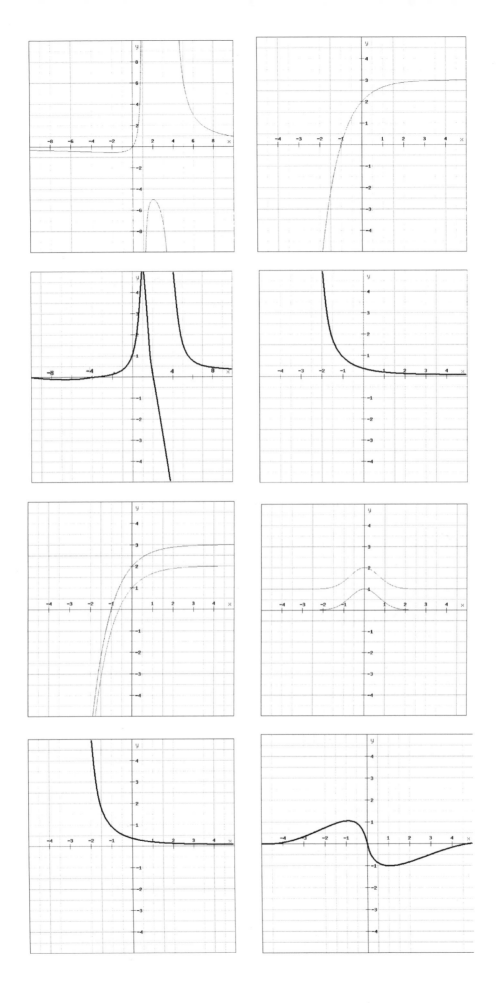

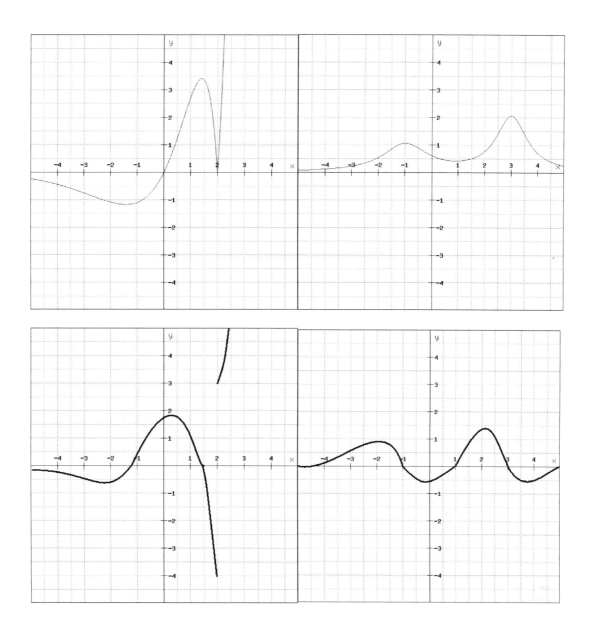

1.4. – GRAPHING THE ANTIDERIVATIVE

Draw the graph of the derivative of the following functions on the graph below:

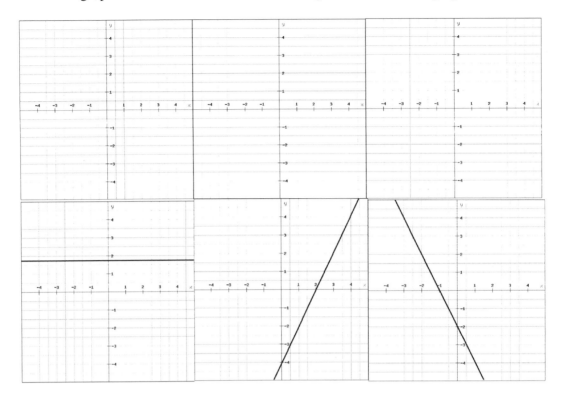

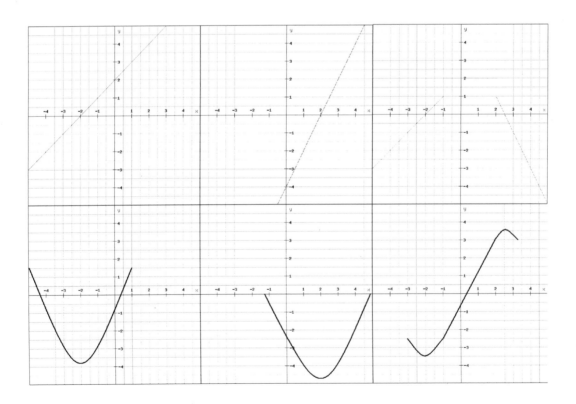

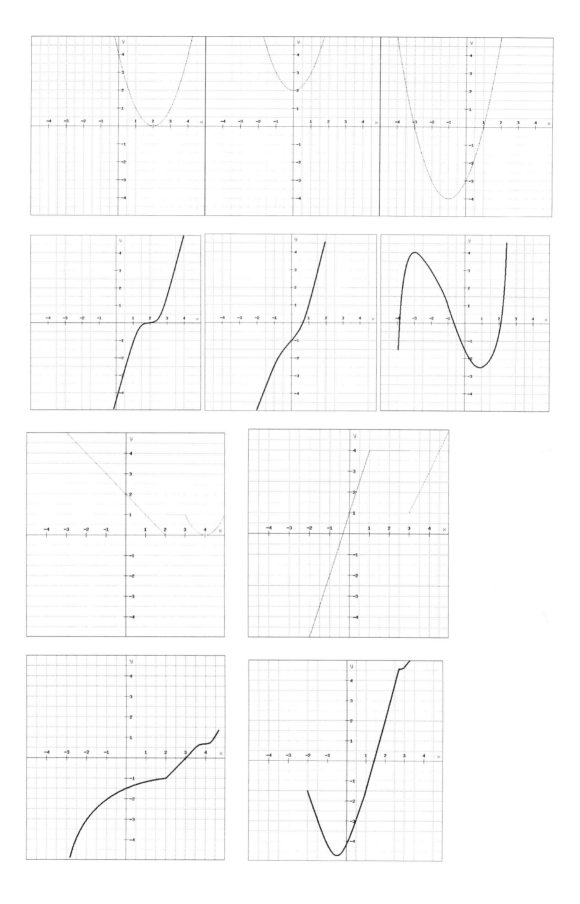

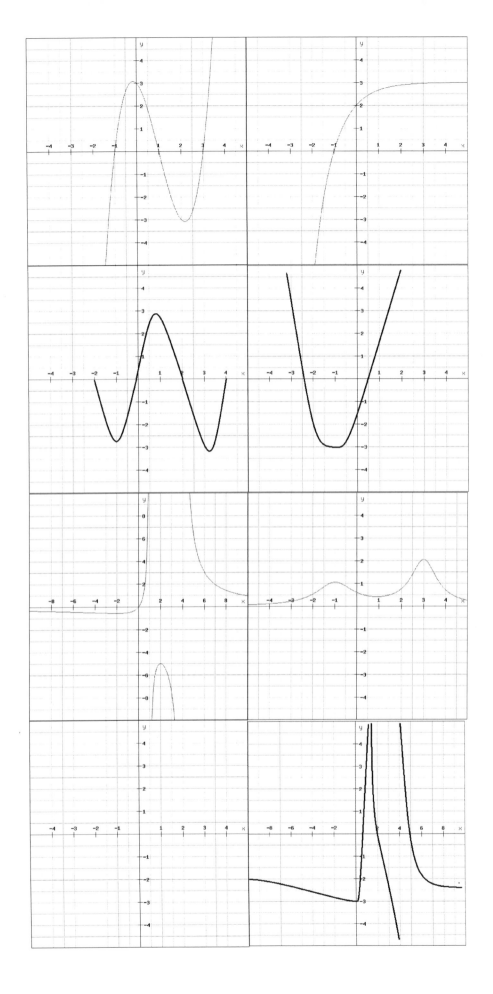

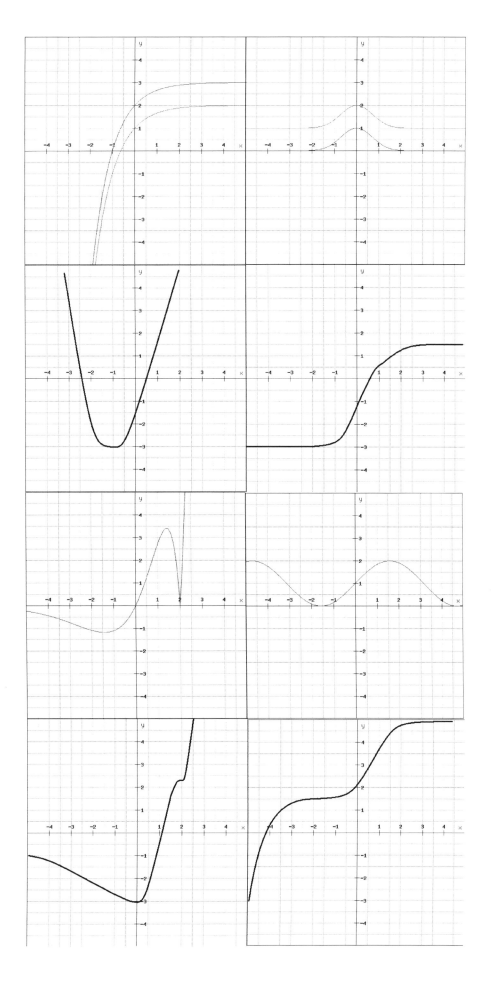

1.5. – TANGENTS AND NORMALS TO FUNCTIONS

1. Given the function $f(x) = 2x^2$. Sketch it.

   a. $f'(x) = \lim_{h \to 0} \dfrac{f(x+h) - f(x)}{h} = \lim_{h \to 0} \dfrac{2(x+h)^2 - 2x^2}{h} = \ldots = 4x$

   b. $f'(1) = 4$

   c. $f'(0) = 0$

   d. $f'(x) = 4x = 3; x = \dfrac{3}{4}; \left(\dfrac{3}{4}, \dfrac{9}{8}\right)$

   e. $f'(x) = 4x = -4; x = -1; (-1, 2)$

   f. $f'(x) = 4x = 2; x = \dfrac{1}{2}; \left(\dfrac{1}{2}, \dfrac{1}{2}\right)$

   g. $f'(x) = 4x = -5; x = -\dfrac{5}{4}; \left(-\dfrac{5}{4}, \dfrac{25}{8}\right)$

   h. $m = f'(1) = 4; point = (1, 2); y = 4x + b; y = 4x - 2$

   i. $Tangent: m = f'(0) = 0; point = (0, 0); y = b; y = 0$
   $Normal: x = 0$

   j. $Tangent: m = f'(-2) = -8; point = (-2, 8); y = -8x + b; y = -8x - 8$
   $Normal: m = \dfrac{1}{8}; point = (-2, 8); y = \dfrac{1}{8}x + b; y = \dfrac{1}{8}x + \dfrac{33}{4}$

2. Given the function $f(x) = -\dfrac{2}{x} + 1$. Sketch it.

   a. $f'(x) = \lim_{h \to 0} \dfrac{f(x+h) - f(x)}{h} = \lim_{h \to 0} \dfrac{\left(-\dfrac{2}{x+h} + 1\right) - \left(-\dfrac{2}{x} + 1\right)}{h} = \ldots = \dfrac{2}{x^2}$

   b. $f'(1) = 2$

   c. Out of domain, not possible.

   d. $f'\left(\dfrac{1}{2}\right) = 8$.

   e. $f'(x) = \dfrac{2}{x^2} = -3$ No such point exists.

   f. $f'(x) = \dfrac{2}{x^2} = \dfrac{1}{2} : x = \pm 2; (2, 0), (-2, 2)$

   g. $f'(x) = \dfrac{2}{x^2} = -\dfrac{5}{3}$ no such point exists.

   h. $f'(x) = \dfrac{2}{x^2} = 6 : x = \pm\dfrac{1}{\sqrt{3}}; \left(\dfrac{1}{\sqrt{3}}, 1 - \dfrac{2\sqrt{3}}{3}\right), \left(\dfrac{1}{\sqrt{3}}, 1 + \dfrac{2\sqrt{3}}{3}\right)$.

   i. $m = f'(1) = 2; point = (1, -1); y = 2x + b; y = 2x - 3$

   j. Out of domain, not possible.

   k. $Tangent: m = f'\left(\dfrac{1}{2}\right) = 8; point = \left(\dfrac{1}{2}, -3\right); y = 8x + b; y = 8x - 7$

   $Normal: m = -\dfrac{1}{8}; point = \left(\dfrac{1}{2}, -3\right); y = -\dfrac{1}{8}x + b; y = -\dfrac{1}{8}x - \dfrac{47}{16}$

3. Given the function $f(x) = -x^2 - x$. Sketch it.

a. $f'(x) = \lim_{h\to 0}\dfrac{f(x+h)-f(x)}{h} = \lim_{h\to 0}\dfrac{\left(-(x+h)^2-(x+h)\right)-\left(-x^2-x\right)}{h} = \ldots = -2x-1$

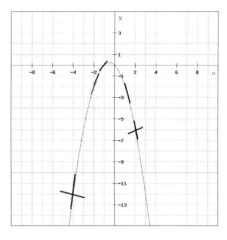

b. $f'(-1) = 1$

c. $f'(2) = -5$

d. $f'(-4) = 7$

e. $f'(x) = -2x-1 = 2; x = -\dfrac{3}{2}; \left(-\dfrac{3}{2}, -\dfrac{3}{4}\right)$

f. $f'(x) = -2x-1 = -2.3; x = 0.65; (0.65, -1.0725)$

g. $f'(x) = -2x-1 = 3; x = -2; (-2, -2)$

h. $f'(x) = -2x-1 = -5; x = 2; (2, -6)$

i. $m = f'(-1) = 1; point = (-1,0); y = x+b; y = x+1$

j. $Tangent: m = f'(2) = -5; point = (2,-6); y = -5x+b; y = -5x+4$

$Normal: m = \dfrac{1}{5}; point = (2,-6); y = \dfrac{1}{5}x+b; y = \dfrac{1}{5}x - \dfrac{32}{5}$

k. $Tangent: m = f'(-4) = 7; point = (-4,-12); y = 7x+b; y = 7x+16$

$Normal: m = -\dfrac{1}{7}; point = (-4,-12); y = -\dfrac{1}{7}x+b; y = -\dfrac{1}{7}x - \dfrac{88}{7}$

4. Given the function $f(x) = -3x^2 + 1$. Sketch it.

a. $f'(x) = \lim_{h\to 0}\dfrac{f(x+h)-f(x)}{h} = \lim_{h\to 0}\dfrac{\left(-3(x+h)^2+1\right)-\left(-3x^2+1\right)}{h} = \ldots = -6x$

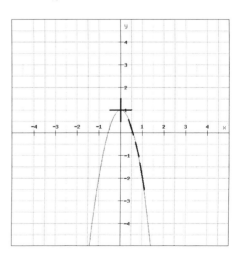

b. $f'(1) = 6$

c. $f'(0) = 0$

d. $f'(2) = -12$

e. $f'(x) = -6x = 3; x = \dfrac{1}{2}; \left(\dfrac{1}{2}, \dfrac{1}{4}\right)$

f. $f'(x) = -6x = -4; x = \dfrac{2}{3}; \left(\dfrac{2}{3}, -\dfrac{1}{3}\right)$

g. $f'(x) = -6x = -5; x = \dfrac{5}{6}; \left(\dfrac{5}{6}, -\dfrac{13}{12}\right)$

h. $Tangent: m = f'(0) = 0; point = (0,1); y = 1$

$Normal: x = 0$

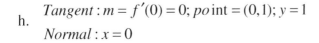

5. Given the function $f(x) = \dfrac{3}{x-2}$. Sketch it.

a. $f'(x) = \lim_{h \to 0} \dfrac{f(x+h) - f(x)}{h} = \lim_{h \to 0} \dfrac{\dfrac{3}{x+h-2} - \dfrac{3}{x-2}}{h} = \ldots = \dfrac{-3}{(x-2)^2}$

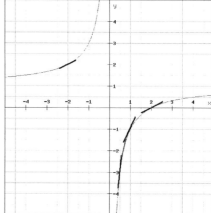

b. $f'(1) = -3$

c. $f'(2) = $ Does not exist.

d. $f'\left(\dfrac{1}{2}\right) = -\dfrac{4}{3}$

e. $f'(x) = \dfrac{-3}{(x-2)^2} = -3; x_1 = 1, x_2 = 3; (1,3),(3,1)$,

f. $f'(x) = \dfrac{-3}{(x-2)^2} = \dfrac{1}{2}$ No solution, no such point.

g. $f'(x) = \dfrac{-3}{(x-2)^2} = -\dfrac{5}{3}; (x-2)^2 = \dfrac{9}{5}; x = 2 \pm \dfrac{3}{\sqrt{5}}; \left(2+\dfrac{3}{\sqrt{5}}, \sqrt{5}\right), \left(2-\dfrac{3}{\sqrt{5}}, -\sqrt{5}\right)$

h. $f'(1) = -3; po\,\mathrm{int} = (1,-3); y = -3x + b; y = -3x$

i. Does not exist, out of domain

j.

$Tangent : m = f'\left(\dfrac{1}{2}\right) = -\dfrac{4}{3}; po\,\mathrm{int} = \left(\dfrac{1}{2}, -2\right); y = -\dfrac{4}{3}x + b; y = -\dfrac{4}{3}x - \dfrac{4}{3}$

$Normal : m = \dfrac{3}{4}; po\,\mathrm{int} = \left(\dfrac{1}{2}, -2\right); y = \dfrac{3}{4}x + b; y = \dfrac{3}{4}x - \dfrac{19}{8}$

1.6. – DERIVATIVES

Polynomial Functions Differentiate the following functions:

1. $f(x) = 5$ $\qquad$ $f'(x) = 0$

2. $f(x) = 3$ $\qquad$ $f'(x) = 0$

3. $f(x) = x$ $\qquad$ $f'(x) = 1$

4. $f(x) = 5x$ $\qquad$ $f'(x) = 5$

5. $f(x) = 5kx+1$ $\qquad$ $f'(x) = 5k$

6. $f(x) = -2x$ $\qquad$ $f'(x) = -2$

7. $f(x) = -2x - 3$ $\qquad$ $f'(x) = -2$

8. $f(x) = -2x + 3$ $\qquad$ $f'(x) = -2$

9. $f(x) = x^2 + 3x - 10$ $\qquad$ $f'(x) = 2x + 3$

10. $f(x) = x^2 + 7x - 1$ $\qquad$ $f'(x) = 2x + 7$

11. $f(x) = bx^6 + 2x + 7$ $\qquad$ $f'(x) = 6bx + 2$

12. $f(x) = x^{22} + x - 1$ $\qquad$ $f'(x) = 22x^{21} + 1$

13. $f(x) = x^4 + 2x + 1$ $\qquad$ $f'(x) = 4x^3 + 2$

14. $f(x) = x^5 + x$ $\qquad$ $f'(x) = 5x^4 + 1$

15. $f(x) = x^{22} - \dfrac{1}{x}$ $\qquad$ $f'(x) = 22x^{21} + x^{-2}$

16. $f(x) = x^2 - 2x + \dfrac{1}{x^2}$ $\qquad$ $f'(x) = 2x - 2 - 2x^{-3}$

17. $f(x) = a\,x^5 - 2x^4 - \dfrac{5}{x^2} + \dfrac{1}{x^3}$ $\qquad$ $f'(x) = 5ax^4 - 8x^3 + 20x^{-3} - 3x^{-4}$

18. $f(x) = 5x^2 - 10x + \dfrac{1}{x^{\frac{2}{3}}} + \dfrac{1}{x^{-2}}$ $\qquad$ $f'(x) = 10x - 10 - \dfrac{2}{3}x^{-\frac{5}{3}} + 2x$

19. $f(x) = -5x^{20} - \dfrac{1}{x^{-2}}$ $\qquad$ $f'(x) = -100x^{19} - 2x$

20. $f(x) = -x^3 + 6x^2 - 8 - \sqrt{x} - \sqrt[3]{x}$ $\qquad$ $f'(x) = 3x^2 + 12x - \dfrac{1}{2}x^{-\frac{1}{2}} - \dfrac{1}{3}x^{-\frac{2}{3}}$

21. $f(x) = -x^5 - 6x^2 + 2x + \sqrt{x^6} - \sqrt[3]{x^4}$ $\qquad$ $f'(x) = -5x^4 - 12x + 2 + \dfrac{1}{6}x^{-\frac{5}{6}} - \dfrac{3}{4}x^{-\frac{1}{4}}$

22. $f(x) = -x^7 + x^2 - 5x - x\sqrt{x} - x\sqrt[3]{x} - \sqrt[3]{x^{-2}}$ $\qquad$ $f'(x) = -7x^6 + 2x - 5 - \dfrac{3}{2}x^{\frac{1}{2}} - \dfrac{4}{3}x^{\frac{1}{3}} + \dfrac{2}{3}x^{-\frac{5}{3}}$

23. $f(x) = -bx^4 - 4x^2 - 4$ $\qquad$ $f'(x) = -4bx^3 - 8x$

24. $f(x) = -x^{-2} + 3x$ $\qquad$ $f'(x) = 2x^{-3} + 3$

25. $f(x) = -15x^{-2} - 3x^{-5}$ $\qquad$ $f'(x) = 30x^{-3} + 3$

26. $f(x) = \dfrac{5}{2}x^{-3} - b6x$ $\qquad$ $f'(x) = -\dfrac{15}{2}x^{-4} - 6b$

27. $f(x) = \dfrac{1}{6}x^3 - 3 + \dfrac{\sqrt{x}+3}{3} - \dfrac{1+x\sqrt{2}}{7}$ $\qquad$ $f'(x) = \dfrac{1}{2}x^2 + \dfrac{1}{6}x^{-\frac{1}{2}} - \dfrac{\sqrt{2}}{7}$

28. $f(x) = \dfrac{2}{3}x^{\frac{2}{3}} - 3x^{\frac{1}{2}} + 2e^2 - x\log(3)$ $f'(x) = \dfrac{4}{9}x^{-\frac{1}{3}} - \dfrac{3}{2}x^{-\frac{1}{2}} - \log(3)$

29. $f(x) = 3x^2 + \dfrac{2}{3}x^{\frac{4}{9}} - 5x^{\frac{2}{5}}$ $f'(x) = 6x + \dfrac{8}{27}x^{-\frac{5}{9}} - 2x^{-\frac{3}{5}}$

30. $f(x) = x^2 + 3x + 4 + 3x^2 + b\dfrac{7}{6}x^{-\frac{4}{9}} - 5x^{\frac{3}{2}}$ $f'(x) = 8x + 3 - \dfrac{28b}{54}x^{-\frac{13}{9}} - \dfrac{15}{2}x^{\frac{1}{2}}$

31. $f(x) = -12x - 13 + 3bx + 4 + 3x^{-3} + \dfrac{7}{6}x^{-\frac{1}{9}} - 5x^{\frac{-7}{2}}$ $f'(x) = -12 + 3b - 9x^{-4} - \dfrac{7}{54}x^{-\frac{10}{9}} + \dfrac{35}{2}x^{-\frac{9}{2}}$

32. $f(x) = -x^3 + 6x^2 - 8 - x\sqrt{x} - \sqrt[3]{x} + \cos(4)x^{-1}$ $f'(x) = -3x^2 + 12x - \dfrac{3}{2}x^{\frac{1}{2}} - \dfrac{1}{3}x^{-\frac{2}{3}} - \cos(4)x^{-2}$

33. $f(x) = x^2 + 9x - 4 + 3x^2 + \dfrac{7}{6}x^{-\frac{4}{9}} - 5x^{\frac{3}{2}} + \ln(2)x^2$ $f'(x) = 8x + 9 - \dfrac{28}{54}x^{-\frac{13}{9}} - \dfrac{15}{2}x^{\frac{1}{2}} + 2\ln(2)x$

34. $f(x) = 8x - x\sqrt{x} - \sqrt[3]{2x}$ $f'(x) = 8 - \dfrac{3}{2}x^{\frac{1}{2}} - \dfrac{\sqrt[3]{2}}{3}x^{-\frac{2}{3}}$

35. $f(x) = -x^3 + 6x^{22} - 8 - x\sqrt{x} - \sqrt[3]{x}x^2$ $f'(x) = -3x^2 + 132x^{21} - \dfrac{3}{2}x^{\frac{1}{2}} - \dfrac{7}{3}x^{\frac{4}{3}}$

Exponential functions

36. $f(x) = 8x - e^x$ $f'(x) = 8 - e^x$

37. $f(x) = 2e^x - x$ $f'(x) = 2e^x - 1$

38. $f(x) = 5e^x - \sqrt{x} - \sqrt[3]{2x}$ $f'(x) = 5e^x - \dfrac{1}{2}x^{-\frac{1}{2}} - \dfrac{\sqrt[3]{2}}{3}x^{-\frac{2}{3}}$

39. $f(x) = -3e^x - x\sqrt{x} - \sqrt[5]{x^2}$ $f'(x) = -3e^x - \dfrac{3}{2}x^{\frac{1}{2}} - \dfrac{2}{5}x^{-\frac{3}{5}}$

Logarithmic functions

40. $f(x) = 2\ln(x) - \sqrt{x\sqrt{x}}$ $f'(x) = \dfrac{2}{x} - \dfrac{3}{4}x^{-\frac{1}{4}}$

41. $f(x) = \dfrac{1}{\sqrt[5]{x}} - \dfrac{\sqrt{x}}{2x} - \dfrac{\sqrt[5]{x^2}}{\sqrt{x}} - \ln(x)$ $f'(x) = -\dfrac{1}{5}x^{-\frac{6}{5}} + \dfrac{1}{4}x^{-\frac{3}{2}} + \dfrac{1}{10}x^{-\frac{11}{10}} - \dfrac{1}{x}$

42. $f(x) = \dfrac{\sqrt{x}+3}{3} - \dfrac{1+x\sqrt{2}}{7} - \dfrac{2}{3x} + \log(x)$ $f'(x) = \dfrac{1}{6}x^{\frac{1}{2}} - \dfrac{\sqrt{2}}{7} + \dfrac{2}{3}x^{-2} + \dfrac{1}{\ln(10)x}$

43. $f(x) = 2e^x - \dfrac{\ln(5)}{\sqrt{2x}} - \log_2(x)$ $f'(x) = 2e^x + \dfrac{\ln(5)}{\sqrt{2}}x^{-2} - \dfrac{1}{\ln(2)x}$

44. $f(x) = \ln(7) - \dfrac{\cos(1)+\sqrt{2}}{7}e^x - x\sqrt{\dfrac{1}{2x}} - 2\log_e(x)$ $f'(x) = -\dfrac{\cos(1)+\sqrt{2}}{7}e^x - \dfrac{1}{2\sqrt{2}}x^{-\frac{1}{2}} - \dfrac{1}{x}$

45. $f(x) = \cos(5) - \ln(7) - \dfrac{x\ln(11)+\sqrt{2}}{\cos(7)} - \dfrac{\sin(1)}{3+\sqrt{2}}x + \log_9(x)$

$$f'(x) = \dfrac{\ln(11)}{\cos(7)} - \dfrac{\sin(1)}{3+\sqrt{2}} + \dfrac{1}{Ln(9)x}$$

Trigonometric functions

46. $f(x) = \ln(8) - 2e^x + \cos(x)$ $\qquad$ $f'(x) = -2e^x - \sin(x)$

47. $f(x) = \cos(2)x^2 - 23.7e^x - \sin(x)$ $\qquad$ $f'(x) = 2\cos(2)x - 23.7e^x - \cos(x)$

48. $f(x) = x^{-\frac{13}{9}} - 33^{\sqrt{2}} - 2\cos(x)$ $\qquad$ $f'(x) = -\frac{13}{9}x^{-\frac{22}{9}} + 2\sin(x)$

49. $f(x) = (1 + 2^{\sqrt{2}})x - e^x + 5\cos(x)$ $\qquad$ $f'(x) = (1 + 2^{\sqrt{2}}) - e^x - 5\sin(x)$

50. $f(x) = 2\sin(x) + \sin(8)\ln(6)x - e^x$ $\qquad$ $f'(x) = 2\cos(x) + \sin(8)\ln(6) - e^x$

51. $f(x) = \cos(x) + \frac{5\sqrt{x}}{3x} - e^x$ $\qquad$ $f'(x) = -\sin(x) - \frac{5}{6}x^{-\frac{3}{2}} - e^x$

PRODUCT RULE $\qquad$ $(fg)' = f'g + fg'$

52. $f(x) = (x + 2)(x + 3)$ $\qquad$ $f'(x) = 1 \cdot (x+2) + (x+3) \cdot 1 = 2x + 5$

53. $f(x) = (x^2 - 2)(x^2 + 3)$ $\qquad$ $f'(x) = 2x \cdot (x^2 + 3) + (x^2 - 2) \cdot 2x$

54. $f(x) = (2x + 2)(5x^2 - 3 + e^x)$ $\qquad$ $f'(x) = 2 \cdot (5x^2 - 3 + e^x) + (2x+2) \cdot (10x + e^x)$

55. $f(x) = (-x + 2 - \cos(x))(5x^8 - 3x)$

$\qquad f'(x) = (-1 + \sin(x)) \cdot (5x^8 - 3x) + (-x + 2 - \cos(x)) \cdot (40x - 3)$

56. $f(x) = (-x^9 + 2 + \sin(x))(x + 3x^2)$

$\qquad f'(x) = (-9x^8 + \cos(x)) \cdot (x + 3x^2) + (-x^9 + 2 + \sin(x)) \cdot (1 + 6x)$

57. $f(x) = (2\ln(x) + 3x^2 + \frac{7}{6}x^{-\frac{4}{9}} - 5x^{\frac{3}{2}})(x^2 - 1 - \cos(x))$

$f'(x) = (\frac{2}{x} + 6x - \frac{28}{54}x^{-\frac{13}{9}} - \frac{15}{2}x^{\frac{1}{2}}) \cdot (x^2 - 1 - \cos(x)) + (2\ln(x) + 3x^2 + \frac{7}{6}x^{-\frac{4}{9}} - 5x^{\frac{3}{2}}) \cdot (2x + \sin(x))$

58. $f(x) = (2\log(x) - \frac{7}{6}\frac{2}{x^{\frac{2}{3}}} - 5\frac{2}{x})(x^2 - 1) + \sin(x)$

$f'(x) = (\frac{2}{\ln(10)x} + 6x + \frac{28}{18}x^{-\frac{5}{3}} + 10x^{-2}) \cdot (x^2 - 1) + (2\log(x) - \frac{14}{6}x^{-\frac{2}{3}} - \frac{10}{x}) \cdot (2x) + \cos(x)$

59. $f(x) = (\log_3(x) + \frac{7}{6}\frac{2}{x^{\frac{2}{3}}} - 5\frac{2}{x})(x^2 - 1 + e^x - \sin(x)) - e^x + \log_2(x)$

$f'(x) = (\frac{1}{\ln(3)x} + \frac{28}{18}x^{-\frac{5}{3}} + 10x^{-2}) \cdot (x^2 - 1 + e^x - \sin(x)) + (\log_3(x) - \frac{14}{6}x^{-\frac{2}{3}} - \frac{10}{x}) \cdot (2x + e^x - \cos(x)) - e^x + \frac{1}{\ln(2)x}$

60. $f(x) = (\frac{1}{6}\frac{1}{x^{-\frac{2}{3}}} - \frac{2}{x^5})(x^2 - \sqrt{x}) + \cos(x)$

$\qquad f'(x) = (\frac{1}{9}x^{-\frac{1}{3}} + 10x^{-6}) \cdot (x^2 - \sqrt{x}) + (\frac{1}{6}x^{\frac{2}{3}} - \frac{2}{x^5}) \cdot (2x - \frac{1}{2}x^{-\frac{1}{2}}) - \sin(x)$

61. $f(x) = (\frac{1}{6}x - \frac{2}{x^2})(x^2 - \frac{1}{\sqrt[3]{x}} - \sin(x) + \cos(x) + e^x) + e^x + \cos(x)$

$f'(x) = (\frac{1}{6} + x^{-\frac{3}{2}}) \cdot (x^2 - x^{-\frac{1}{3}} - \sin(x) + \cos(x) + e^x) + (\frac{1}{6}x - 2x^{-\frac{1}{2}}) \cdot (2x + \frac{1}{3}x^{-\frac{4}{3}} - \cos(x) - \sin(x) + e^x) + e^x - \sin(x)$

QUOTIENT RULE $\left(\dfrac{f}{g}\right)' = \dfrac{f'g - fg'}{g^2}$

62. $f(x) = \dfrac{x+1}{2x^2}$ $f'(x) = \dfrac{1 \cdot 2x^2 - (x+1) \cdot 4x}{(2x^2)^2}$

63. $f(x) = \dfrac{2x^2 + x}{x^2}$ $f'(x) = \dfrac{(4x+1) \cdot x^2 - (2x^2 + x) \cdot 2x}{(x^2)^2}$

64. $f(x) = \dfrac{x^2 + \sqrt{x} + 1}{-x^4}$ $f'(x) = \dfrac{(2x + \frac{1}{2}x^{-\frac{1}{2}}) \cdot (-x^4) - (x^2 + \sqrt{x} + 1) \cdot (-4x^3)}{(-x^4)^2}$

65. $f(x) = \dfrac{x^{\frac{2}{3}} - x}{2x^2 + x}$ $f'(x) = \dfrac{(\frac{2}{3}x^{-\frac{1}{3}} - 1) \cdot (2x^2 + x) - (x^{\frac{2}{3}} - x) \cdot (4x + 1)}{(2x^2 + x)^2}$

66. $f(x) = -4\dfrac{\sin(x) + x}{3x}$ $f'(x) = -4 \cdot \dfrac{(\cos(x) + 1) \cdot (3x) - (\sin(x) + x) \cdot (3)}{(3x)^2}$

67. $f(x) = \dfrac{x - \log(x)}{\log(x) + 1}$ $f'(x) = \cdot \dfrac{(1 - \frac{1}{\ln(10)x}) \cdot (\log(x) + 1) - (x - \log(x)) \cdot (\frac{1}{\ln(10)x})}{(\log(x) + 1)^2}$

68. $f(x) = \tan(x)$ $f'(x) = \dfrac{\cos(x) \cdot \cos(x) + \sin(x) \cdot \sin(x)}{(\cos(x))^2} = \dfrac{1}{(\cos(x))^2}$

69. $f(x) = 2\dfrac{x + e^x}{\cos(x)}$ $f'(x) = 2 \cdot \dfrac{(1 + e^x) \cdot \cos(x) + (x + e^x) \cdot \sin(x)}{(\cos(x))^2}$

70. $f(x) = \sec(x)$ $f'(x) = \dfrac{\sin(x)}{(\cos(x))^2}$

71. $f(x) = \cos ec(x)$ $f'(x) = \dfrac{-\cos(x)}{(\sin(x))^2}$

72. $f(x) = \dfrac{\sin(x) + \ln(x)}{x^4}$ $f'(x) = \dfrac{(\cos(x) + \frac{1}{x}) \cdot x^4 - (\sin(x) + \ln(x)) \cdot 4x^3}{(x^4)^2}$

73. $f(x) = \dfrac{x^{-\frac{2}{5}} + \sin(x) + \ln(x)}{2x^{3.2} + 1}$ $f'(x) = \dfrac{(-\frac{2}{5}x^{-\frac{7}{5}} + \cos(x) + \frac{1}{x}) \cdot (2x^{3.2} + 1) - (x^{-\frac{2}{5}} + \cos(x) + \frac{1}{x}) \cdot 4.6x^{2.2}}{(2x^{3.2} + 1)^2}$

74. $f(x) = \dfrac{\sin(x)(x+1)}{2x^2}$

$f'(x) = \dfrac{(\cos(x) \cdot (x+1) + \sin(x) \cdot 1) \cdot 2x^2 - (\sin(x) \cdot (x+1)) \cdot 4x}{(2x^2)^2}$

75. $f(x) = \dfrac{(3x+1)(2x+2)}{e^x}$

$$f'(x) = \dfrac{\left(3\cdot(2x+2)+(3x+1)\cdot2\right)\cdot e^x - \left((3x+1)\cdot(2x+2)\right)\cdot e^x}{(e^x)^2}$$

76. $f(x) = \dfrac{e^x}{2x}$ $f'(x) = \dfrac{e^x\cdot 2x - e^x\cdot 2}{(2x)^2}$

$$\left(f(g)\right)' = f'(g)\,g'$$

CHAIN RULE

77. f(x) = sin(3x) $f'(x) = \cos(3x)\cdot 3$

78. f(x) = −3tan(−2x) $f'(x) = \dfrac{-3\cdot(-2)}{\left(\cos(-2x)\right)^2}$

79. f(x) = 2cos(6x²) $f'(x) = -2\sin(6x^2)\cdot 12x$

80. f(x) = − (4x + 5)² $f'(x) = -2(4x+5)\cdot 4$

81. f(x) = −3(6x − 1)⁻¹⁰ $f'(x) = 30(6x-1)^{-11}\cdot 6$

82. f(x) = 2(3x² + 3)⁸⁰ $f'(x) = 160(3x^2+3)^{79}\cdot 6$

83. f(x) = e⁴ˣ + 2²ˣ $f'(x) = e^{4x}\cdot 4 + 2^{2x}\cdot \ln(2)\cdot 2$

84. f(x) = 5e⁴ˣ − 3⁴ˣ $f'(x) = 5e^{4x}\cdot 4 - 3^{4x}\cdot \ln(3)\cdot 4$

85. f(x) = eˢⁱⁿ⁽ˣ⁾ $f'(x) = e^{\sin(x)}\cdot \cos(x)$

86. f(x) = (5 − 3x²·³)⁻⁶ $f'(x) = -6(5-3x^{2.3})^{-7}\cdot(-6.9)$

87. f(x) = 5ˣ $f'(x) = 5^x\cdot \ln(5)$

88. f(x) = 5ˢⁱⁿ⁽ˣ⁾ $f'(x) = 5^{\sin(x)}\cdot \ln(5)\cdot \cos(x)$

89. f(x) = 5ᶜᵒˢ⁽²ˣ⁾ $f'(x) = 5^{\cos(2x)}\cdot \ln(5)\cdot(-\sin(2x))\cdot 2$

90. f(x) = (7 − x)⁻² $f'(x) = -2(7-x)^{-3}(-1)$

91. f(x) = xsin(2x) $f'(x) = \sin(2x) + x\cos(2x)\cdot 2$

92. f(x) = 4xe³ˣ $f'(x) = 4e^{3x} + 4x\cdot e^{3x}\cdot 3$

93. f(x) = 3x²cos(5x²) $f'(x) = 6x\cdot \cos(5x^2) + 6x\cdot \sin(5x^2)\cdot 10x$

94. f(x) = eˣ − 4ˣ $f'(x) = e^x - 4^x\cdot \ln(4)$

95. f(x) = −2ˣ + x $f'(x) = -2^x\cdot \ln(2) + 1$

96. f(x) = 7ˣ − x¹⁰ $f'(x) = 7^x\cdot \ln(7) - 10x^9$

97. f(x) = 5eˣ + 3ˣ $f'(x) = 5e^x + 3^x\cdot \ln(3)$

98. $f(x) = \left(\dfrac{2}{3}\right)^x$ $f'(x) = \left(\dfrac{2}{3}\right)^x\cdot \ln\!\left(\dfrac{2}{3}\right)$

99. $f(x) = \left(\dfrac{1}{4}\right)^{x+1}$ $f'(x) = \left(\dfrac{1}{4}\right)^{x+1}\cdot \ln\!\left(\dfrac{1}{4}\right)$

100. f(x) = −3xlog₂(3x + 2) $f'(x) = -3\cdot \log_2(3x+2) - 3x\cdot \dfrac{3}{(3x+2)\ln(2)}$

101. f(x) = 4x⁵log₄(5x² + x) $f'(x) = 20x^4\cdot \log_4(5x^2+x) + 4x^5\cdot \dfrac{10x}{(5x^2+x)\ln(4)}$

$$f'(x) = (-3)(4+5x)^{-3} + (2-3x)\cdot(-3)(4+5x)^{-4}\cdot 5$$

102. $f(x) = (2 - 3x)(4 + 5x)^{-3}$

103. $f(x) = (5 - \ln(x))e^{\sin(x)}$
$\qquad f'(x) = -\dfrac{1}{x} \cdot e^{\sin(x)} + (5 - \ln(x)) \cdot e^{\sin(x)} \cdot \cos(x)$

104. $f(x) = (\sin(3x))^3$
$\qquad f'(x) = 3(\sin(3x))^2 \cdot \cos(3x) \cdot 3$

105. $f(x) = (4x^2 + 3x + 2 - e^x)^{\frac{5}{4}}$
$\qquad f'(x) = \dfrac{5}{4}(4x^2 + 3x + 2 - e^x)^{\frac{1}{4}} \cdot (8x + 3 - e^x)$

106. $f(x) = \sqrt{(\sin(3x) + 2x)}$
$\qquad f'(x) = \dfrac{1}{2}(\sin(3x) + 2x)^{-\frac{1}{2}} \cdot (\cos(3x) \cdot 3 + 2)$

107. $f(x) = \dfrac{3}{\sqrt{(\ln(x))}}$
$\qquad f'(x) = -\dfrac{3}{2}(\ln(x))^{-\frac{3}{2}} \cdot \dfrac{1}{x}$

108. $f(x) = x^2(\sin(3x^2 - 5x + 3) + 2x)$
$\qquad f'(x) = 2x \cdot (\sin(3x^2 - 5x + 3) + 2x) + x^2 \cdot (\sin(3x^2 - 5x + 3) \cdot (6x - 5) + 2)$

109. $f(x) = \sqrt{\dfrac{2x + 1}{2^x}}$
$\qquad f'(x) = \dfrac{1}{2}\left(\dfrac{2x + 1}{2^x}\right)^{-\frac{1}{2}} \cdot \dfrac{2 \cdot 2^x - (2x + 1) \cdot 2^x \ln(2)}{(2^x)^2}$

110. $f(x) = 3^{\sqrt{x}}$
$\qquad f'(x) = 3^{\sqrt{x}} \cdot \ln(3) \cdot \dfrac{1}{2}x^{-\frac{1}{2}}$

111. $f(x) = 3^{\sqrt[3]{x}} + x$
$\qquad f'(x) = 3^{\sqrt[3]{x}} \cdot \ln(3) \cdot \dfrac{1}{3}x^{-\frac{2}{3}} + 1$

112. $f(x) = (\ln(3x^2 + x))^{-2}$
$\qquad f'(x) = -2(\ln(3x^2 + x))^{-3} \cdot \dfrac{6x + 1}{3x^2 + x}$

113. $f(x) = \sin(\ln(x^2))$
$\qquad f'(x) = \cos(\ln(x^2)) \cdot \dfrac{2x}{x^2} = \dfrac{2\cos(\ln(x^2))}{x}$

114. $f(x) = 2^{\cos(x^2)}$
$\qquad f'(x) = 2^{\cos(x^2)} \cdot \ln(2) \cdot (-\sin(x^2)) \cdot 2x$

115. $f(x) = \ln(x + \cos(\sqrt{x})$
$\qquad f'(x) = \dfrac{1 - \sin(\sqrt{x}) \cdot \dfrac{1}{2}x^{-\frac{1}{2}}}{x + \cos(\sqrt{x})}$

116. $f(x) = \dfrac{\sin(3x^2) - \ln(2x - 1)}{e^{2x} + 4x}$

$\qquad f'(x) = \dfrac{\left(\cos(3x^2) \cdot 6x - \dfrac{2}{2x - 1}\right) \cdot \left(e^{2x} + 4x\right) - \left(\sin(3x^2) - \ln(2x - 1)\right) \cdot \left(2e^{2x} + 4\right)}{\left(e^{2x} + 4x\right)^2}$

117. $f(x) = \dfrac{Ln(\sin(3x + 1)^{-2})}{\left(\dfrac{1}{\cos(2x)}\right)} = Ln(\sin(3x + 1)^{-2}) \cdot \cos(2x)$

$\qquad f'(x) = \dfrac{\cos((3x + 1)^{-2}) \cdot (-2(3x + 1)^{-3} \cdot 3)}{\sin((3x + 1)^{-2})} \cdot \cos(2x) + Ln(\sin((3x + 1)^{-2}) \cdot (-\sin(2x) \cdot 2)$

Derivative of inverse trigonometric functions

1. Find the derivative of $f(x) = y = \arccos(x)$

$x = \cos(y)$, $\dfrac{dx}{dy} = -\sin(y)$, $\dfrac{dx}{dy} = -\sqrt{1-(\cos)^2}$, $\dfrac{dy}{dx} = \dfrac{-1}{\sqrt{1-(\cos(y))^2}}$, $\dfrac{dy}{dx} = \dfrac{-1}{\sqrt{1-x^2}}$

2. Find the derivative of $f(x) = y = \arctan(x)$

$x = \tan(y)$, $\dfrac{dx}{dy} = \dfrac{1}{\cos^2(y)} = \dfrac{1}{\cos^2(y)} = 1+\tan^2(y) = 1+x^2$, And Finally: $\dfrac{dy}{dx} = \dfrac{1}{1+x^2}$

3. $f(x) = \arccos(2x)$

$$f'(x) = \dfrac{-2}{\sqrt{1-4x^2}}$$

$$f'(x) = \dfrac{-x^{-\frac{5}{4}}}{4\left(1+(x)^{-\frac{1}{2}}\right)}$$

4. $f(x) = \arcsin(\dfrac{x}{3})$

$$f'(x) = \dfrac{1}{3\sqrt{1-\dfrac{x^2}{9}}}$$

10. $f(x) = \arccos(\sin(x))$

$$f'(x) = \dfrac{-\cos(x)}{\sqrt{1-(\sin(x))^2}} = \pm 1$$

11. $f(x) = \arccos(e^x)$

5. $f(x) = \arccos(\dfrac{2-x}{3})$

$$f'(x) = \dfrac{-1}{3\sqrt{1-\left(\dfrac{2-x}{3}\right)^2}}$$

$$f'(x) = \dfrac{-e^x}{\sqrt{1-(e^x)^2}}$$

12. $f(x) = \dfrac{2}{\arctan(2x)} = 2(\arctan(2x))^{-1}$

$$f'(x) = -2(\arctan(2x))^{-2}\dfrac{2}{\left(1+(2x)^2\right)}$$

6. $f(x) = \arctan(\dfrac{x-2}{3})$

$$f'(x) = \dfrac{-2}{3\left(1+\left(\dfrac{x-2}{3}\right)^2\right)}$$

13. $f(x) = \dfrac{\arccos(x^2)}{2x}$

$$f'(x) = \dfrac{\left(\dfrac{-2x\cdot 2x}{\sqrt{1-x^4}}\right) - 2\arccos(x^2)}{4x^2}$$

7. $f(x) = \arccos(-5x)$

$$f'(x) = \dfrac{5}{\sqrt{1-25x^2}}$$

14. $f(x) = 4^{\arcsin(x)}$

$$f'(x) = 4^{\arcsin(x)} Ln(4)\dfrac{1}{\sqrt{1-x^2}}$$

8. $f(x) = \arcsin(\dfrac{1}{x})$

$$f'(x) = \dfrac{-x^{-2}}{\sqrt{1-x^{-2}}}$$

15. $f(x) = \sin(2x)\arcsin(x^2 - 5x)$

9. $f(x) = \arctan(\dfrac{1}{\sqrt[4]{x}})$

$$f'(x) = 2\cos(2x)\arcsin(x^2-5x) + \sin(2x)\dfrac{2x-5}{\sqrt{1-(x^2-5x)^2}}$$

IMPLICIT DIFFERENTIATION

1. $y^2 + x = y$

   $2yy' + 1 = y'$

   $\dfrac{dy}{dx} = y' = \dfrac{1}{1 - 2y}$

2. $y^2 + 3xy = y^3$

   $2yy' + 3y + 2xy' = 3y^2 y'$

   $\dfrac{dy}{dx} = y' = \dfrac{3y}{3y^2 - 2y - 2x}$

3. $5xy^2 + x + 2 = y$

   $5y^2 + 10xyy' + 1 = y'$

   $\dfrac{dy}{dx} = y' = \dfrac{5y^2 + 1}{1 - 10xy}$

4. $y^2 - 2x = y - 3x$

   $2yy' - 2 = y' - 3x$

   $\dfrac{dy}{dx} = y' = \dfrac{2 - 3x}{2y - 1}$

5. $4y^2 + 2x^4 = e^y$

   $8yy' + 8x = e^y y'$

   $\dfrac{dy}{dx} = y' = \dfrac{8x}{e^y - 8y}$

6. $2y^4 + x = y + x$

   $8y^3 y' + 1 = y' + 1$

   $\dfrac{dy}{dx} = y' = 0$

7. $y^2 - x = yx - x$

   $2yy' - 1 = y'x + y - 1$

   $\dfrac{dy}{dx} = y' = \dfrac{y}{2y - x}$

8. $y + yx + y^2 x^2 = 2 - x$

   $y' + y'x + y + 2yy'x^2 + 2y^2 x = -1$

   $\dfrac{dy}{dx} = y' = \dfrac{2y^2 x - y - 1}{1 + x + 2yx^2}$

9. $xy^2 + \ln(yx) = x$

   $y^2 + 2xyy' + \dfrac{y'x + y}{xy} = 1$

   $xy^3 + 2x^2 y^2 y' + y'x + y = xy$

   $\dfrac{dy}{dx} = y' = \dfrac{xy - xy^3 - y}{2x^2 y^2 + x}$

10. $x\sin(xy) = y$

    $\sin(xy) + x\cos(xy)(y + xy') = y'$

    $\sin(xy) + x\cos(xy)y + x^2 y\cos(xy)y' = y'$

    $\dfrac{dy}{dx} = y' = \dfrac{\sin(xy) + x\cos(xy)y}{1 - x^2 y\cos(xy)}$

11. Given the relation $y^3 + 2x^3 = 1$

a. Find $\dfrac{dy}{dx}$.

   $3y^2 y' + 6x^2 = 0$

   $\dfrac{dy}{dx} = y' = -\dfrac{2x^2}{y^2}$

b. Make y a function of x

   $y = \sqrt[3]{1 - 2x^3}$

c. Differentiate

   $\dfrac{dy}{dx} = \dfrac{1}{3}\left(1 - 2x^3\right)^{-\frac{2}{3}}(-6x^2) = \left(1 - 2x^3\right)^{-\frac{2}{3}}(-2x^2)$

d. Show that derivative obtained in a is identical to the one obtained in c

$\dfrac{dy}{dx} = y' = -\dfrac{2x^2}{y^2} = -\dfrac{2x^2}{\left(\sqrt[3]{1 - 2x^3}\right)^2} =$

$\left(1 - 2x^3\right)^{-\frac{2}{3}}(-2x^2)$

e. Tangent to the curve at x = 1

   $x = 1; \; y = -1$

   $\dfrac{dy}{dx} = y' = -\dfrac{2}{1} = -2$

   $y = -2x + 1$

f. Normal to the curve at x = -1

   $x = -1; \; y = \sqrt[3]{3}$

   $\dfrac{dy}{dx} = y' = -\dfrac{2}{\sqrt[3]{9}}; m_{normal} = \dfrac{\sqrt[3]{9}}{2}$

   $y = \dfrac{\sqrt[3]{9}}{2}x + \sqrt[3]{3} + \dfrac{\sqrt[3]{9}}{2}$

12. Given the relation $x + \sin(y) = 1$

a. Find $\dfrac{dy}{dx}$.

$1 + \cos(y)\, y' = 0$

$\dfrac{dy}{dx} = y' = -\dfrac{1}{\cos(y)}$

b. The equation of the <u>tangent</u> and <u>normal</u> to the function at $y = \dfrac{\pi}{6}$.

$x = \dfrac{1}{2}; \; y = \dfrac{\pi}{6}$

$\dfrac{dy}{dx} = y' = -\dfrac{2}{\sqrt{3}}$

$Tangent: y = -\dfrac{2}{\sqrt{3}}x + \dfrac{1}{\sqrt{3}} + \dfrac{\pi}{6}$

$Normal: y = \dfrac{\sqrt{3}}{2}x - \dfrac{\sqrt{3}}{4} + \dfrac{\pi}{6}$

13. Given the relation $x + \ln(y) = 1$

a. Find $\dfrac{dy}{dx}$.

$1 + \dfrac{y'}{y} = 0$

$\dfrac{dy}{dx} = y' = -y$

b. The equation of the <u>tangent</u> and <u>normal</u> to the function at $x = 1$.

$x = 1; \; y = 1$

$\dfrac{dy}{dx} = y' = -1$

$Tangent: y = -x + 2$

$Normal: y = x$

14. Given the function $f(x) = (x+1)^2 \cos(\ln(x))$

a. Obtain its derivative.

$f'(x) = 2(x+1)\cos(\ln(x)) - \dfrac{(x+1)^2 \sin(\ln(x))}{x}$

b. The equation of the <u>tangent</u> and <u>normal</u> to the function at $x = 1$.

$x = 1; \; y = 4$

$f'(1) = 4$

$Tangent: y = 4x \qquad Normal: y = -\dfrac{1}{4}x + \dfrac{17}{4}$

15. Given the function $f(x) = \cos(2^x - 2) + x^{\frac{3}{2}}$

a. Obtain its derivative.

$f'(x) = -\sin(2^x - 2)\cdot 2^x \cdot Ln(2) + \dfrac{3}{2}x^{\frac{1}{2}}$

b. The equation of the <u>tangent</u> and <u>normal</u> to the function at $x = 1$.

$x = 1; \; y = 2$

$f'(1) = \dfrac{3}{2}$

$Tangent: y = \dfrac{3}{2}x + \dfrac{1}{2} \qquad Normal: y = -\dfrac{2}{3}x + \dfrac{8}{3}$

HIGHER DERIVATIVES

1. $f(x) = x^2$

$$\frac{df}{dx} = f'(x) = 2x$$

$$\frac{d^2 f}{dx^2} = f''(x) = 2$$

2. $f(x) = \ln(x)$

$$\frac{df}{dx} = f'(x) = x^{-1}$$

$$\frac{d^2 f}{dx^2} = f''(x) = -x^{-2}$$

3. $f(x) = \sin(x)$

$$\frac{df}{dx} = f'(x) = \cos(x)$$

$$\frac{d^2 f}{dx^2} = f''(x) = -\sin(x)$$

4. $f(x) = e^{2x}$

$$\frac{df}{dx} = f'(x) = 2e^{2x}$$

$$\frac{d^2 f}{dx^2} = f''(x) = 4e^{2x}$$

$$\frac{d^3 f}{dx^3} = f'''(x) = 8e^{2x}$$

$$\frac{d^n f}{dx^n} = f^{(n)}(x) = 2^n e^{2x}$$

5. $f(x) = xe^x$

$$\frac{df}{dx} = f'(x) = e^x(x+1)$$

$$\frac{d^2 f}{dx^2} = f''(x) = e^x(x+2)$$

$$\frac{d^3 f}{dx^3} = f'''(x) = e^x(x+3)$$

$$\frac{d^n f}{dx^n} = f^{(n)}(x) = e^x(x+n)$$

6. $f(x) = \sin(e^x)$

$$\frac{df}{dx} = f'(x) = \cos(e^x) \cdot e^x$$

$$\frac{d^2 f}{dx^2} = f''(x) = e^x(\cos(e^x) - e^x \sin(x))$$

$$\frac{d^3 f}{dx^3} = f'''(x) = e^x(\cos(e^x) - 3e^x \sin(x) - e^{2x} \cos(e^x))$$

$$\frac{d^4 f}{dx^4} = f^{(4)}(x) = e^x(\cos(e^x) - 7e^x \sin(x) - 6e^{2x} \cos(e^x) + e^{3x} \sin(x))$$

7. $f(x) = \ln(2x)$

$$\frac{df}{dx} = f'(x) = \frac{1}{x}$$

$$\frac{d^2 f}{dx^2} = f''(x) = -\frac{1}{x^2}$$

$$\frac{d^3 f}{dx^3} = f'''(x) = \frac{2}{x^3}$$

$$\frac{d^n f}{dx^n} = f^{(n)}(x) = \frac{(n-1)!}{x^n}$$

1.7. – STATIONARY (OR CRITICAL) POINTS

1. In a maximum or minimum point of a "smooth" function the slope of the tangent

    to the function is **zero**. Sketch an example:

2. There is one more situation in which the slope of the tangent to the function is

    zero, such point is called: horizontal inflection point. An example:

3. In order to find a stationary points´ x coordinate we equal the **derivative** to **zero**.
    For example the function $f(x) = 2x^2 + 2x$, $f'(x) = 4x+2=0$, $x = -0.5$

4. To find the stationary points´ y coordinate we **plug the x found into the function**. In the last example $f(-2) = 4$

5. Once we found the stationary point we have to decide if it's a **maximum**, **minimum** or **horizontal inflection point**.

6. We will discuss 3 methods to check if a function has minimum, maximum or horizontal inflection point at a certain point.

The 3 methods are:

1. Check the **value of the function** on both "sides" of the point and close to it. If both sides' values are higher the point is **a minimum** if both sides are lower the point is **a maximum** and if one side is higher and the other lower we have a **horizontal inflection point** Example: $f(x) = 2x^2 + 2x$

   $$f'(x) = 4x + 2 = 0; x = -\frac{1}{2}$$

   $$f(-0.51) = -0.4998; f(-0.5) = -0.5; f(-0.49) = -0.4998$$

   As both adjacent points are higher the point is a minimum.

2. Build a diagram including all the zeros in the first derivative and all the places it is not defined, indicating **the sign of the derivative**. Example: $f(x) = 2x^4 + x^2$

   Sign of the derviative

   As can be seen the function decreases and then increases around the stationary point and therefore it is a minimum.

3. Use the 2nd derivative. As you could see if the 2nd derivative, at the point in which the 1st derivative is 0, is positive the function is **concave up** and the point would be a **minimum**. if the 2nd derivative, at the point in which the 1st derivative is 0, is negative the function is **concave down** and the point would be a **maximum.** if the 2nd derivative is also 0 this test is **inconclusive**.
   Example: $f(x) = 2x^3 + x^2$

   $$f'(x) = 6x^2 + 2x = 0; x = 0, -\frac{1}{3}; (0,0), (-\frac{1}{3}, \frac{1}{27})$$

   $$f''(x) = 12x + 2; f''(0) = 2; f''(-\frac{1}{3}) = -2$$

   As can be seen the function is concave up at x = 0 so (0, 0) is a minimum and concave down at x = − 1/3 so (− 1/3, 1/27) is a maximum.
   Example: $f(x) = x^4$
   $$f'(x) = 4x^3 = 0; x = 0; (0,0)$$
   $$f''(x) = 12x^2; f''(0) = 0$$

   As can be seen the function is not concave up nor down at x = 0 (2nd derivative is 0) so we cannot determine in this case what kind of stationary point is (0, 0) using this test. If we sketch the function using the GDC we can see that (0, 0) is a minimum.

SECOND DERIVATIVE

1. The 1st derivative of a function gives **the slope of the tangent to the function at a point.**

2. In case $f(x) = x^2$, the first derivative is **2x** and the 2nd derivative is **2**. As you can see the second derivative is always **positive**. and that means that the function is always **concave up**.

3. In case $f(x) = x^3 - 3x^2$:
   The first derivative is **$3x^2 - 6x$** and the 2nd derivative is **$6x - 6$**. As you can see the second derivative is positive for **$x > 1$**, negative for **$x < 1$** and exactly 0 for **$x = 1$** That means that when the 2nd derivative is positive the function is **concave up** when the 2nd derivative is negative the function is **concave down** and when the 2nd derivative is 0 the function <u>might have</u> an **inflection point**.

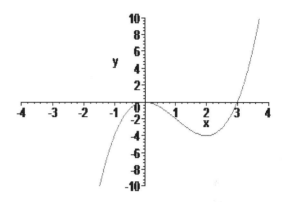

4. In case $f(x) = x^4$
   The first derivative is **$4x^3$** and the 2nd derivative is **$12x^2$**. As you can see the second derivative is positive for **$x > 0$**, negative for **$x < 0$** and exactly 0 for **$x = 0$** That means that when the 2nd derivative is positive the function is **concave up** when the 2nd derivative is negative the function is **concave down** and when the 2nd derivative is 0 the function <u>might have</u> an **inflection point** but in this case it has a **minimum.**

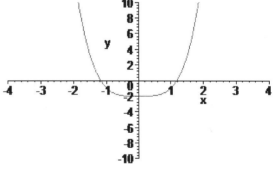

5. If $f'(a) = 0$ it means the function has a **stationary point** at a.

6. If f'$(a) < 0$ it means the function is **decreaseing** at a.

7. If $f'(a) \neq$ and $f''(a) = 0$ it means the function **may have an inflection point** at a.

8. If possible, fill the following table with a sketch of the function around the point where $x = a$.

	$f''(a) = 0$	$f''(a) > 0$	$f''(a) < 0$
$f'(a)=0$			
$f'(a) > 0$			
$f'(a) < 0$			

4. A certain function satisfies: $f(a) = 2, f'(a) = 1, f''(a) < 0$

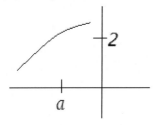

5. A certain function satisfies: $f(a) = -2, f'(a) = -2, f''(a) < 0$

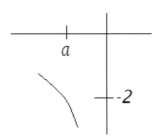

6. A certain function satisfies: $f(a) = 0$ $f'(a) = -2, f''(a) = 0$

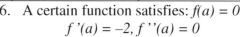

7. A certain function satisfies: $f(a) = 3$ $f'(a) = 3, \quad f''(a) = 0$

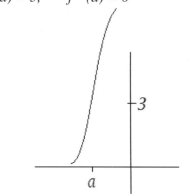

8. Sketch the graph of a function which has all the following properties:

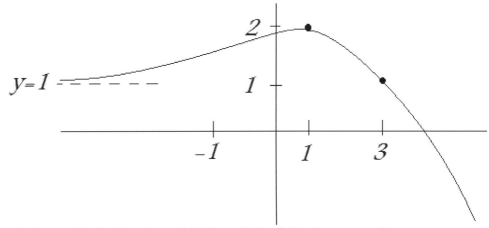

9. Sketch the graph of a function which has all the following properties:

a. $\lim\limits_{x \to 2^-} f(x) = -\infty$

b. $\lim\limits_{x \to 2^+} f(x) = \infty$

c. $\lim\limits_{x \to -\infty} f(x) = 0$

d. $f(-2) = 2, f(5) = 1, f(0) = 0$

e. $f'(x) > 0$ if $x < -2$ or $x > 5$

f. $f'(x) > 0$ if $-2 < x < 2, 2 < x < 5$

g. $f'(5) = 0, f'(-2) = 0$

h. $f''(x) > 0$ if $x < -3$ or $x > 2$

i. $f''(x) < 0$ if $-3 < x < 2$

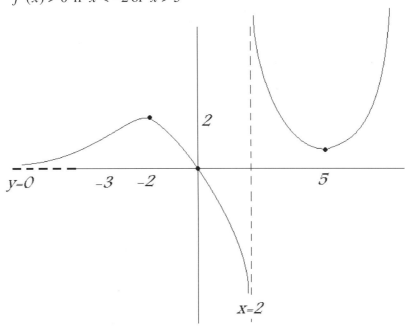

10. Sketch the graph of a function which has all the following properties:

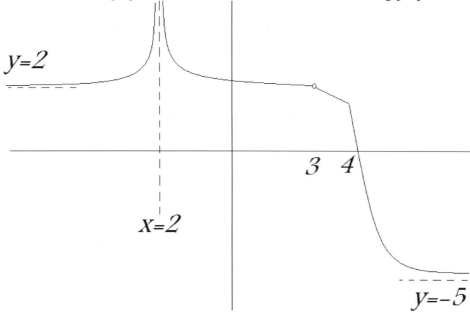

11.
$$f(1) = 1 \implies a+b+c = 1$$
$$f'(1) = 0; \implies 2a+b = 0$$
$$f'(2) = -2; \implies 4a+b = -2$$
$$a = -1$$
$$b = 2$$
$$c = 0$$

12.
$$f(0) = -1 \implies c = -1$$
$$f'(1) = 0; \implies 3+2a+b = 0$$
$$f''(\tfrac{2}{3}) = 0; \implies 4+2a = 0$$
$$a = -2$$
$$b = 1$$
$$c = 0$$

13.
$$f(0) = 0 \implies 0 = 0$$
$$f'(0) = 0 \implies c = 0$$
$$f(2) = 16; \implies 8a+4b = 16$$
$$f''(2) = 0; \implies 12a+2b = 0$$
$$a = -1$$
$$b = 6$$
$$c = 0$$

14.
$$f(1) = 3 \implies a+b = 3$$
$$f'(1) = 0 \implies -a+2b = 0$$
$$a = 2$$
$$b = 1$$

1.8. – FUNCTION ANALYSIS

A. POLYNOMIALS WITH NATURAL POWER

1. Graph the following functions. Obtain and indicate all x and y intercepts maximum, minimum and inflection points on the graph (include their coordinates)

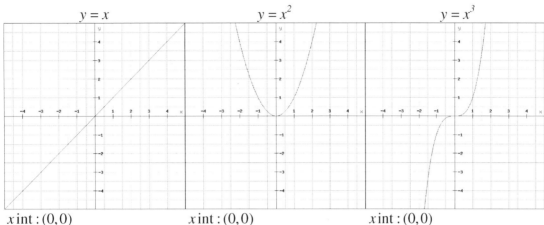

$x\,\text{int}:(0,0)$	$x\,\text{int}:(0,0)$	$x\,\text{int}:(0,0)$
$y\,\text{int}:(0,0)$	$y\,\text{int}:(0,0)$	$y\,\text{int}:(0,0)$
$Max:None$	$Max:None$	$Max:None$
$Min:None$	$Min:(0,0)$	$Min:None$
$Inflection\ po\text{int}\,s:None$	$Inflection\ po\text{int}\,s:None$	$Inflection\ po\text{int}\,s:(0,0)$

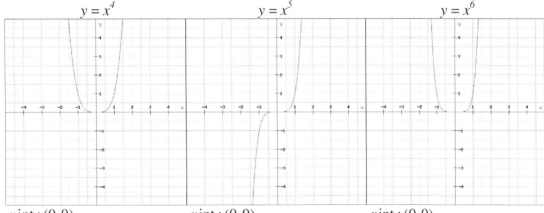

$x\,\text{int}:(0,0)$	$x\,\text{int}:(0,0)$	$x\,\text{int}:(0,0)$
$y\,\text{int}:(0,0)$	$y\,\text{int}:(0,0)$	$y\,\text{int}:(0,0)$
$Max:None$	$Max:None$	$Max:None$
$Min:(0,0)$	$Min:None$	$Min:(0,0)$
$Inflection\ po\text{int}\,s:None$	$Inflection\ po\text{int}\,s:(0,0)$	$Inflection\ po\text{int}\,s:None$

Conclusion: Even Powers have similar end behaviour (up – up or down – down). Odd powers have similar end behaviour (up – down or down – up)

2. Graph the following functions. Obtain and indicate all x and y intercepts maximum, minimum and inflection points on the graph (include their coordinates)

$$y = (x+2)^2 + 1 \qquad\qquad y = (x-2)^3 - 3 \qquad\qquad y = (x+3)^4 - 6$$

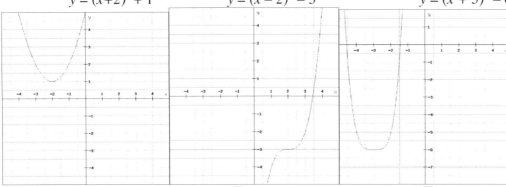

x int : *None* $\qquad\qquad$ x int : $(\sqrt[3]{3}+2, 0)$ $\qquad\qquad$ x int : $(\pm\sqrt[4]{6}-3, 0)$

y int : $(0, 5)$ $\qquad\qquad$ y int : $(0, -11)$ $\qquad\qquad$ y int : $(0, 75)$

Max : *None* $\qquad\qquad$ *Max* : *None* $\qquad\qquad$ *Max* : *None*

Min : $(-2, 1)$ $\qquad\qquad$ *Min* : *None* $\qquad\qquad$ *Min* : $(-3, -6)$

Inflection points : *None* $\quad$ *Inflection points* : $(2, -3)$ $\quad$ *Inflection points* : *None*

Conclusion: These are the same functions as in the previous part after an application of horizontal and vertical translations.

3. Graph the following functions. Obtain and indicate all x and y intercepts maximum, minimum and inflection points on the graph (include their coordinates)

$$y = -(x+2)^2 + 1 \qquad\qquad y = -(x-2)^3 - 3 \qquad\qquad y = -(x+3)^4 - 6$$

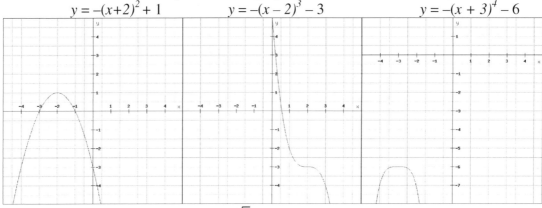

x int : *None* $\qquad\qquad$ x int : $(-\sqrt[3]{3}+2, 0)$ $\qquad\qquad$ x int : *None*

y int : $(0, -3)$ $\qquad\qquad$ y int : $(0, 5)$ $\qquad\qquad$ y int : $(0, -87)$

Max : $(-2, 1)$ $\qquad\qquad$ *Max* : *None* $\qquad\qquad$ *Max* : $(-3, -6)$

Min : *None* $\qquad\qquad$ *Min* : *None* $\qquad\qquad$ *Min* : *None*

Inflection points : *None* $\quad$ *Inflection points* : $(2, -3)$ $\quad$ *Inflection points* : *None*

Conclusion: These are the same functions as in the previous part after an application of horizontal and vertical translations and a reflection in the x axis.

4. Graph the following functions. Obtain and indicate all x and y intercepts:

$y = x(x^2+1)=$ $y = x(x+1)(x+1)$ $y = x(x+1)(x-1)$

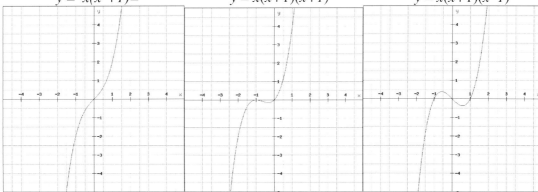

$y = -x(x+2)(x-3)$ $y = x(x^3+1)$ $y = x(x^3-1)$

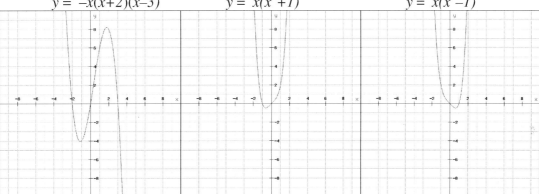

$y = x^2(x+1)(x+1)$ $y = x^2(x+1)(x-2)$ $y = -x^2(x+1)(x-2)$

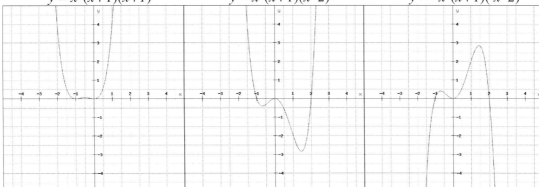

$y = (x-0)(x-1)(x-2)(x-3)$ $y = 2(x-0)(x-1)(x-2)(x-3)$ $y = -4(x-0)(x-1)(x-2)(x-3)$

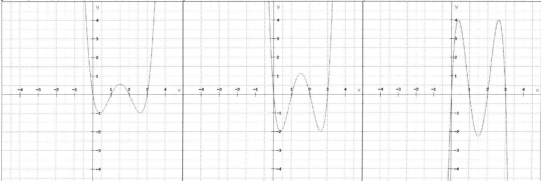

347

5. Fill the blanks (expand)

    a) $y = x^3$

    b) $y = x(x^2+1) = x^3 + x$

    c) $y = x(x+1)(x+1) = x^3 + 2x^2 + x$

    d) $y = x(x+1)(x-1) = x^3 - x$

    e) $y = -x(x+2)(x-3) = -x^3 - x^2 - 6x$

    f) $y = -(x-1)^3 = -x^3 + 3x^2 - 3x + 1$

All the functions in this section are of the **3rd** degree. They all have an **inflection point** They all have at least 1 **x intercept**. Sometimes they have **2 or 3 x intercepts.** If at one end the function tends to **infinity** then on the other end it will tend to **negative infinity**.

6. Fill the blanks (expand)

    a) $y = x^4$

    b) $y = x(x^3+1) = x^4 + x$

    c) $y = x(x^3-1) = x^4 - x$

    d) $y = x^2(x+1)(x+1) = x^4 + 2x^3 + x^2$

    e) $y = x^2(x+1)(x-1) = x^4 - x^2$

    f) $y = x^2(x+1)(x-2) = x^4 - x^3 - 2x^2$

    g) $y = -x^2(x+1)(x-2) = -x^4 + x^3 + 2x^2$

    h) $y = -(x-2)^4 = -x^4 + 8x^3 - 24x^2 + 32x - 16$

All the functions in this section are of the **4th** degree. They all have at least one **stationary point**. Sometimes they have two **minimums** and one **maximum** or two **maximum** and one **minimum**. If one end the function tends to **infinity** then on the other end it will tend to **infinity** as well.

7. Given the functions:

    a) $y = (x-1)(x-2)(x-3)(x-4)$

    b) $y = 2(x-1)(x-2)(x-3)(x-4)$

    c) $y = 3(x-1)(x-2)(x-3)(x-4)$

    d) $y = -4(x-1)(x-2)(x-3)(x-4)$

All the functions in this section are of the **4th** degree. On multiplying a function by a number, the **x intercepts stay** the same. The **y intercept changes**. The general aspect of the function is **similar**/very different

8. Graph the following functions

    $y = -(x-1)(x-2)^2(x-4)^3$ $y = -(x-2)^3(x-4)^4$ $y = (x-2)(x^2-1)(x^2+1)$

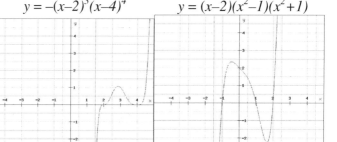

In case a factor is of 1st degree on the graph it will correspond an **x intercept**

In case a factor is of even degree on the graph it will correspond a **max** or **min**

In case a factor is of odd (> 1) degree on the graph it will correspond an **inflection point**

9. Graph the following functions. Obtain and indicate all x and y intercepts on the graph (include their coordinates). <u>Sketch a dashed line</u> (use a pen or pencil) to indicate horizontal and/or vertical asymptotes.

a. $y = \dfrac{2x}{x-1}$

Vertical asymptote(s): x = 1
Horizontal asymptote(s): y = 2

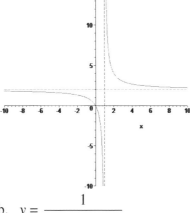

c. $y = \dfrac{3x^2}{(x+1)(x-4)}$

Vertical asymptote(s): x = –1, 4
Horizontal asymptote(s): y = 3

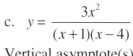

b. $y = \dfrac{1}{(x+1)(x-2)}$

Vertical asymptote(s): x = –1, 2
Horizontal asymptote(s): y = 0

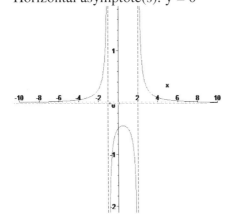

d. $y = xe^x$

Vertical asymptote(s): None
Horizontal asymptote(s): y = 0

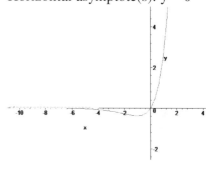

10. Given the following function, fill the table:

x = a	x = –3	x = –2	x = – 1	x = –0.6	x = 0	x =1	x = 1.5	x = 2
f(x)	21	0	≈–1.5	≈–1.7	0	13	24	0
f'(x)	≈–10	0	≈–0.5	0	0	≈8	0	D.E.
f''(x)	≈1	0	≈2	≈2	0	0	≈–4	D.E.

Conclusions:
a. In a "smooth" maximum or minimum the **derivative is 0**
b. In a horizontal inflection point both **first and second derivatives are zero.**
c. In a non–horizontal inflection point **first derivative is different than 0 and second derivatives iszero.**.

11. Use GDC to sketch the functions $f(x) = x^3$ and $g(x) = 4^x + 2^{-x} - 8$

f(x) > g(x) for $x \in (-1.8, 2)$

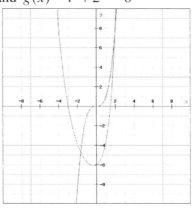

12. Use GDC to sketch the functions $f(x) = x^2$ and $g(x) = \ln(x)$

f(x) > g(x) for $x \in \Re$

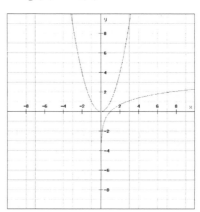

13. $f(x) = x^4, x \in [-1, 2]$

Domain : $x \in [-1, 2]$ *Extrema* : $(0,0)$, min, *Absolute*   max : $(2,16)$

Vertical   Asymptotes : *None*   *Range* : $f(x) \in [0, 16]$

Horizontal   Asymptotes : *None*   *Increase* : $x \in (0, 2)$

Slant   Asymptotes : *None*   *Decrease* : $x \in (-1, 0)$

$y - $int : $(0,0)$ *Concave* $-up$: $x \in (-1, 2)$

$x - $int : $(0,0)$ *Concave* $-down$: *Never*

*Inflection   po*int*s* : *None*

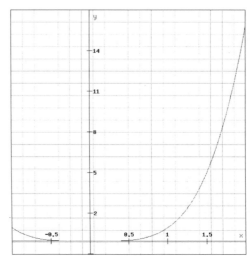

350

14. $f(x) = -x^6 + 6, x \in \mathbb{R}$

Domain : $x \in \Re$

Vertical   Asymptotes : None

Horizontal   Asymptotes : None

Slant   Asymptotes : None

$y - \text{int} : (0, 6)$

$x - \text{int} : (\pm\sqrt[6]{6}, 0)$

Inflection   points : None

Extrema : $(0, 6), \max$

Range : $f(x) \in [-\infty, 6]$

Increase : $x \in (-\infty, 0)$

Decrease : $x \in (0, \infty)$

Concave - up : Never

Concave - down : $x \in \Re$

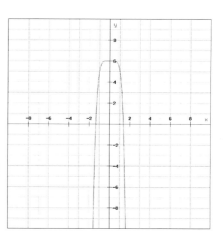

15. $f(x) = x^2(x + 2), x \in [-\frac{3}{2}, \frac{1}{2}]$

Domain : $x \in [-\frac{3}{2}, \frac{1}{2}]$

Vertical   Asymptotes : None

Horizontal   Asymptotes : None

Slant   Asymptotes : None

$y - \text{int} : (0, 0)$

$x - \text{int} : None$

Inflection   points : $(-\frac{2}{3}, \frac{16}{27})$

Extrema : $(0, 0), \min; (-\frac{4}{3}, \frac{32}{27}), \max$

Range : $f(x) \in [0, \frac{32}{27}]$

Increase : $x \in (-\frac{3}{2}, -\frac{4}{3}) \cup (0, \frac{1}{2})$

Decrease : $x \in (-\frac{4}{3}, 0)$

Concave - up : $x \in (-\frac{2}{3}, \frac{1}{2})$

Concave - down : $x \in (-\frac{3}{2}, -\frac{2}{3})$

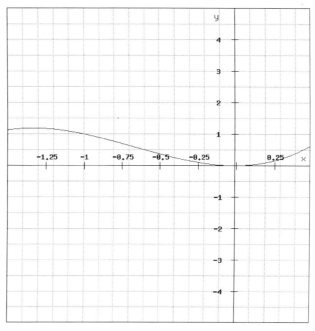

16. $f(x) = x(x+2)(x-1), x \in \mathbb{R}$

$Domain: x \in \Re$

$Vertical \quad Asymptotes: None$

$Horizontal \quad Asymptotes: None$

$Slant \quad Asymptotes: None$

$y-\text{int}: (0,0)$

$x-\text{int}: (0,0), (-2,0), (1,0)$

$Inflection \quad po\text{int}s: (-\frac{1}{3}, \frac{20}{27})$

$Extrema: (\frac{-1+\sqrt{7}}{3}, \approx -0.631), \min, (\frac{-1-\sqrt{7}}{3}, \approx 2.11), \max$

$Range: f(x) \in \Re$

$Increase: x \in (-\infty, \frac{-1-\sqrt{7}}{3}) \cup (\frac{-1+\sqrt{7}}{3}, \infty)$

$Decrease: x \in (\frac{-1-\sqrt{7}}{3}, \frac{-1+\sqrt{7}}{3})$

$Concave-up: x \in (-\frac{1}{3}, \infty)$

$Concave-down: x \in (-\infty, -\frac{1}{3})$

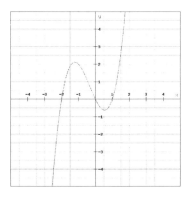

17. $f(x) = 2x^3 + 11x^2 + 10x - 8, x \in \mathbb{R}$

$Domain: x \in \Re$

$Vertical \quad Asymptotes: None$

$Horizontal \quad Asymptotes: None$

$Slant \quad Asymptotes: None$

$y-\text{int}: (0,-8)$

$x-\text{int}: (\frac{1}{2},0), (-2,0), (-4,0)$

$Inflection \quad po\text{int}s: (-\frac{11}{6}, -\frac{91}{54})$

$Extrema: (\frac{-11+\sqrt{61}}{6}, \approx -10.5), \min, (\frac{-11-\sqrt{61}}{6}, \approx 7.14), \max$

$Range: f(x) \in \Re$

$Increase: x \in (-\infty, \frac{-11-\sqrt{61}}{6}) \cup (\frac{-11+\sqrt{61}}{6}, \infty)$

$Decrease: x \in (\frac{-11-\sqrt{61}}{6}, \frac{-11+\sqrt{61}}{6})$

$Concave-up: x \in (-\frac{11}{6}, \infty)$

$Concave-down: x \in (-\infty, -\frac{11}{6})$

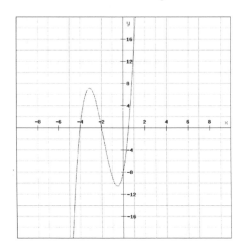

18. $f(x) = x^3 - x^2, x \in [0,2]$

$Domain : x \in [0,2]$

$Extrema : (0,0), \max; (\frac{2}{3}, -\frac{4}{27}), Absolute \quad Max : (2,4)$

$Vertical \quad Asymptotes : None$

$Range : f(x) \in [-\frac{4}{27}, 4]$

$Horizontal \quad Asymptotes : None$

$Increase : x \in (-\frac{2}{3}, 4)$

$Slant \quad Asymptotes : None$

$Decrease : x \in (0, \frac{2}{3})$

$y - int : (0,0)$

$Concave - up : x \in (\frac{1}{3}, 2)$

$x - int : (0,0), (1,0)$

$Concave - down : x \in (0, \frac{1}{3})$

$Inflection \quad points : (\frac{1}{3}, -\frac{2}{27})$

19. $f(x) = 2x^4 - 4x^2, x \in \mathbb{R}$

$Domain : x \in \mathbb{R}$

$Extrema : (0,0), \max; (-1, -2)(1, -2), \min$

$Vertical \quad Asymptotes : None$

$Range : f(x) \in [-2, \infty)$

$Horizontal \quad Asymptotes : None$

$Increase : x \in (-1, 0) \cup (1, \infty)$

$Slant \quad Asymptotes : None$

$Decrease : x \in (-\infty, -1) \cup (0, 1)$

$y - int : (0,0)$

$Concave - up : x \in (-\infty, -\frac{1}{\sqrt{3}}) \cup (\frac{1}{\sqrt{3}}, \infty)$

$x - int : (0,0), (\pm 1, 0)$

$Concave - down : x \in (-\frac{1}{\sqrt{3}}, \frac{1}{\sqrt{3}})$

$Inflection \quad points : (-\frac{1}{\sqrt{3}}, -\frac{10}{9}), (\frac{1}{\sqrt{3}}, -\frac{10}{9})$

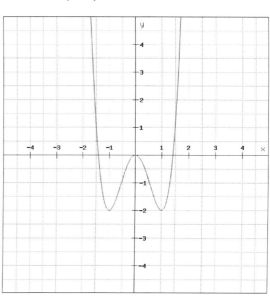

353

20. $f(x) = x^4 - 2x^3, x \in \mathbb{R}$

$Domain: x \in \mathbb{R}$

$Vertical \ \ Asymptotes: None$

$Horizontal \ \ Asymptotes: None$

$Slant \ \ Asymptotes: None$

$y - \text{int}: (0,0)$

$x - \text{int}: (0,0), (2,0)$

$Inflection \ \ points: (0,0) Horizontal, (1,-1)$

$Extrema(\dfrac{3}{2}, -\dfrac{27}{16}), min$

$Range: f(x) \in [-\dfrac{27}{16}, \infty)$

$Increase: x \in (\dfrac{3}{2}, \infty)$

$Decrease: x \in (-\infty, \dfrac{3}{2})$

$Concave - up: x \in (-\infty, 0) \cup (1, \infty)$

$Concave - down: x \in (0,1)$

21. A function of the 3rd degree that intercepts the x axis at (2, 0), (–3, 0) and (–0.5, 0). Is it possible to make this function have a y intercept (0, 10)? Yes:

$$f(x) = a(x-2)(x+3)(x+\dfrac{1}{2}); f(0) = 10; a = -\dfrac{10}{3}; f(x) = -\dfrac{10}{3}(x-2)(x+3)(x+\dfrac{1}{2})$$

22. A function of the 4th degree that intercepts the x axis at (1, 0), (2, 0), (5, 0) and (–1, 0). Is it possible to make this function have a y intercept (0, 5)? Yes:

$$f(x) = a(x-1)(x-2)(x-5)(x+1); f(0) = 5; a = -\dfrac{1}{2}; f(x) = -\dfrac{1}{2}(x-1)(x-2)(x-5)(x+1)$$

23. The expression of f(x) = x^3 shifted 2 positions to the right and 3 positions down.

   $f(x) = (x-2)^3 - 3$

24. The expression of f(x) = x^4 shifted 4 positions to the left and 6 positions up.

   $f(x) = (x+4)^4 + 6$

25. In case the first derivative of a function is 0 at a certain point, this point can be a **maximum** or a **minimum** or a **horizontal inflection point**

26. In case the 1st derivative is 0 and the 2nd derivative is positive at a certain point, the point must be a **minimum**

27. In case the 1st derivative is 0 and the 2nd derivative is negative at a certain point, the point must be a **maximum**

28. In case the 1st derivative is 0 and the 2nd derivative is also 0 at a certain point, the point can be a **maximum** or a **minimum** or a **horizontal inflection point**

29. In the parts where $f'(x) > 0$ the function is **increasing**

30. In the parts where $f''(x) > 0$ the function is **decreasing**

B. POLYNOMIALS WITH RATIONAL POWER

31. $f(x) = x^{\frac{2}{3}}, x \in \mathbb{R}$

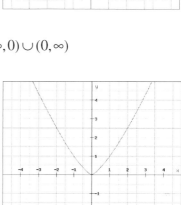

$Domain : x \in \mathbb{R}$ $Extrema : (0,0), \min$

$Vertical \quad Asymptotes : None$ $Range : f(x) \in [0, \infty)$

$Horizontal \quad Asymptotes : None$ $Increase : x \in (0, \infty)$

$Lim_{x \to -\infty} (f(x)) = \infty \quad Lim_{x \to \infty} (f(x)) = \infty$

$Slant \quad Asymptotes : None$ $Decrease : x \in (-\infty, 0)$

$y - \text{int} : (0,0)$ $Concave - up : Never$

$x - \text{int} : (0,0)$ $Concave - down : x \in (-\infty, 0) \cup (0, \infty)$

$Inflection \quad po \text{int} s : None$

$*Attention : Derivative \quad is \quad undefined \quad at \quad x = 0$

32. $f(x) = x^{\frac{4}{3}}, x \in \mathbb{R}$

$Domain : x \in \mathbb{R}$ $Extrema : (0,0), \min$

$Vertical \quad Asymptotes : None$ $Range : f(x) \in [0, \infty)$

$Horizontal \quad Asymptotes : None$ $Increase : x \in (0, \infty)$

$Lim_{x \to -\infty} (f(x)) = \infty \quad Lim_{x \to \infty} (f(x)) = \infty$

$Slant \quad Asymptotes : None$ $Decrease : x \in (-\infty, 0)$

$y - \text{int} : (0,0)$ $Concave - up : x \in (-\infty, 0) \cup (0, \infty)$

$x - \text{int} : (0,0)$ $Concave - down : Never$

$Inflection \quad po \text{int} s : None$

33. $f(x) = 2x^{-\frac{4}{3}}, x \in \mathbb{R}$

$Domain : x \in (-\infty, 0) \cup (0, \infty)$ $Extrema : None$

$Vertical \quad Asymptotes : x = 0$ $Range : f(x) \in (0, \infty)$

$Lim_{x \to 0^-} (f(x)) = \infty \quad Lim_{x \to 0^+} (f(x)) = \infty$ $Increase : x \in (-\infty, 0)$

$Horizontal \quad Asymptotes : y = 0$ $Decrease : x \in (0, \infty)$

$Lim_{x \to \infty} (f(x)) = 0 \quad Lim_{x \to \infty} (f(x)) = 0$ $Concave - up : x \in (-\infty, 0) \cup (0, \infty)$

$Slant \quad Asymptotes : None$ $Concave - down : Never$

$y - \text{int} : None$

$x - \text{int} : None$

$Inflection \quad po \text{int} s : None$

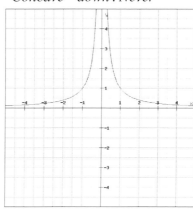

34. $f(x) = x - x^{\frac{2}{3}}, x \in \mathbb{R}$

$Domain: x \in \mathbb{R}$　　　　$Extrema: (0,0), min, (\frac{8}{27}, \approx -0.148)$

$Vertical\ \ Asymptotes: None$　　$Range: f(x) \in (-\infty, \infty)$

$Horizontal\ \ Asymptotes: None$　$Increase: x \in (-\infty, 0) \cup (\frac{8}{27}, \infty)$

$Lim_{x \to -\infty}(f(x)) = -\infty$　$Lim_{x \to \infty}(f(x)) = \infty$

$Slant\ \ Asymptotes: None$　　$Decrease: x \in (0, \frac{8}{27})$

$y-int: (0,0)$　　　$Concave-up: x \in (-\infty, 0) \cup (0, \infty)$

$x-int: (0,0), (1,0)$　　　$Concave-down: Never$

$Inflection\ \ points: None$

$*Attention: Derivative\ \ is\ \ undefined\ \ at\ \ x = 0$

35. $f(x) = x + x^{-\frac{2}{3}}, x \in \mathbb{R}$

$Domain: x \in (-\infty, 0) \cup (0, \infty)$　　　$Extrema: (\frac{\sqrt[5]{72}}{3}, \approx 1.96)$

$Vertical\ \ Asymptotes: x = 0$　　　$Range: f(x) \in (-\infty, \infty)$

$Lim_{x \to 0^-}(f(x)) = \infty$　$Lim_{x \to 0^+}(f(x)) = \infty$　$Increase: x \in (-\infty, 0) \cup (\frac{\sqrt[5]{72}}{3}, \infty)$

$Horizontal\ \ Asymptotes: None$　　　$Decrease: x \in (0, \frac{\sqrt[5]{72}}{3})$

$Lim_{x \to -\infty}(f(x)) = -\infty$　$Lim_{x \to \infty}(f(x)) = \infty$　$Concave-up: x \in (-\infty, 0) \cup (0, \infty)$

$Slant\ \ Asymptotes: y = x$　　　$Concave-down: Never$

$y-int: None$

$x-int: (-1, 0)$

$Inflection\ \ points: None$

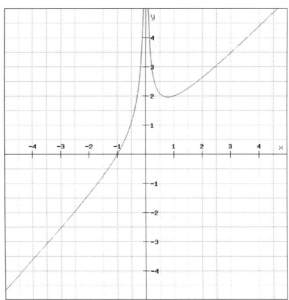

C. RATIONAL FUNCTIONS

36. $f(x) = \dfrac{3(x+2)}{(x-5)(x+2)} + 4, x \in \mathbb{R}$

$Domain: x \in (-\infty, -2) \cup (-2, 5) \cup (5, \infty)$

$Vertical \quad Asymptotes: x = 5$

$Lim_{x \to 2^-}(f(x)) = \dfrac{7}{2} \quad Lim_{x \to -2^+}(f(x)) = \dfrac{7}{2}$

$Lim_{x \to 5^-}(f(x)) = -\infty \quad Lim_{x \to 5^+}(f(x)) = \infty$

$Horizontal \quad Asymptotes: y = 4$

$Lim_{x \to -\infty}(f(x)) = 4 \quad Lim_{x \to \infty}(f(x)) = 4$

$Slant \quad Asymptotes: None$

$y-int: (0, \dfrac{17}{5})$

$x-int: (\dfrac{17}{4}, 0)$

$Inflection \quad points: None$

$Extrema: None$

$Range: f(x) \in (-\infty, \dfrac{7}{2}) \cup (\dfrac{7}{2}, 4) \cup (4, \infty)$

$Increase: x \in Never$

$Decrease: x \in (-\infty, -2) \cup (-2, 5) \cup (5, \infty)$

$Concave-up: x \in (-\infty, -2) \cup (-2, 5)$

$Concave-down: x \in (5, \infty)$

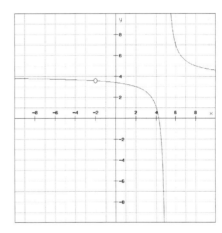

37. $f(x) = \dfrac{2x}{x+1}, x \in \mathbb{R}$

$Domain: x \in (-\infty, -1) \cup (-1, \infty)$

$Vertical \quad Asymptotes: x = -1$

$Lim_{x \to -1^-}(f(x)) = \infty \quad Lim_{x \to -1^+}(f(x)) = -\infty$

$Horizontal \quad Asymptotes: y = 2$

$Lim_{x \to -\infty}(f(x)) = 2 \quad Lim_{x \to \infty}(f(x)) = 2$

$Slant \quad Asymptotes: None$

$y-int: (0, 0)$

$x-int: (0, 0)$

$Inflection \quad points: None$

$Extrema: None$

$Range: f(x) \in (-\infty, 2) \cup (2, \infty)$

$Increase: x \in (-\infty, -1) \cup (-1, \infty)$

$Decrease: Never$

$Concave-up: x \in (-\infty, -1)$

$Concave-down: x \in (-1, \infty)$

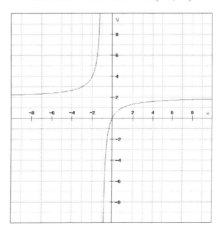

357

38. $f(x) = \dfrac{1}{x^2}, x \in \mathbb{R}$

$Domain: x \in (-\infty, 0) \cup (0, \infty)$

$Vertical \quad Asymptotes: x = 0$

$Lim_{x \to 0^-}(f(x)) = \infty \quad Lim_{x \to 0^+}(f(x)) = \infty$

$Horizontal \quad Asymptotes: y = 0$

$Lim_{x \to -\infty}(f(x)) = 0 \quad Lim_{x \to \infty}(f(x)) = 0$

$Slant \quad Asymptotes: None$

$y-\mathrm{int}: None$

$x-\mathrm{int}: None$

$Inflection \quad po\mathrm{int}s: None$

$Extrema: None$

$Range: f(x) \in (0, \infty)$

$Increase: x \in (-\infty, 0)$

$Decrease: x \in (0, \infty)$

$Concave-up: x \in (-\infty, 0) \cup (0, \infty)$

$Concave-down: Never$

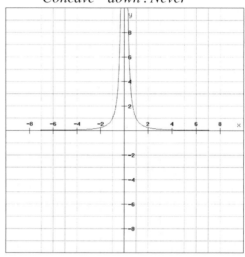

39. $f(x) = \dfrac{2}{(x-3)^2} - 4, x \in \mathbb{R}$

$Domain: x \in (-\infty, 3) \cup (3, \infty)$

$Vertical \quad Asymptotes: x = 3$

$Lim_{x \to 3^-}(f(x)) = \infty \quad Lim_{x \to 3^+}(f(x)) = \infty$

$Horizontal \quad Asymptotes: y = -4$

$Lim_{x \to -\infty}(f(x)) = -4 \quad Lim_{x \to \infty}(f(x)) = -4$

$Slant \quad Asymptotes: None$

$y-\mathrm{int}: (0, -\dfrac{34}{9})$

$x-\mathrm{int}: (\pm \dfrac{1}{\sqrt{2}} + 3, 0)$

$Inflection \quad po\mathrm{int}s: None$

$Extrema: None$

$Range: f(x) \in (-4, \infty)$

$Increase: x \in (-\infty, 3)$

$Decrease: x \in (3, \infty)$

$Concave-up: x \in (-\infty, 3) \cup (3, \infty)$

$Concave-down: Never$

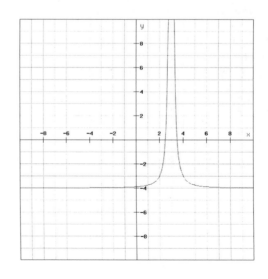

40. $f(x) = \dfrac{1}{x^2+1}, x \in \mathbb{R}$

$Domain: x \in \mathbb{R}$

$Vertical \quad Asymptotes: None$

$Horizontal \quad Asymptotes: y = 0$

$Lim_{x \to -\infty}(f(x)) = 0 \quad Lim_{x \to \infty}(f(x)) = 0$

$Slant \quad Asymptotes: None$

$y - \text{int}: (0,1)$

$x - \text{int}: None$

$Inflection \quad po\text{int}s: (\pm\dfrac{1}{\sqrt{3}}, \dfrac{3}{4})$

$Extrema: (0,1), max$

$Range: f(x) \in (0,1]$

$Increase: x \in (-\infty, 0)$

$Decrease: x \in (0, \infty)$

$Concave - up: x \in (-\infty, -\dfrac{1}{\sqrt{3}}) \cup (\dfrac{1}{\sqrt{3}}, \infty)$

$Concave - down: x \in (-\dfrac{1}{\sqrt{3}}, \dfrac{1}{\sqrt{3}})$

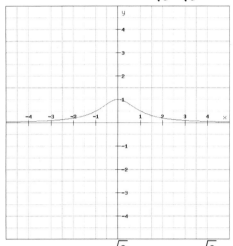

41. $f(x) = \dfrac{x}{x^2+2}, x \in \mathbb{R}$

$Domain: x \in \mathbb{R}$

$Vertical \quad Asymptotes: None$

$Horizontal \quad Asymptotes: y = 0$

$Lim_{x \to -\infty}(f(x)) = 0 \quad Lim_{x \to \infty}(f(x)) = 0$

$Slant \quad Asymptotes: None$

$y - \text{int}: (0,0)$

$x - \text{int}: (0,0)$

$Inflection \quad po\text{int}s: (\pm\sqrt{6}, \dfrac{\pm\sqrt{6}}{8})$

$Extrema: (-\sqrt{2}, -\dfrac{\sqrt{2}}{4}), min, (\sqrt{2}, \dfrac{\sqrt{2}}{4}), max$

$Range: f(x) \in [-\dfrac{\sqrt{2}}{4}, \dfrac{\sqrt{2}}{4}]$

$Increase: x \in (-\sqrt{2}, \sqrt{2})$

$Decrease: x \in (-\infty, -\sqrt{2}) \cup (\sqrt{2}, \infty)$

$Concave - up: x \in (-\sqrt{6}, 0) \cup (\sqrt{6}, \infty)$

$Concave - down: x \in (-\infty, -\sqrt{6}) \cup (0, \sqrt{6})$

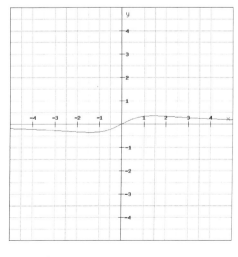

42. $f(x) = \dfrac{2}{(x-2)(x+3)}, x \in \mathbb{R}$

$Domain: x \in (-\infty, -3) \cup (-3, 2) \cup (2, \infty)$

$Extrema: (-\dfrac{1}{2}, -\dfrac{8}{25})$

$Vertical \quad Asymptotes: x = 3, x = 2$

$Range: f(x) \in (-\infty, -\dfrac{8}{25}] \cup (0, \infty)$

$Lim_{x \to -3^-}(f(x)) = \infty \quad Lim_{x \to -3^+}(f(x)) = -\infty$

$Increase: x \in (-\infty, -3) \cup (-3, -\dfrac{1}{2})$

$Lim_{x \to 2^-}(f(x)) = -\infty \quad Lim_{x \to 2^+}(f(x)) = \infty$

$Decrease: x \in (-\dfrac{1}{2}, 2) \cup (2, \infty)$

$Horizontal \quad Asymptotes: y = 0$

$Lim_{x \to -\infty}(f(x)) = 0 \quad Lim_{x \to \infty}(f(x)) = 0$

$Concave-up: x \in (-\infty, -3) \cup (2, \infty)$

$Slant \quad Asymptotes: None$

$Concave-down: x \in (-3, 2)$

$y-int: (0, -\dfrac{1}{3})$

$x-int: None$

$Inflection \quad points: None$

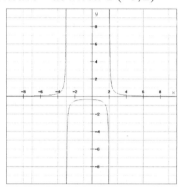

43. $f(x) = \dfrac{-3}{x^2 - 5x - 6}, x \in \mathbb{R}$

$Domain: x \in (-\infty, -1) \cup (-1, 6) \cup (6, \infty)$

$Extrema: (\dfrac{5}{2}, -\dfrac{8}{49})$

$Vertical \quad Asymptotes: x = -1, x = 6$

$Range: f(x) \in (-\infty, -\dfrac{8}{49}] \cup (0, \infty)$

$Lim_{x \to -1^-}(f(x)) = \infty \quad Lim_{x \to -1^+}(f(x)) = -\infty$

$Increase: x \in (-\infty, -1) \cup (-1, \dfrac{5}{2})$

$Lim_{x \to 6^-}(f(x)) = -\infty \quad Lim_{x \to 6^+}(f(x)) = \infty$

$Decrease: x \in (\dfrac{5}{2}, 6) \cup (6, \infty)$

$Horizontal \quad Asymptotes: y = 0$

$Lim_{x \to -\infty}(f(x)) = 0 \quad Lim_{x \to \infty}(f(x)) = 0$

$Concave-up: x \in (-\infty, -1) \cup (6, \infty)$

$Slant \quad Asymptotes: None$

$Concave-down: x \in (-1, 6)$

$y-int: (0, -\dfrac{1}{3})$

$x-int: None$

$Inflection \quad points: None$

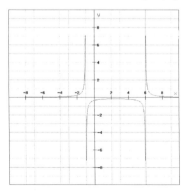

44. $f(x) = \dfrac{x^2}{x-1}, x \in \mathbb{R}$

Domain: $x \in (-\infty, 1) \cup (1, \infty)$

Vertical Asymptotes: $x = 1$

$Lim_{x \to -1^-}(f(x)) = \infty$ $Lim_{x \to -1^+}(f(x)) = -\infty$

Horizontal Asymptotes: *None*

$Lim_{x \to -\infty}(f(x)) = -\infty$ $Lim_{x \to \infty}(f(x)) = \infty$

Slant Asymptotes: $y = x + 1$

$y - $int: $(0, 0)$

$x - $int: $(0, 0)$

Inflection points: *None*

Extrema: $(0, 0), \max, (2, 4), \min$

Range: $f(x) \in (-\infty, 0] \cup [4, \infty)$

Increase: $x \in (-\infty, 0) \cup (2, \infty)$

Decrease: $x \in (0, 1) \cup (1, 2)$

Concave-up: $x \in (1, \infty)$

Concave-down: $x \in (-\infty, 1)$

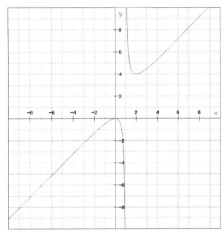

45. $f(x) = \dfrac{2x^2}{(x+3)(x-1)}, x \in \mathbb{R}$

Domain: $x \in (-\infty, -3) \cup (-3, 1) \cup (1, \infty)$

Vertical Asymptotes: $x = -3, x = 1$

$Lim_{x \to -3^-}(f(x)) = \infty$ $Lim_{x \to -3^+}(f(x)) = -\infty$

$Lim_{x \to 1^-}(f(x)) = -\infty$ $Lim_{x \to 1^+}(f(x)) = \infty$

Horizontal Asymptotes: $y = 2$

$Lim_{x \to -\infty}(f(x)) = 2$ $Lim_{x \to \infty}(f(x)) = 2$

Slant Asymptotes: *None*

$y - $int: $(0, 0)$

$x - $int: $(0, 0)$

Inflection points: $(\approx 4.70, \approx 1.55)$

Extrema: $(0, 0), \max, (3, \dfrac{3}{2}), \min$

Range: $f(x) \in (-\infty, 0] \cup [\dfrac{3}{2}, \infty)$

Increase: $x \in (-\infty, -3) \cup (-3, 0) \cup (3, \infty)$

Decrease: $x \in (0, 1) \cup (1, 3)$

Concave-up: $x \in (-\infty, -3) \cup (1, \approx 4.70)$

Concave-down: $x \in (-3, 1) \cup (\approx 4.70, \infty)$

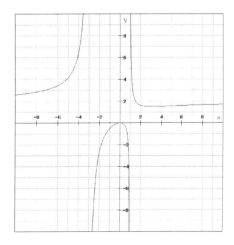

46. $f(x) = \dfrac{x^2 + 3}{x - 1}, x \in \mathbb{R}$

$Domain: x \in (-\infty, 1) \cup (1, \infty)$

$Vertical \quad Asymptotes: x = 1$

$Lim_{x \to 1^-}(f(x)) = -\infty \quad Lim_{x \to 1^+}(f(x)) = \infty$

$Horizontal \quad Asymptotes: None$

$Lim_{x \to -\infty}(f(x)) = -\infty \quad Lim_{x \to \infty}(f(x)) = \infty$

$Slant \quad Asymptotes: y = x + 1$

$y-\text{int}: (0, -3)$

$x-\text{int}: None$

$Inflection \quad po \text{int} s: None$

$Extrema: (-1, -2), \min, (3, 6), \min$

$Range: f(x) \in (-\infty, -2] \cup [6, \infty)$

$Increase: x \in (-\infty, -1) \cup (3, \infty)$

$Decrease: x \in (-1, 1) \cup (1, 3)$

$Concave-up: x \in (-\infty, 1) \cup (1, \infty)$

$Concave-down: Never$

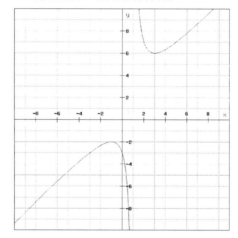

47. $f(x) = \dfrac{-1}{x^2 - x}, x \in \mathbb{R}$

$Domain: x \in (-\infty, 0) \cup (0, 1) \cup (1, \infty)$

$Vertical \quad Asymptotes: x = 0, x = 1$

$Lim_{x \to 0^-}(f(x)) = -\infty \quad Lim_{x \to 0^+}(f(x)) = \infty$

$Lim_{x \to 1^-}(f(x)) = \infty \quad Lim_{x \to 1^+}(f(x)) = -\infty$

$Horizontal \quad Asymptotes: y = 0$

$Lim_{x \to -\infty}(f(x)) = 0 \quad Lim_{x \to \infty}(f(x)) = 0$

$Slant \quad Asymptotes: None$

$y-\text{int}: None$

$x-\text{int}: None$

$Inflection \quad po \text{int} s: None$

$Extrema: (\dfrac{1}{2}, 4), \max$

$Range: f(x) \in (-\infty, -2] \cup [6, \infty)$

$Increase: x \in (\dfrac{1}{2}, 1) \cup (1, \infty)$

$Decrease: x \in (-\infty, 0) \cup (0, \dfrac{1}{2})$

$Concave-down: (-\infty, 0) \cup (1, \infty)$

$Concave-up: x \in (0, 1)$

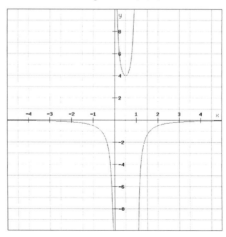

48. $f(x) = \dfrac{3x+1}{x^2 - x}, x \in \mathbb{R}$

$Domain : x \in (-\infty, 0) \cup (0,1) \cup (1,\infty)$

$Vertical\quad Asymptotes : x = 0, x = 1$

$Lim_{x \to 0^-}(f(x)) = \infty \quad Lim_{x \to 0^+}(f(x)) = -\infty$

$Lim_{x \to 1^-}(f(x)) = -\infty \quad Lim_{x \to 1^+}(f(x)) = \infty$

$Horizontal\quad Asymptotes : y = 0$

$Lim_{x \to -\infty}(f(x)) = 0 \quad Lim_{x \to \infty}(f(x)) = 0$

$Slant\quad Asymptotes : None$

$y - \text{int} : None$

$x - \text{int} : (-\dfrac{1}{3}, 0)$

$Inflection\quad po\text{int} s : (\approx -1.70, \approx -0.893)$

$Extrema : (-1,-1), \max, (\dfrac{1}{3}, -9), \min$

$Range : f(x) \in (-\infty, -9] \cup [-1, \infty)$

$Increase : x \in (-1, 0) \cup (0, \dfrac{1}{3})$

$Decrease : x \in (-\infty, -1) \cup (\dfrac{1}{3}, 1) \cup (1, \infty)$

$Concave - up : x \in (-0.893, 0) \cup (1, \infty)$

$Concave - down : x \in (-\infty, -0.893) \cup (0,1)$

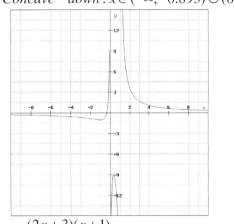

49. The function $f(x) = 2x + 3$, 2nd graph, $f(x) = \dfrac{(2x+3)(x+1)}{(x+1)}$

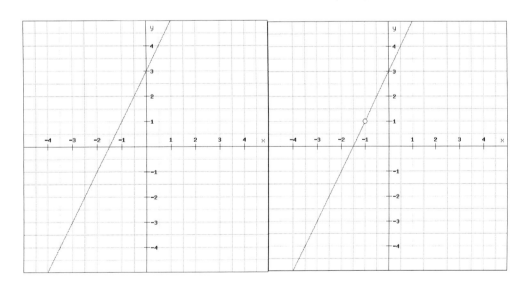

50. Determine the equations of all the asymptotes of the following functions and discuss their continuity:

a. $f(x) = \dfrac{2x^3 + 3x + 1}{x^3 - x}$, in consequence f(x) is continuous $x \in \mathbb{R}, x \notin \{-1, 0, 1\}$,

infinite jump discontinuity at $x = -1, 0, 1$

$Domain : x \notin \{-1, 0, 1\}$

$Lim_{x \to -1^-}(f(x)) = \infty \quad Lim_{x \to -1^+}(f(x)) = -\infty$

$Lim_{x \to 0^-}(f(x)) = \infty \quad Lim_{x \to 0^+}(f(x)) = -\infty$

$Lim_{x \to 1^-}(f(x)) = -\infty \quad Lim_{x \to 1^+}(f(x)) = \infty$

$Vertical \quad Asymptotes : x = 0, x = 1, x = -1$

$Lim_{x \to -\infty}(f(x)) = 2 \quad Lim_{x \to \infty}(f(x)) = 2$

$Horizontal \quad Asymptotes : y = 2$

$Slant \quad Asymptotes : None$

b. $f(x) = \dfrac{x^3 - x^2}{x^2 - 3x + 2} = \dfrac{x^2(x-1)}{(x-1)(x-2)}$, in consequence f(x) is continuous

$x \in \mathbb{R}, x \notin \{-1, 0, 1\}$, infinite jump discontinuity at $x = 2$, removable discontinuity at

$x = 1$

$Domain : x \notin \{1, 2\}$

$Lim_{x \to 1^-}(f(x)) = -1 \quad Lim_{x \to 1^+}(f(x)) = -1$

$Lim_{x \to 2^-}(f(x)) = -\infty \quad Lim_{x \to 2^+}(f(x)) = \infty$

$Vertical \quad Asymptotes : x = 2$

$Lim_{x \to -\infty}(f(x)) = -\infty \quad Lim_{x \to \infty}(f(x)) = \infty$

$Horizontal \quad Asymptotes : None$

$Slant \quad Asymptotes : y = x + 2$

c. $f(x) = \dfrac{5x^3 + 3x^2 + 1}{x^2 - 2}$, in consequence f(x) is continuous $x \in \mathbb{R}, x \notin \{-\sqrt{2}, \sqrt{2}\}$,

infinite discontinuity at $x = \sqrt{2}, \sqrt{2}$

$Domain : x \notin \{1, 2\}$

$Lim_{x \to -\sqrt{2}^-}(f(x)) = -\infty \quad Lim_{x \to -\sqrt{2}^+}(f(x)) = \infty$

$Lim_{x \to 2^-}(f(x)) = -\infty \quad Lim_{x \to 2^+}(f(x)) = \infty$

$Vertical \quad Asymptotes : x = \sqrt{2}, x = -\sqrt{2}$

$Lim_{x \to -\infty}(f(x)) = -\infty \quad Lim_{x \to \infty}(f(x)) = \infty$

$Horizontal \quad Asymptotes : None$

$Slant \quad Asymptotes : y = 5x + 3$

d. $f(x) = \dfrac{x - 2x^2}{3x^2 - 9x + 6} = \dfrac{x(1 - 2x)}{3(x - 2)(x - 1)}$, in consequence f(x) is continuous

$x \in \mathbb{R}, x \notin \{1, 2\}$, infinite jump discontinuity at $x = 1, 2$

Domain: $x \notin \{1, 2\}$

$Lim_{x \to 1^-}(f(x)) = -\infty \qquad Lim_{x \to 1^+}(f(x)) = \infty$

$Lim_{x \to 2^-}(f(x)) = \infty \qquad Lim_{x \to 2^+}(f(x)) = -\infty$

Vertical Asymptotes: $x = 1, x = 2$

$Lim_{x \to -\infty}(f(x)) = -\dfrac{2}{3} \qquad Lim_{x \to \infty}(f(x)) = -\dfrac{2}{3}$

Horizontal Asymptotes: $y = 2 - \dfrac{2}{3}$

Slant Asymptotes: *None*

51. Vertical asymptotes are of the form **x = a** Their origin is a function in which a certain value of **x** makes the denominator of the function **0** and the numerator **different than 0**

52. Horizontal asymptotes are of the form Their meaning is significant for **large negative** and **large positive values** of x. Sometimes a function can have a certain horizontal asymptote for **large negative values** and a different horizontal asymptote for **large positive values**. In a rational function which is of the form

$f(x) = \dfrac{a_1 x^n + a_2 x^{n-1} + \ldots}{b_1 x^m + b_2 x^{m-1} + \ldots}$ when **n = m** the function will have a horizontal asymptote of

the form $y = \dfrac{a_1}{b_1}$

53. Slant (or oblique) asymptotes are of the form **y = mx + b** Their meaning is significant for **large negative** and **large positive values** of x. Sometimes a function can have a certain horizontal asymptote for **large negative values** and a different horizontal asymptote for **large positive values**. In a rational function which is of the form $f(x) = \dfrac{a_1 x^n + a_2 x^{n-1} + \ldots}{b_1 x^m + b_2 x^{m-1} + \ldots}$, when **n = m + 1** the function will have a slant asymptote.

54. (T/**F**) All functions must have at least one vertical asymptote.
55. (T/**F**) All functions must have at least one horizontal asymptote.
56. (T/**F**) All functions must have at least one slant asymptote.
57. (T/**F**) A function that has two vertical asymptotes cannot have a slant asymptote.
58. (**T**/F) A function that has two slant asymptotes cannot have a horizontal asymptote.

D. GENERAL FUNCTIONS

59. $f(x) = e^x - x, x \in \mathbb{R}$

$Domain: x \in (-\infty, \infty)$ $Extrema: (0,1), \min$

$Vertical \quad Asymptotes: None$ $Range: f(x) \in [1, \infty)$

$Horizontal \quad Asymptotes: None$ $Increase: x \in (0, \infty)$

$Lim_{x \to -\infty}(f(x)) = \infty \quad Lim_{x \to \infty}(f(x)) = \infty$ $Decrease: x \in (-\infty, 0)$

$Slant \quad Asymptotes: y = -x(Left)$ $Concave - down: Never$

$y - \text{int}: (0,1)$ $Concave - up \in (-\infty, \infty)$

$x - \text{int}: None$

$Inflection \quad points: None$

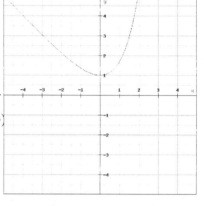

60. $f(x) = e^x + x, x \in \mathbb{R}$

$Domain: x \in (-\infty, \infty)$ $Extrema: None$

$Vertical \quad Asymptotes: None$ $Range: f(x) \in (-\infty, \infty)$

$Horizontal \quad Asymptotes: None$ $Increase: x \in (-\infty, \infty)$

$Lim_{x \to -\infty}(f(x)) = -\infty \quad Lim_{x \to \infty}(f(x)) = \infty$ $Decrease: Never$

$Slant \quad Asymptotes: y = x(Left)$ $Concave - down: Never$

$y - \text{int}: (0,1)$ $Concave - up \in (-\infty, \infty)$

$x - \text{int}: (-0.567, 0)$

$Inflection \quad points: None$

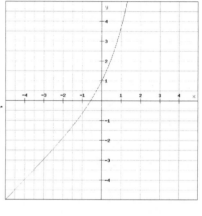

61. $f(x) = \dfrac{2}{1 + e^x}$

$Domain: x \in (-\infty, \infty)$ $Extrema: None$

$Vertical \quad Asymptotes: None$ $Range: f(x) \in (0, 2)$

$Horizontal \quad Asymptotes: y = 2(Left), y = 0(Right)$ $Increase: Never$

$Lim_{x \to -\infty}(f(x)) = 2 \quad Lim_{x \to \infty}(f(x)) = 0$ $Decrease: x \in (-\infty, \infty)$

$Slant \quad Asymptotes: None$ $Concave - down: x \in (-\infty, 0)$

$y - \text{int}: (0,1)$ $Concave - up: x \in (0, \infty)$

$x - \text{int}: None$

$Inflection \quad points: (0,1)$

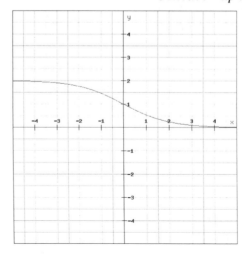

62. $f(x) = \dfrac{2}{2 - e^x}$

Domain : $x \in (-\infty, \ln(2)) \cup (\ln(2), -\infty)$

Vertical   Asymptotes : $x = \ln(2)$

$Lim_{x \to \ln(2)^-} (f(x)) = \infty \ Lim_{x \to \ln(2)^+} (f(x)) = -\infty$

Horizontal   Asymptotes : $y = 1(Left), \ y = 0(Right)$

$Lim_{x \to -\infty} (f(x)) = 1 \ \ Lim_{x \to \infty} (f(x)) = 0$

Slant   Asymptotes : *None*

$y - \text{int} : (0, 2)$

$x - \text{int} : None$

*Inflection   po*int *s* : *None*

Extrema : *None*

Range : $f(x) \in (-\infty, 0) \cup (1, \infty)$

Increase : $x \in (-\infty, \ln(2)) \cup (\ln(2), -\infty)$

Decrease : *Never*

  Concave − *down* : $x \in (\ln(2), \infty)$

  Concave − *up* : $x \in (-\infty, \ln(2))$

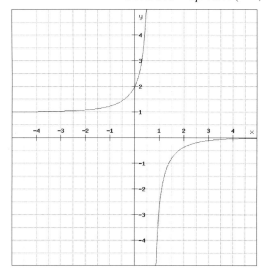

63. $f(x) = x \ln(x), x \in \mathbb{R}$

Domain : $x \in (0, \infty)$

Vertical   Asymptotes : *None*

$Lim_{x \to 0^+} (f(x)) = 0$

Horizontal   Asymptotes : *None*

$Lim_{x \to \infty} (f(x)) = \infty$

Slant   Asymptotes : *None*

$y - \text{int} : None$

$x - \text{int} : (1, 0)$

*Inflection   po*int *s* : *None*

Extrema : $(e^{-1}, -e^{-1}), \min$

Range : $f(x) \in [-e^{-1}, \infty)$

Increase : $x \in (e^{-1}, \infty)$

Decrease : $x \in (0, e^{-1})$

Concave − *down* : *Never*

Concave − *up* : $x \in (0, \infty)$

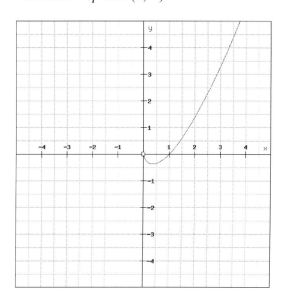

64. $f(x) = x\ln(x^2), x \in \mathbb{R}$

$Domain: x \in (-\infty, 0) \cup (0, \infty)$

$Extrema: (e^{-1}, -2e^{-1}), \min, (-e^{-1}, 2e^{-1}), \max$

$Vertical \quad Asymptotes: None$

$Range: f(x) \in (-\infty, \infty)$

$Lim_{x \to 0^-}(f(x)) = 0 \quad Lim_{x \to 0^+}(f(x)) = 0$

$Increase: x \in (-\infty, -e^{-1}) \cup (e^{-1}, \infty)$

$Horizontal \quad Asymptotes: None$

$Decrease: x \in (-e^{-1}, e^{-1})$

$Lim_{x \to -\infty}(f(x)) = -\infty \quad Lim_{x \to \infty}(f(x)) = \infty$

$Concave - down: x \in (-\infty, 0)$

$Slant \quad Asymptotes: None$

$Concave - up: x \in (0, \infty)$

$y - \text{int}: None$

$x - \text{int}: (1, 0), (-1, 0)$

$Inflection \quad po\text{int}s: None$

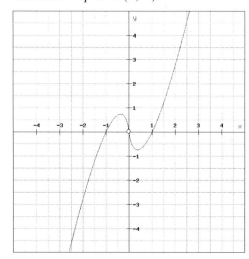

65. $f(x) = x^2 \ln(x), x \in \mathbb{R}$

$Domain: x \in (0, \infty)$

$Extrema: (e^{-\frac{1}{2}}, -\frac{1}{2}e^{-1}), \min$

$Vertical \quad Asymptotes: None$

$Range: f(x) \in [-\frac{1}{2}e^{-1}, \infty)$

$Lim_{x \to 0^+}(f(x)) = 0$

$Increase: x \in (e^{-\frac{1}{2}}, \infty)$

$Horizontal \quad Asymptotes: None$

$Decrease: x \in (0, e^{-\frac{1}{2}})$

$Lim_{x \to \infty}(f(x)) = \infty$

$Concave - down: Never$

$Slant \quad Asymptotes: None$

$Concave - up: x \in (0, \infty)$

$y - \text{int}: None$

$x - \text{int}: (1, 0)$

$Inflection \quad po\text{int}s: None$

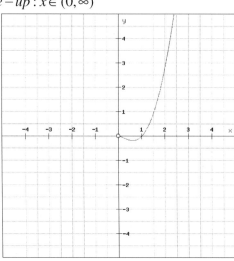

66. $f(x) = x(\ln(x))^2, x \in \mathbb{R}$

Domain : $x \in (0, \infty)$

Vertical Asymptotes : None

$Lim_{x \to 0^+}(f(x)) = 0$

Horizontal Asymptotes : None

$Lim_{x \to \infty}(f(x)) = \infty$

Slant Asymptotes : None

$y - \text{int} : None$

$x - \text{int} : (1, 0)$

Inflection points : (e^{-1}, e^{-1})

Extrema : $(e^{-2}, 4e^{-2}), \max, (1, 0), \min$

Range : $f(x) \in [0, \infty)$

Increase : $x \in (0, e^{-2}) \cup (1, \infty)$

Decrease : $x \in (e^{-2}, 1)$

Concave $-$ down : $x \in (0, e^{-1})$

Concave $-$ up : $x \in (e^{-1}, \infty)$

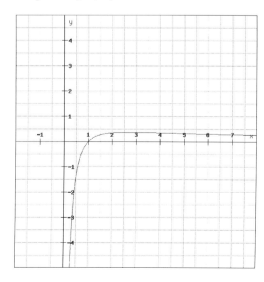

67. $f(x) = \dfrac{\ln(x)}{x}, x \in \mathbb{R}$

Domain : $x \in (0, \infty)$

Vertical Asymptotes : $x = 0$

$Lim_{x \to 0^+}(f(x)) = -\infty$

Horizontal Asymptotes : $y = 0$

$Lim_{x \to \infty}(f(x)) = 0$

Slant Asymptotes : None

$y - \text{int} : None$

$x - \text{int} : (1, 0)$

Inflection points : $(e^{\frac{3}{2}}, \frac{3}{2}e^{-\frac{3}{2}})$

Extrema : $(e, e^{-1}), \max$

Range : $f(x) \in (-\infty, e^{-1}]$

Increase : $x \in (0, e)$

Decrease : $x \in (e, \infty)$

Concave $-$ down : $x \in (0, e^{\frac{3}{2}})$

Concave $-$ up : $x \in (e^{\frac{3}{2}}, \infty)$

68. $f(x) = \sqrt{x} - x, x \in \mathbb{R}$

$Domain : x \in [0, \infty)$

$Vertical \quad Asymptotes : None$

$Lim_{x \to 0^+}(f(x)) = 0$

$Horizontal \quad Asymptotes : None$

$Lim_{x \to \infty}(f(x)) = -\infty$

$Slant \quad Asymptotes : None$

$y - int : (0, 0)$

$x - int : (0, 0), (1, 0)$

$Inflection \quad points : None$

$Extrema : (\dfrac{1}{4}, \dfrac{1}{4}), max$

$Range : f(x) \in (-\infty, \dfrac{1}{4}]$

$Increase : x \in (0, \dfrac{1}{4})$

$Decrease : x \in (\dfrac{1}{4}, \infty)$

$Concave - down : x \in (0, \infty)$

$Concave - up : Never$

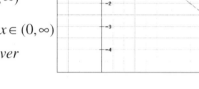

69. $f(x) = x^2 - \dfrac{1}{x}, x \in \mathbb{R}$

$Domain : x \in (-\infty, 0) \cup (0, \infty)$

$Vertical \quad Asymptotes : x = 0$

$Lim_{x \to 0^-}(f(x)) = \infty \quad Lim_{x \to 0^+}(f(x)) = -\infty$

$Horizontal \quad Asymptotes : None$

$Lim_{x \to -\infty}(f(x)) = \infty \quad Lim_{x \to \infty}(f(x)) = \infty$

$Slant \quad Asymptotes : None$

$y - int : None$

$x - int : (1, 0)$

$Inflection \quad points : (1, 0)$

$Extrema : (-2^{-\frac{1}{3}}, \dfrac{3}{2} 2^{\frac{1}{3}}), min$

$Range : f(x) \in (-\infty, \infty)$

$Increase : x \in (-2^{-\frac{1}{3}}, 0) \cup (0, \infty)$

$Decrease : x \in (-\infty, -2^{-\frac{1}{3}})$

$Concave - down : x \in (0, 1)$

$Concave - up : x \in (-\infty, 0) \cup (1, \infty)$

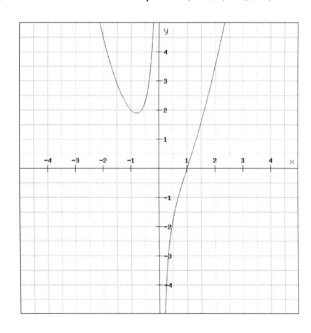

70. $f(x) = x^2 + \dfrac{2}{x}, x \in \mathbb{R}$

$Domain : x \in (-\infty, 0) \cup (0, \infty)$ $Extrema : (1, 3), \min$

$Vertical \quad Asymptotes : x = 0$ $Range : f(x) \in (-\infty, \infty)$

$Lim_{x \to 0^-}(f(x)) = -\infty \quad Lim_{x \to 0^+}(f(x)) = \infty$ $Increase : x \in (1, \infty)$

$Horizontal \quad Asymptotes : None$ $Decrease : x \in (-\infty, 0) \cup (0, 1)$

$Lim_{x \to -\infty}(f(x)) = \infty \quad Lim_{x \to \infty}(f(x)) = \infty$ $Concave - down : x \in (-2^{\frac{1}{3}}, 0)$

$Slant \quad Asymptotes : None$ $Concave - up : x \in (-\infty, -2^{\frac{1}{3}}) \cup (0, \infty)$

$y - int : None$

$x - int : (-2^{\frac{1}{3}}, 0)$

$Inflection \quad po\text{int}s : (-2^{\frac{1}{3}}, 0)$

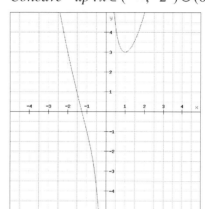

71. $f(x) = \sin(x^2), x \in \mathbb{R}$

$Domain : x \in (-\infty, \infty) \quad Extrema : \min : (0, 0), (\dfrac{\pm\sqrt{6\pi + 8\pi k}}{2}, -1), k \in \mathbb{N} \, \max : (\dfrac{\pm\sqrt{2\pi + 8\pi k}}{2}, 1), k \in \mathbb{N})$

$Vertical \quad Asymptotes : None \quad Range : f(x) \in [-1, 1]$

$Horizontal \quad Asymptotes : None$

$Lim_{x \to -\infty}(f(x)) = D.E. \quad Lim_{x \to \infty}(f(x)) = D.E.$

$Decrease : x \in (\dfrac{-\sqrt{2\pi + 8\pi k}}{2}, \dfrac{-\sqrt{6\pi + 8\pi k}}{2}) \cup (\dfrac{-\sqrt{2\pi + 8\pi k}}{2}, 0) \cup (\dfrac{\sqrt{2\pi + 8\pi k}}{2}, \dfrac{\sqrt{6\pi + 8\pi k}}{2}), k \in \mathbb{N}$

$Increase : x \in (\dfrac{-\sqrt{6\pi + 8\pi k}}{2}, \dfrac{-\sqrt{2\pi + 8\pi k}}{2}) \cup (0, \dfrac{\sqrt{2\pi + 8\pi k}}{2}, 0) \cup (\dfrac{\sqrt{6\pi + 8\pi k}}{2}, \dfrac{\sqrt{2\pi + 8\pi k}}{2}), k \in \mathbb{N}$

$Concave - down : Beyond \quad Level \quad Concave - up : Beyond \quad Level$

$Slant \quad Asymptotes : None$

$y - int : (0, 0)$

$x - int : (\pm\sqrt{\pi k}, 0), k \in \mathbb{N}$

$Inflection \quad po\text{int}s : Beyond \quad Level$

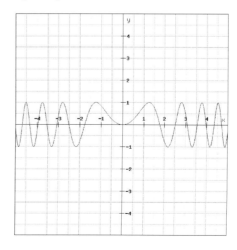

72. $f(x) = \sin(x) + x, x \in \mathbb{R}$

$Domain : x \in (-\infty, \infty)$ $Extrema : (\pi + 2\pi k, \pi + 2\pi k), k \in \mathbb{Z}, Inflection\ points$

$Vertical\ Asymptotes : None$ $Range : f(x) \in (-\infty, \infty)$

$Horizontal\ Asymptotes : None$ $Increase : x \in (-\infty, \infty)$

$Lim_{x \to -\infty}(f(x)) = \infty\ \ Lim_{x \to \infty}(f(x)) = -\infty$ $Decrease : Never$

$Slant\ Asymptotes : None$ $Concave-down : x \in (2\pi k, \pi + 2\pi k), k \in \mathbb{Z}$

$y - \mathrm{int} : (0, 0)$ $Concave-up : x \in (\pi + 2\pi k, 2\pi + 2\pi k), k \in \mathbb{Z}$

$x - \mathrm{int} : (0, 0)$

$Inflection\ points : (\pi + 2\pi k, \pi + 2\pi k), k \in \mathbb{Z}, Horizontal\ Inflection\ points$

$(2\pi k, 2\pi k), k \in \mathbb{Z}, Non-Horizontal\ Inflection\ points$

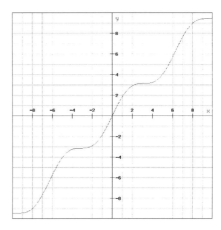

73. $f(x) = x(1 - \ln(x^2)), x \in \mathbb{R}$

$Domain : x \in (-\infty, 0) \cup (0, \infty)$ $Extrema : (e^{-\frac{1}{2}}, 2e^{-\frac{1}{2}}), \max, (-e^{-\frac{1}{2}}, -2e^{-\frac{1}{2}}), \min$

$Vertical\ Asymptotes : None$ $Range : f(x) \in (-\infty, \infty)$

$Lim_{x \to 0^-}(f(x)) = 0\ \ Lim_{x \to 0^+}(f(x)) = 0$ $Increase : x \in (-e^{-\frac{1}{2}}, e^{-\frac{1}{2}})$

$Horizontal\ Asymptotes : None$ $Decrease : x \in (-\infty, -e^{-\frac{1}{2}}) \cup (e^{-\frac{1}{2}}, \infty)$

$Lim_{x \to -\infty}(f(x)) = \infty\ \ Lim_{x \to \infty}(f(x)) = -\infty$ $Concave-down : x \in (0, \infty)$

$Slant\ Asymptotes : None$ $Concave-up : x \in (-\infty, 0)$

$y - \mathrm{int} : None$

$x - \mathrm{int} : (e^{\frac{1}{2}}, 0), (-e^{\frac{1}{2}}, 0)$

$Inflection\ points : None$

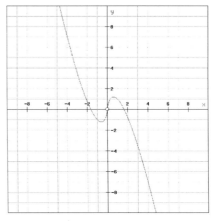

74. $f(x) = e^{x - x^2}, x \in \mathbb{R}$

$Domain : x \in (-\infty, \infty)$ $Extrema : (\frac{1}{2}, e^{\frac{1}{4}}), \max$

$Vertical \quad Asymptotes : None$ $Range : f(x) \in (0, e^{\frac{1}{4}}]$

$Horizontal \quad Asymptotes : y = 0$ $Increase : x \in (-\infty, \frac{1}{2})$

$Lim_{x \to -\infty}(f(x)) = 0 \quad Lim_{x \to \infty}(f(x)) = 0 \quad Decrease : x \in (\frac{1}{2}, \infty)$

$Slant \quad Asymptotes : None$

$y - \text{int} : (0, 1)$

$x - \text{int} : None$

$Inflection \quad po\text{int} s : (\frac{1 - \sqrt{2}}{2}, 0), (\frac{1 + \sqrt{2}}{2}, 0)$

$Concave - up : x \in (-\infty, \frac{1 - \sqrt{2}}{2}) \cup (\frac{1 + \sqrt{2}}{2}, \infty)$

$Concave - down : x \in (\frac{1 - \sqrt{2}}{2}, \frac{1 + \sqrt{2}}{2})$

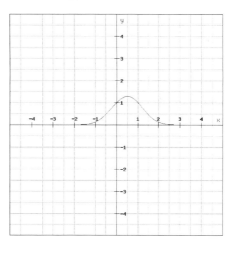

75. $f(x) = x^3(1 - \ln(x^2)), x \in \mathbb{R}$

$Domain : x \in (-\infty, 0) \cup (0, \infty)$ $Extrema : (e^{\frac{1}{6}}, \frac{2}{3}e^{\frac{1}{2}}), \max, (-e^{\frac{1}{6}}, -\frac{2}{3}e^{\frac{1}{2}}), \min$

$Vertical \quad Asymptotes : None$ $Range : f(x) \in (-\infty, \infty)$

$Lim_{x \to 0^-}(f(x)) = 0 \quad Lim_{x \to 0^+}(f(x)) = 0 \quad Increase : x \in (-e^{\frac{1}{6}}, e^{\frac{1}{6}})$

$Horizontal \quad Asymptotes : None$ $Decrease : x \in (-\infty, -e^{\frac{1}{6}}) \cup (e^{\frac{1}{6}}, \infty)$

$Lim_{x \to -\infty}(f(x)) = \infty \quad Lim_{x \to \infty}(f(x)) = -\infty \quad Concave - down : x \in (-\frac{5}{3}e^{-1}, 0) \cup (\frac{5}{3}e^{-1}, \infty)$

$Slant \quad Asymptotes : None$ $Concave - up : x \in (-\infty, -\frac{5}{3}e^{-1}) \cup (0, \frac{5}{3}e^{-1})$

$y - \text{int} : None$

$x - \text{int} : (e^{\frac{1}{2}}, 0), (-e^{\frac{1}{2}}, 0)$

$Inflection \quad po\text{int} s : (e^{-\frac{1}{3}}, \frac{5}{3}e^{-1},), (-e^{-\frac{1}{3}}, -\frac{5}{3}e^{-1})$

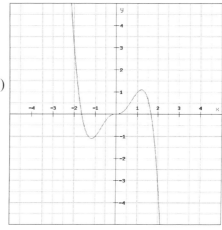

373

76. $f(x) = e^{x^3 - x^2}, x \in \mathbb{R}$

$Domain: x \in (-\infty, \infty)$

$Extrema: (0,1), \max, (\frac{2}{3}, e^{-\frac{4}{27}}), \max$

$Vertical\ \ Asymptotes: None$

$Range: f(x) \in (0, \infty)$

$Horizontal\ \ Asymptotes: y = 0$

$Increase: x \in (-\infty, 0) \cup (\frac{2}{3}, \infty)$

$Lim_{x \to -\infty} (f(x)) = 0 \quad Lim_{x \to \infty} (f(x)) = \infty$

$Decrease: x \in (0, \frac{2}{3})$

$Slant\ \ Asymptotes: None$

$Concave-up: x \in (-\infty, \approx -0.620) \cup (\approx 0.315, \infty)$

$y-\text{int}: (0,1)$

$Concave-down: x \in (\approx -0.620, \approx 0.315)$

$x-\text{int}: None$

$Inflection\ \ points: (\approx 0.315, \approx 0.934), (\approx -0.620, \approx 0.536)$

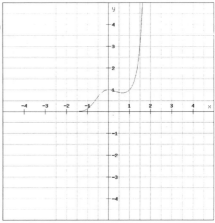

77. $f(x) = \ln(x^2 - 1), x \in \mathbb{R}$

$Domain: x \in (-\infty, -1) \cup (1, \infty)$

$Extrema: None$

$Vertical\ \ Asymptotes: x = -1, x = 1$

$Range: f(x) \in (-\infty, \infty)$

$Lim_{x \to -1^-} (f(x)) = -\infty \quad Lim_{x \to 1^+} (f(x)) = -\infty$

$Increase: x \in (1, \infty)$

$Horizontal\ \ Asymptotes: None$

$Decrease: x \in (-\infty, -1)$

$Lim_{x \to -\infty} (f(x)) = \infty \quad Lim_{x \to \infty} (f(x)) = \infty$

$Concave-down: x \in (-\infty, -1) \cup (1, \infty)$

$Slant\ \ Asymptotes: None$

$Concave-up: Never$

$y-\text{int}: None$

$x-\text{int}: (\sqrt{2}, 0), (-\sqrt{2}, 0)$

$Inflection\ \ points: None$

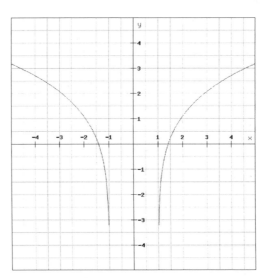

78. $f(x) = \ln(4 - x^2), x \in \mathbb{R}$

$Domain: x \in (-2, 2)$ $\qquad$ $Extrema: (0, \ln(4)), \max$

$Vertical \quad Asymptotes: x = -2, x = 2$ $\qquad$ $Range: f(x) \in (-\infty, \infty)$

$Lim_{x \to -2^+}(f(x)) = -\infty \quad Lim_{x \to 2^-}(f(x)) = -\infty$ $\quad$ $Increase: x \in (-2, 0)$

$Horizontal \quad Asymptotes: None$ $\qquad$ $Decrease: x \in (0, 2)$

$Lim_{x \to -\infty}(f(x)) = D.E. \quad Lim_{x \to \infty}(f(x)) = D.E.$ $\quad$ $Concave - down: x \in (-2, 2)$

$Slant \quad Asymptotes: None$ $\qquad$ $Concave - up: Never$

$y - \text{int}: (0, \ln(4))$

$x - \text{int}: (\sqrt{3}, 0), (-\sqrt{3}, 0)$

$Inflection \quad po\text{int}s: None$

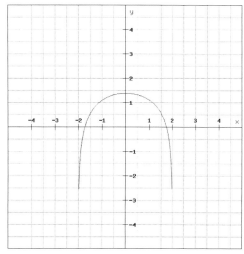

79. $f(x) = \sqrt{3x - x^2}$

$Domain: x \in [0, 3]$ $\qquad$ $Extrema: (\frac{3}{2}, \frac{3}{2}), \max$

$Vertical \quad Asymptotes: None$ $\qquad$ $Range: f(x) \in (0, \frac{3}{2})$

$Lim_{x \to 0^+}(f(x)) = 0 \quad Lim_{x \to 3^-}(f(x)) = 0$ $\quad$ $Increase: x \in (0, \frac{3}{2})$

$Horizontal \quad Asymptotes: None$ $\qquad$ $Decrease: x \in (\frac{3}{2}, 3)$

$Lim_{x \to -\infty}(f(x)) = D.E. \quad Lim_{x \to \infty}(f(x)) = D.E.$ $\quad$ $Concave - down: x \in (0, 3)$

$Slant \quad Asymptotes: None$ $\qquad$ $Concave - up: Never$

$y - \text{int}: (0, 0)$

$x - \text{int}: (0, 0), (3, 0)$

$Inflection \quad po\text{int}s: None$

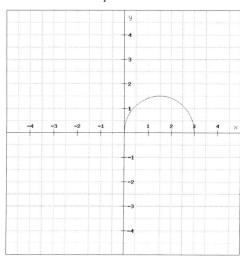

80. $f(x) = \dfrac{1}{\sqrt{3x - x^2}}$

$Domain : x \in (0,3)$

$Extrema : (\dfrac{3}{2}, \dfrac{2}{3}), \min$

$Vertical \quad Asymptotes : x = 0, x = 3$

$Range : f(x) \in [\dfrac{2}{3}, \infty)$

$Lim_{x \to 0^+}(f(x)) = \infty \quad Lim_{x \to 3^-}(f(x)) = \infty$

$Increase : x \in (\dfrac{3}{2}, 3)$

$Horizontal \quad Asymptotes : None$

$Decrease : x \in (0, \dfrac{3}{2})$

$Lim_{x \to -\infty}(f(x)) = D.E. \quad Lim_{x \to \infty}(f(x)) = D.E.$

$Concave - down : Never$

$Slant \quad Asymptotes : None$

$Concave - up : x \in (0,3)$

$y - \text{int} : None$

$x - \text{int} : None$

$Inflection \quad po\text{int} s : None$

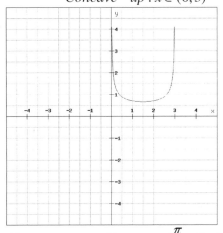

81. $f(x) = \dfrac{1}{\sin(x) + 1}$

$Domain : x \in \mathbb{R}, x \neq \dfrac{3\pi}{2} + 2\pi k, k \in \mathbb{Z}$

$Extrema : (\dfrac{\pi}{2} + 2\pi k, \dfrac{1}{2}), k \in \mathbb{Z}, \min$

$Vertical \quad Asymptotes : x = \dfrac{3\pi}{2} + 2\pi k, k \in \mathbb{Z}$

$Range : f(x) \in [\dfrac{1}{2}, \infty)$

$Lim_{x \to \frac{3\pi}{2} + 2\pi k^+}(f(x)) = \infty \quad Lim_{x \to \frac{3\pi}{2} + 2\pi k^-}(f(x)) = \infty$

$Increase : x \in (\dfrac{\pi}{2} + 2\pi k, \dfrac{3\pi}{2} + 2\pi k), k \in \mathbb{Z}$

$Horizontal \quad Asymptotes : None$

$Decrease : x \in (\dfrac{3\pi}{2} + 2\pi k, \dfrac{5\pi}{2} + 2\pi k), k \in \mathbb{Z}$

$Lim_{x \to -\infty}(f(x)) = D.E. \quad Lim_{x \to \infty}(f(x)) = D.E.$

$Concave - down : Never$

$Slant \quad Asymptotes : None$

$Concave - up : x \neq \dfrac{3\pi}{2} + 2\pi k, k \in \mathbb{Z}$

$y - \text{int} : (0,1)$

$x - \text{int} : None$

$Inflection \quad po\text{int} s : None$

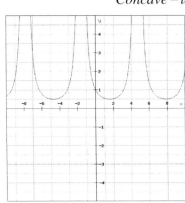

1.9. – INDEFINITE INTEGRATION

1. $\int x^{75} - 12x + 2\,dx = \dfrac{x^{76}}{76} - \dfrac{12x^2}{2} + 2x + C$

2. $\int \dfrac{1}{x^3} - 3x^{\frac{2}{3}} + 31x\,dx = \dfrac{x^{-2}}{-2} - \dfrac{9x^{\frac{5}{3}}}{5} + 31\dfrac{x^2}{2} + C$

3. $\int \sqrt[4]{\dfrac{1}{x^3}} - x + 1 + \pi + \cos(1) + e\,dx = 4x^{\frac{1}{4}} - \dfrac{x^2}{2} + x + \pi x + \cos(1)x + ex + C$

4. $\int \dfrac{1}{x^3} - 3x + 3\,dx = \dfrac{x^{-2}}{-2} - \dfrac{3x^2}{2} + 3x + C$

5. $\int \dfrac{1}{x^2} - \dfrac{3}{\sqrt{2x^3}}\,dx = \dfrac{x^{-1}}{-1} + \dfrac{6x^{-\frac{1}{2}}}{\sqrt{2}} + C$

6. $\int \dfrac{4}{x^5} - \dfrac{3}{2x^2}\,dx = \dfrac{4x^{-4}}{-4} - \dfrac{3x^{-1}}{-2} + C$

7. $\int \dfrac{-5}{x^{55}} - \dfrac{5}{7x^{211}}\,dx = \dfrac{5x^{-54}}{54} + \dfrac{5x^{-210}}{7 \cdot 210} + C$

8. $\int \dfrac{2}{x} - \dfrac{5}{x}\,dx = -3Ln(x) + C$

9. $\int \dfrac{2}{x^3} + \dfrac{5}{3x^{10}} - \dfrac{2}{x}\,dx = \dfrac{2x^{-2}}{-2} + \dfrac{5x^{-9}}{-27} - 2Ln(x) + C$

10. $\int \dfrac{15}{x} - x^{12}\,dx = 15Ln(x) - \dfrac{x^{13}}{13} + C$

11. $\int \dfrac{2}{x^3} + \dfrac{5}{3x^{10}} - \dfrac{2}{x}\,dx = \dfrac{2x^{-2}}{-2} + 5\dfrac{x^{-9}}{-27} - 2Ln(x) + C$

12. $\int \sqrt{\dfrac{a}{x}} + \dfrac{a}{x} + \dfrac{x}{a} - ae^x + \dfrac{1}{a} + x^a\,dx = 2\sqrt{a}x^{\frac{1}{2}} + aLn(x) + \dfrac{x^2}{2a} - ae^x + \dfrac{x}{a} + \dfrac{x^{a+1}}{a+1} + C$

13. $\int 0.1x - 0.2e^x\,dx = \dfrac{x^2}{20} - \dfrac{1}{5}e^x + C$

14. $\int \dfrac{1}{x} - 15e^x + 0.2\,dx = Ln(x) - 15e^x + 0.2x + C$

15. $\int \sqrt{\dfrac{2}{x}} + \dfrac{2}{3} - e^x\,dx = 2\sqrt{2}x^{\frac{1}{2}} + \dfrac{2}{3}x - e^x + C$

16. $\int \frac{2}{x^{40}} + \frac{2}{7x^{12}} - 5e^x\,dx = -\frac{2x^{-39}}{41\cdot 39} - \frac{2x^{-11}}{7\cdot 11} - 5e^x + C$

17. $\int 7\cos(x) + 12x\,dx = 7\sin(x) + 6x^2 + C$

18. $\int -\cos(x) - \sin(x) - \frac{2}{x} + \frac{2}{x^2} - e^x\,dx = -\sin(x) + \cos(x) - 2Ln(x) - 2x^{-1} - e^x + C$

19. $\int \cos(4) + 7e^x + \frac{3}{x^{12}}\,dx = \cos(4)\cdot x + 7e^x + \frac{3x^{-11}}{-11} + C$

20. $\int \cos(x) + \sin(x) + \frac{3}{x}\,dx = \sin(x) - \cos(x) + 3\ln(x) + C$

21. $\int \cos(4) + \sin(x) + \frac{3}{\sqrt{x^7}}\,dx = \cos(4)\cdot x - \cos(x) + \frac{3x^{\frac{9}{2}}}{\left(\frac{9}{2}\right)} + C$

22. $\int 7 - \frac{a}{x} + \frac{b}{2x^5} + 4\,dx = 3x - a\ln(x) + \frac{bx^{-4}}{-8} + C$

23. $\int \frac{1}{3}\cos(x) + \frac{1}{2} - \sqrt{3}e^x + \sqrt{3} + \sqrt{2}x - \frac{2}{x} + \frac{1}{2x} + 1 + x\,dx =$

$$\frac{1}{3}\sin(x) + \frac{1}{2}x - \sqrt{3}e^x + \sqrt{3}\cdot x + \sqrt{2}\frac{x^2}{2} - \frac{3}{2}\ln(x) + x + \frac{x^2}{2} + C$$

24. $\int \frac{1}{3}\sin(x) + \frac{5}{2} - \sqrt{3}e^x + \sqrt{7} + \sqrt{2}x - \frac{a}{x} + \frac{1}{bx} + 1 + x\,dx =$

$$-\frac{1}{3}\cos(x) + \frac{5}{2}x - \sqrt{3}e^x + \sqrt{7}\cdot x + \sqrt{2}\frac{x^2}{2} - a\ln(x) + \frac{1}{b}\ln(x) + x + \frac{x^2}{2} + C$$

Exercises:

25. $\int 2x\cos(x^2)\,dx = \sin(x^2) + C$

26. $\int -2\sin(-x^3)x^2\,dx = \frac{-2\cos(-x^3)}{3} + C$

27. $\int xe^{x^2+3}\,dx = \frac{e^{x^2+3}}{2} + C$

28. $\int \cos(x^3 + 1)x^2\,dx = \frac{\sin(x^3+1)}{3} + C$

29. $\int \frac{4x}{x^2+2}\,dx = 2Ln(x^2 + 2) + C$

30. $\int x^3\sin(x^4 + 5)\,dx = -\frac{\cos(x^4 + 5)}{4} + C$

31. $\int \frac{4}{(3x+5)^7}\,dx = \frac{4(3x+5)^{-6}}{-6\cdot 3} + C$

32. $\int e^{\frac{x}{2}}\,dx = 2e^{\frac{x}{2}} + C$

33. $\int 2x\sin(3x^2 + 52)\,dx = -\frac{\cos(3x^2+52)}{3} + C$

378

34. $\int 5\cos(3x+5)\,dx = \dfrac{5\sin(3x+5)}{3} + C$

45. $\int \dfrac{4}{7}\cos(-7x+11)\,dx = \dfrac{4}{-49}\sin(-7x+11) + C$

35. $\int \dfrac{20x+2}{5x^2+x}\,dx = 2Ln(5x^2+x) + C$

46. $\int \dfrac{4x}{3}\cos(3x^2+15)\,dx = \dfrac{4}{18}\sin(3x^2+15) + C$

36. $\int \dfrac{2}{5}\cos(\dfrac{x}{2}+5)\,dx = \dfrac{4}{5}\sin(\dfrac{x}{2}+5) + C$

37. $\int \dfrac{x^2}{x^3+3}\,dx = \dfrac{Ln(x^3+3)}{3} + C$

47. $\int \dfrac{4}{7}\sin(3x+5)\,dx = -\dfrac{4}{21}\cos(3x+5) + C$

38. $\int (3x^2-4)e^{x^3-4x}\,dx = e^{x^3-4x} + C$

48. $\int \dfrac{4x}{3(x^2-5)^4}\,dx = -\dfrac{4}{18}(x^2-5)^{-3} + C$

39. $\int 5x(x^2-4)^{-6}\,dx = \dfrac{-(x^2-4)^{-5}}{2} + C$

49. $\int \dfrac{2x-5}{(x^2-5x)^5}\,dx = \dfrac{(x^2-5x)^{-4}}{-8} + C$

40. $\int 15(e^x-4)^{11}e^x\,dx = \dfrac{15(e^x-4)^{12}}{12} + C$

50. $\int -\dfrac{2x^3}{(x^4-3)^5}\,dx = \dfrac{(x^4-3)^{-4}}{8} + C$

51. $\int -\dfrac{2x}{3(x^2-3)}\,dx = -\dfrac{1}{3}Ln(x^2-3) + C$

41. $\int x^2 e^{4x^3+17}\,dx = \dfrac{e^{4x^3+17}}{12} + C$

42. $\int e^{-5x+7}\,dx = \dfrac{e^{-5x+7}}{-5} + C$

52. $\int \dfrac{3x^2+5x}{x}\,dx = \int 3x+5\,dx = \dfrac{3x^2}{2}+5x + C$

43. $\int \dfrac{2x+3}{x^2+3x}\,dx = Ln(x^2+3x) + C$

44. $\int \dfrac{4x+2}{2x^2+2x+7}\,dx = Ln(2x^2+2x+7) + C$

53. $\int \dfrac{x^3+x^2-2\sqrt{x}+1}{\sqrt[3]{x}}\,dx = \int x^{\frac{8}{3}}+x^{\frac{5}{3}}-2x^{\frac{1}{6}}+x^{-\frac{1}{3}}\,dx = \dfrac{3x^{\frac{11}{3}}}{11}+\dfrac{3x^{\frac{8}{3}}}{8}-3x^{\frac{4}{6}}+\dfrac{3x^{\frac{2}{3}}}{2}+C$

54. $\int \dfrac{\sqrt{x}}{x^4}\,dx = \int x^{-\frac{7}{2}}\,dx = -\dfrac{2x^{-\frac{5}{2}}}{5}+C$

55. $\int (\sqrt{x}+\sqrt{\dfrac{1}{x}})\,dx = \dfrac{2x^{\frac{3}{2}}}{3}+2x^{\frac{1}{2}}+C$

56. $\int \dfrac{\sqrt{x}+\sqrt[3]{x^2}}{\sqrt[6]{x^5}}\,dx = \int x^{-\frac{1}{3}}+x^{-\frac{1}{6}}\,dx = \dfrac{3x^{\frac{2}{3}}}{2}+\dfrac{6x^{\frac{5}{6}}}{5}+C$

57. $\int \dfrac{x^2+\sqrt[3]{x^2}}{\sqrt{x}}\,dx = \int x^{\frac{3}{2}}+x^{\frac{1}{6}}\,dx = \dfrac{2x^{\frac{5}{2}}}{5}+\dfrac{6x^{\frac{7}{6}}}{7}+C$

58. $\displaystyle\int \frac{dx}{x^2 \sqrt[5]{x^2}} = \int x^{-\frac{12}{5}}\,dx = \frac{-5x^{-\frac{7}{5}}}{7} + C$

59. $\displaystyle\int (3x+5)\,dx = \frac{3x^2}{2} + 5x + C$

60. $\displaystyle\int (5x-7)^{-3}\,dx = \frac{(5x-7)^{-2}}{-10} + C$

61. $\displaystyle\int (15x-7)^{-\frac{1}{2}}\,dx = \frac{2(15x-7)^{\frac{1}{2}}}{15} + C$

62. $\displaystyle\int (12x+3)^{\frac{4}{7}}\,dx = \frac{7(12x+3)^{\frac{11}{7}}}{12\cdot 11} + C$

63. $\displaystyle\int (12x+3)^{-\frac{1}{12}}\,dx = \frac{(12x+3)^{\frac{11}{12}}}{11} + C$

64. $\displaystyle\int 6x(3x^2+5)^2\,dx = \frac{(3x^2+5)^3}{3} + C$

65. $\displaystyle\int 18x(6x^3+5)^{-1}\,dx = Ln(6x^3+5) + C$

66. $\displaystyle\int (60x^3-7)(15x^4-7x)^{-3}\,dx = \frac{(15x^4-7x)^{-2}}{-2} + C$

67. $\displaystyle\int (\frac{1}{x}+1)(\ln(x)+x)^{-\frac{1}{2}}\,dx = 2(\ln(x)+x)^{\frac{1}{2}} + C$

68. $\displaystyle\int 3x^4(2x^5+3)^{\frac{4}{7}}\,dx = \frac{21(2x^5+3)^{\frac{11}{7}}}{110} + C$

69. $\displaystyle\int (\frac{1}{\sqrt{x}}+2)(\sqrt{x}+x)^{\frac{2}{5}}\,dx = \frac{10(\sqrt{x}+x)^{\frac{7}{5}}}{7} + C$

70. $\displaystyle\int x^{-1}\,dx = Ln(x) + C$

71. $\displaystyle\int x^{-2}\,dx = -x^{-1} + C$

72. $\displaystyle\int e^{2x}(e^{2x}+2)^{-\frac{21}{4}}\,dx = \frac{-4(e^{2x}+2)^{-\frac{17}{4}}}{34} + C$

73. $\displaystyle\int \frac{2}{x+1}\,dx = 2Ln(x+1)+C$

74. $\displaystyle\int \frac{1}{5x+1}\,dx = \frac{Ln(5x+1)}{5}+C$

75. $\displaystyle\int \frac{x}{3x^2+5}\,dx = \frac{Ln(3x^2+5)}{6}+C$

76. $\displaystyle\int \frac{2x}{x^2+1}\,dx = Ln(x^2+1)+C$

77. $\displaystyle\int \frac{x^2}{x^3-5}\,dx = \frac{Ln(x^3-5)}{3}+C$

78. $\displaystyle\int \frac{2x^3}{3x^4-5}\,dx = \frac{Ln(3x^4-5)}{6}+C$

79. $\displaystyle\int \frac{x^{-\frac{1}{2}}-2}{x^{\frac{1}{2}}-x}\,dx = 2Ln(x^{\frac{1}{2}}-x)+C$

80. $\displaystyle\int \frac{3x^2+1}{x^3+x}\,dx = Ln(x^3+x)+C$

81. $\displaystyle\int \frac{3x^7}{2x^8+1}\,dx = \frac{3Ln(2x^8+1)}{16}+C$

82. $\displaystyle\int \frac{5x^{\frac{3}{2}}-4x}{x^{\frac{5}{2}}-x^2}\,dx = 2Ln(x^{\frac{5}{2}}-x^2)+C$

83. $\displaystyle\int \frac{-5e^x}{e^x-4}\,dx = -5Ln(e^x-4)+C$

84. $\displaystyle\int \frac{2e^{3x+1}}{e^{3x+1}-3}\,dx = \frac{2Ln(e^{3x+1}-3)}{3}+C$

85. $\displaystyle\int \frac{14e^{7x+2}-2}{e^{7x+2}-x}\,dx = 2Ln(e^{7x+2}-x)+C$

86. $\displaystyle\int \frac{4x+1}{8x^2+4x+4}\,dx = \frac{Ln(8x^2+4x+4)}{4}+C$

87. $\displaystyle\int \frac{(\tan(x)+3)^{-2}}{(\cos(x))^2}\,dx = -(\tan(x)+3)^{-1}+C$

88. $\displaystyle\int\frac{\sin(x)}{\cos(x)}dx=\int\tan(x)dx=-Ln(\cos(x))+C$

89. $\displaystyle\int\frac{1-\sin(x)}{x+\cos(x)}dx=\int\frac{1-\sin(x)}{x+\cos(x)}dx=Ln(x+\cos(x))+C$

90. $\displaystyle\int\frac{1}{x\ln(x)}dx=Ln(Ln(x))+C$

91. $\displaystyle\int\frac{1}{x\ln(2x)}dx=Ln(Ln(2x))+C$

92. $\displaystyle\int\frac{1}{(3x+1)\ln(3x+1)}dx=\frac{Ln(Ln(3x+1))}{3}+C$

93. $\displaystyle\int\frac{3x^2+5x-1}{x}dx=\int 3x+5-\frac{1}{x}dx=\frac{3x^2}{2}+5x-Ln(x)+C$

94. $\displaystyle\int\frac{x^3+x^2-2\sqrt{x}+1}{\sqrt[3]{x}}dx=\int x^{\frac{8}{3}}+x^{\frac{5}{3}}-2x^{\frac{1}{6}}+x^{-\frac{1}{3}}dx=\frac{3x^{\frac{11}{3}}}{11}+\frac{3x^{\frac{5}{3}}}{5}-\frac{12x^{\frac{7}{6}}}{7}+\frac{3x^{\frac{2}{3}}}{2}+C=$

95. $\displaystyle\int\frac{\sqrt{\sqrt{x}}}{x^4}dx=\int x^{-\frac{15}{4}}dx=-\frac{4x^{-\frac{11}{4}}}{11}+C$

96. $\displaystyle\int(x\sqrt{x}+\sqrt[5]{\frac{1}{x}})dx=\int(x^{\frac{3}{2}}+x^{-\frac{1}{5}})dx=\frac{2x^{\frac{5}{2}}}{5}+\frac{5x^{\frac{4}{5}}}{4}+C$

97. $\displaystyle\int\frac{\sqrt{\sqrt{x}}+\sqrt[3]{x^2}}{\sqrt[6]{x^2}}dx=\int x^{-\frac{1}{12}}+x^{\frac{1}{3}}dx=\frac{12x^{\frac{11}{12}}}{11}+\frac{3x^{\frac{4}{3}}}{4}+C$

98. $\displaystyle\int\frac{2x^3+2\sqrt[3]{x^4}}{\sqrt{x}}dx=\int 2x^{\frac{5}{2}}+2x^{\frac{5}{6}}dx=\frac{4x^{\frac{7}{2}}}{7}+\frac{12x^{\frac{11}{6}}}{11}+C$

99. $\displaystyle\int\frac{\sqrt[3]{x^4}}{x\cdot\sqrt{x}}dx=\int x^{-\frac{3}{4}}dx=4x^{\frac{1}{4}}+C$

100. $\displaystyle\int(\frac{1}{x^2}-\frac{1}{x+1})dx=-x^{-1}-Ln(x+1)+C$

101. $\displaystyle\int\left(\sqrt{x}+\frac{1}{\sqrt{x}}\right)^2dx=\int x+2+\frac{1}{x}dx=\frac{x^2}{2}+2x+Ln(x)+C=$

102. $\displaystyle\int\left(x^2+\frac{1}{x}\right)^3dx=\int x^6+3x^3+3+x^{-3}dx=\frac{x^7}{7}+\frac{3x^4}{4}+3x+\frac{x^{-2}}{-2}+C=$

103. $\int\left(\dfrac{1}{x^2}+\dfrac{1}{1+x^2}\right)dx=-x^{-1}+\arctan(x)+C$

104. $\int\left(\sqrt{x}+\dfrac{1}{x}\right)^2 dx=\int x+2x^{\frac{3}{2}}+x^{-2}\,dx=\dfrac{x^2}{2}+\dfrac{4x^{\frac{5}{2}}}{5}-x^{-1}+C=$

105. $\int (nx)^{\frac{1-n}{n}}\,dx=\int n^{\frac{1-n}{n}}x^{\frac{1-n}{n}}\,dx=\dfrac{n^{\frac{1-n}{n}}x^{\frac{1-n}{n}+1}}{\frac{1-n}{n}+1}=n^{\frac{1}{n}}x^{\frac{1}{n}}+C$

106. $\int (a^{\frac{2}{3}}-x^{\frac{2}{3}})^3\,dx=\int a^2-3a^{\frac{4}{3}}x^{\frac{2}{3}}+3a^{\frac{2}{3}}x^{\frac{4}{3}}-x^2\,dx=a^2 x-\dfrac{9a^{\frac{4}{3}}x^{\frac{5}{3}}}{5}+\dfrac{9a^{\frac{2}{3}}x^{\frac{7}{3}}}{7}-\dfrac{x^3}{3}+C$

107. $\int (\sqrt{x}+1)(x-\sqrt{x}+1)dx=\int x^{\frac{3}{2}}+1\,dx=\dfrac{2x^{\frac{5}{2}}}{5}+x+C$

108. $\int \dfrac{(x^2+1)(x^2-2)}{\sqrt[3]{x^2}}\,dx=\int x^{\frac{10}{3}}-x^{\frac{4}{3}}-2x^{-\frac{2}{3}}\,dx=\dfrac{3x^{\frac{13}{3}}}{13}-\dfrac{3x^{\frac{7}{3}}}{7}-6x^{\frac{1}{3}}+C$

109. $\int \sqrt{\dfrac{5}{x^3}}\,dx=\int \sqrt{5}\cdot x^{-\frac{3}{2}}\,dx=-2\sqrt{5}\cdot x^{-\frac{1}{2}}+C$

110. $\int (x+\sqrt{x})^2\,dx=\int x^2+2x^{\frac{3}{2}}+x\,dx=\dfrac{x^3}{3}+\dfrac{4x^{\frac{5}{2}}}{5}+\dfrac{x^2}{2}+C$

111. $\int \dfrac{5}{x+4}\,dx=5Ln(x+4)+C=$

112. $\int (x+\dfrac{1}{x^2})^3\,dx=\int x^3-3+3x^{-3}-x^{-6}\,dx=\dfrac{x^4}{4}-3x+\dfrac{3x^{-2}}{-2}-\dfrac{x^{-5}}{-5}+C$

113. $\int \dfrac{2}{2x+3}\,dx=Ln(2x+3)+C$

114. $\int \dfrac{e^x}{e^x+4}\,dx=Ln(e^x+4)+C$

115. $\int \dfrac{x^2}{x^3+8}\,dx=\dfrac{Ln(x^3+8)}{3}+C$

116. $\int \dfrac{a\,dx}{a-x}=-aLn(a-x)+C$

117. $\int \dfrac{e^{2x}}{e^{2x}+2}\,dx=\dfrac{Ln(e^{2x}+2)}{2}+C$

118. $\int \dfrac{sin(x)}{2+cos(x)}dx = -Ln(2+cos(x))+C$

119. $\int \dfrac{sin(Ln(x))}{x}dx = cos(Ln(x))+C$

120. $\int \dfrac{dx}{tg\left(\frac{x}{5}\right)} = \int \dfrac{cos(\frac{x}{5})}{sin(\frac{x}{5})}dx = 5Ln(sin(\frac{x}{5}))+C$

121. $\int \dfrac{tg\left(\sqrt{x}\right)}{\sqrt{x}}dx = \int \dfrac{sin\left(\sqrt{x}\right)}{\sqrt{x}\cdot cos\left(\sqrt{x}\right)}dx = -2Ln(cos(\sqrt{x}))+C$

122. $\int x\cot g\,(x^2+1)\,dx = \int \dfrac{x\cos(x^2+1)}{sin(x^2+1)}dx = \dfrac{Ln(sin(x^2+1))}{2}+C$

123. $\int \dfrac{Ln^3(x)}{x}dx = \dfrac{Ln^4(x)}{4}+C$

124. $\int \dfrac{e^x}{e^x-1}dx = Ln(e^x-1)+C =$

125. $\int \dfrac{\sqrt{x}+Ln^2(x)}{x}dx = \int x^{-\frac{1}{2}}+\dfrac{Ln^2(x)}{x}dx = 2x^{\frac{1}{2}}+\dfrac{Ln^3(x)}{3}+C =$

126. $\int \dfrac{x}{\sqrt{x^2+1}}dx = (x^2+1)^{\frac{1}{2}}+C$

127. $\int \sqrt{2-5x}\,dx = -\dfrac{2(2-5x)^{\frac{3}{2}}}{15}+C$

128. $\int \sqrt{5x^2-4x+3}\,(10x-4)dx = \dfrac{2(5x^2-4x+3)^{\frac{3}{2}}}{3}+C$

129. $\int \dfrac{x^2}{\sqrt{x^3+2}}dx = \dfrac{2(x^3+2)^{\frac{1}{2}}}{6}+C$

130. $\int \dfrac{3x^2}{\sqrt{1-2x^3}}dx = \dfrac{2(1-2x^3)^{\frac{1}{2}}}{-6}+C$

131. $\int 3x\sqrt{1-2x^2}\,dx = \dfrac{2(1-2x^2)^{\frac{3}{2}}}{-4}+C$

132. $\int \dfrac{x+3}{\sqrt{x^2+6x+4}}dx = (x^2+6x+4)^{\frac{1}{2}}+C$

133. $\displaystyle\int \frac{dx}{\sqrt{x+3}-\sqrt{x+2}} \cdot \frac{\sqrt{x+3}+\sqrt{x+2}}{\sqrt{x+3}+\sqrt{x+2}} = \int \frac{\sqrt{x+3}+\sqrt{x+2}}{1}dx = \frac{2(x+3)^{\frac{3}{2}}}{3} + \frac{2(x+2)^{\frac{3}{2}}}{3} + C$

134. $\displaystyle\int \frac{\sqrt{x^2+4}+x}{\sqrt{x^2+4}}dx = \int 1 + \frac{x}{\sqrt{x^2+4}}dx = x + (x^2+4)^{\frac{1}{2}} + C =$

135. $\displaystyle\int \frac{dx}{\sqrt{x}\sqrt{1+\sqrt{x}}} = 4(1+\sqrt{x})^{\frac{1}{2}} + C$

136. $\displaystyle\int \frac{e^x}{\sqrt{1+e^x}}dx = 2(1+e^x)^{\frac{1}{2}} + C$

137. $\displaystyle\int (\cos(x) - \sin(x))dx = \sin(x) + \cos(x) + C =$

138. $\displaystyle\int \frac{2 - 2\sin^2(x) + 3\cos(x)}{\cos(x)}dx = \int \frac{2\cos^2(x) + 3\cos(x)}{\cos(x)}dx = \int 2\cos(x) + 3\,dx = 2\sin(x) + 3x + C$

139. $\displaystyle\int \sin(x) \cdot \cos(x)\,dx = \frac{\sin^2(x)}{2} + C$

140. $\displaystyle\int \frac{\sin^2(x) - 1 + 5\sin^3(x)}{2\sin^2(x)}dx = \int \frac{1}{2} - \frac{1}{2\sin^2(x)} + \frac{5}{2}\sin(x)\,dx = \frac{x}{2} + \frac{\cot(x)}{2} - \frac{5}{2}\cos(x) + C$

141. $\displaystyle\int 4^x dx = \frac{4^x}{Ln(4)} + C$

142. $\displaystyle\int 7^x dx = \frac{7^x}{Ln(7)} + C$

143. $\displaystyle\int 5^{2x} dx = \frac{5^{2x}}{2\,Ln(5)} + C$

144. $\displaystyle\int x \cdot 6^{x^2} dx = \frac{6^{x^2}}{2\,Ln(6)} + C =$

145. $\displaystyle\int (\cos 3x)2^{\sin 3x} dx = \frac{2^{\sin 3x}}{3\,Ln(2)} + C$

146. $\displaystyle\int e^x \cdot 9^{e^x} dx = \frac{9^{e^x}}{Ln(9)} + C$

147. $\displaystyle\int x^2 \cdot 6^{4x^3+1} dx = \frac{6^{4x^3+1}}{12\,Ln(6)} + C$

148. $\int \dfrac{4^{\sqrt{x}}}{\sqrt{x}}dx = \dfrac{2\cdot 4^{\sqrt{x}}}{Ln(4)}+C$

149. $\int e^{3x}dx = \dfrac{e^{3x}}{3}+C$

150. $\int xe^{3x^2}dx = \dfrac{e^{3x^2}}{6}+C$

151. $\int \dfrac{e^x+e^{-x}}{\left(e^x-e^{-x}\right)^2}dx = -(e^x-e^{-x})^{-1}+C$

152. $\int \dfrac{e^{3x}+e^x+2}{e^x}dx = \int e^{2x}+1+2\cdot e^{-x}dx = \dfrac{e^{2x}}{2}+x-2\cdot e^{-x}+C$

153. $\int e^x\left(e^x+2\right)^2 dx = \dfrac{\left(e^x+2\right)^3}{3}+C$

154. $\int \cos(x)\cdot e^{\sin(x)}dx = e^{\sin(x)}+C$

155. $\int \dfrac{e^{\frac{1}{x}}}{x^2}dx = -e^{\frac{1}{x}}+C$

156. $\int e^x\sqrt{1-e^x}\,dx = \dfrac{-2(1-e^x)^{\frac{3}{2}}}{3}+C$

157. $\int \left(x^2-2\right)e^{x^3-6x+5}dx = \dfrac{e^{x^3-6x+5}}{3}+C$

158. $\int \left(e^x-e^{-x}\right)\left(e^x+e^{-x}\right)^4 dx = \dfrac{\left(e^x+e^{-x}\right)^5}{5}+C$

159. $\int \dfrac{1}{2x+3}dx = \dfrac{Ln(2x+3)}{2}+C$

160. $\int \dfrac{1}{2-3x}dx = \dfrac{Ln(2-3x)}{-3}+C$

161. $\int \dfrac{x^2+2x+3}{x}dx = \int x+2+\dfrac{3}{x}dx = \dfrac{x^2}{2}+2x+3Ln(x)+C$

162. $\int \dfrac{e^x}{1+e^x}dx = Ln(1+e^x)+C$

163. $\displaystyle\int \frac{\left(\ln(x)\right)^3}{x}dx = \frac{(Ln(x))^4}{4}+C$

164. $\displaystyle\int \frac{x+2}{x-1}dx = Dividing \quad polynomials... = \int 1+\frac{3}{x-1}dx = x+3Ln(x-1)+C$

165. $\displaystyle\int \frac{x^2+2x+3}{x+1}dx = Dividing \quad polynomials... = \int x+1+\frac{2}{x+1}dx = \frac{x^2}{2}+x+2Ln(x+1)+C$

166. $\displaystyle\int (e^x-e^{-x})^2 dx = \int e^{2x}-2+e^{-2x}dx = \frac{e^{2x}}{2}-2x+\frac{e^{-2x}}{-2}+C$

167. $\displaystyle\int \frac{\cos(x)}{\sin(x)}dx = Ln(\sin(x))+C$

168. $\displaystyle\int \frac{\ln(x)}{x}dx = \frac{(\ln(x))^2}{2}+C$

169. $\displaystyle\int \frac{xdx}{x+1} = \int 1-\frac{1}{x+1}dx = x-Ln(x+1)+C$

170. $\displaystyle\int x^2 e^{x^3} dx = \frac{e^{x^3}}{3}+C$

171. $\displaystyle\int \frac{x-2}{x+1}dx = \int 1-\frac{3}{x+1}dx = x-3Ln(x+1)+C$

172. $\displaystyle\int \frac{2x-3}{x+1}dx = \int 2-\frac{5}{x+1}dx = 2x-5Ln(x+1)+C$

INTEGRATION BY PARTS

$$\int f'(x)g(x) = f(x)g(x)-\int f(x)g'(x)$$

173. $\displaystyle\int \ln(x)dx = x\ln(x)-\int 1dx = x\ln(x)-x+C$

174. $\displaystyle\int \frac{Ln(x)}{x^2}dx = -x^{-1}Ln(x)-\int -x^{-2}dx = -x^{-1}Ln(x)-x^{-1}+C$

175. $\displaystyle\int x\ln(x)dx = \frac{x^2}{2}\ln(x)-\int \frac{x}{2}dx = \frac{x^2}{2}\ln(x)-\frac{x^2}{4}+C$

176. $\displaystyle\int x^2 \ln(x)dx = \frac{x^3}{3}\ln(x)-\int \frac{x^2}{3}dx = \frac{x^3}{3}\ln(x)-\frac{x^3}{9}+C$

177. $\displaystyle\int x\sin(x)dx = -x\cos(x)-\int -\cos(x)dx = -x\cos(x)+\sin(x)+C$

178. $$\int x^2 \sin(2x)dx = -\frac{x^2 \cos(2x)}{2} - \int -x\cos(2x)dx = -\frac{x^2 \cos(2x)}{2} - \left(-\frac{x\sin(2x)}{2} - \int -\frac{\sin(2x)}{2}dx \right) =$$

$$-\frac{x^2 \cos(2x)}{2} - \left(-\frac{x\sin(2x)}{2} - \frac{\cos(2x)}{4} \right) = -\frac{x^2 \cos(2x)}{2} + \frac{x\sin(2x)}{2} + \frac{\cos(2x)}{4} + C$$

179. $$\int \mathrm{tg}^2\, x\, dx = \int \frac{\sin^2(x)}{\cos^2(x)}\, dx = \int \frac{1-\cos^2(x)}{\cos^2(x)}\, dx = \int \frac{1}{\cos^2(x)} - 1\, dx = \tan(x) - x + C$$

180. $$\int (x^2+x)e^{-3x}dx = \frac{e^{-3x}}{-3}(x^2+x) - \int \frac{e^{-3x}}{-3}(2x+1)dx = \frac{e^{-3x}}{-3}(x^2+x) - \left(\frac{e^{-3x}}{9}(2x+1) - \int \frac{e^{-3x}}{9}2dx \right) =$$

$$\frac{e^{-3x}}{-3}(x^2+x) - \left(\frac{e^{-3x}}{9}(2x+1) - \frac{2e^{-3x}}{-27} \right) = \frac{e^{-3x}}{-3}(x^2+x) - \frac{e^{-3x}}{9}(2x+1) + \frac{2e^{-3x}}{-27} + C$$

181. $$\int (2-x^2)\cos(-3x)dx = \frac{(2-x^2)\sin(-3x)}{-3} - \int \frac{-2x\sin(-3x)}{-3}dx =$$

$$\frac{(2-x^2)\sin(-3x)}{-3} - \left(\frac{2x\cos(-3x)}{-9} - \int \frac{2\cos(-3x)}{-9}dx \right) =$$

$$\frac{(2-x^2)\sin(-3x)}{-3} - \frac{2x\cos(-3x)}{9} + \frac{2\sin(-3x)}{27} + C$$

182. $$\int e^x \cos(x)dx = e^x \cos(x) + \int e^x \sin(x)dx = e^x \cos(x) + \left(e^x \sin(x) - \int e^x \cos(x)dx \right)$$

$$\int e^x \cos(x)dx = e^x \cos(x) + e^x \sin(x) - \int e^x \cos(x)dx$$

$$2\int e^x \cos(x)dx = e^x \cos(x) + e^x \sin(x); \int e^x \cos(x)dx = \frac{1}{2}\left(e^x \cos(x) + e^x \sin(x) + C \right)$$

183. $$\int e^{2x} \sin(3x)dx = \frac{e^{2x}}{2}\sin(3x) - \int \frac{e^{2x}}{2}3\cos(3x)dx = \frac{e^{2x}}{2}\sin(3x) - \left(\frac{e^{2x}}{4}3\cos(3x) - \int \frac{e^{2x}}{4}9(-\sin(3x))dx \right)$$

$$\int e^{2x} \sin(3x)dx = \frac{e^{2x}}{2}\sin(3x) - \frac{e^{2x}}{4}3\cos(3x) - \frac{e^{2x}}{4}9(-\sin(3x))$$

$$\frac{13}{4}\int e^{2x} \sin(3x)dx = \frac{e^{2x}}{2}\sin(3x) - \frac{e^{2x}}{4}3\cos(3x); \int e^{2x} \sin(3x)dx = \frac{4}{13}\left(\frac{e^{2x}}{2}\sin(3x) - \frac{e^{2x}}{4}3\cos(3x) + C \right)$$

184. $$\int (\ln(x))^2\, dx = x(\ln(x))^2 - \int \ln(x)dx = x(\ln(x))^2 - x\ln(x) + x + C$$

INTEGRALS ARCSIN, ARCOS, ARCTAN TYPE

185. $$\int \frac{2}{x^2+1}\cdot dx = 2\arctan(x) + C$$

186. $$\int \frac{2x}{x^2+1}\cdot dx = Ln(x^2+1) + C$$

187. $$\int \frac{-11}{x^2+4}dx = \frac{-11}{2}\int \frac{1}{\left(\frac{x}{2}\right)^2+1}dx = \frac{-11}{2}\arctan\left(\frac{x}{2}\right) + C$$

188. $\displaystyle\int\frac{7}{2x^2+3}\,dx=\frac{7}{3}\int\frac{1}{\left(\sqrt{\frac{2}{3}}x\right)^2+1}\,dx=\frac{7}{3}\sqrt{\frac{3}{2}}\arctan\left(\sqrt{\frac{2}{3}}x\right)+C$

189. $\displaystyle\int\frac{1}{x^2+2x+2}\,dx=\int\frac{1}{(x+1)^2+1}\,dx=\arctan(x+1)+C$

190. $\displaystyle\int\frac{-15}{x^2+4x+10}\,dx=\int\frac{-15}{(x+2)^2+6}\,dx=\frac{-15}{6}\int\frac{1}{\left(\frac{x+2}{\sqrt{6}}\right)^2+1}\,dx=\frac{-15\sqrt{6}}{6}\arctan\left(\frac{x+2}{\sqrt{6}}\right)+C$

191. $\displaystyle\int\frac{2}{x^2-6x+10}\,dx=\int\frac{2}{(x-3)^2+1}\,dx=2\arctan(x-3)+C$

192. $\displaystyle\int\frac{1}{\sqrt{1-4x^2}}\,dx=\frac{\arcsin(\sqrt{2}x)}{\sqrt{2}}+C$

193. $\displaystyle\int\frac{1}{1+9x^2}\,dx=\frac{\arctan(3x)}{3}+C$

194. $\displaystyle\int\frac{x}{\sqrt{1-x^4}}\,dx=\frac{\arcsin(x^2)}{2}+C$

195. $\displaystyle\int\frac{e^x}{1+e^{2x}}\,dx=\arctan(e^x)+C$

196. $\displaystyle\int\frac{x^2}{1+x^6}\,dx=\frac{\arctan(x^3)}{3}+C$

197. $\displaystyle\int\frac{1}{\sqrt{1-\frac{x^2}{4}}}\,dx=2\arcsin(\frac{x}{2})+C$

198. $\displaystyle\int\frac{1}{1+\frac{x^2}{9}}\,dx=3\arctan(\frac{x}{3})+C$

INTEGRATION USING A CHANGE OF VARIABLE

199. $\displaystyle\int\frac{e^x}{e^x+1}\,dx=\int\frac{t}{t+1}\frac{dt}{t}=Ln(1+t)=Ln(1+e^x)+C$

$t=e^x;\,dt=e^x\,dx;\,\dfrac{dt}{t}=dx$

200. $\displaystyle\int\frac{1}{x\sqrt{x-1}}\cdot dx=\int\frac{1}{(t^2+1)t}2t\,dt=\int\frac{1}{(t^2+1)}2\,dt=2\arctan(t)=2\arctan(e^x)+C$

$t=\sqrt{x-1};\,x=t^2+1;\,dt=\dfrac{1}{2}\left(x-1\right)^{-\frac{1}{2}}dx;\,dx;\,2t\,dt=dx$

$$\int \frac{x^5}{(1+x^2)^4} \cdot dx = \int \frac{(t-1)^{\frac{5}{4}}}{t^4} \cdot \frac{dt}{2\sqrt{t-1}} = \int \frac{(t-1)^2}{2t^4} dt = \int \frac{t^2-2t+1}{2t^4} dt =$$

201.
$$\frac{1}{2}\int t^{-2} - 2t^{-3} + t^{-4} dt = \frac{1}{2}(Ln(t) + t^{-2} - \frac{t^{-3}}{3}) + C = \frac{1}{2}(-(1+x^2)^{-1} + (1+x^2)^{-2} - \frac{(1+x^2)^{-3}}{3}) + C$$

$$t = 1 + x^2; x = \sqrt{t-1}; dt = 2x dx; \frac{dt}{2\sqrt{t-1}} = dx$$

202.
$$\int x\sqrt{x-1} \cdot dx = \int (t^2+1)t \cdot 2t dt = 2\int (t^4+t^2) dt = 2(\frac{t^5}{5} + \frac{t^3}{3}) = 2(\frac{(x-1)^{\frac{5}{2}}}{5} + \frac{(x-1)^{\frac{3}{2}}}{3}) + C$$

$$t = \sqrt{x-1}; x = t^2 + 1; dx = 2t dt$$

203.
$$\int \frac{x}{(x-2)^3} \cdot dx = \int \frac{t+2}{t^3} \cdot dt = \int t^{-2} + 2t^{-3} \cdot dt = -t^{-1} - \frac{t^{-2}}{2} = -(x-2)^{-1} - \frac{(x-2)^{-2}}{2} + C$$

$$t = x - 2; x = t + 2; dx = dt$$

$$\int \sqrt{4-x^2} \, dx = 2\int \sqrt{4-4\sin^2(t)} \, \cos(t) dt = 2\int 2\cos^2(t) dt = 4\int \frac{\cos(2t)+1}{2} dt =$$

204.
$$\sin(2t) + 2t = \sin(2\arcsin(\frac{x}{2})) + 2\arcsin(\frac{x}{2}) = x\cos(\arcsin(\frac{x}{2})) + 2\arcsin(\frac{x}{2}) =$$

$$x\sqrt{1-\frac{x^2}{4}} + 2\arcsin(\frac{x}{2}) + C$$

$$x = 2\sin(t); t = \arcsin(\frac{x}{2}); dx = 2\cos(t) dt$$

$$\int \cos(\sqrt{x}) dx = \int \cos(t) 2t dt = \sin(t) \cdot 2t - 2\int \sin(t) dt = \sin(t) \cdot 2t + 2\cos(t) =$$

205.
$$\sin(\sqrt{x}) \cdot 2\sqrt{x} + 2\cos(\sqrt{x}) + C$$

$$x = t^2; t = \sqrt{x}; dx = 2t dt$$

PRACTICE

206.
$$\int x\sin(1-x^2) \, dx = \frac{\cos(1-x^2)}{2} + C$$

207.
$$\int \frac{1}{1+x^2} dx = \arctan(x) + C$$

208.
$$\int (tg(x) + \cot g(x))^2 dx = \int (tg^2(x) + 2 + \cot g^2(x)) dx =$$

$$\int (\frac{1-\cos^2(x)}{\cos^2(x)} + 2 + \frac{1-\sin^2(x)}{\sin^2(x)}) dx = \tan(x) - \cot g(x) + C =$$

209.
$$\int \frac{dx}{sin(x)} = \frac{1}{2}\int \frac{sin^2(\frac{x}{2})+cos^2(\frac{x}{2})}{sin(\frac{x}{2})cos(\frac{x}{2})}dx = \frac{1}{2}\int \frac{sin(\frac{x}{2})}{cos(\frac{x}{2})}+\frac{cos(\frac{x}{2})}{sin(\frac{x}{2})}dx =$$

$$-Ln(cos(\frac{x}{2}))+Ln(sin(\frac{x}{2})) = Ln(tan(\frac{x}{2}))+C$$

210.
$$\int \frac{dx}{sin(x)\cdot cos(x)} = \int \frac{(sin^2(x)+cos^2(x))}{sin(x)\cdot cos(x)}dx = \int \frac{sin(x)}{cos(x)}+\frac{cos(x)}{sin(x)}dx =$$

$$-Ln(cos(x)+Ln(sin(x)) = Ln(tan(x))+C$$

211.
$$\int \frac{e^x}{\sqrt{1-e^{2x}}}dx = arcsin(e^x)+C$$

212.
$$\int \frac{dx}{e^x\sqrt{1-e^{-2x}}} = -arcsin(e^{-x})+C$$

213.
$$\int \frac{dx}{x(Ln^2(x)+1)} = arctan(Ln(x))+c$$

214.
$$\int \frac{e^{\sqrt{x}}+x}{\sqrt{x}}dx = \int \frac{e^{\sqrt{x}}}{\sqrt{x}}+x^{\frac{1}{2}}dx = 2e^{\sqrt{x}}+\frac{2}{3}x^{\frac{3}{2}}+C$$

215.
$$\int \frac{x-\sqrt{arctg\,(2x)}}{1+4x^2}dx = \int \frac{x}{1+4x^2}-\frac{\sqrt{arctg\,(2x)}}{1+4x^2}dx = \frac{1}{8}Ln(1+4x^2)-\frac{2}{3}\left(arctg\,(2x)\right)^{\frac{3}{2}}+C$$

216.
$$\int \frac{x^2}{\sqrt{1-x^6}}dx = \frac{arc\,sin(x^3)}{3}+C$$

217.
$$\int \frac{dx}{\sqrt{4-x^2}} = \frac{1}{2}\int \frac{dx}{\sqrt{1-\left(\frac{x}{2}\right)^2}} = arcsin(\frac{x}{2})+C$$

218.
$$\int \frac{dx}{9+x^2} = \frac{1}{9}\int \frac{dx}{1+\left(\frac{x}{3}\right)^2} = \frac{1}{3}arctan(\frac{x}{3})+C$$

219.
$$\int \frac{dx}{\sqrt{25-x^2}} = \frac{1}{5}\int \frac{dx}{\sqrt{1-\left(\frac{x}{5}\right)^2}} = arcsin(\frac{x}{5})+C$$

220.
$$\int \frac{dx}{16+x^2} = \frac{1}{4}arctan(\frac{x}{4})+C$$

222.
$$\int \frac{dx}{1+16x^2} = \frac{1}{4}arctan(4x)+C$$

221.
$$\int \frac{dx}{\sqrt{1-9x^2}} = \frac{1}{3}arcsin(3x)+c$$

223.
$$\int \frac{e^{2x}}{\sqrt{1-e^{4x}}}dx = \frac{1}{2}arcsin(e^{2x})+C$$

224. $\displaystyle\int \frac{x}{4+x^4}\,dx = \frac{1}{4}\int \frac{x}{1+\left(\dfrac{x^2}{2}\right)^2}\,dx = \frac{1}{4}\arctan\left(\frac{x^2}{2}\right)+C$

225. $\displaystyle\int \frac{x^2}{\sqrt{100-x^6}}\,dx = \frac{1}{10}\int \frac{x^2}{\sqrt{1-\left(\dfrac{x^3}{10}\right)^2}}\,dx = \frac{1}{3}\arcsin\left(\frac{x^3}{10}\right)+C$

226. $\displaystyle\int \frac{x^3}{1+x^8}\,dx = \frac{1}{4}\arctan(x^4)+C$

227. $\displaystyle\int \frac{\sin(\theta)}{1+\cos^2(\theta)}\,d\theta = -\arctan(\cos(\theta))+C$

228. $\displaystyle\int \sqrt{\frac{arcsin(x)}{1-x^2}}\,dx = \frac{2}{3}\left(arcsin(x)\right)^{\frac{3}{2}}+C$

229. $\displaystyle\int \frac{a^x}{1+a^{2x}}\,dx = \frac{1}{Ln(a)}\arctan(a^x)+C$

230. $\displaystyle\int \frac{x}{\cos^2\left(x^2\right)}\,dx = -\frac{1}{2}\left(\cos(x^2)\right)^{-1}+C$

231. $\displaystyle\int \frac{e^t}{\sqrt{1-e^{2t}}}\,dt = \arcsin(e^t)+C$

232. $\displaystyle\int \frac{dx}{x^2\left(1+\left(\frac{1}{x}\right)^2\right)} = -\arctan(x^{-1})+C$

233. $\displaystyle\int \frac{dx}{x^2+7} = \frac{1}{7}\int \frac{dx}{\left(\dfrac{x}{\sqrt{7}}\right)^2+1} = \frac{\sqrt{7}}{7}\arctan\left(\frac{x}{\sqrt{7}}\right)+C$

234. $\displaystyle\int \frac{dx}{\sqrt{4-x^2}} = \frac{1}{2}\int \frac{dx}{\sqrt{1-\left(\dfrac{x}{2}\right)^2}} = \arcsin\left(\frac{x}{2}\right)+C$

235. $\displaystyle\int \frac{\sqrt{2+x^2}}{\sqrt{4-x^4}}\,dx = \int \frac{\sqrt{2+x^2}}{\sqrt{2+x^2}\,\sqrt{2-x^2}}\,dx = \int \frac{1}{\sqrt{2-x^2}}\,dx = \arcsin\left(\frac{x}{\sqrt{2}}\right)+C$

236. $\displaystyle\int \frac{dx}{x\sqrt{x^2-2}} = \int \frac{2t}{(t^2+2)t}\,dt = 2\int \frac{1}{(t^2+2)}\,dt = \sqrt{2}\arctan\left(\frac{t}{\sqrt{2}}\right) = \sqrt{2}\arctan\left(\frac{\sqrt{x^2-2}}{\sqrt{2}}\right)+C$

$t=\sqrt{x^2-2}; x=t^2+2; dx=2tdt$

237. $\displaystyle\int \frac{x}{a^4+x^4}\,dx = \frac{1}{a^4}\int \frac{x}{1+\left(\dfrac{x^2}{a^2}\right)^2}\,dx = \frac{1}{2a^2}\arctan\left(\frac{x^2}{a^2}\right)+C$

238. $\int \dfrac{1+2x}{1+x^2}\,dx = \int \dfrac{1}{1+x^2} + \dfrac{2x}{1+x^2}\,dx = \arctan(x) + Ln(1+x^2) + C$

239. $\int \dfrac{dx}{3x^2+5} = \dfrac{1}{5}\int \dfrac{dx}{\left(\sqrt{\dfrac{3}{5}}x\right)^2+1} = \dfrac{1}{\sqrt{15}}\arctan\left(\sqrt{\dfrac{3}{5}}x\right) + C$

240. $\int \dfrac{2x+3}{2x+1}\,dx = \int 1 + \dfrac{2}{2x+1}\,dx = x + Ln(2x+1) + C$

241. $\int \dfrac{2x-5}{3x^2+2}\,dx = \int \dfrac{2x}{3x^2+2} - \dfrac{5}{3x^2+2}\,dx = 3Ln(3x^2+2) - \dfrac{5}{\sqrt{6}}\arctan\left(x\sqrt{\dfrac{3}{2}}\right) + C$

242. $\int \dfrac{x^3}{\sqrt{a^4-x^4}}\,dx = -\dfrac{1}{2}\left(a^4-x^4\right)^{\frac{1}{2}} + C$

243. $\int \dfrac{dx}{\sqrt{9-16x^2}} = \dfrac{1}{3}\int \dfrac{dx}{\sqrt{1-\left(\dfrac{4x}{3}\right)^2}} = \dfrac{1}{4}\arcsin\left(\dfrac{4x}{3}\right) + C$

244. $\int \dfrac{x}{(x+1)^2}\,dx = \int \dfrac{t-1}{t^2}\,dt = \int \dfrac{1}{t} - t^{-2}\,dt = Ln(t) + t^{-1} = Ln(x+1) + (x+1)^{-1} + C$

$t = x+1; \; x = t-1; \; dt = dx$

245. $\int 3^{2+x}\,dx = \dfrac{3^{2+x}}{Ln(3)} + C$

246. $\int \dfrac{3^x + 4^{x+1}}{5^x}\,dx = \int \left(\dfrac{3}{5}\right)^x + 4\left(\dfrac{4}{5}\right)^x\,dx = \dfrac{\left(\dfrac{3}{5}\right)^x}{Ln\left(\dfrac{3}{5}\right)} + 4\dfrac{\left(\dfrac{4}{5}\right)^x}{Ln\left(\dfrac{4}{5}\right)} + C$

247. $\int 3^x e^x\,dx = \int (3e)^x\,dx = \dfrac{(3e)^x}{Ln(3e)} + C$

251. $\int \dfrac{dx}{\sqrt{a-bx}} = -\dfrac{2}{b}\left(a-bx\right)^{\frac{1}{2}} + C$

248. $\int a^{5x^2} 10x\,dx = \dfrac{a^{5x^2}}{Ln(a)} + C$

252. $\int x^{n-1} \cdot \sqrt{a+bx^n}\,dx = \dfrac{2}{3bn}\left(a+bx^n\right)^{\frac{3}{2}} + C$

249. $\int x7^{x^2}\,dx = \dfrac{7^{x^2}}{2Ln(7)} + C$

253. $\int \dfrac{e^x}{e^{2x}+1}\,dx = \arctan(e^x) + C$

250. $\int e^x\sqrt{a-be^x}\,dx = -\dfrac{2}{3b}\left(a-be^x\right)^{\frac{3}{2}} + C$

254. $\int \dfrac{x}{\sqrt{3x^2-3}}\,dx = \dfrac{1}{3}\left(3x^2-3\right)^{\frac{1}{2}} + C$

255.
$\int \dfrac{2+\sqrt[6]{x-1}}{\sqrt[3]{(x-1)^2} - \sqrt{x-1}}\,dx = \int \dfrac{2+t}{t^4-t^3}6t^5\,dt = \int \dfrac{t^5(12+t)}{t^3(t-1)}\,dt = \int \dfrac{12t^2+t^3}{t-1}\,dt =$

$\dfrac{t^3}{3} + \dfrac{13t^2}{2} + 13t + 13\ln(t-1) = \dfrac{(x-1)^{\frac{1}{2}}}{3} + \dfrac{13(x-1)^{\frac{1}{3}}}{2} + 13(x-1)^{\frac{1}{6}} + 13\ln\left((x-1)^{\frac{1}{6}} - 1\right) + C$

$x-1 = t^6; \; dx = 6t^5\,dt$

$$\int \frac{x-\sqrt{x-1}}{x+\sqrt{x-1}}dx = \int \frac{1+t^2-t}{1+t^2+t}2tdt = \int \frac{t^3-t^2+t}{t^2+t+1}dt = \frac{t^2}{2}-2t+\ln(t^2+t+1)+\frac{2}{\sqrt{3}}\arctan(\frac{1+2t}{\sqrt{3}})$$

256. $$\frac{(x-1)}{2}-2(x-1)^{\frac{1}{2}}+\ln((x-1)+(x-1)^{\frac{1}{2}}+1)+\frac{2}{\sqrt{3}}\arctan(\frac{1+2(x-1)^{\frac{1}{2}}}{\sqrt{3}})$$

$$x-1=t^2;t=(x-1)^{\frac{1}{2}};dx=2tdt$$

257. $$\int \frac{x\ln(2x^2+2)}{x^2+1}dx = \int \frac{x\ln(2(x^2+1))}{x^2+1}dx = \int \frac{x\ln(2)+xLn(x^2+1)}{x^2+1}dx =$$
$$\frac{\ln(2)}{2}Ln(x^2+1)+\frac{\left(Ln(x^2+1)\right)^2}{4}+C$$

258. $$\int \frac{2x}{x-4}dx = \int 2+\frac{8}{x-4}dx = 2x+8\ln(x-4)+C$$

259. $$\int \frac{e^x}{1+e^x}dx = Ln(1+e^x)+C$$

260. $$\int \frac{5x}{(x-4)^3}dx = \int \frac{5t+20}{t^3}dx = \int 5t^{-2}+20t^{-3}dx = -5t^{-1}-10t^{-2} = -5(x-4)^{-1}-10(x-4)^{-2}+C$$

$$t=x-4;x=t+4;dx=dt$$

261. $$\int (-2x+5)^{\frac{3}{2}}dx = -\frac{1}{5}(-2x+5)^{\frac{5}{2}}+C$$

262. $$\int xe^{-2x}dx = \frac{e^{-2x}}{-2}x-\int \frac{e^{-2x}}{-2}dx = \frac{e^{-2x}}{-2}x-\frac{e^{-2x}}{4}+C$$

263. $$\int \frac{\ln(x)}{x}dx = \frac{(Ln(x))^2}{2}+C$$

264. $$\int x^2e^{-2x}dx = -\frac{1}{4}(1+2x+2x^2)e^{-2x}+C$$

265. $$\int \frac{t}{t^4+16}dt = \frac{1}{16}\int \frac{t}{\left(\frac{t^2}{4}\right)^2+1}dt = \frac{1}{8}\arctan(\frac{t^2}{4})+C$$

266. $$\int \frac{e^x}{\sqrt{1-e^{2x}}}dx = \arcsin(e^x)+C$$

267. $$\int \frac{1}{x^2+6x+13}dx = \int \frac{1}{(x+3)^2+4}dx = \frac{1}{4}\int \frac{1}{(\frac{x+3}{2})^2+1}dxdx = \frac{1}{2}\arctan(\frac{x+3}{2})+C$$

268. $$\int \frac{\cos(x)}{\sqrt{4-\sin^2(x)}}dx = \frac{1}{2}\int \frac{\cos(x)}{\sqrt{1-\left(\frac{\sin(x)}{2}\right)^2}}dx = \arcsin(\frac{\sin(x)}{2})+C$$

1.10. – DEFINITE INTEGRTION

The result of indefinite integration is a: <u>function</u> $= F(x) = \int f(x)dx$

The result of definite integration is <u>a number</u> $= \int_{a}^{b} f(x)dx = F(b) - F(a)$

Definite integration represents the "**area under the graph**".

1. Above the x axis definite integrals have a <u>positive sign.</u>

2. Below the x axis definite integrals have a <u>negative sign.</u>

3. $\int_{2}^{3} \frac{1}{x} + 2x \, dx = \left[Ln(x) + x^2 \right]_{2}^{3} = \left[Ln(3) + 9 \right] - \left[Ln(2) + 4 \right] = Ln(\frac{3}{2}) + 5$

4. $\int_{\pi}^{\frac{3\pi}{2}} \cos(x) + x \, dx = \left[\sin(\frac{3\pi}{2}) + \frac{1}{2}\left(\frac{3\pi}{2}\right)^2 \right] - \left[\sin(\pi) + \frac{1}{2}\pi^2 \right] = -1 + \frac{5}{8}\pi^2$

5. $\int_{1}^{e} (\ln(x)) \, dx = 1$

6. $\int_{2}^{6} x^2 + 1 \, dx = \left[\frac{x^3}{3} + x \right]_{2}^{6} = \left[\frac{216}{3} + 6 \right] - \left[\frac{8}{3} + 2 \right] = \frac{220}{3}$

7. $\int_{0}^{2} 3^x \, dx = \left[\frac{3^x}{Ln(3)} \right]_{0}^{2} = \left[\frac{9}{Ln(3)} \right] - \left[\frac{1}{Ln(3)} \right] = \frac{8}{Ln(3)}$

8. $\int_{1}^{\sqrt{2}} x \cdot 2^{-x^2} \, dx = \left[\frac{2^{-x^2}}{-2Ln(2)} \right]_{1}^{\sqrt{2}} = \left[\frac{2^{-2}}{-2Ln(2)} \right] - \left[\frac{2^{-1}}{-2Ln(2)} \right] = \frac{1}{8Ln(2)}$

9. $\int_{0}^{\frac{\pi}{6}} (\cos(\theta)) 4^{-\sin(\theta)} \, d\theta = \left[\frac{-4^{-\sin(\theta)}}{Ln(4)} \right]_{0}^{\frac{\pi}{6}} = \left[\frac{-4^{-\sin(\frac{\pi}{6})}}{Ln(4)} \right] - \left[\frac{-4^{-\sin(0)}}{Ln(4)} \right] = \left[\frac{1}{2Ln(4)} \right]$

10. $\int_{-3}^{-1} 10^{-x} \, dx = \left[\frac{-10^{-x}}{Ln(10)} \right]_{-3}^{-1} = \left[\frac{-10}{Ln(10)} \right] - \left[\frac{-10^3}{Ln(10)} \right] = \frac{990}{Ln(10)}$

11. $\int_{0}^{\frac{1}{2}} \frac{1}{\sqrt{1-x^2}} \, dx \approx 0.524$

12. $\int_{\sqrt{2}}^{2} \frac{1}{x\sqrt{x^2-1}} \, dx \approx 0.268$

13. $\int_{-1}^{1} \frac{1}{1+x^2} \, dx \approx 1.57$

14. $\int_{0}^{3} e^{3-x} \, dx = \left[e^{3-x} \right]_{0}^{3} = \left[e^0 \right] - \left[e^3 \right] = 1 - e^3$

15. $\int_{0}^{1} \frac{x^3}{x^4+1} \, dx = \left[\frac{Ln(x^4+1)}{4} \right]_{0}^{1} = \left[\frac{Ln(2)}{4} \right] - \left[\frac{Ln(1)}{4} \right] = \frac{Ln(2)}{4}$

16. $\int_{\frac{\pi}{6}}^{\frac{\pi}{2}} \frac{\cos(x)}{\sin(x)} dx = \left[Ln(\sin(x)) \right]_{\frac{\pi}{6}}^{\frac{\pi}{2}} = \left[Ln(\sin(\frac{\pi}{2})) \right] - \left[Ln(\sin(\frac{\pi}{6})) \right] = Ln(2)$

17. $\int_{0}^{\frac{1}{6}} \frac{1}{\sqrt{1-9x^2}} dx \approx 0.175$

18. $\int_{\sqrt{3}}^{3} \frac{1}{9+x^2} dx \approx 0.0873$

19. $\int_{1}^{e^2} \frac{3}{x} dx = \left[3Ln(x) \right]_{1}^{e^2} = \left[3Ln(e^2) \right] - \left[3Ln(1) \right] = 6$

BOUNDARY CONDITION

20. Given that $\int \frac{1}{x} dx = F(x)$ and that $F(1) = 2$ find $F(x)$.

$\int \frac{1}{x} dx = Ln(x) + C; Ln(1) + C = 2; C = 2; F(x) = Ln(x) + 2$

21. Given that $\int \sin(2x) dx = F(x)$ and that $F(\pi) = 1$ find $F(x)$.

$\int \sin(2x) dx = \frac{-\cos(2x)}{2} + C; \frac{-\cos(2\pi)}{2} + C = 1; C = \frac{3}{2}; F(x) = \frac{-\cos(2x)}{2} + \frac{3}{2}$

22. Given that $\int e^{2x} + (x-1)^6 dx = F(x)$ and that $F(0) = 1$ find $F(x)$.

$\int e^{2x} + (x-1)^6 dx = \frac{e^{2x}}{2} + \frac{(x-1)^7}{7} + C; \frac{e^0}{2} - \frac{1}{7} + C = 1; F(x) = \frac{e^{2x}}{2} + \frac{(x-1)^7}{7} + \frac{9}{14}$

23. Given that $\int \sqrt{x} + x dx = F(x)$ and that $F(1) = 1$ find $F(x)$.

$\int \sqrt{x} + x dx = \frac{2x^{\frac{3}{2}}}{3} + \frac{x^2}{2} + C; \frac{2}{3} + \frac{1}{2} + C = 1; C = -\frac{1}{6}; F(x) = \frac{2x^{\frac{3}{2}}}{3} + \frac{x^2}{2} - \frac{1}{6}$

FINDING AREAS

24. Find the area enclosed between the functions $f(x) = x^2 - x$ and the x axis. Make a sketch to show the mentioned area.

$\int_{0}^{1} x^2 - x dx = \left[\frac{1}{3} - 1 \right] - [0] = -\frac{2}{3}$

So area enclosed is $\frac{2}{3}$

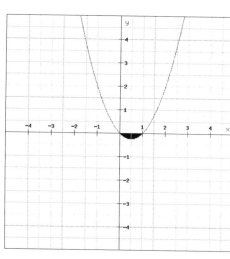

25. Find the area enclosed between the function $f(x) = x^3 - 6x^2 + 8x$ and the x axis.
Make a sketch to show the mentioned area.

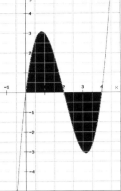

$$\int_0^2 x^3 - 6x^2 + 8x\,dx = \left[\frac{16}{4} - 16 + 16\right] - [0] = 4$$

$$\int_2^4 x^3 - 6x^2 + 8x\,dx = \left[\frac{256}{4} - 128 + 64\right] - \left[\frac{16}{4} - 16 + 16\right] = -4$$

So area enclosed is 8

26. Find the area enclosed between the function $f(x) = -x^3 + 3x^2 - 4$ and the axes
Make a sketch to show the mentioned area.

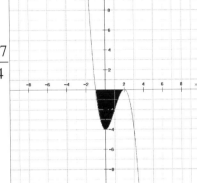

$$-x^3 + 3x^2 - 4 = 0; x = -1, 2$$

$$\int_{-1}^2 -x^3 + 3x^2 - 4\,dx = \left[-\frac{16}{4} + \frac{24}{3} - 8\right] - \left[-\frac{1}{4} - \frac{3}{3} + 4\right] = -\frac{27}{4}$$

So area enclosed is $\dfrac{27}{4}$

27. Find the area enclosed between the functions $f(x) = x^2 + x$ and $g(x) = x + 2$.
Make a sketch to show the mentioned area.

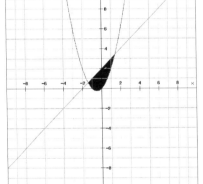

$$x^2 + x = x + 2; x = \pm\sqrt{2}$$

$$\int_{-\sqrt{2}}^{\sqrt{2}} (x+2) - (x^2 + x)\,dx = \left[2\sqrt{2} - \frac{2\sqrt{2}}{3}\right] - \left[-2\sqrt{2} + \frac{2\sqrt{2}}{3}\right]$$

$$= \frac{8\sqrt{2}}{3}$$

So area enclosed is $\dfrac{8\sqrt{2}}{3}$

28. Find the area enclosed between the functions $f(x) = x^2 + 2$ and $g(x) = -x^2 + 3$.
Make a sketch to show the mentioned area.

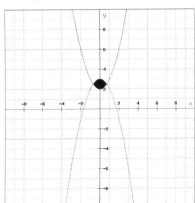

$$x^2 + 2 = -x^2 + 3; x = \pm\sqrt{\frac{1}{2}}$$

$$\int_{-\sqrt{\frac{1}{2}}}^{\sqrt{\frac{1}{2}}} (-x^2 + 3) - (x^2 + 2)\,dx = \frac{2\sqrt{2}}{3}$$

So area enclosed is $\dfrac{2\sqrt{2}}{3}$

397

29. Find the area enclosed between the functions $f(x) = x^4 - 2x + 1$ and $g(x) = -x^2 + 1$. Make a sketch to show the mentioned area.

$$x^4 - 2x + 1 = -x^2 + 1; x = 0,1$$

$$\int_0^1 (-x^2 + 1) - (x^4 - 2x + 1)dx = \left[-\frac{1}{5} - \frac{1}{3} + 1\right] - [0] = \frac{7}{15}$$

So area enclosed is $\dfrac{7}{15}$

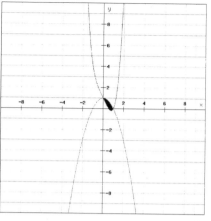

30. Find the area enclosed between the functions $f(x) = 2 - x^2$ and $g(x) = |x|$. Make a sketch to show the mentioned area.

$$2 - x^2 = x; x = 1 (other \quad solution \quad irrelevant)$$

$$\int_0^1 (2 - x^2) - (x)dx = \left[2 - \frac{1}{3} - 1\right] - [0] = \frac{2}{3}$$

So area enclosed is trice as big (because of symmetry)

$$2 \cdot \frac{2}{3} = \frac{4}{3}$$

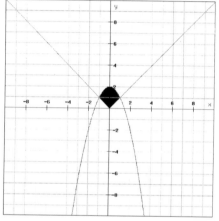

31. Find the area enclosed between the function $f(x) = x^2 + 2x + 2$, the tangent to $f(x)$ at its extrema and the tangent to $f(x)$ with a slope 6. Make a sketch to show the mentioned area.

$$f'(x) = 2x + 2 = 0; x = -1; f(-1) = 1; y = 1 (Tangent)$$
$$f'(x) = 2x + 2 = 6; x = 2; f(2) = 10; y = 6x + b; y = 6x - 2 (Tangent)$$

$$6x - 2 = 1; x = \frac{1}{2}$$

$$\int_{-1}^{\frac{1}{2}} (x^2 + 2x + 2) - (1)dx = \frac{9}{8}$$

$$\int_{\frac{1}{2}}^{2} (x^2 + 2x + 2) - (6x - 2)dx = \frac{9}{8}$$

So area enclosed is $\dfrac{18}{8} = \dfrac{9}{4}$

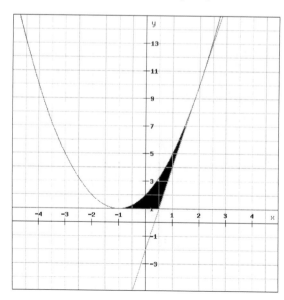

32. Find the area enclosed between the functions $f(x) = 5 - x^2 + 4x$ and $g(x) = 5$. Make a sketch to show the mentioned area.

$5 - x^2 + 4x = 5; x = 0, 4$

$$\int_0^4 (5 - x^2 + 4x) - (5)dx = \frac{32}{3}$$

So area enclosed is $\frac{32}{3}$

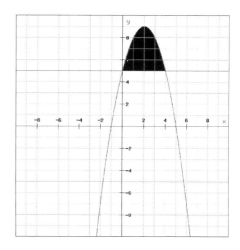

33. Find the area enclosed between the functions $f(x) = x^2 - 2x$ and $g(x) = x$. Make a sketch to show the mentioned area.

$x^2 - 2x = x; x = 0, 3$

$$\int_0^3 (x) - (x^2 - 2x)dx = \frac{9}{2}$$

So area enclosed is $\frac{9}{2}$

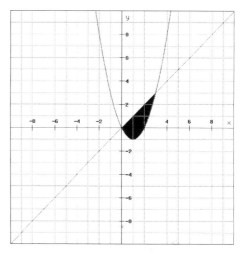

34. The area enclosed between the curve $y = a(1 - (x - 2)^2)$ with $a > 0$ and the x axis is 12. Find a. Make a sketch to show the mentioned area.

$y = -a(x - 2)^2 + a = 0; x = 1, 3$

$$\int_1^3 (-a(x - 2)^2 + a)dx = \left[-\frac{a(x - 2)^3}{3} + ax \right]_1^3 =$$

$$= \left[-\frac{a}{3} + 3a \right] - \left[\frac{a}{3} + a \right] = \frac{4a}{3} = 12; a = 9$$

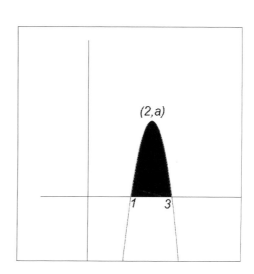

35. Given the function $f(x) = ae^{\frac{x}{3}} + \dfrac{1}{x^2}, x \neq 0$, find:

a. $\displaystyle\int_1^2 f(x)dx$ in terms of a.

$$\int_1^2 ae^{\frac{x}{3}} + \frac{1}{x^2}dx = \left[3ae^{\frac{x}{3}} - \frac{1}{x}\right]_1^2 = \left[3ae^{\frac{2}{3}} - \frac{1}{2}\right] - \left[3ae^{\frac{1}{3}} - \frac{1}{1}\right] = 3ae^{\frac{1}{3}}(e^{\frac{1}{3}} - 1) + \frac{1}{2}$$

b. If F(x) is a primitive of f(x) find a knowing that F(1) = 0 and F(2) = $\dfrac{1}{2}$

$$F(x) = 3ae^{\frac{x}{3}} - \frac{1}{x} + C;$$
$$I)\, F(1) = 3ae^{\frac{1}{3}} - 1 + C = 0$$

$$II) - I)\ 3a(e^{\frac{2}{3}} - e^{\frac{1}{3}}) = \frac{1}{2}; a = \frac{1}{6}(e^{\frac{2}{3}} - e^{\frac{1}{3}})^{-1} \qquad II)\, F(2) = 3ae^{\frac{2}{3}} - \frac{1}{2} + C = \frac{1}{2}$$

36. Find the area bounded by: $y = e^{-x}$; $x = 0$; $y = 0$ and $x = 1$. Make a sketch to show the mentioned area.

$$\int_0^1 (e^{-x})dx = \left[-e^{-1}\right] - [1] = 1 - \frac{1}{e}$$

So area enclosed is $1 - \dfrac{1}{e}$

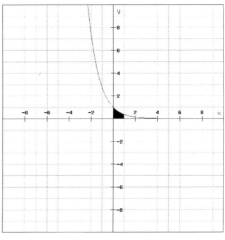

37. Find the area enclosed between the function $f(x) = 1 - e^{-x}$, the tangent to f(x) at the point where x = 0 and the line x = 2. Make a sketch to show the mentioned area.

$$f'(x) = e^{-x}; f'(0) = 1; f(0) = 0; y = x (Tangent)$$

$$\int_0^2 (x) - (1 - e^{-x})dx = 1 - \frac{1}{e^2}$$

So area enclosed is $1 - \dfrac{1}{e^2}$

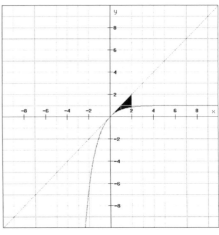

VOLUMES OF REVOLUTION

$$V = \int_a^b \pi\left(f(x)\right)^2 dx \text{ (around the x axis)} \qquad V = \int_c^d \pi\left(f(y)\right)^2 dy \text{ (around the y axis)}$$

1. Find the volume of revolution formed by the function $f(x) = x+1, x \in [0,5]$
   a. Around the x axis.

   $$V = \int_0^5 \pi(x+1)^2 dx = \pi\left[\frac{(x+1)^3}{3}\right]_0^5 = \pi\left[\left[\frac{216}{3}\right] - \left[\frac{1}{3}\right]\right] = \frac{215\pi}{3}$$

   b. Around the y axis.

   $$V = \int_{-1}^4 \pi(y-1)^2 dy = \pi\left[\frac{(y-1)^3}{3}\right]_{-1}^4 = \pi\left[\left[\frac{9}{3}\right] - \left[\frac{-8}{3}\right]\right] = \frac{17\pi}{3}$$

2. Find the volume of revolution formed by the function $f(x) = e^x, x \in [0,1]$
   a. Around the x axis.

   $$V = \int_0^5 \pi e^{2x} dx = \pi\left[\frac{e^{2x}}{2}\right]_0^1 = \pi\left[\left[\frac{e^2}{2}\right] - \left[\frac{1}{2}\right]\right] = \frac{\pi\left(e^2-1\right)}{2}$$

   b. Around the y axis. $x = Ln(y), y \in [1,e]$

   $$V = \int_1^e \pi\left(Ln(y)\right)^2 dy = \pi\left[y\left(Ln(y)\right)^2 - 2y\ln(y) + 2y\right]_1^e = \pi\left[\left[e-2e+2e\right] - \left[0+2\right]\right] = \pi(e-2)$$

3. Find the volume of revolution formed by the function

   $f(x) = \sqrt{\sin(2x)}, x \in [0, \frac{\pi}{6}]$ Around the x axis.

   $$V = \int_0^{\frac{\pi}{6}} \pi\sin(2x) dx = \pi\left[\frac{-\cos(2x)}{2}\right]_0^{\frac{\pi}{6}} = \pi\left[\left[-\frac{1}{4}\right] - \left[-\frac{1}{2}\right]\right] = \frac{\pi}{4}$$

4. Find the volume of revolution formed by the function $f(x) = \sqrt{x-1}, x \in [2,3]$

   a. Around the x axis.

   $$V = \int_2^3 \pi(x-1) dx = \pi\left[\frac{x^2}{2} - x\right]_2^3 = \pi\left[\left[\frac{9}{2} - 3\right] - \left[\frac{4}{2} - 2\right]\right] = \frac{3\pi}{2}$$

   b. Around the y axis. $x = y^2 + 1, y \in [1, \sqrt{2}]$

   $$V = \int_1^{\sqrt{2}} \pi(y^2+1)^2 dy = \pi\left[\frac{y^5}{5} + \frac{2y^3}{3} + y\right]_1^{\sqrt{2}} = \pi\left[\left[\frac{4\sqrt{2}}{5} + \frac{4\sqrt{2}}{3} + \sqrt{2}\right] - \left[\frac{1}{5} + \frac{2}{3} + 1\right]\right] = \pi\frac{47\sqrt{2} - 28}{15}$$

1.11. – KINEMATICS

1. The displacement of an object is measured in <u>meters</u>.
2. The velocity of an object is the <u>change in the position per unit of time</u> and it is measured in meters/second. Mathematically it is the <u>derivative</u> of the displacement.
3. The acceleration of an object is the and it is <u>change in the velocity per unit of time</u> measured in meters/second^2. Mathematically it is the <u>derivative</u> of the velocity or the <u>2nd derivative</u> of the displacement.
4. An object accelerates from rest with a = 2 m/s^2 during 4 seconds, write down its velocity: <u>8 m/s</u>
5. An object moves at 12 m/s and accelerates with a = –3 m/s^2 during 2 seconds, write down its final velocity: <u>6 m/s</u>
6. If the distance run by an object after t seconds is given by $d(t) = 2t^2 + 3t + 5$, find:

    a. Its initial position: <u>d(0) = 5m</u>
    b. Its position after 2 seconds: <u>d(2) = 19m</u>
    c. Its velocity after 2 seconds: $v(t) = d'(t) = 4t + 3; v(2) = 11m / s$,
    d. Its acceleration after 2 seconds: $a(t) = v'(t) = 4; a(2) = 4m / s^2$

7. The velocity of an object after t seconds is given by $v(t) = 2s\,in(3t)$, find:

    a. Its initial velocity: $v(0) = 2s\,in(0) = 0m / s$
    b. Its initial acceleration: $a(t) = v'(t) = 6\cos(3t); a(0) = 6m / s^2$
    c. The period of its motion: $d(t) = \int 2s\,in(3t)dt = -\dfrac{2\cos(3t)}{3} + C; T = \dfrac{2\pi}{3}s$

8. The velocity of an object after t seconds is given by $v(t) = e^{-\frac{t}{a}}$, find:

    a. Its initial velocity: $v(0) = e^0 = 1m / s$

    b. Given that its initial acceleration is –3 m/s^2, find a:

$$a(t) = v'(t) = \frac{-e^{-\frac{t}{a}}}{a}; a(0) = \frac{-1}{a} = -3; a = \frac{1}{3}s$$

    c. Given that the initial displacement of the object is 2m, find its displacement after 3 seconds.

$$d(t) = \int e^{-3t}dt = \frac{-e^{-3t}}{3} + C; d(0) = \frac{-1}{3} + C = 2; C = \frac{7}{3}$$

$$d(t) = \frac{-e^{-3t}}{3} + \frac{7}{3}; d(3) = \frac{7 - e^{-9}}{3}m$$

9. The acceleration of an object is given by $a(t) = \dfrac{1}{(t+1)^2}$, find:

a. Given that v(0) = 0, find its velocity as a function time.

$$v(t) = \int \frac{1}{(t+1)^2} dt = -(t+1)^{-1} + C; v(0) = -1 + C = 0; C = 1$$

$$v(t) = -(t+1)^{-1} + 1$$

b. Given that d(0) = 0, find its displacement as a function time.

$$d(t) = \int (-(t+1)^{-1} + 1) dt = -Ln(t+1) + t + K; d(0) = K = 0;$$

$$d(t) = -Ln(t+1) + t$$

c. Write the acceleration and the velocity of the object after a long period

$$a(t \to \infty) \approx 0 m/s^2$$

$$v(t \to \infty) \approx 1 m/s$$

10. The acceleration of an object is given by $a(t) = 3\cos(2t)$, find:

a. Given that v(0) = 0, find its velocity as a function time.

$$v(t) = \int 3\cos(2t) dt = \frac{3\sin(2t)}{2} + C; v(0) = 0 + C = 0; C = 0$$

$$v(t) = \frac{3\sin(2t)}{2}$$

b. Given that d(0) = 0, find its displacement as a function time.

$$d(t) = \int \frac{3\sin(2t)}{2} dt = -\frac{3\cos(2t)}{4} + K; d(0) = -\frac{3}{4} + K = 0; K = \frac{3}{4}$$

$$d(t) = -\frac{3\cos(2t)}{4} + \frac{3}{4}$$

2.1. – VECTORS

Transposing a vector means changing <u>Row(s)</u> to <u>Column(s)</u> or <u>Column(s)</u> to <u>Row(s)</u>

What is a null vector?

A null vector is a vector with all the components of the vector equal to <u>zero</u>

Exercises

1. Give an example of a 3–dimensional column vector: $\begin{pmatrix} 2 \\ 0 \\ -3 \end{pmatrix}$

2. Give an example of a 4–dimensional row null vector: $\begin{pmatrix} 0 & 0 & 0 & 0 \end{pmatrix}$

3. Give an example of a 1–dimensional <u>Row/Column</u> vector: 5

4. Sketch the vectors: $(1, 3), (-3, 1), (-3, -4). (5, -2)$ on the following diagram:

    Important note: Vectors are "free" they do not start or end in any particular point. The point in the centre is meaningless in the context of this exercise. Points however, do refer to a particular point of reference.

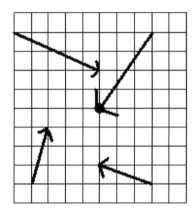

5. Circle the points: $(1, 3), (-3, 1), (-3, -4). (5, -2)$ on the previous system.

    Assume that the origin is the blackened dot. The notation of vectors is identical to the notation of <u>points</u> when they are written in <u>Cartesian form</u>. However on sketching a free vector there is an <u>infinite</u> number of possibilities while on sketching a point only <u>one</u> possibility that makes reference to a chosen <u>Origin</u>.

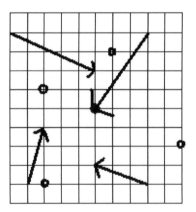

6. The vectors from exercises 4 are <u>bidimensional</u> (they have <u>2</u> dimensions).

7. A vector starts at the point $(2, -7)$ and ends at the point $(1, 3)$, the vector is $(-1, 10)$

8. A vector starts at the point $(12, 3, 0)$ and ends at the point $(11, -3. -2)$, the vector is $(-1, -6, -2)$

Magnitude of a vector

9. Find the magnitude of the vectors: (1, 3), (–3, 1), (–3, –4). (0, –2).

   |(1, 3)| = $\sqrt{10}$ |(–3, 1)| = $\sqrt{10}$ |(–3, –4)| = 5 |(0, –2)| = 2

10. The magnitude of a vector is always <u>Positive</u>
11. Find the magnitude of the vectors:

   $\vec{A} = (1, 0, -3, -4)$ $|\vec{A}| = \sqrt{26}$

   $\vec{B} = (-3, -2, -4)$ $|\vec{B}| = \sqrt{29}$

   $\vec{C} = (1, 2)$ $|\vec{C}| = \sqrt{5}$

   $\vec{D} = (3, 4)$ $|\vec{D}| = 5$

   $\vec{E} = (1, 2, -3)$ $|\vec{E}| = \sqrt{14}$

   $\vec{F} = (0,0,0,-12,0,0,0,0,0)$ $|\vec{F}| = 12$

12. <u>In 1D 2 directions exist, in 2D infinite directions exist</u>

13. Given the vector $\vec{a} = (1, 1)$. Its magnitude is $\sqrt{2}$. Sketch it on the following diagram (Assume is "starts" at the centre).

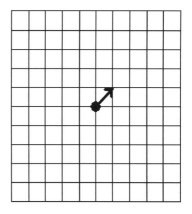

14. Given the vector (–4, 3). Its magnitude is <u>5</u>. Sketch it on the following diagram (Assume is "starts" at the centre). It forms an angle of

   $\alpha = \arctan(\dfrac{3}{4}) \approx 36.9°$ with the <u>West</u>, therefore

   its direction is W36.9°N and an   angle of 53.1° with the <u>North</u> therefore its direction can also be written as   N53.1°W. The form (–4, 3) of the vector is called **Algebraic notation**. The vector can also be written as: <u>5, W36.9°N</u> that is the **geometrical notation**.

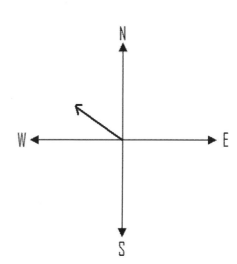

When are two vectors equal?

15. Given $\vec{A} = \begin{bmatrix} 2 \\ a_2 \\ -4 \\ 1 \end{bmatrix}$ $\vec{B} = \begin{bmatrix} b_1 \\ 3 \\ 4 \\ b_4 \end{bmatrix}$ and $\vec{A} = \vec{B}$. Find all the missing components.

These vectors cannot be equal even if $b_1 = 2$, $a_2 = 3$ and $b_4 = 1$ as 4 is different than –4

16. Which of the following vectors are equal:

How can two vectors be added?

Analytically:

17. Given that $\vec{A} = \begin{bmatrix} 2 \\ 3 \\ 4 \\ 1 \end{bmatrix}$, $\vec{B} = \begin{bmatrix} 5 \\ -2 \\ 3 \\ 7 \end{bmatrix}$ Find $\vec{A} + \vec{B} = \begin{bmatrix} 7 \\ 1 \\ 7 \\ 8 \end{bmatrix}$

Graphically:

18. Sketch the vector $\vec{a} = (3. \ 4)$ on the following diagram (start at point A):

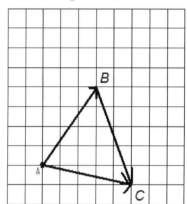

19. Where it ends (denote the point as B), sketch the vector $(2, -5)$, where it ends denote the point as C. Sketch the vector that connects the points A and C, that vector is $(5, -1)$

20. Sum the vectors $(3, 4)$ and $(2, -5)$ analytically. What is your conclusion?

$(3 \quad 4) + (2 \quad -5) = (5 \quad -1)$

Vector obtained in the graphical sum is of course identical.

21. Another conclusion is that the vectors $\overrightarrow{AB} + \overrightarrow{BC} = \overrightarrow{AC}$ (independently of point B)

22. Consider

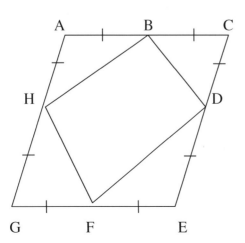

Determine each vector sum:

a) $\overrightarrow{AH} + \overrightarrow{HG} = \overrightarrow{AG}$

b) $\overrightarrow{HB} + \overrightarrow{BD} = \overrightarrow{HD}$

c) $\overrightarrow{GF} + \overrightarrow{BC} = \overrightarrow{GE}$

d) $\overrightarrow{GF} + \overrightarrow{CB} = \vec{0}$

e) $\overrightarrow{FD} + \overrightarrow{DE} = \overrightarrow{FE}$

f) $\overrightarrow{GH} - \overrightarrow{AH} = \overrightarrow{GA}$

g) $\overrightarrow{HF} - \overrightarrow{DF} = \overrightarrow{HD}$

h) $\overrightarrow{GF} + \overrightarrow{FD} + \overrightarrow{DH} + \overrightarrow{HE} = \overrightarrow{GE}$

i) $\overrightarrow{GF} - \overrightarrow{FD} + \overrightarrow{FD} + \overrightarrow{FB} = \overrightarrow{GB}$

406

23. Sum the vectors (1,–2), (3, 1), (2, 5) analytically and graphically. Did you obtain the same result? <u>Yes!</u>

$$\begin{pmatrix} 1 & -2 \end{pmatrix} + \begin{pmatrix} 3 & 1 \end{pmatrix} + \begin{pmatrix} 2 & 5 \end{pmatrix} = \begin{pmatrix} 6 & 4 \end{pmatrix}$$

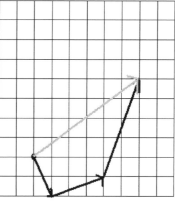

24. Vectors start at a <u>point</u> and end in a different <u>point</u>
25. The only situation in which the coordinates of a vector are identical to the coordinates of the point it ends at, is the case in which the vector starts at the <u>origin</u>
26. Given the vectors $\vec{A} = (10,0)$ and $\vec{B}$.

$\left|\vec{B}\right| = 5$ and the angle between the vectors is 60°.

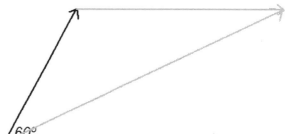

   a. Draw the 2 vectors on a plane.
   b. Sum the 2 vectors **graphically**.
   c. Sum the 2 vectors **analytically.**

$$\vec{A} + \vec{B} = (10,0) + (5\cos(60°), 5\sin(60°)) = (12.5, \frac{5\sqrt{3}}{2})$$

How can 2 vectors be subtracted?

27. Given the two vectors $\vec{A} = \begin{bmatrix} 2 \\ 3 \\ 4 \\ 1 \end{bmatrix}, \vec{B} = \begin{bmatrix} 5 \\ -2 \\ 3 \\ 7 \end{bmatrix}; \vec{A} - \vec{B} = \begin{bmatrix} -3 \\ 5 \\ 1 \\ -6 \end{bmatrix}$

<u>Graphically:</u>

28. Given the vectors $\vec{a} = (3. 4)$ and $\vec{b} = (2, -1)$. Find $\vec{a} - \vec{b}$ using the graphical method. On the following diagram (start at point A) sketch the vector $\vec{a}$:

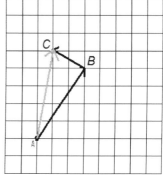

29. Where it ends (denote the point as B), sketch the vector $-\vec{b}$, where it ends denote the point as C. Sketch the vector that connects the points A and C, that vector is $\vec{a} - \vec{b}$, its coordinates are (1 , 5).
30. Consequently we can say that subtraction of the vector $\vec{d}$ is done by adding the vector $-\vec{d}$

407

How can a vector be multiplied by a scalar?

31. Given the row vectors $\vec{A} = \begin{bmatrix} 25 & 20 & 5 \end{bmatrix}$ and $\vec{B} = \begin{bmatrix} 7 & 5 & -3 \end{bmatrix}$:

    a. $2\vec{A} = \begin{bmatrix} 50 & 40 & 10 \end{bmatrix}$

    b. $-\vec{A} = \begin{bmatrix} -25 & -20 & -5 \end{bmatrix}$

    c. $3\vec{A} - 2\vec{B} = \begin{bmatrix} 61 & 50 & 24 \end{bmatrix}$

    d. $-\vec{A} + 4\vec{B} = \begin{bmatrix} 3 & 0 & -17 \end{bmatrix}$

What is a unit vector?

32. The magnitude of a unit vector is <u>1</u>.

33. $\vec{U} = k(2, -3)$. Find k so that $\vec{U}$ would be a unit vector. $k = \dfrac{1}{\sqrt{13}}$

34. $\vec{U} = k(1, -4, 6)$. Find k so that $\vec{U}$ would be a unit vector. $k = \dfrac{1}{\sqrt{53}}$

35. Draw a conclusion of the last 2 exercises, what is the value of k in general?

    Given the vector $\vec{A}$, the unit vector that has the same direction. $\vec{U}_{\vec{A}} = \dfrac{\vec{A}}{|\vec{A}|}$

36. Given the vector $\vec{a} = (\dfrac{1}{\sqrt{3}}, \dfrac{\sqrt{5}}{3}, \dfrac{1}{3})$. Is it a unit vector? $|\vec{a}| = \sqrt{\dfrac{1}{3} + \dfrac{5}{9} + \dfrac{1}{9}} = 1$, <u>yes</u>

37. Given the vector $\vec{a} = (1, 0, \dfrac{1}{10})$. Is it a unit vector? If not, find a unit vector that

    has the same direction. $|\vec{a}| = \sqrt{1 + \dfrac{1}{100}} > 1$ not a unit vector.

    $\vec{U}_{\vec{a}} = \dfrac{1}{\sqrt{1 + \dfrac{1}{100}}} (1, 0, \dfrac{1}{10}) = \dfrac{10}{\sqrt{101}} (1, 0, \dfrac{1}{10})$

38. Given the vector $\vec{a} = (1, 1, 1)$. Is it a unit vector? If not, find a unit vector that has

    the same direction. $|\vec{a}| = \sqrt{3} > 1$ not a unit vector. $\vec{U}_{\vec{a}} = \dfrac{1}{\sqrt{3}} (1, 1, 1)$

39. 2 examples of bidmensional unit vectors. $\vec{a} = (\dfrac{1}{\sqrt{2}}, \dfrac{1}{\sqrt{2}})$, $\vec{b} = (\dfrac{1}{\sqrt{3}}, \sqrt{\dfrac{2}{3}})$

40. 2 examples of tridmensional unit vectors: $\vec{a} = (\dfrac{1}{\sqrt{3}}, \dfrac{1}{\sqrt{3}}, \dfrac{1}{\sqrt{3}})$, $\vec{b} = (\dfrac{1}{\sqrt{2}}, \dfrac{1}{2}, \dfrac{1}{2})$

41. Given the vector $\vec{A} = (a, \dfrac{-1}{3}, \dfrac{1}{3})$.

    a. Find a so $\vec{A}$ is a unit vector: $1 = a^2 + \left(-\dfrac{1}{3}\right)^2 + \left(\dfrac{1}{3}\right)^2$; $a = \dfrac{\sqrt{7}}{3}$

    b. In case a = 1, find a vector with magnitude 5 that has the same direction.

    $\vec{B} = k(1, \dfrac{-1}{3}, \dfrac{1}{3})$; $|\vec{B}| = k\sqrt{1 + \dfrac{2}{9}} = 5$; $k = \dfrac{15}{\sqrt{11}}$; $\vec{B} = \dfrac{15}{\sqrt{11}} (1, \dfrac{-1}{3}, \dfrac{1}{3})$

    c. In case a = 2, find a vector with magnitude 4 that with opposite direction.

    $\vec{C} = k(2, \dfrac{-1}{3}, \dfrac{1}{3})$; $|\vec{B}| = k\sqrt{4 + \dfrac{2}{9}} = 4$; $k = \dfrac{15}{\sqrt{38}}$; $\vec{C} = -\dfrac{15}{\sqrt{38}} (2, \dfrac{-1}{3}, \dfrac{1}{3})$

42. Given the points A = (1, 2, 5), B = (−2, 4, 4), C = (1, −1, −3). Assuming these points form a parallelogram, find the 4th vertex of this parallelogram.

$$\overrightarrow{CD} = \overrightarrow{BA} = (3,-2,1)$$

$$\overrightarrow{OD} = \overrightarrow{OC} + \overrightarrow{CD} = \overrightarrow{OC} + \overrightarrow{BA} = (1,-1,3) + (3,-2,1) = (4,-3,4)$$

43. An object is located at point A = (1, 2, 5) in front of a mirror whose nearest point to A is B = (3, 4, 6). Sketch a diagram of the situation and find the point in which the reflection of the object is observed.

$$\overrightarrow{OA'} = \overrightarrow{OA} + 2\overrightarrow{AB} = (1,2,5) + 2(2,2,1) = (5,6,7)$$

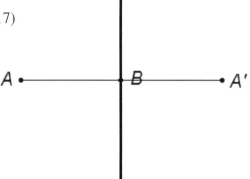

44. A lost airplane was detected at 10pm on radar located at the point A = (−30, 22, 13) (in km) with velocity (12, 120, 22) (in km/h). Assuming the airplane continued with the same velocity for 30 more minutes find its last known location.

$$\vec{d} = \vec{v} \cdot t$$

$$\overrightarrow{OB} = \overrightarrow{OA} + \overrightarrow{AB} = (-30,22,13) + \frac{1}{2}(12,120,22) = (-24,82,24)$$

45. Given the point A = (10, 12, 5). Find a point distanced 2 units from this point in the direction (1, 1, 1).

$$\left| k(1,1,1) \right| = 2; k = \frac{2}{\sqrt{3}}$$

$$\overrightarrow{OB} = \overrightarrow{OA} + \overrightarrow{AB} = (10,12,5) + \frac{2}{\sqrt{3}}(1,1,1) = (10 + \frac{2}{\sqrt{3}}, 12 + \frac{2}{\sqrt{3}}, 5 + \frac{2}{\sqrt{3}})$$

What is meant by vectors being linearly independent?

46. $\vec{A} = \begin{bmatrix} 5 \\ 2 \end{bmatrix}$ and $\vec{B} = \begin{bmatrix} 3 \\ 0 \end{bmatrix}$ are linearly independent? <u>yes,</u> $\frac{2}{5} \neq \frac{0}{3}$

47. $\vec{A} = \begin{bmatrix} 12 \\ 3 \end{bmatrix}$ and $\vec{B} = \begin{bmatrix} 4 \\ 1 \end{bmatrix}$ are linearly independent? <u>no,</u> $\frac{12}{3} = \frac{4}{1}$

48. $\vec{A} = \begin{bmatrix} 1 \\ 0 \\ 2 \end{bmatrix}$ and $\vec{B} = \begin{bmatrix} 1 \\ 3 \\ 0 \end{bmatrix}$ are linearly independent? <u>yes,</u> $\frac{1}{1} \neq \frac{0}{3} \neq \frac{2}{0}$

49. $\vec{A} = \begin{bmatrix} -4 \\ 2 \\ 6 \end{bmatrix}$ and $\vec{B} = \begin{bmatrix} -6 \\ 3 \\ 9 \end{bmatrix}$ are linearly independent? <u>no, $\dfrac{-4}{-6} = \dfrac{2}{3} = \dfrac{6}{9}$</u>

50. $\vec{A} = \begin{bmatrix} 1 \\ 3 \end{bmatrix}, \vec{B} = \begin{bmatrix} 4 \\ 1 \end{bmatrix}$ and $\vec{C} = \begin{bmatrix} 12 \\ -25 \end{bmatrix}$ are linearly independent? <u>no, since $\vec{A}$ and $\vec{B}$</u>

<u>are independent any 3rd vector in 2D can be expressed as a linear combination of</u>
<u>those 2.</u>

51. $\vec{A} = \begin{bmatrix} -1 \\ 9 \end{bmatrix}, \vec{B} = \begin{bmatrix} 5 \\ -3 \end{bmatrix}$ and $\vec{C} = \begin{bmatrix} -4 \\ -2 \end{bmatrix}$ are linearly independent? <u>no, since $\vec{A}$ and $\vec{B}$</u>

<u>are independent any 3rd vector in 2D can be expressed as a linear combination of</u>
<u>those 2.</u>

52. $\vec{A} = \begin{bmatrix} 2 \\ 4 \end{bmatrix}, \vec{B} = \begin{bmatrix} 6 \\ 12 \end{bmatrix}$ and $\vec{C} = \begin{bmatrix} -9 \\ -18 \end{bmatrix}$ are linearly independent? <u>no, $\dfrac{2}{4} = \dfrac{6}{12} = \dfrac{-9}{-18}$</u>

53. $\vec{A}_1 = \begin{bmatrix} 25 \\ 64 \\ 144 \end{bmatrix}, \vec{A}_2 = \begin{bmatrix} 5 \\ 8 \\ 12 \end{bmatrix}, \vec{A}_3 = \begin{bmatrix} 1 \\ 1 \\ 1 \end{bmatrix}$ are linearly independent? <u>yes, the only solution</u>

<u>of the system</u> $k_1 \begin{bmatrix} 25 \\ 64 \\ 144 \end{bmatrix} + k_2 \begin{bmatrix} 5 \\ 8 \\ 12 \end{bmatrix} + k_3 \begin{bmatrix} 1 \\ 1 \\ 1 \end{bmatrix} = \begin{bmatrix} 0 \\ 0 \\ 0 \end{bmatrix}$ <u>is $k_1 = k_2 = k_3 = 0$</u>

54. $\vec{A}_1 = \begin{bmatrix} 1 \\ 2 \\ 5 \end{bmatrix}, \vec{A}_2 = \begin{bmatrix} 2 \\ 5 \\ 7 \end{bmatrix}, A_3 = \begin{bmatrix} 6 \\ 14 \\ 24 \end{bmatrix}$ are linearly independent? <u>no, there are many</u>

<u>solutions to the system</u> $k_1 \begin{bmatrix} 1 \\ 2 \\ 5 \end{bmatrix} + k_2 \begin{bmatrix} 2 \\ 5 \\ 7 \end{bmatrix} + k_3 \begin{bmatrix} 6 \\ 14 \\ 24 \end{bmatrix} = \begin{bmatrix} 0 \\ 0 \\ 0 \end{bmatrix}$

55. $\vec{A}_1 = \begin{bmatrix} 25 \\ 64 \\ 89 \end{bmatrix}, \vec{A}_2 = \begin{bmatrix} 5 \\ 8 \\ 13 \end{bmatrix}, \vec{A}_3 = \begin{bmatrix} 1 \\ 1 \\ 2 \end{bmatrix}$ are linearly independent? <u>no, there are many</u>

<u>solutions to the system</u> $k_1 \begin{bmatrix} 25 \\ 64 \\ 89 \end{bmatrix} + k_2 \begin{bmatrix} 5 \\ 8 \\ 13 \end{bmatrix} + k_3 \begin{bmatrix} 1 \\ 1 \\ 2 \end{bmatrix} = \begin{bmatrix} 0 \\ 0 \\ 0 \end{bmatrix}$

56. **Important note:** n linearly independent vectors in an n–dimensional vector space form a <u>base</u>

57. In 2D space <u>2</u> vectors are needed to form a **base**.

58. In 3D space <u>3</u> vectors are needed to form a **base**.

59. Given the vectors $\vec{A} = \begin{bmatrix} 2 \\ 4 \end{bmatrix}, \vec{B} = \begin{bmatrix} 6 \\ 12 \end{bmatrix}$ form a base in 2D? <u>no, these are not</u>

<u>independent vectors: $\dfrac{2}{4} = \dfrac{6}{12}$</u>

60. $\vec{A} = \begin{bmatrix} 2 \\ 3 \\ -1 \end{bmatrix}, \vec{B} = \begin{bmatrix} 2 \\ -4 \\ 5 \end{bmatrix}, \vec{C} = \begin{bmatrix} 4 \\ 20 \\ -14 \end{bmatrix}$, form a base in 3D? <u>no, vectors are not</u>

<u>independent, there are many solutions to the system</u>

$$k_1 \begin{bmatrix} 2 \\ -1 \\ 5 \end{bmatrix} + k_2 \begin{bmatrix} 2 \\ -4 \\ 5 \end{bmatrix} + k_3 \begin{bmatrix} 4 \\ 20 \\ -14 \end{bmatrix} = \begin{bmatrix} 0 \\ 0 \\ 0 \end{bmatrix}$$

Cartesian Notation:

In 2D:

1. The vector $\vec{a} = (2, -3)$ can be written in the following way:

$$\vec{a} = (2, -3) = 2\vec{i} + (-3)\vec{j} = 2(1,0) - 3(0,1) = (2,0) - (0,3) = (2,-3)$$

2. ABC is equilateral, AB = 2cm, AE = 1cm, in terms of $\vec{i}$ and $\vec{j}$

$\overrightarrow{AB} = \vec{i} + \sqrt{3}\vec{j} = (1, \sqrt{3})$

$\overrightarrow{AC} = 2\vec{i} + 0\vec{j} = (2, 0)$

$\overrightarrow{AD} = 2\vec{i} - \vec{j} = (2, -1)$

$\overrightarrow{AE} = 0\vec{i} - \vec{j} = (0, -1)$

$\overrightarrow{EB} = \vec{i} + (1+\sqrt{3})\vec{j} = (1, 1+\sqrt{3})$

$\overrightarrow{EC} = 2\vec{i} + \vec{j} = (2, 1)$

$\overrightarrow{ED} = 2\vec{i} + 0\vec{j} = (2, 0)$

$\overrightarrow{BD} = \vec{i} - (1+\sqrt{3})\vec{j} = (1, -1-\sqrt{3})$

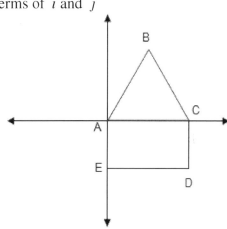

In 3D:

3. The vector $\vec{a} = (2, -3, 5)$ can be written in the following way:

$\vec{a} = (2, -3, 5) = 2\vec{i} + (-3)\vec{j} + 5\vec{k} = 2(1,0,0) - 3(0,1,0) + 5(0,0,1) = (2,0,0) + (0,-3,0) + (0,0,5)$

Write the following vectors in the Cartesian notation:

$(6, 7, -8) = 6\vec{i} + 7\vec{j} - 8\vec{k} = 6(1,0,0) + 7(0,1,0) - 8(0,0,1) = (6,0,0) + (0,7,0) + (0,0,-8)$

$(-3, 4, 7) = -3\vec{i} + 4\vec{j} + 7\vec{k} = -3(1,0,0) + 4(0,1,0) + 7(0,0,1) = (-3,0,0) + (0,4,0) + (0,0,7)$

$(-1, 0, 1) = = -3\vec{i} + 4\vec{j} + 7\vec{k} = -(1,0,0) + 0(0,1,0) + 1(0,0,1) = (-1,0,0) + (0,0,1)$

$(0, 0, 7) = = 0\vec{i} + 0\vec{j} + 7\vec{k} = 0(1,0,0) + 0(0,1,0) + 7(0,0,1) = (0,0,7)$

Some algebraic properties of vectors:

If **u**, **v** and **w** are vectors, α and β are two scalars and **0** is the zero vector:

(i)   **u + v = v + u**   Example: $(6,1,3) + (2,7,0) = (2,7,0) + (6,1,3)$

(ii)   **u + (v + w) = (u + v) + w**   Example:

$$(1,-1,1) + \big((6,1,3) + (2,7,0)\big) = \big((1,-1,1) + (6,1,3)\big) + (2,7,0)$$

(iii)   **v + (−v) = 0**   Example: $(6,1,3) + (-6,-1,-3) = (0,0,0)$

(iv)   **(αβv) = α(βv)**   Example: $5 \cdot 2 \cdot (6,1,3) = 2 \cdot 5 \cdot (6,1,3)$

(v)   **(α+β)v = αv + βv**   Example: $(5+2) \cdot (6,1,3) = 5(6,1,3) + 2(6,1,3) = 7(6,1,3)$

(vi)   **α(u + v) = αu + αv**   Example: $2 \cdot ((6,1,3) + (3,-1,2)) = 2(6,1,3) + 2(3,-1,2)$

(vii)   **$|\alpha v| = \alpha |v|$**   Example:

$$2 \cdot |(6,1,3)| = |2 \cdot (6,1,3)| = |(12,2,6)| = 2\sqrt{6^2 + 1^2 + 3^2} = \sqrt{12^2 + 2^2 + 6^2} = 2\sqrt{46}$$

2.2. – THE SCALAR OR DOT OR INNER PRODUCT

Exercises

1. If the angle between two vectors is <u>90°</u> their dot product is 0.

2. If the angle between two vectors $\vec{a}$ and $\vec{b}$ is <u>0°</u> their dot product is $\left|\vec{a}\right|\left|\vec{b}\right|$

3. If the angle between two vectors $\vec{a}$ and $\vec{b}$ is <u>180°</u> their dot product is $-\left|\vec{a}\right|\left|\vec{b}\right|$

4. Calculate: $\vec{i}\cdot\vec{i} = \left|\vec{i}\right|\left|\vec{i}\right|\cos(0°) = 1$ $\vec{i}\cdot\vec{j} = \left|\vec{i}\right|\left|\vec{j}\right|\cos(90°) = 0$

5. Given that $\vec{A} = A_x\vec{i} + A_y\vec{j} + A_z\vec{k}$ and $\vec{B} = B_x\vec{i} + B_y\vec{j} + B_z\vec{k}$ find

   $\vec{A}\cdot\vec{B} = \left(A_x\vec{i} + A_y\vec{j} + A_z\vec{k}\right)\cdot\left(B_x\vec{i} + B_y\vec{j} + B_z\vec{k}\right) = A_xB_x + A_yB_y + A_zB_z$ <u>(All other dot products are 0)</u>

6. Given the vectors: $\vec{a} = (-1,5,3)$, $\vec{b} = (-1,2,-4)$, $\vec{c} = (5,-4)$, $\vec{d} = (1,-8)$, $\vec{g} = (-5,-1,7)$. Find:

   a. $\vec{a}\cdot\vec{b} = -2$

   b. $\vec{b}\cdot\vec{a} = -2$

   c. $\vec{a}\cdot\vec{c} =$ Not possible, do not have the same dimensions.

   d. $\vec{d}\cdot\vec{c} = 37$

   e. $\vec{a}\cdot\vec{g} = 21$

   f. $\vec{g}\cdot\vec{g} = 75$

   g. $\vec{g}\cdot\vec{b} = -25$

7. Given the vectors: $\vec{a} = (-1,1,1)$, $\vec{b} = (-1,2,-4)$, find the angle between them.

   $(-1,1,1)\cdot(-1,2,-4) = \sqrt{3}\sqrt{21}\cos(\alpha)$

   $\alpha = \arccos(\dfrac{7}{\sqrt{3}\sqrt{21}}) \approx 0.491 rad$

8. Given the vectors: $\vec{a} = (-1,6)$, $\vec{b} = (-1,-4)$, find the angle between them.

   $(-1,6)\cdot(-1,-4) = \sqrt{37}\sqrt{17}\cos(\alpha)$

   $\alpha = \arccos(\dfrac{-25}{\sqrt{37}\sqrt{17}}) \approx 3.06 rad$

9. Given the vectors: $\vec{a} = (-1,5,3)$, $\vec{b} = (2,-10,-6)$, find the angle between them.

   $(-1,5,3)\cdot(2,-10,-6) = \sqrt{35}\sqrt{140}\cos(\alpha)$

   $\alpha = \arccos(\dfrac{-70}{\sqrt{35}\sqrt{140}}) = \arccos(-1) = \pi_{rad}$

10. Given the vectors: $\vec{a} = (-1,5,3)$, $\vec{b} = (5,-2,5)$, find the angle between them.

    $(-1,5,3)\cdot(5,-2,5) = \sqrt{35}\sqrt{54}\cos(\alpha)$

    $\alpha = \arccos(\dfrac{0}{\sqrt{35}\sqrt{54}}) = \dfrac{\pi}{2}_{rad}$

11. Given the vectors: $\vec{a} = (t, -h, 0)$, $\vec{b} = (-t, h, 0)$, find the angle between them.

$(t, -h, 0) \cdot (-t, h, 0) = \sqrt{t^2 + h^2} \sqrt{t^2 + h^2} \cos(\alpha)$

$\alpha = \arccos(\dfrac{-(t^2 + h^2)}{t^2 + h^2}) = \arccos(-1) = \pi_{rad}$

12. Given the vector: $\vec{a} = (1, 4, -3)$, Write down a vector that is perpendicular to it.
Write down a vector that is parallel to it.
Parallel : $(2, 8, -6)$ *Perpendicular* : $(0, 3, 4)$

13. Given the vector: $\vec{a} = (a, a, a)$, Write down a vector that is perpendicular to it.
Write down a vector that is parallel to it (in terms of a).
Parallel : $(3a, 3a, 3a)$ *Perpendicular* : $(b, -b, 0)$

14. Given the vector: $\vec{a} = (7, -3)$, Write down a vector that is perpendicular to it.
Write down a vector that is parallel to it.
Parallel : $(70, -30)$ *Perpendicular* : $(3, 7)$

15. Given the vector: $\vec{a} = (t, h, m)$, Write down a vector that is perpendicular to it.
Write down a vector that is parallel to it (in terms of t, h and m).
Parallel : $(5t, 5h, 5m)$ *Perpendicular* : $(0, -m, h)$

16. Given the vectors: $\vec{a} = (-1, 1, 1)$, $\vec{b} = (-1, 2, -4)$. Find
$\vec{a} \cdot \vec{a} = 3$ $\vec{b} \cdot \vec{b} = 21$ Conclusion: The dot product of a vector with itself is equal to <u>the magnitude squared</u>

17. Given the vectors $\vec{a} = (1, 5, k)$ and $\vec{b} = (-1, 2, 4)$

    a. Find their dot product if k = 1. $\vec{a} \cdot \vec{b} = 13$
    b. Find the angle between them in case k = 2.

       $(1, 5, 2) \cdot (-1, 2, 4) = \sqrt{30}\sqrt{21} \cos(\alpha)$

       $\alpha = \arccos(\dfrac{17}{\sqrt{30}\sqrt{21}}) \approx 0.827_{rad}$

    c. Find the value of k to make these 2 vectors perpendicular.

       $(1, 5, k) \cdot (-1, 2, 4) = 4k + 9 = 0; k = -\dfrac{9}{4}$

    d. Find the value of k to make these 2 vectors parallel. <u>Not possible, since</u>

       <u>$\dfrac{1}{-1} \neq \dfrac{5}{2}$ these vectors cannot be parallel.</u>

18. Given the vectors $\vec{a} = (7, 2, -4)$ and $\vec{b} = (-1, b, a)$

    a. Calculate their dot product if a = 1, b = 2 $\vec{a} \cdot \vec{b} = -11$

    b. Calculate the angle between them in the same case

       $(7, 2, -4) \cdot (-1, 2, 1) = \sqrt{69}\sqrt{6} \cos(\alpha)$

       $\alpha = \arccos(\dfrac{-7}{\sqrt{69}\sqrt{6}}) \approx 1.92_{rad}$

c. Calculate what value of a will make these 2 vectors perpendicular in case a = b.

$(7, 2, -4) \cdot (-1, a, a) = 0$

$-7 - 2a = 0$

$a = -\dfrac{7}{2}$

d. Calculate what values of a and b will make these 2 vectors parallel.

$\dfrac{7}{-1} = \dfrac{b}{2} = \dfrac{a}{-4}; b = -14; a = 28$

19. Given the vectors $\vec{a} = (3, -1)$ and $\vec{b} = (5, b)$

a. Calculate their dot product if b = 15 $\qquad \vec{a} \cdot \vec{b} = 40$

b. Calculate the angle between them in the same case.

$(3, -1) \cdot (5, 15) = \sqrt{10}\sqrt{230} \cos(\alpha)$

$\alpha = \arccos(\dfrac{0}{\sqrt{69}\sqrt{6}}) = 90°$

c. Calculate what value of b will make these 2 vectors parallel.

$\dfrac{5}{3} = \dfrac{b}{-1}; b = -\dfrac{5}{3}$

Some Properties of Dot Product

For some vectors **u**, **v** and **w**,

(i) $\mathbf{u \bullet v = v \bullet u}$ $\qquad\qquad$ Example: $(1, 5, 2) \cdot (-1, 2, 4) = (-1, 2, 4) \cdot (1, 5, 2)$

(ii) $\mathbf{(u + v) \bullet w = u \bullet w + v \bullet w}$ $\qquad$ Example:

$$\big((1, 5, 2) + (-3, 0, 1)\big) \cdot (7, 8, 3) = (1, 5, 2) \cdot (7, 8, 3) + (-3, 0, 1) \cdot (7, 8, 3)$$

(iii) $(\alpha\mathbf{u}) \bullet \mathbf{v} = \alpha(\mathbf{u \bullet v})$, α is scalar $\qquad$ Example:

$$(6 \cdot (1, 1, -2)) \cdot (7, 8, 3) = 6 \cdot ((1, 1, -2) \cdot (7, 8, 3))$$

(iv) $\mathbf{u \bullet u} \geq 0$ and $\mathbf{u \bullet u} = 0$ if $\mathbf{u = 0}$ $\qquad$ Example: $(1, 1, -2) \cdot (1, 1, -2) > 0$

(v) $|\mathbf{u}|^2 = \mathbf{u \bullet u}$ $\qquad\qquad$ Example:

$$(1, 1, -2) \cdot (1, 1, -2) = 6 = \left(\sqrt{1^2 + 1^2 + (-2)^2}\right)^2$$

2.3. – THE VECTOR OR CROSS PRODUCT

1. The cross product between 2 vectors is a <u>vector</u>
2. The cross product between 2 parallel vectors is: $\vec{0} = (0,0,0)$
3. Given the vectors $\vec{a} = (4,2,-1)$, $\vec{b} = (-8,-4,2)$, find:

   a. $\vec{a} \times \vec{b} = \vec{0}$ (parallel vectors)

   b. $\vec{a} \times \vec{a} = \vec{0}$

4. Given the vectors $\vec{a} = (1,5,0)$, $\vec{b} = (1,0,1)$, $\vec{c} = (1,1,1)$, find:

   a. $\vec{a} \times \vec{c} = \begin{vmatrix} \vec{i} & \vec{j} & \vec{k} \\ 1 & 5 & 0 \\ 1 & 1 & 1 \end{vmatrix} = (5,-1,-4)$

   b. $\vec{c} \times \vec{a} = \begin{vmatrix} \vec{i} & \vec{j} & \vec{k} \\ 1 & 1 & 1 \\ 1 & 5 & 0 \end{vmatrix} = (-5,1,4)$

   c. $2\vec{b} \times \vec{c} = \begin{vmatrix} \vec{i} & \vec{j} & \vec{k} \\ 2 & 0 & 2 \\ 1 & 1 & 1 \end{vmatrix} = (-2,0,2)$

   d. $\vec{a} \times (\vec{b} \times \vec{c}) = \vec{a} \times \begin{vmatrix} \vec{i} & \vec{j} & \vec{k} \\ 1 & 0 & 1 \\ 1 & 1 & 1 \end{vmatrix} = \vec{a} \times (-1,0,1) = \begin{vmatrix} \vec{i} & \vec{j} & \vec{k} \\ 1 & 5 & 0 \\ -1 & 0 & 1 \end{vmatrix} = (5,-1,5)$

5. Given the vectors $\vec{a} = (1,5,0)$, $\vec{b} = (1,0,1)$, $\vec{c} = (1,1,1)$. State whether the following expressions are vectors, scalars or meaningless. Calculate the values of the expressions that are <u>not</u> meaningless:

   a. Scalar $\vec{a} \bullet (\vec{b} \times \vec{c}) = \vec{a} \bullet \begin{vmatrix} \vec{i} & \vec{j} & \vec{k} \\ 1 & 0 & 1 \\ 1 & 1 & 1 \end{vmatrix} = (-1,0,1) \cdot (-1,0,1) = 2$

   b. Vector $3\vec{a} \times (\vec{b} \times \vec{c}) = \begin{vmatrix} \vec{i} & \vec{j} & \vec{k} \\ 1 & 0 & 1 \\ 1 & 1 & 1 \end{vmatrix} = 3\vec{a} \times (-1,0,1) = \begin{vmatrix} \vec{i} & \vec{j} & \vec{k} \\ 3 & 15 & 0 \\ -1 & 0 & 1 \end{vmatrix} = (15,-3,15)$

   c. Vector $\vec{a} \times (\vec{b} + 2\vec{c}) = \begin{vmatrix} \vec{i} & \vec{j} & \vec{k} \\ 1 & 5 & 0 \\ 3 & 2 & 3 \end{vmatrix} = (15,-3,-13)$

   d. Vector $(\vec{a} \times \vec{c}) \times (\vec{b} + \vec{c}) = \begin{vmatrix} \vec{i} & \vec{j} & \vec{k} \\ 1 & 5 & 0 \\ 1 & 1 & 1 \end{vmatrix} \times (\vec{b} + \vec{c}) = \begin{vmatrix} \vec{i} & \vec{j} & \vec{k} \\ 5 & -1 & -4 \\ 2 & 1 & 2 \end{vmatrix} = (2,-18,7)$

   e. Meaningless $4\vec{a} + (\vec{b} \bullet \vec{c})$

   f. Meaningless $\vec{a} \times (\vec{a} \bullet \vec{a})$

   g. Scalar $(\vec{b} \times (\vec{b} + \vec{b})) \bullet \vec{b} = \vec{0}$

   h. Scalar $(\vec{a} \bullet \vec{a})^{\vec{b} \bullet \vec{c}} = 26^2$

6. Find a vector perpendicular to the vector $(1, 2, -1)$: $(0,1,2)$

7. Find a vector that will be perpendicular to <u>both</u> $(1, 2, -1)$ and the vector you found in 6)

$$\begin{vmatrix} \vec{i} & \vec{j} & \vec{k} \\ 1 & 2 & -1 \\ 0 & 1 & 2 \end{vmatrix} = (3,-2,1)$$

8. Find a **unit** vector parallel to the vector you found in 6. $\dfrac{1}{\sqrt{5}}(0,1,2)$

9. If **u** and **v** are parallel, then $\quad\quad\quad$ **u** × **v** $= \vec{0}$

10. For any **u**: $\quad\quad\quad\quad\quad\quad$ $(\mathbf{u} \times \mathbf{u}) = \vec{0}$

11. For any **u**, **v**: $\quad\quad\quad\quad\quad$ |**u** × (**u** × **v**)| = |**u**||**u** × **v**|

12. Given the vectors $\vec{a} = (1,-5,-2)$ and $\vec{b} = (7,7,1)$, find a vector perpendicular to both of them.

$$\begin{vmatrix} \vec{i} & \vec{j} & \vec{k} \\ 1 & -5 & -2 \\ 7 & 7 & 1 \end{vmatrix} = (9,-15,42)$$

13. Given the points A = (0, 1, 1), B = (–2, 1, 2) and C = (1, 1, –3). Find a vector perpendicular to the plane formed by these points.

$$\overrightarrow{AB} = \overrightarrow{OB} - \overrightarrow{OA} = (-2,0,1)$$
$$\overrightarrow{AC} = \overrightarrow{OC} - \overrightarrow{OA} = (1,0,-4)$$
$$\overrightarrow{AB} \times \overrightarrow{AC} = \begin{vmatrix} \vec{i} & \vec{j} & \vec{k} \\ -2 & 0 & 1 \\ 1 & 0 & -4 \end{vmatrix} = (0,-7,0)$$

Graphical interpretation of cross product

$|\vec{a} \times \vec{b}| = |\vec{a}||\vec{b}|\sin(\theta)$ = **The area of the parallelogram formed by the vectors** $\vec{a}$ **and** $\vec{b}$

14. The area of the triangle with the vertices: A = (0, 1, 1), B = (–2, 1, 2) and C = (1, 1, –3)

$$\overrightarrow{AB} = \overrightarrow{OB} - \overrightarrow{OA} = (-2,0,1)$$
$$\overrightarrow{AC} = \overrightarrow{OC} - \overrightarrow{OA} = (1,0,-4)$$
$$\left|\overrightarrow{AB} \times \overrightarrow{AC}\right| = \frac{1}{2}\begin{Vmatrix} \vec{i} & \vec{j} & \vec{k} \\ -2 & 0 & 1 \\ 1 & 0 & -4 \end{Vmatrix} = \frac{|(0,-7,0)|}{2} = \frac{7}{2}$$

15. The area of the quadrilateral with the vertices A = (2, 1, 3), B = (-5, -1, 2), C = (1, 1, -3) and D = (-2, -5, -6)

$$\overrightarrow{AB} = \overrightarrow{OB} - \overrightarrow{OA} = (-7,-2,-1)$$
$$\overrightarrow{AC} = \overrightarrow{OC} - \overrightarrow{OA} = (-1,0,-6)$$
$$\left|\overrightarrow{AB} \times \overrightarrow{AC}\right| = \frac{1}{2}\begin{Vmatrix} \vec{i} & \vec{j} & \vec{k} \\ -7 & -2 & -1 \\ -1 & 0 & -6 \end{Vmatrix} = \frac{|(12,-41,-2)|}{2} = \frac{\sqrt{1829}}{2}$$

$$\overrightarrow{AD} = \overrightarrow{OD} - \overrightarrow{OA} = (-4,-6,-9)$$
$$\overrightarrow{AC} = \overrightarrow{OC} - \overrightarrow{OA} = (-1,0,-6)$$
$$\left|\overrightarrow{AD} \times \overrightarrow{AC}\right| = \frac{1}{2}\begin{Vmatrix} \vec{i} & \vec{j} & \vec{k} \\ -4 & -6 & -9 \\ -1 & 0 & -6 \end{Vmatrix} = \frac{|(36,-15,-6)|}{2} = \frac{\sqrt{1557}}{2}$$

$$A_{ABCD} = \frac{\sqrt{1829}}{2} + \frac{\sqrt{1557}}{2}$$

16. Find the area of the triangle with the vertices A = (5, 1, 1), B = (0, –1, 2) and C = (1, 1, –3)

$$\overrightarrow{AB} = \overrightarrow{OB} - \overrightarrow{OA} = (-5, -2, 1)$$
$$\overrightarrow{AC} = \overrightarrow{OC} - \overrightarrow{OA} = (-4, 0, -4)$$

$$\left|\overrightarrow{AB} \times \overrightarrow{AC}\right| = \frac{1}{2}\begin{Vmatrix} \vec{i} & \vec{j} & \vec{k} \\ -5 & -2 & 1 \\ -4 & 0 & -4 \end{Vmatrix} = \left|\frac{(8, -24, -8)}{2}\right| = \frac{\sqrt{704}}{2}$$

17. Find the area of the quadrilateral with the vertices A = (1, 1, 1), B = (2, 2, 2), C = (-1, -1, 1) and D = (-2, -2, 2)

$$\overrightarrow{AB} = \overrightarrow{OB} - \overrightarrow{OA} = (1, 1, 1)$$
$$\overrightarrow{AC} = \overrightarrow{OC} - \overrightarrow{OA} = (-2, -2, 0)$$

$$\left|\overrightarrow{AB} \times \overrightarrow{AC}\right| = \frac{1}{2}\begin{Vmatrix} \vec{i} & \vec{j} & \vec{k} \\ 1 & 1 & 1 \\ -2 & -2 & 0 \end{Vmatrix} = \left|\frac{(-2, -2, 0)}{2}\right| = \frac{\sqrt{8}}{2} = \sqrt{2}$$

$$\overrightarrow{AD} = \overrightarrow{OD} - \overrightarrow{OA} = (-3, -3, 1)$$
$$\overrightarrow{AC} = \overrightarrow{OC} - \overrightarrow{OA} = (-2, -2, 0)$$

$$\left|\overrightarrow{AD} \times \overrightarrow{AC}\right| = \frac{1}{2}\begin{Vmatrix} \vec{i} & \vec{j} & \vec{k} \\ -3 & -3 & 1 \\ -2 & -2 & 0 \end{Vmatrix} = \left|\frac{(2, -2, 0)}{2}\right| = \frac{\sqrt{8}}{2} = \sqrt{2}$$

$$A_{ABCD} = \sqrt{2} + \sqrt{2} = 2\sqrt{2}$$

Some properties of cross product:

(i) $\mathbf{u} \times \mathbf{v} = -(\mathbf{v} \times \mathbf{u})$ Example: $\begin{vmatrix} \vec{i} & \vec{j} & \vec{k} \\ u_1 & u_2 & u_3 \\ v_1 & v_2 & v_3 \end{vmatrix} = -\begin{vmatrix} \vec{i} & \vec{j} & \vec{k} \\ v_1 & v_2 & v_3 \\ u_1 & u_2 & u_3 \end{vmatrix}$

(ii) $(\alpha\mathbf{u}) \times \mathbf{v} = \alpha(\mathbf{u} \times \mathbf{v})$ Example: $\begin{vmatrix} \vec{i} & \vec{j} & \vec{k} \\ \alpha u_1 & \alpha u_2 & \alpha u_3 \\ v_1 & v_2 & v_3 \end{vmatrix} = \alpha\begin{vmatrix} \vec{i} & \vec{j} & \vec{k} \\ u_1 & u_2 & u_3 \\ v_1 & v_2 & v_3 \end{vmatrix}$

(iii) $\mathbf{u} \times (\mathbf{v} + \mathbf{w}) = (\mathbf{u} \times \mathbf{v}) + (\mathbf{u} \times \mathbf{w})$ Example:

$$\begin{vmatrix} \vec{i} & \vec{j} & \vec{k} \\ u_1 & u_2 & u_3 \\ v_1 + w_1 & v_2 + w_2 & v_3 + w_3 \end{vmatrix} = \begin{vmatrix} \vec{i} & \vec{j} & \vec{k} \\ u_1 & u_2 & u_3 \\ v_1 & v_2 & v_3 \end{vmatrix} + \begin{vmatrix} \vec{i} & \vec{j} & \vec{k} \\ u_1 & u_2 & u_3 \\ w_1 & w_2 & w_3 \end{vmatrix}$$

(iv) $(\mathbf{u} \times \mathbf{v}) \bullet \mathbf{w} = \mathbf{u} \bullet (\mathbf{v} \times \mathbf{w})$ (mixed product)

$$\begin{vmatrix} \vec{i} & \vec{j} & \vec{k} \\ u_1 & u_2 & u_3 \\ v_1 & v_2 & v_3 \end{vmatrix} \cdot (w_1, w_2, w_3) = (u_1, u_2, u_3) \cdot \begin{vmatrix} \vec{i} & \vec{j} & \vec{k} \\ v_1 & v_2 & v_3 \\ w_1 & w_2 & w_3 \end{vmatrix}$$

2.4. – LINES

Exercises

1. Given the vector $\vec{a} = (1,3)$ and $\vec{d} = (1,-2)$. Find following vectors, sketch them on the diagram, start at the origin. Connect the end points of all the vectors.

   a. $\vec{r_1} = \vec{a} + \vec{d}$
   b. $\vec{r_2} = \vec{a} + 2\vec{d}$
   c. $\vec{r_3} = \vec{a} + 3\vec{d}$
   d. $\vec{r_4} = \vec{a} - \vec{d}$
   e. $\vec{r_5} = \vec{a} - 2\vec{d}$
   f. $\vec{r_6} = \vec{a} - 3\vec{d}$

   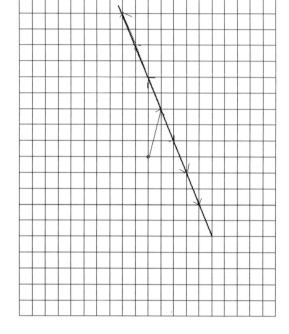

   g. Conclusion: The line has the same direction as the vector $\vec{d}$. $\vec{a}$ is arbitrary.

   h. The equation of the line:
   $(x, y) = \vec{r} = (1,3) + t(1,-2)$

   i. $\vec{a} = (2,1)$ and $\vec{d} = (-2,4)$: $(x, y) = \vec{r} = (2,1) + t(-2,4)$

2. A line in 2D or 3D using the vector form can be written in <u>an infinite</u> number of ways. The reason is that: <u>$\vec{a}$ is any vector from the origin to the line, $\vec{d}$ is any vector parallel to the line, so infinite choices for both.</u>

3. To describe a certain line, if we choose the direction vector to be a unity vector we have <u>two</u> possibilities for our choice.

4. The vector and parametric equations for the line passing through the points P = (2, –1, 6) and Q = (3, 1, –2).

   $(x, y, z) = \vec{r} = (2,-1,6) + t(1,2,-8)$

   $x = 2 + t \qquad t = x - 2$

   $y = -1 + 2t \qquad t = \dfrac{y+1}{2}$

   $z = 6 - 8t \qquad t = \dfrac{z-6}{-8}$

   $\dfrac{z-6}{-8} = \dfrac{y+1}{2} = \dfrac{x-2}{1}$

5. Write the equation of the straight line that passing through the points (1,2), (2, 8)

   a. In the vector form $(x, y) = \vec{r} = (1,2) + t(1,6)$

   b. In the parametric form: $\begin{array}{l} x = 1 + t \\ y = 2 + 6t \end{array}$

   c. In the symmetric (continuous) form: $\dfrac{y-2}{6} = \dfrac{x-1}{1}$

6. Find the parametric equation and the symmetric equations for the line L passing through $(1, -2, 4)$ and parallel to $\mathbf{v} = \mathbf{i} + \mathbf{j} - \mathbf{k}$

$(x, y, z) = \vec{r} = (1, -2, 4) + t(1, 1, -1)$

$x = 1 + t$

$y = -2 + t$

$z = 4 - t$

$\dfrac{x-1}{1} = \dfrac{y+2}{1} = \dfrac{z-4}{-1}$

7. Which one of the following points lies on the given line (show your answer)

$x = 3t,$
$y = 2t - 5$
$z = -t + 1$

   a. $(1, -3, 1)$
   b. $(30, 15, 9)$
   c. $(-6, -1, 3)$
   d. $(-12, -13, 5)$

$-12 = 3t; t = -4$
$-13 = 2t - 5; t = -4$
$5 = -t + 1; t = -4$

8. The equation of <u>a line (there are many)</u> perpendicular to the line passing thorough the points $A = (1, 1, 1)$ and $B = (7, 2, 2)$. Find the equation of a line perpendicular to both of the lines.

$\overrightarrow{AB} = (6, 1, 1); \overrightarrow{AB} \perp \vec{d} = (0, -1, 1)$

$(x, y, z) = \vec{r} = (1, 1, 1) + t(0, -1, 1)$

$\begin{vmatrix} \vec{i} & \vec{j} & \vec{k} \\ 6 & 1 & 1 \\ 0 & -1 & 1 \end{vmatrix} = (2, -6, -6) \qquad (x, y, z) = \vec{r} = (a_1, a_2, a_3) + t(2, -6, -6)$

9. Equation of a line parallel to the z axis in the vector form in 3 different ways.

$(x, y, z) = \vec{r} = (1, 1, 1) + t(0, 0, 1)$

$(x, y, z) = \vec{r} = (1, 1, 2) + t(0, 0, 7)$

$(x, y, z) = \vec{r} = (0, 0, 0) + t(0, 0, -121)$

10. Write the equation of a line parallel to the xy plane in the vector form in 3 different ways.

$(x, y, z) = \vec{r} = (1, 0, -2) + t(2, 3, 0)$

$(x, y, z) = \vec{r} = (4, 0, -2) + t(\sqrt{2}, 0, 0)$

$(x, y, z) = \vec{r} = (0, 0, 2) + t(1, 1, 0)$

11. The angle between the lines $\dfrac{x-1}{4} = \dfrac{y+5}{-4} = \dfrac{2z-3}{2}$ and $\dfrac{2x-1}{4} = \dfrac{2y+5}{-1} = \dfrac{z-3}{2}$

Lines are:

$(x, y, z) = (1, -5, \dfrac{3}{2}) + t(4, -4, 1)$

$(x, y, z) = (\dfrac{1}{2}, -\dfrac{5}{2}, 3) + t(2, -\dfrac{1}{2}, 2)$

$(4, -4, 1) \cdot (2, -\dfrac{1}{2}, 2) = \sqrt{33}\sqrt{\dfrac{33}{4}} \cos(\theta) \qquad \cos(\theta) = \dfrac{24}{33} \qquad \theta \approx 43.3°$

12. Find the angle between the lines $(x, y, z) = (0,0,1) + t(1,1,1)$ and

$$(1,1,1) \cdot (-1,2,1) = \sqrt{3}\sqrt{6} \cos(\alpha)$$

$$(x, y, z) = (1,-1,1) + t(-1,2,1)$$

$$\alpha = \arccos(\frac{2}{\sqrt{3}\sqrt{6}}) \approx 1.08 rad$$

13. Given that the lines $(x, y, z) = (0,0,1) + t(a,0,-1)$ and
$(x, y, z) = (1,-1,1) + t(3,4,0)$ form an angle of 60°, find a.

$$(a,0,-1) \cdot (3,4,0) = \sqrt{a^2+1}\sqrt{25} \cos(60°) \qquad 3a = \sqrt{a^2+1} \cdot 5 \cdot \frac{1}{2}; a = \frac{5\sqrt{11}}{11}$$

14. The position of a car in reference to its last known position is given by the equation $(x, y, z) = (10,-4) + t(-1,3)$. Position in km, velocity in km/h, t in hours.

a. The initial position of the car: $(x, y, z) = (10,-4) + 0(-1,3) = (10,-4)$

b. Initial distance between the car and its last destination. $|(10,-4)| = \sqrt{116}km$

c. The position of the car 2 hours later and its distance from the last known position.

$$(x, y, z) = (10,-4) + 2(-1,3) = (8,2)$$

$$|(8,2)| = \sqrt{68}km$$

d. The speed of a car: $\vec{v} = (-1,3); |\vec{v}| = \sqrt{10}km/h$

e. Sketch a diagram of the situation for the 2 hours mentioned:

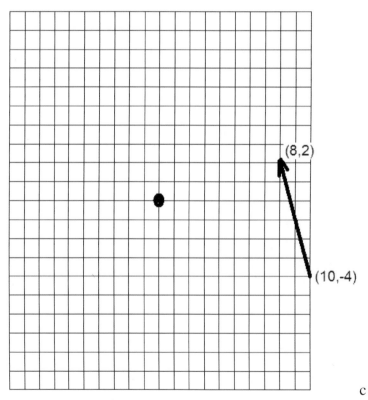

(8,2)

(10,-4)

c

420

15. An airplane is located at position $\vec{p} = (200, 150, 10)$ km from a certain control tower. It is moving with velocity vector $\vec{v} = (-160, -120, -8)$ km/h. The x coordinate is oriented east/west and the y coordinate north/south. The z coordinate is the vertical coordinate.

a. A diagram that includes the control tower and the location of the airplane.

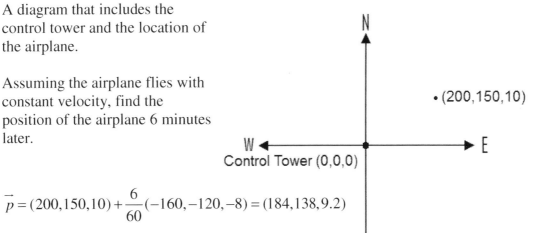

b. Assuming the airplane flies with constant velocity, find the position of the airplane 6 minutes later.

$$\vec{p} = (200, 150, 10) + \frac{6}{60}(-160, -120, -8) = (184, 138, 9.2)$$

c. The air distance between the airplane and the tower.

$$\left|\vec{p}\right| = \sqrt{(200)^2 + (150)^2 + (10)^2} = \sqrt{62600}\,km$$

d. The ground distance between the airplane and the tower (the distance between the shadow of the airplane and the tower).

$$\left|\vec{p}\right| = \sqrt{(200)^2 + (150)^2} = \sqrt{62500}\,km$$

e. The air speed of the airplane: $\left|\vec{v_{air}}\right| = \sqrt{(-160)^2 + (-120)^2 + (-8)^2} = \sqrt{40064} \approx 200\,km/h$

f. The ground speed of the airplane (the speed of the shadow of the airplane on the ground).

$$\left|\vec{v_{ground}}\right| = \sqrt{(-160)^2 + (-120)^2} = 200\,km/h$$

g. In case the airplane does not change its velocity, how long will it take it to reach the airport? The direction of the airplane is correct as its velocity vector points to the airport (proportional to the position vector and opposite direction). The height of the airplane should decrease to 0km. It starts at 10km.

$$10 = 8t; t = \frac{10}{8} = 1.25h(1h, 15\,min)$$

h. What will be the position of the airplane at that moment?

$$\vec{p} = (200, 150, 10) + 1.25(-160, -120, -8) = (0, 0, 0)$$

2.5. – RELATIVE POSITON BETWEEN LINES

TWO DIMENSIONS

1. Two lines can be <u>parallel, intersecting or coincident</u>. In order to find the relative position of the lines the system of equations needs to be solved.
2. If the system has <u>zero</u> solutions the lines are <u>parallel</u>
    $\vec{d_1} \cdot \vec{d_2} = \left|\vec{d_1}\right| \cdot \left|\vec{d_2}\right| \neq 0$ Direction vectors are <u>parallel</u>.

3. If the system has 1 solution the lines are intersecting. $\vec{d_1} \cdot \vec{d_2} \leq \left|\vec{d_1}\right| \cdot \left|\vec{d_2}\right|$. Direction vectors are <u>not parallel</u>.

4. If the system has <u>infinite</u> solutions the lines are <u>coincident</u>. $\vec{d_1} \cdot \vec{d_2} = \left|\vec{d_1}\right| \cdot \left|\vec{d_2}\right| \neq 0$
    Direction vectors are <u>parallel</u>

Given the following lines, write them in all possible forms, find their relative position. In case they intersect find their point of intersection and the angle between them.

5. $(x, y) = (1, -2) + k\,(3, -2)$ and $(x, y) = (-3, -2) + s\,(-6, 4)$

$x = 1 + 3k$

$y = -2 - 2k$

$\dfrac{x}{1} = \dfrac{y+2}{-2}$

$y = -2x - 2$

$x = -3 - 6s$

$y = -2 + 4s$

$\dfrac{x+3}{-6} = \dfrac{y+2}{4}$

$y = -\dfrac{2}{3}x$

$\dfrac{4}{-2} = \dfrac{-6}{3} \Rightarrow \vec{d_1} \parallel \vec{d_2}$ Solving the system: $\begin{matrix} 1 + 3k = -3 - 6s \\ -2 - 2k = -2 + 4s \end{matrix}$, no solution, lines are parallel, the angle is 0°.

6. $(x, y) = (0, 3) + k\,(-1, 2)$ and $(x, y) = (-1, 2) + s\,(-1, 4)$

$x = -k$

$y = 3 + 2k$

$\dfrac{x}{-1} = \dfrac{y-3}{2}$

$y = -2x + 3$

$x = -1 - s$

$y = 2 + 4s$

$\dfrac{x+1}{-1} = \dfrac{y-2}{4}$

$y = -4x - 2$

$\dfrac{-1}{-1} \neq \dfrac{4}{2} \Rightarrow \vec{d_1}$ not parallel to $\vec{d_2}$. Solving the system: $\begin{matrix} -k = -1 - s \\ 3 + 2k = 2 + 4s \end{matrix}$

$s = \dfrac{3}{2}, k = \dfrac{5}{2}$, one solution, lines are intersecting at the point $(\dfrac{3}{2}, 8)$

$(-1, 2) \cdot (-1, 4) = \sqrt{5}\sqrt{17} \cos(\alpha)$

$\alpha = \arccos(\dfrac{9}{\sqrt{5}\sqrt{17}}) \approx 0.219_{rad}$

7. $(x, y) = (0, 0) + k (-1, -3)$ and $(x, y) = (2, 2) + s (3, -1)$

$x = -k$ $x = 2 + 3s$

$y = -3k$ $y = 2 - s$

$\dfrac{x}{-1} = \dfrac{y}{-3}$ $\dfrac{x-2}{3} = \dfrac{y-2}{-1}$

$y = 3x$ $y = -\dfrac{x}{3} + \dfrac{8}{3}$

$\dfrac{3}{-1} \neq \dfrac{-1}{-3} \Rightarrow \vec{d_1}$ not parallel to $\vec{d_2}$. Solving the system: $\begin{aligned} -k &= 2 + 3s \\ -3k &= 2 - s \end{aligned}$

$s = -\dfrac{2}{5}, k = -\dfrac{4}{5}$, one solution, lines are intersecting at the point $(\dfrac{4}{5}, \dfrac{12}{5})$

$(-1, -3) \cdot (3, -1) = \sqrt{10}\sqrt{10} \cos(\alpha)$ $\alpha = \arccos(\dfrac{0}{100}) = \dfrac{\pi}{2}_{rad}$

8. $(x, y) = (2, -5) + k (-3, -4)$ and $(x, y) = (8, 3) + s (6, 8)$

$x = 2 - 3k$ $x = 8 + 6s$

$y = -5 - 4k$ $y = 3 + 8s$

$\dfrac{x-2}{-3} = \dfrac{y+5}{-4}$ $\dfrac{x-8}{6} = \dfrac{y-3}{8}$

$y = -\dfrac{4}{3}x + \dfrac{23}{3}$ $y = \dfrac{4}{3}x - \dfrac{23}{3}$

$\dfrac{6}{-3} = \dfrac{8}{-4} \Rightarrow \vec{d_1} \parallel \vec{d_2}$. Solving the system: $\begin{aligned} 2 - 3k &= 8 + 6s \\ -5 - 4k &= 3 + 8s \end{aligned}$, infinite solutions,

lines are coincident, the angle is $0°$.

9. $3x + 2y = 5$ and $-2x + y = 1$

$y = -\dfrac{3}{2}x + \dfrac{5}{2}$ $y = 2x + 1$

$(x, y) = (0, \dfrac{5}{2}) + t(2, -3)$ $(x, y) = (0, 1) + b(1, 2)$

                        $x = b$

$x = 2t$ $y = 1 + 2b$

$y = \dfrac{5}{2} - 3t$ $\dfrac{x}{1} = \dfrac{y-1}{2}$

$\dfrac{x}{2} = \dfrac{y - \dfrac{5}{2}}{-3}$

$\dfrac{1}{2} \neq \dfrac{2}{-3} \Rightarrow \vec{d_1}$ not parallel to $\vec{d_2}$. Solving the system: $\begin{aligned} 2t &= b \\ \dfrac{5}{2} - 3t &= 1 + 2b \end{aligned}$

$t = \dfrac{3}{14}, b = \dfrac{3}{7}$, one solution, lines are intersecting at the point $(\dfrac{3}{7}, \dfrac{13}{7})$

$(2, -3) \cdot (1, 2) = \sqrt{13}\sqrt{5} \cos(\alpha)$ $\alpha = \arccos(\dfrac{-4}{\sqrt{13}\sqrt{5}}) \approx 2.09_{rad}$

THREE DIMENSIONS

10. Two lines paronsparallel, intersecting skew or coincident. In order to find the relative position of the lines the system of equations needs to be solved by equaling the x, y and z coordinates of the lines and solving for s and t.

11. If the system has zero solutions the lines are parallel if $\left|\vec{d_1} \cdot \vec{d_2}\right| = \left|\vec{d_1}\right| \cdot \left|\vec{d_2}\right| \neq 0$

    Direction vectors are parallel $\vec{d_1} \parallel \vec{d_2}$

12. If the system has zero solutions the lines are skew if $\left|\vec{d_1} \cdot \vec{d_2}\right| < \left|\vec{d_1}\right| \cdot \left|\vec{d_2}\right|$

    Direction vectors are not parallel

13. If the system has one solution the lines are intersecting. $\vec{d_1} \cdot \vec{d_2} \leq \left|\vec{d_1}\right| \cdot \left|\vec{d_2}\right|$

    Direction vectors are not parallel

14. If the system has infinite solutions the lines are coincident. $\left|\vec{d_1} \cdot \vec{d_2}\right| = \left|\vec{d_1}\right| \cdot \left|\vec{d_2}\right| \neq 0$.

    Direction vectors are parallel $\vec{d_1} \parallel \vec{d_2}$

15. $\vec{r} = (1,3,2) + s(-1,2,3)$ and $\vec{c} = (1,3,2) + t(5,-10,1)$

    $\dfrac{5}{-1} = \dfrac{-10}{2} \neq \dfrac{1}{3}$ Lines are not parallel nor coincident, skew or intersecting.

    Solving system:

    $1 - s = 1 + 5t$

    $3 + 2s = 3 - 10t \qquad \begin{matrix} s = 0 \\ \\ t = 0 \end{matrix}$ The lines intersect at the point $(1, 3, 2)$

    $2 + 3s = 2 + t$

    $(-1,2,3) \cdot (5,-10,1) = \sqrt{14}\sqrt{126}\cos(\alpha) \qquad \alpha = \arccos(\dfrac{-22}{\sqrt{14}\sqrt{126}}) \approx 2.12_{rad}$

16. $\vec{r} = (2,1,0) + s(2,2,1)$ and $\vec{c} = (-4,-5,-3) + t(10,10,5)$

    $\dfrac{10}{2} = \dfrac{10}{2} = \dfrac{5}{1}$ Lines are parallel or coincident, solving system:

    $2 + 2s = -4 + 10t$

    $1 + 2s = -5 + 10t \qquad$ Infinite solutions the lines are coincident, angle $0°$

    $s = -3 + 5t$

17. $\vec{r} = (2,1,0) + s(2,2,0)$ and $\vec{c} = (6,5,0) + t(1,1,5)$

    $\dfrac{1}{2} = \dfrac{1}{2} \neq \dfrac{5}{0}$ Lines are not parallel nor coincident, skew or intersecting.

    Solving system:

    $2 + 2s = 6 + t$

    $1 + 2s = 5 + t \qquad \begin{matrix} s = 2 \\ \\ t = 0 \end{matrix}$ The lines intersect at the point $(6, 5, 0)$

    $0 = 5t$

    $(2,2,0) \cdot (1,1,5) = \sqrt{8}\sqrt{27}\cos(\alpha)$

    $\alpha = \arccos(\dfrac{4}{\sqrt{8}\sqrt{27}}) \approx 1.30_{rad}$

18. $(x, y, z) = (-9, 2, 3) + k\,(3, -2, -1)$ and $(x, y, z) = (-3, -2, 1) + s\,(-6, 4, 2)$

$\dfrac{-6}{3} = \dfrac{4}{-2} = \dfrac{2}{-1}$ Lines are parallel or coincident. Solving system:

$-9 + 3k = -3 - 6s$

$2 - 2k = -2 + 4s$ Infinite solutions the lines are coincident, angle 0°

$3 - k = 1 + 2s$

19. $(x, y, z) = (1, 0, 1) + k\,(1, -2, 1)$ and $(x, y, z) = (1, -5, 3) + s\,(1, 3, -1)$

$\dfrac{1}{1} \neq \dfrac{3}{0} \neq \dfrac{-1}{1}$ Lines are not parallel nor coincident, skew or intersecting

Solving system:

$1 + k = 1 + s$

$-2k = -5 + 3s$ No solutions, lines are Skew.

$1 + k = 1 - s$

$(1, -2, 1) \cdot (1, 3, -1) = \sqrt{6}\sqrt{11}\cos(\alpha)$

$\alpha = \arccos\left(\dfrac{-6}{\sqrt{6}\sqrt{11}}\right) \approx 2.40_{rad}$

20. $\dfrac{x-1}{-1} = \dfrac{y}{2} = \dfrac{3z+2}{3}$ and $\dfrac{2x-1}{-1} = \dfrac{y}{2} = \dfrac{z-1}{2}$

$\vec{r} = (1, 0, -\tfrac{2}{3}) + t(-1, 2, 1)$ $\vec{r} = (\tfrac{1}{2}, 0, 1) + k(-\tfrac{1}{2}, 2, 2)$

$\dfrac{-1/2}{1} \neq \dfrac{2}{2} \neq \dfrac{2}{1}$ Not parallel nor coincident, skew or intersecting Solving system:

$1 - t = \dfrac{1}{2} - \dfrac{1}{2}k;$

$2t = 2k$ No solutions, lines are Skew.

$-\dfrac{2}{3} + t = 1 + 2k$

$(-1, 2, 1) \cdot (-1, 4, 4) = \sqrt{6}\sqrt{33}\cos(\alpha)$

$\alpha = \arccos\left(\dfrac{13}{\sqrt{6}\sqrt{33}}\right) \approx 0.393_{rad}$

21. $\dfrac{x-2}{3} = \dfrac{y-1}{-1} = \dfrac{z+1}{2}$ and $\dfrac{x-1}{-6} = \dfrac{y+1}{2} = \dfrac{z+2}{-4}$

$\vec{r} = (2, 1, -1) + t(3, -1, 2)$ $\vec{r} = (1, -1, -2) + k(-6, 2, -4)$

$\dfrac{3}{-6} = \dfrac{-1}{2} = \dfrac{2}{-4}$ Lines are parallel or coincident. Solving system:

$2 + 3t = 1 - 6k$

$1 - t = -1 + 2k$ No solutions, lines are parallel, angle is 0°.

$-1 + 2t = -2 - 4k$

22. Write different equations of 2 lines in 3D such that:

    a. The lines will be coincident:
$$(x, y, z) = (1, 2, 0) + t(3, -2, 1) \quad (x, y, z) = (-2, 4, -1) + k(6, -4, 2)$$

    b. The lines will be parallel:
$$(x, y, z) = (1, 2, 0) + t(3, -2, 1) \quad (x, y, z) = (-2, 4, 0) + k(6, -4, 2)$$

    c. The lines will be intersecting:
$$(x, y, z) = (1, 2, 0) + t(3, -2, 1) \quad (x, y, z) = (5, 5, 5) + k(-4, -3, -5)$$

    d. The lines will be skew:
$$(x, y, z) = (1, 2, 0) + t(3, -2, 0) \quad (x, y, z) = (1, 2, 5) + k(-4, -3, -5)$$

    e. The lines will intersect with an angle of 60°
$$(x, y, z) = (1, 2, 0) + k(0, 0, 1)$$
$$(x, y, z) = (1, 2, 0) + t(0, a, 1)$$
$$(0, 0, 1) \cdot (0, a, 1) = \sqrt{a^2 + 1} \cos(60°)$$
$$2 = \sqrt{a^2 + 1}$$
$$a = \pm\sqrt{3}$$
$$(x, y, z) = (1, 2, 0) + t(0, 0, 1) \quad (x, y, z) = (1, 2, 0) + t(0, \sqrt{3}, 1)$$
Lines intersect at (1, 2, 0) with an angle of 60°

    f. The lines will intersect with an angle of 90° (perpendicular)
$$(x, y, z) = (1, 2, 0) + t(0, 5, -3)$$
$$(x, y, z) = (1, 2, 0) + k(-4, -3, -5)$$

23. Write the equations of 3 lines that intersect at a point.

$$(x, y, z) = (1, 2, 0) + t(1, 1, 1)$$
$$(x, y, z) = (2, 3, 1) + k(0, 5, -3)$$
$$(x, y, z) = (0, 0, 0) + s(2, 3, 1)$$
All 3 lines intersect at (2, 3, 1)

24. Write the equations of 3 parallel lines
$$(x, y, z) = (1, 2, 0) + t(1, 1, 1)$$
$$(x, y, z) = (1, 2, 1) + k(2, 2, 2)$$
$$(x, y, z) = (1, 2, 2) + s(-1, -1, -1)$$

25. Write the equations of 3 lines, 2 parallel and a 3rd line that intersects both of them with an angle of 30°.
2 parallel lines:
$$(x, y, z) = (0, 0, 0) + s(0, 0, 1)$$
$$(x, y, z) = (1, 0, 0) + k(0, 0, 1)$$
Line that intersect them with an angle of 30°:
$$(x, y, z) = (0, 0, 0) + t(1, 0, a)$$
$$(0, 0, 1) \cdot (1, 0, a) = \sqrt{a^2 + 1} \cos(30°)$$
$$2a = \sqrt{a^2 + 1}\sqrt{3} \qquad 4a^2 = 3a^2 + 3 \qquad a = \pm\sqrt{3}$$
$$(x, y, z) = (0, 0, 0) + t(1, 0, \sqrt{3})$$

2.6. – PLANES IN 3D
Exercises

1. A plane in 3D using the <u>vector form</u> can be written in <u>an infinite</u> number of ways. The reason is that: <u>infinite possibilities for each one of the vectors **P**, **v** and **w**</u>

2. To describe a certain plane, if we choose the "direction vectors" to be unity vectors, we have <u>infinite</u> possibilities for our choice.

3. To describe a plane using points, we need 3 points that are not on the same <u>line</u>.

4. The equation of the plane that contains the three points: F(1, 2, 1), G(–2, 0, 2) and H(–1, 4, 3) in the vector form and parametric form in 2 different ways.

$$(x, y, z) = \vec{r} = (1, 2, 1) + t(-3, -2, 1) + k(-2, 2, 2) \quad (x, y, z) = \vec{r} = (1, 2, 1) + t(-5, 0, 3) + k(-2, 2, 2)$$

$$x = 1 - 3t - 2k \qquad\qquad\qquad x = 1 - 5t - 2k$$

$$y = 2 - 2t + 2k \qquad\qquad\qquad y = 2 + 2k$$

$$z = 1 + t + 2k \qquad\qquad\qquad z = 1 + 3t + 2k$$

5. Find an equation of the plane passing through the point D = (2, 5, 1) and normal to the vector **n** = **i** – 2**j** + 3**k**. Use the fact as seen in the following diagram that

$$\overrightarrow{AD} \cdot \vec{n} = 0 \qquad (x - 2, y - 5, z - 1) \cdot (1, -2, 3) = 0 \qquad x - 2y + 3z = -5$$

6. In order to write the Cartesian equation of the plane we need to know the <u>Normal</u> vector to the plane and a <u>Point.</u>

7. Find an equation of the plane passing through the points P = (1, 2, 1), Q = (–2, 3, –1) and R = (1, 0, 4) in the Cartesian form.

$$\vec{n} = \overrightarrow{PQ} \times \overrightarrow{PR} = \begin{vmatrix} \vec{i} & \vec{j} & \vec{k} \\ -3 & 1 & -2 \\ 0 & -2 & 3 \end{vmatrix} = (-1, 9, 6)$$

$$\overrightarrow{AD} \cdot \vec{n} = 0$$
$$(x - 1, y - 2, z - 1) \cdot (-1, 9, 6) = 0$$
$$-x + 9y + 6z = 23$$

8. A plane parallel to the z axis in the vector, parametric and Cartesian form.

$$(x, y, z) = \vec{r} = (1, 1, 0) + t(0, 0, 1) + k(1, 1, 0)$$
$$x = 1 + k \qquad y = 1 + k \qquad z = t$$

$$\vec{n} = \begin{vmatrix} \vec{i} & \vec{j} & \vec{k} \\ 0 & 0 & 1 \\ 1 & 1 & 0 \end{vmatrix} = (-1, 1, 0)$$

$$(x - 1, y - 1, z) \cdot (-1, 1, 0) = 0$$
$$-x + y = 0$$

9. A plane parallel to the xy plane in the vector, parametric and Cartesian form.

$$(x, y, z) = \vec{r} = (0, 0, 1) + t(1, 0, 0) + k(0, 1, 0)$$
$$x = t \qquad y = k \qquad z = 1$$

$$\vec{n} = \begin{vmatrix} \vec{i} & \vec{j} & \vec{k} \\ 1 & 0 & 0 \\ 0 & 1 & 0 \end{vmatrix} = (0, 0, 1)$$

$$(x, y, z - 1) \cdot (0, 0, 1) = 0$$
$$z = 1$$

10. A plane parallel to the zy plane in the vector, parametric and Cartesian form.

$$(x, y, z) = \vec{r} = (1, 0, 0) + t(0, 0, 1) + k(0, 1, 0)$$
$$x = 1 \qquad y = k \qquad z = t$$

$$\vec{n} = \begin{vmatrix} \vec{i} & \vec{j} & \vec{k} \\ 0 & 0 & 1 \\ 0 & 1 & 0 \end{vmatrix} = (-1, 0, 0)$$

$$(x - 1, y, z) \cdot (-1, 0, 0) = 0$$
$$x = -1$$

11. Equation of the plane containing the lines and write it in all possible forms:

$$\vec{r} = (1, 3, 2) + s(-1, 2, 3), \vec{c} = (-5, 5, 6) + t(-2, 4, 6) \qquad \frac{-2}{-1} = \frac{4}{2} = \frac{6}{3} \text{ parallel or coincide.}$$

solving system: No solution, parallel lines. Plane contains both lines.

$$(x, y, z) = \vec{r} = (1, 3, 2) + t(-1, 2, 3) + k(-6, 2, 4)$$
$$x = 1 - t - 6k \qquad y = 3 + 2t + 2k \qquad z = 2 + 3t + 4k$$

$$\vec{n} = \begin{vmatrix} \vec{i} & \vec{j} & \vec{k} \\ -1 & 2 & 3 \\ -6 & 2 & 4 \end{vmatrix} = (2, -14, 10)$$

$$\overrightarrow{AD} \cdot \vec{n} = 0 \qquad (x - 1, y - 3, z - 2) \cdot (2, -14, 10) = 0 \qquad 2x - 14y + 10z = -20$$

427

2.7. – RELATIVE POSITIONS BETWEEN LINES AND PLANES
Exercises
1. In 2D, a line and a plane can be: <u>Any line is contained in the plane (xy plane)</u>
2. In 3D, a line and a plane can be <u>intersecting, parallel</u> or <u>contained</u> In order to find the relative position of the line and plane the system of equations needs to be solved by plugging the parametric equations of the line into the plane..
3. If the system has <u>0</u> solutions the line and plane are <u>parallel</u> $\vec{n} \cdot \vec{d} = 0$.
4. If the system has <u>1</u> solution the line and plane are <u>intersecting</u> $\vec{n} \cdot \vec{d} \neq 0$
5. If the system has <u>infinite</u> solutions the line is <u>contained</u> in the plane. $\vec{n} \cdot \vec{d} = 0$.

Given the following lines and planes, find their relative position. If possible find their point of intersection and/or angle between them.

6. $\dfrac{x-1}{-1} = \dfrac{y}{2} = \dfrac{3z+2}{3}$ and $2x - y + 2z = 1$ $\qquad \vec{n} = (2, -1, 2)$

$\vec{r} = (1, 0, \dfrac{-2}{3}) + t(-1, 2, 1)$ $\qquad \vec{n} \cdot \vec{d} \neq 0$, intersecting $\qquad 2 - 2t - 2t - \dfrac{4}{3} + 2t = 1$

$x = 1 - t \qquad y = 2t \qquad z = \dfrac{-2}{3} + t \qquad\qquad\qquad t = -\dfrac{1}{6}$

$(2, -1, 2) \cdot (-1, 2, 1) = 3\sqrt{6} \cos(\alpha)$

Point of intersection $(\dfrac{7}{6}, -\dfrac{1}{3}, -\dfrac{5}{6})$ $\quad \alpha = \arccos(\dfrac{2}{3\sqrt{6}}) = 1.30_{rad}$, Angle: $\dfrac{\pi}{2} - 1.30_{rad}$

7. $(x, y, z) = (1, -2, 0) + k(3, -9, 1)$ and $3x + y = 2$ $\qquad \vec{n} = (3, 1, 0)$

$x = 1 + 3k \qquad y = -2 - 9k \qquad z = k \qquad \vec{n} \cdot \vec{d} = 0$, parallel, contained

$3 + 9k - 2 - 9k = 2$

No Solution $\qquad$ Line is parallel to plane, angle is $0°$

8. $(x, y, z) = (3, 2, 2) + s(-3, -2, 0)$ and $-2x + 3y + z = 2$ $\qquad \vec{n} = (-2, 3, 1)$

$x = 3 - 3s \qquad y = 2 - 2s \qquad z = 2 \qquad \vec{n} \cdot \vec{d} = 0$, parallel, contained

$-6 + 6s + 6 - 6s + 2 = 2 \qquad 2 = 2$

Infinite Solutions $\qquad$ Line is contained in plane, angle is $0°$

9. $(x, y, z) = (1, 0, 1) + k(1, -2, 1)$ and $2x - 4y + 2z = 4$ $\qquad \vec{n} = (2, -4, 2)$

$x = 1 + k \qquad y = -2k \qquad z = 1 + k \qquad \vec{n} \cdot \vec{d} \neq 0$, intersecting

$2 + 2k + 8k + 2 + 2k = 4$

$k = 0$ $\qquad$ Point of intersection $(1, 0, 1)$

$(1, -2, 1) \cdot (2, -4, 2) = \sqrt{6}\sqrt{24} \cos(\alpha)$

$\alpha = \arccos(\dfrac{12}{12}) = 0_{rad}$, Angle: $\dfrac{\pi}{2}_{rad}$

10. $\dfrac{x-1}{-1} = \dfrac{y}{-2} = \dfrac{z-1}{4}$ and $2x + y + z = 5$ $\qquad \vec{n} = (2,1,1)$

$x = 1 - k$ $\qquad y = -2k$ $\qquad z = 1 + 4k$ $\qquad \vec{n}\cdot\vec{d} = 0, \ parallel, \ contained$

$2 - 2k - 2k + 1 + 4k = 5$

No Solution $\qquad\qquad$ Lines and plane are parallel angle is $0°$

11. $\dfrac{x-2}{3} = \dfrac{y-1}{-1} = \dfrac{z+1}{2}$ and $z = -1$ $\qquad \vec{n} = (0,0,1)$

$x = 2 + 3k$ $\qquad y = 1 - k$ $\qquad z = -1 + 2k$ $\qquad \vec{n}\cdot\vec{d} \neq 0, \ intersecting$

$-1 + 2k = -1$ $\qquad$ Point of intersection $(2,1,-1)$

$k = 0$

$(0,0,1)\cdot(3,-1,2) = \sqrt{14}\cos(\alpha)$

$\alpha = \arccos(\dfrac{1}{\sqrt{14}}) = 1.30_{rad}, Angle : (\dfrac{\pi}{2} - 1.30)_{rad}$

12. $\dfrac{x-1}{-6} = \dfrac{y+1}{2} = \dfrac{z+2}{-4}$ and $3x - y + 2z = 0$ $\quad \vec{n} = (3,-1,2)$

$x = 1 - 6k$ $\qquad y = -1 + 2k$ $\qquad z = -2 - 4k$ $\qquad \vec{n}\cdot\vec{d} \neq 0, \ intersecting$

$3 - 18k + 1 - 2k - 4 - 8k = 0$

$k = 0$ $\qquad\qquad$ Point of intersection $(1,-1,-2)$

$(3,-1,2)\cdot(-6,2,-4) = \sqrt{14}\sqrt{56}\cos(\alpha)$

$\alpha = \arccos(\dfrac{-28}{\sqrt{14}\sqrt{56}}) = \pi_{rad}, Angle : \dfrac{\pi}{2}_{rad}$

13. Write the equation of a line and a plane in 3D such that:

a. The line will intersect the plane.

$\vec{r} = (0,0,0) + t(1,1,1)$ $\qquad x + y + z = 10$

b. The line will be parallel to the plane

$\vec{r} = (0,0,0) + t(0,1,-1)$ $\qquad x + y + z = 10$

c. The line will be contained in the plane

$\vec{r} = (10,0,0) + t(0,1,-1)$ $\qquad x + y + z = 10$

d. The line will intersect the plane with an angle of $60°$

$\vec{r} = (10,0,0) + t(a,1,a)$ $\qquad x + y + z = 10$ $\qquad (a,1,a)\cdot(1,1,1) = \sqrt{1 + 2a^2}\sqrt{3}\cos(30°)$

$2 + 4a = 3\sqrt{1 + a^2}; a = 4\pm\dfrac{3\sqrt{6}}{2}$ $\qquad \vec{r} = (10,0,0) + t(4\pm\dfrac{3\sqrt{6}}{2}, 1, 4\pm\dfrac{3\sqrt{6}}{2})$

e. The line will intersect the plane with an angle of $90°$

$\vec{r} = (10,0,0) + t(1,1,1)$ $\qquad x + y + z = 10$

14. Summarizing, in case of a line and a plane if the system has <u>0 solutions</u> there is no intersection and the line is <u>parallel</u> to the <u>plane.</u> if the system has 1 solution the line <u>intersects the plane</u> and if the system has <u>infinite solutions</u> the line is <u>contained</u> in the plane.

2.8. – SYSTEMS OF EQUATIONS

TWO DIMENSIONAL SYSTEMS

1. One equation with 2 variables has <u>infinite</u> number of solution(s).
    Each solution graphically is represented by a <u>point</u>.

2. In a system of 2 equations with 2 variables each equation represents a <u>line</u>.

3. The possible situations between 2 lines are <u>intersecting</u>, <u>parallel</u> and <u>coincident</u>

4. In case the lines are parallel and we try to solve the system we will get
    <u>0</u> solution(s).

5. In case the lines are intersecting and we try to solve the system we will get
    <u>1</u> solution(s).

6. In case the lines are <u>coincident</u> and we try to solve the system we will get
    <u>Infinite</u> solution(s).

7. In case we have 3 lines the only situation in which the system will have a
    solution <u>is if all three intersect at the same point (assuming different lines)</u>

8. Given the system: x + y = 1, x + y = 2
    In this case the lines are <u>parallel</u> and the system has <u>0</u> Solution(s)

9. Given the system : x + y = 1, 2x + 2y = 2
    In this case the lines are <u>coincident</u> and the system has <u>infinite</u> solution(s)

10. Given the system : x + y = 1, x + 2y = 2
    In this case the lines are <u>intersecting</u> and the system has <u>1</u> solution(s)

1. Given the following system 4x – 2y = 3, x – y = 1
    Solve or express solution properly, indicate the number of solutions.
    $$I - 4II \quad 2y = -1; y = -\frac{1}{2}; x = \frac{3}{2} \quad 1 \ Solution, \text{Intersecting} \ Lines$$

2. Given the following system – 3x – 2y = 2, 9x + 6y = 5
    Solve or express solution properly, indicate the number of solutions.
    $$3I + II \quad 0 = 1 No \ Solution, Parallel \ Lines$$

3. Given the following system – 3x – 2y = 2, 9x + 6y = 6
    Solve or express solution properly, indicate the number of solutions.
    $$3I + II \quad 0 = 0 \ Infinite \ Solutions, Coincident \ Lines$$

THREE DIMENSIONAL SYSTEMS

1. Each equation represents a: <u>Plane</u>

2. Can you think about the different relative positions of 2 planes?
   <u>Intersect in a line, Parallel, Coincident</u>

3. When a system of 2 equations, each with 3 variables, is given the possible number of solutions is:

   a. <u>Infinite</u> solutions, that means the planes intersect in a line.

   b. <u>Infinite</u> solutions, means the planes intersect in a plane.

   c. <u>0</u> solutions, that means the planes are parallel.

4. Can you think about the different relative positions of 3 planes? There are 8 different positions. See Question 15.

5. Given the system, use normal vectors to check the relative position of the planes. Solve or express solution properly.

   $x - 4y + 8z = -2$ $Checking\ \ if\ \overrightarrow{n_1} \parallel \overrightarrow{n_2} : \dfrac{1}{3} \neq \dfrac{-4}{3}, No$, Planes intersect in a line

   $$II - 3I \qquad 15y - 23z = 7;\ y = \dfrac{23}{15}z;\ z \equiv \lambda;\ x = \dfrac{92}{15}\lambda - 8\lambda - 2$$

   $3x + 3y + z = 1$

   $$(x, y, z) = (-2 - \dfrac{28}{15}\lambda, \dfrac{23}{15}\lambda, \lambda)$$

6. Given the system, use normal vectors to check the relative position of the planes. Solve or express solution properly.

   $2x - y + z = -2$ $Checking\ \ if\ \overrightarrow{n_1} \parallel \overrightarrow{n_2} : \dfrac{2}{4} = \dfrac{-1}{-2} = \dfrac{1}{2}, Yes$, PlanesParallel/Coincident

   $4x - 2y + 2z = 3$ Solving: No Solution, planes are parallel.

7. Given the system, use normal vectors to check the relative position of the planes. Solve or express solution properly.

   $7x - y + 2z = -5$ $Checking\ \ if\ \overrightarrow{n_1} \parallel \overrightarrow{n_2} : \dfrac{2}{4} = \dfrac{-1}{-2} = \dfrac{1}{2}, Yes$, PlanesParallel/Coincident

   $-21x + 3y - 6z = -9$ Solving: No Solution, planes are parallel.

8. Given the system, find a,b, and c so that the planes are coincident. find a,b, and c so that the planes are parallel.

   $ax - by + 2z = 1$

   $18x + 6y - cz = 3$ $Checking\ \ if\ \overrightarrow{n_1} \parallel \overrightarrow{n_2} : \dfrac{a}{18} = \dfrac{-b}{6} = \dfrac{2}{-c}$

   $$x = y = 0, z = \dfrac{1}{2} \Rightarrow c = -6 \Rightarrow b = -2, a = 6 (Coincident)$$

   $$c = 6, b = 2, a = -6 (Parallel)$$

9. Given the planes $3x + 2y - z = 5$ and $-6x + 3y + z = 2$, find their relative position. In case they intersect, find the line of intersection.

Checking if $\overrightarrow{n_1} \parallel \overrightarrow{n_2} : \dfrac{3}{-6} \neq \dfrac{2}{3}, No$, Planes intersect in a line

$II + 2I \quad 7y - z = 12; z = 7y - 12; y \equiv \lambda; x = \dfrac{5}{3}\lambda - \dfrac{7}{3}$

$(x, y, z) = (\dfrac{5}{3}\lambda - \dfrac{7}{3}, \lambda, 7\lambda - 12)$

10. Given the planes $7x + 2y - 3z = 2$ and $-14x + 4y - 6z = 2$, find their relative position. In case they intersect, find the line of intersection.

Checking if $\overrightarrow{n_1} \parallel \overrightarrow{n_2} : \dfrac{7}{-14} \neq \dfrac{2}{4}, No$, Planes intersect in a line

$II + 2I \quad 8y - 12z = 6; y = \dfrac{3}{2}z + \dfrac{3}{4}; z \equiv \lambda; x = \dfrac{3}{7}\lambda - \dfrac{3}{7}\lambda - \dfrac{3}{14}\lambda + 2$

$(x, y, z) = (\dfrac{1}{14}, \dfrac{3}{2}\lambda \dfrac{3}{4}, \lambda)$

11. Given the planes $7x + 2y - 3z = 2$ and $-14x + 4y - 6z = 4$, find their relative position. In case they intersect, find the line of intersection.

Checking if $\overrightarrow{n_1} \parallel \overrightarrow{n_2} : \dfrac{7}{-14} \neq \dfrac{2}{4}, No$, Planes intersect in a line

$II + 2I \quad 8y - 12z = 8; y = \dfrac{3}{2}z + 1; z \equiv \lambda; x = \dfrac{3}{7}\lambda - \dfrac{3}{7}\lambda - \dfrac{2}{7} + \dfrac{2}{7}$

$(x, y, z) = (0, \dfrac{3}{2}\lambda + 1, \lambda)$

12. A plane parallel to the plane $x + 2y - z = 2$ would be <u>$x + 2y - z = 3$</u>, an identical plane would be <u>$2x + 4y - 2z = 4$</u> an intersecting plane would be <u>$5x + 2y - z = 2$</u>

13. Given the plane $\vec{r} = (1, 3, 2) + w(-1, 2, 3) + t(0, 2, 2)$ Find, using vector notation:
    a. A parallel plane.
       $\vec{r} = (1, 3, 10) + w(-1, 2, 3) + t(0, 2, 2)$
    b. An identical plane using different vectors and different point.
       $\vec{r} = (0, 5, 5) + w(-1, 4, 5) + t(1, 0, -1)$
    c. An intersecting plane.
       $\vec{r} = (1, 3, 2) + w(-1, 2, 3) + t(0, 2, 10)$
    d. A plane that intersects this plane with an angle of 30°.

$\overrightarrow{n_1} = \begin{vmatrix} \vec{i} & \vec{j} & \vec{k} \\ -1 & 2 & 3 \\ 0 & 2 & 2 \end{vmatrix} = (-2, 2, -2) \qquad \overrightarrow{n_1} \cdot \overrightarrow{n_2} = (-2, 2, -2) \cdot (0, 1, a) = \sqrt{8}\sqrt{1+a^2} \cos(30°)$

$4 - 4a = \sqrt{24}\sqrt{1+a^2} \qquad a = -2 \pm \dfrac{\sqrt{12}}{2} \qquad y + \left(\dfrac{\sqrt{12}}{2} - 2\right)z = \sqrt{12} - 1$

14. Given the planes: $\vec{r} = (1, 0, -2) + s(1, 4, 1) + t(1, -2, 5)$ and

$\vec{r} = (-1, -1, 2) + s(3, 1, 1) + t(-1, 1, 2)$. Find their relative position.

$$\vec{n_1} = \begin{vmatrix} \vec{i} & \vec{j} & \vec{k} \\ 1 & 4 & 1 \\ 1 & -2 & 5 \end{vmatrix} = (22, 4, -6) \qquad \vec{n_2} = \begin{vmatrix} \vec{i} & \vec{j} & \vec{k} \\ 3 & 1 & 1 \\ -1 & 1 & 2 \end{vmatrix} = (1, 7, 4)$$

$22x + 4y - 6z = 34 \qquad\qquad x + 7y + 4z = 0$

Normal vectors not parallel, planes intersect in a line.

15. There are 8 different possibilities for question 4, these possibilities are grouped to 3 groups:

Gauss's Method: Consists in creating a matrix with a triangle of zeros under the diagonal (upper triangular matrix).

Example 1: System with unique solution

    x + 2y + 4z = 5
    x + 4y + 8z = 9
    x + 3y +   z = 2

The objective was to obtain a triangle of <u>zeros</u> From here, multiplying we see that $-5z = -5$ so <u>z = 1</u> We also see $2y + 4z = 4$ so <u>y = 0</u> From here x is easily obtained, <u>x = 1</u>

So the solution for the system is: (<u>1, 0, 1</u>)

Example 2: System infinite solutions (intersection of the planes is a line)

    2x – 3y + 4z = 5
    x + 4y + 8z = 9   can be written as:
    3x + y + 12z = 14

The objective was to obtain a triangle of <u>zeros</u> as can be observed that is not possible

and a row of zeros was obtained, that means only 2 equations are independent and third

one was a linear combination of those 2. The system will have <u>infinite</u> solutions.

The equations remaining can be written as:

x + 2y + 4z = 5

11y + 12z = 13

Making $z = \lambda$, $y = \dfrac{13 - \lambda}{11}$ $x = 5 - 2\dfrac{(13 - \lambda)}{11} - \lambda = \dfrac{29}{11} - \dfrac{46}{11}\lambda$

So the solution is the line given by: $(\dfrac{29}{11} - \dfrac{46}{11}\lambda, \dfrac{13 - \lambda}{11}, \lambda)$

16. Solve or express solution properly, indicate the number of solutions.

$$\begin{aligned}2x+2y+4z&=4\\x+4y+8z&=5\\x+3y+z&=4\end{aligned}\quad \begin{pmatrix}2&2&4\\1&4&8\\1&3&1\end{pmatrix}\begin{pmatrix}x\\y\\z\end{pmatrix}=\begin{pmatrix}4\\5\\4\end{pmatrix}\Rightarrow\begin{pmatrix}2&2&4\\1&4&8\\0&-1&-7\end{pmatrix}\begin{pmatrix}x\\y\\z\end{pmatrix}=\begin{pmatrix}4\\5\\-1\end{pmatrix}\Rightarrow$$

$$\begin{pmatrix}2&2&4\\0&6&12\\0&-1&-7\end{pmatrix}\begin{pmatrix}x\\y\\z\end{pmatrix}=\begin{pmatrix}4\\6\\-1\end{pmatrix}\Rightarrow\begin{pmatrix}2&2&4\\0&6&12\\0&0&-30\end{pmatrix}\begin{pmatrix}x\\y\\z\end{pmatrix}=\begin{pmatrix}4\\6\\0\end{pmatrix}\Rightarrow\begin{pmatrix}x\\y\\z\end{pmatrix}=\begin{pmatrix}1\\1\\0\end{pmatrix}$$

1 Solution

17. Solve or express solution properly, indicate the number of solutions.

$$\begin{aligned}2x+2y+4z&=4\\x-4y+8z&=-2\\3x+3y+z&=1\end{aligned}\quad \begin{pmatrix}2&2&4\\1&-4&8\\3&3&1\end{pmatrix}\begin{pmatrix}x\\y\\z\end{pmatrix}=\begin{pmatrix}4\\-2\\1\end{pmatrix}\Rightarrow\begin{pmatrix}2&2&4\\1&-4&8\\0&15&-23\end{pmatrix}\begin{pmatrix}x\\y\\z\end{pmatrix}=\begin{pmatrix}4\\-2\\7\end{pmatrix}\Rightarrow$$

$$\begin{pmatrix}2&2&4\\0&-10&12\\0&15&-23\end{pmatrix}\begin{pmatrix}x\\y\\z\end{pmatrix}=\begin{pmatrix}4\\-8\\7\end{pmatrix}\Rightarrow\begin{pmatrix}2&2&4\\0&-10&12\\0&0&-10\end{pmatrix}\begin{pmatrix}x\\y\\z\end{pmatrix}=\begin{pmatrix}4\\-8\\-10\end{pmatrix}\Rightarrow\begin{pmatrix}x\\y\\z\end{pmatrix}=\begin{pmatrix}-2\\2\\1\end{pmatrix}$$

1 solution

18. Solve or express solution properly, indicate the number of solutions.

$$\begin{aligned}x+y+z&=1\\x+2y+z&=3\\x+y+z&=2\end{aligned}\quad \begin{pmatrix}1&1&1\\1&2&1\\1&1&1\end{pmatrix}\begin{pmatrix}x\\y\\z\end{pmatrix}=\begin{pmatrix}1\\3\\2\end{pmatrix}\Rightarrow\begin{pmatrix}1&1&1\\1&2&1\\0&0&0\end{pmatrix}\begin{pmatrix}x\\y\\z\end{pmatrix}=\begin{pmatrix}1\\3\\1\end{pmatrix}\Rightarrow 0\text{ Solutions}$$

19. Solve or express solution properly, indicate the number of solutions.

$$\begin{aligned}x+z&=1\\x+2y+z&=3\\x+y+z&=2\end{aligned}\quad \begin{pmatrix}1&0&1\\1&2&1\\1&1&1\end{pmatrix}\begin{pmatrix}x\\y\\z\end{pmatrix}=\begin{pmatrix}1\\3\\2\end{pmatrix}\Rightarrow\begin{pmatrix}1&0&1\\0&2&0\\0&1&0\end{pmatrix}\begin{pmatrix}x\\y\\z\end{pmatrix}=\begin{pmatrix}1\\2\\1\end{pmatrix}\Rightarrow\begin{pmatrix}x\\y\\z\end{pmatrix}=\begin{pmatrix}t\\1\\1-t\end{pmatrix}$$

∞ solutions(Line)

20. Solve or express solution properly, indicate the number of solutions.

$$\begin{aligned}x+z&=1\\x+2y+z&=3\\x+2z&=2\end{aligned}\quad \begin{pmatrix}1&0&1\\1&2&1\\1&0&2\end{pmatrix}\begin{pmatrix}x\\y\\z\end{pmatrix}=\begin{pmatrix}1\\3\\2\end{pmatrix}\Rightarrow\begin{pmatrix}1&0&1\\0&2&0\\0&0&1\end{pmatrix}\begin{pmatrix}x\\y\\z\end{pmatrix}=\begin{pmatrix}1\\2\\2\end{pmatrix}\Rightarrow\begin{pmatrix}x\\y\\z\end{pmatrix}=\begin{pmatrix}-1\\1\\2\end{pmatrix}$$

1 solution

21. Solve or express solution properly, indicate the number of solutions.

$$\begin{aligned}x+z&=1\\x+2y+z&=2\\-x+z&=2\end{aligned}\quad \begin{pmatrix}1&0&1\\1&2&1\\-1&0&1\end{pmatrix}\begin{pmatrix}x\\y\\z\end{pmatrix}=\begin{pmatrix}1\\2\\2\end{pmatrix}\Rightarrow\begin{pmatrix}1&0&1\\0&2&0\\0&0&2\end{pmatrix}\begin{pmatrix}x\\y\\z\end{pmatrix}=\begin{pmatrix}1\\1\\3\end{pmatrix}\Rightarrow\begin{pmatrix}x\\y\\z\end{pmatrix}=\begin{pmatrix}-\frac{1}{2}\\\frac{1}{2}\\\frac{3}{2}\end{pmatrix}$$

1 solution

22. Solve or express solution properly, indicate the number of solutions.

$$x + z = 1$$
$$-2x + 3y + 7z = 2$$
$$-x + y + 2z = 2$$

$$\begin{pmatrix} 1 & 0 & 1 \\ -2 & 3 & 7 \\ -1 & 1 & 2 \end{pmatrix} \begin{pmatrix} x \\ y \\ z \end{pmatrix} = \begin{pmatrix} 1 \\ 2 \\ 2 \end{pmatrix} \Rightarrow \begin{pmatrix} 1 & 0 & 1 \\ -2 & 3 & 7 \\ 0 & 1 & 3 \end{pmatrix} \begin{pmatrix} x \\ y \\ z \end{pmatrix} = \begin{pmatrix} 1 \\ 2 \\ 3 \end{pmatrix} \Rightarrow$$

$$\begin{pmatrix} 1 & 0 & 1 \\ 0 & 3 & 9 \\ 0 & 1 & 3 \end{pmatrix} \begin{pmatrix} x \\ y \\ z \end{pmatrix} = \begin{pmatrix} 1 \\ 4 \\ 3 \end{pmatrix} \Rightarrow \begin{pmatrix} 1 & 0 & 1 \\ 0 & 3 & 9 \\ 0 & 0 & 0 \end{pmatrix} \begin{pmatrix} x \\ y \\ z \end{pmatrix} = \begin{pmatrix} 1 \\ 4 \\ 5 \end{pmatrix} \Rightarrow 0$$ Solutions, system incompatible

23. Solve or express solution properly, indicate the number of solutions.

$$x + z = 0$$
$$-2x + 3y + 7z = 0$$
$$-x + y + 2z = 0$$

$$\begin{pmatrix} 1 & 0 & 1 \\ -2 & 3 & 7 \\ -1 & 1 & 2 \end{pmatrix} \begin{pmatrix} x \\ y \\ z \end{pmatrix} = \begin{pmatrix} 0 \\ 0 \\ 0 \end{pmatrix} \Rightarrow \begin{pmatrix} 1 & 0 & 1 \\ -2 & 3 & 7 \\ 0 & 1 & 3 \end{pmatrix} \begin{pmatrix} x \\ y \\ z \end{pmatrix} = \begin{pmatrix} 0 \\ 0 \\ 0 \end{pmatrix} \Rightarrow$$

$$\begin{pmatrix} 1 & 0 & 1 \\ 0 & 3 & 9 \\ 0 & 1 & 3 \end{pmatrix} \begin{pmatrix} x \\ y \\ z \end{pmatrix} = \begin{pmatrix} 0 \\ 0 \\ 0 \end{pmatrix} \Rightarrow \begin{pmatrix} 1 & 0 & 1 \\ 0 & 3 & 9 \\ 0 & 0 & 0 \end{pmatrix} \begin{pmatrix} x \\ y \\ z \end{pmatrix} = \begin{pmatrix} 0 \\ 0 \\ 0 \end{pmatrix} \Rightarrow \begin{pmatrix} x \\ y \\ z \end{pmatrix} = \begin{pmatrix} t \\ -3t \\ -t \end{pmatrix}$$

∞ solutions(Line)

24. Solve or express solution properly, indicate the number of solutions.

$$x + z = 2$$
$$-2x + 3y + 7z = 8$$
$$-x + y + 2z = -2$$

$$\begin{pmatrix} 1 & 0 & 1 \\ -2 & 3 & 7 \\ -1 & 1 & 2 \end{pmatrix} \begin{pmatrix} x \\ y \\ z \end{pmatrix} = \begin{pmatrix} 2 \\ 8 \\ -2 \end{pmatrix} \Rightarrow \begin{pmatrix} 1 & 0 & 1 \\ -2 & 3 & 7 \\ 0 & 1 & 3 \end{pmatrix} \begin{pmatrix} x \\ y \\ z \end{pmatrix} = \begin{pmatrix} 2 \\ 8 \\ 0 \end{pmatrix} \Rightarrow$$

$$\begin{pmatrix} 1 & 0 & 1 \\ 0 & 3 & 9 \\ 0 & 1 & 3 \end{pmatrix} \begin{pmatrix} x \\ y \\ z \end{pmatrix} = \begin{pmatrix} 2 \\ 12 \\ 0 \end{pmatrix} \Rightarrow \begin{pmatrix} 1 & 0 & 1 \\ 0 & 3 & 9 \\ 0 & 0 & 0 \end{pmatrix} \begin{pmatrix} x \\ y \\ z \end{pmatrix} = \begin{pmatrix} 2 \\ 12 \\ -12 \end{pmatrix} \Rightarrow 0$$ Solutions, system incompatible

3.1. – INTRODUCTION TO STATISTICS

In Statistics we try to obtain some conclusions by observing and/or analyzing data.

1. The set of objects that we are trying to study is called <u>Population</u>, the number of elements in the population can be <u>finite</u> or <u>infinite.</u>

2. Usually the <u>population</u> is too big and therefore we obtain a <u>sample.</u> This process is called <u>Sampling.</u>

3. We use the <u>sample</u> to obtain conclusions about the <u>population.</u>

Types of DATA

1. <u>Categorical</u> data.

2. <u>Numerical</u> data that can be divided to <u>discrete</u> or <u>continuous</u>

3. <u>Discrete data</u> can be counted while <u>continuous</u> data can be <u>measured.</u>

4. Give 5 examples of <u>Categorical</u> data: eye color, favorite food, type of car, type of sport, name of child etc.

5. Give 3 examples of <u>Numerical</u> <u>discrete</u> data: shoe size, number of students in the classroom, number of cars in a parking lot.

6. Give 3 examples of <u>Numerical</u> <u>continuous</u> data: height, weight, value of a stock.

3.2. – FREQUENCY DIAGRAMS

1. In a certain math class the following grades were obtained:
    68, 79, 75, 89, 54, 81, 88, 62, 67, 75, 64, 85, 97, 77, 79, 90, 75, 89, 76, 68
    a. State the number of elements in the set: <u>20</u>
    b. What kind of data is this? <u>Numerical discrete</u>
    c. Fill the table:

Grade	Mid – Grade (Mi)	Frequency (fi)	fi · Mi	Cumulative Frequency (Fi)	Fi (%)
51 – 60	55.5	1	55.5	1	5
61 – 70	65.5	5	327.5	6	30
71 – 80	75.5	7	528.5	13	65
81 – 90	85.5	6	513	19	95
91 – 100	95.5	1	95.5	20	100
Total		20	1520		

    d. Is this the only possible choice for the left column of the table? Why?
        Discuss the advantages and disadvantages of organizing information in
        such a way.
        <u>No it is not the only possibility. Narrower or wider intervals can be
        chosen. Narrower interval implies higher accuracy but information may
        be harder to understand and/or analyze. It also implies more work.
        Wider interval implies lower level of accuracy but information may be
        easier to understand and/or analyze. It also implies less work.</u>
    e. Design a new table with a different <u>interval width</u>

Grade	Mid – Grade (Mi)	Frequency (fi)	fi · Mi	Cumulative Frequency (Fi)	Fi (%)
51 – 55	53	1	53	1	5
56 – 60	58	0	0	1	5
61 – 65	63	2	126	3	15
66 – 70	68	3	204	6	30
71 – 75	73	3	219	9	45
76 – 80	78	4	312	13	65
81 – 85	83	2	166	15	75
86 – 90	88	4	352	19	95
91 – 95	93	0	0	19	95
96 – 100	98	1	98	20	100
Total		20	1530		

    f. The mean in both cases: <u>Table 1</u> $\mu = \dfrac{1520}{20} = 76$ <u>Table 2</u> $\mu = \dfrac{1530}{20} = 76.5$

g. State a formula for the mean: $\mu = \dfrac{\sum_n M_i f_i}{n}$

h. The mean of the <u>population</u> is denoted with the Greek letter mu: μ and typically it is <u>unknown</u>. The mean of the <u>sample</u> is denoted by $\bar{x}$

i. State the mode of the set: <u>75</u>

j. Find the modal interval in both cases:
Table 1: <u>71 – 80</u>   Table 2: <u>76 – 80, 86 – 90 (Bimodal)</u>

k. Find the Median using the original data: <u>76.5</u>
Since there are 20 elements, the mean of elements 10 and 11 is the median. First elements must be put in order:
54 62 64 67 68 68 75 75 75 **76 77** 79 79 81 85 88 89 89 90 97
<u>So median is 76.</u>

l. Find the median using the tables, discuss your answer.
The median is the center of interval where F% $\geq$ 50% for the first time.
Table 1: <u>75.5</u>   Table 2: <u>78</u>

m. In general this method of organizing information is called <u>grouping</u>

n. The 1st column is called <u>class</u> with upper interval boundary and <u>lower</u> interval boundary.

o. The 2nd column is called <u>Mid - Class</u>

p. On the following grid paper sketch the corresponding points.

Cumulative frequency   **OGIVE**

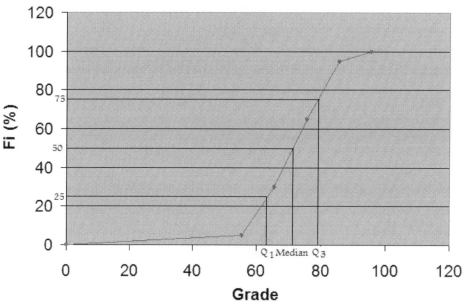

q. This graph is called cumulative frequency curve or <u>Ogive</u>

r. Find the median using the graph: ~ 72

s. Find the first quartile (Q_1) using the graph: $Q_1 = $ ~ 64

t. Find the first quartile (Q_1) using the original data: $Q_1 = $ <u>68</u>

u. Find the third quartile (Q_3) using the graph: $Q_3 = $ ~ 79

v. Find the first quartile (Q_3) using the original data: $Q_3 = $ <u>86.5</u>

w. Find P_{30} using the graph: ~ 67 Find P_{65} using the graph: ~ 75

x. The <u>Inter Quartile Range</u> is in general $Q_3 - Q_1$ in this case <u>86.5–68= 18.5</u>

438

2. In a certain class the following heights (in m) of students were collected:
   1.77, 1.60, 1.89, 1.54, 1.77, 1.65, 1.86, 1.51, 1.67, 1.94, 1.73, 1.70, 1.66
   a. State the number of elements in the set: 13
   b. What kind of data is this? Numerical continuous
   c. Fill the table:

Height	Mid – Height (Mi)	Frequency (fi)	fi · Mi	Cumulative Frequency (Fi)	Fi (%)
[1.50 , 1.60)	1.55	2	3.1	2	15.4
[1.60 , 1.70)	1.65	4	6.6	6	46.2
[1.70 , 1.80)	1.75	4	7	10	76.9
[1.80 , 1.90)	1.85	2	3.7	12	92.3
[1.90 , 2.00)	1.95	1	1.95	13	100
Total			22.35		

   d. Obtain the mean: $\mu = \dfrac{22.35}{13} \approx 1.72m$

   e. State the mode of the set: 1.77m
   f. Find the modal interval: bimodal, [1.60 – 1.70), [1.70– 1.80)
   g. Find the Median using the original data: We order the data:
      1.51 1.54 1.60 1.65 1.66 1.67 **1.70** 1.73 1.77 1.77 1.86 1.89 1.94
      There are 13 terms so the median is the 7th, 1.70m
   h. Find the median using the table, discuss your answer.
      The median according to table is the centre of the interval in which Fi%
      is greater than 50% for the first time. The interval is [1.70– 1.80) so
      median 1.75.
   i. On the following grid paper sketch the corresponding points.

   Cumulative frequency

   OGIVE

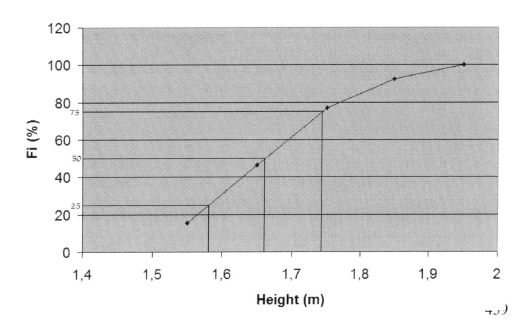

j. This graph is called cumulative frequency curve or <u>ogive</u>

k. Find the median using the graph: $\sim 1.66m$

l. Find the first quartile (Q_1) using the graph: $Q_1 = \sim 1.58m$

m. Find the first quartile (Q_1) using the original data: $Q_1 = \underline{1.625m}$
   We use the ordered data; the middle of the first half of data is 1.625m
   1.51 1.54 **1.60 1.65** 1.66 1.67 <u>1.70</u> 1.73 1.77 1.77 1.86 1.89 1.94

n. Find the third quartile (Q_3) using the graph: $Q_3 = \sim 1.74m$

o. Find the first quartile (Q_3) using the original data: $Q_3 = \underline{1.815m}$
   We use the ordered data; the middle of the second half of data is 1.815m
   1.51 1.54 <u>1.60 1.65</u> 1.66 1.67 <u>1.70</u> 1.73 1.77 **1.77 1.86** 1.89 1.94

p. Find P_{20} using the graph: $\sim 1.67m$ Find P_{80} using the graph: $\sim 1.78m$

q. The <u>Inter Quartile Range</u> is in general $Q_3 - Q_1$ in this case $\underline{1.815 - 1.625}$
   $= 0.190m$

3. In a certain class students eye color was collected:
   Brown, Black, Brown, Blue, Brown, Blue, Green, Brown, Black, Green
   a. State the number of elements in the set: <u>10</u>
   b. What kind of data is this? <u>Categorical</u>
   c. Fill the table:

Eye Color	Mid – Color (Mi)	Frequency (fi)	Fi x Mi	Cumulative Frequency (Fi)	Fi (%)
Brown	N/A	4	N/A	N/A	N/A
Blue	N/A	2	N/A	N/A	N/A
Green	N/A	2	N/A	N/A	N/A
Black	N/A	2	N/A	N/A	N/A
Total	N/A	10	N/A	N/A	N/A

d. Obtain the mean: <u>N/A</u>
e. State the mode of the set: <u>Brown</u>
f. Find the modal interval: <u>N/A</u>
g. Find the Median using the original data: <u>N/A</u>
h. Find the median using the table, discuss your answer. <u>N/A</u>
i. Find the answers to all the different parts using your GDC. <u>N/A</u>
j. Represent the information in a histogram:

HISTOGRAM

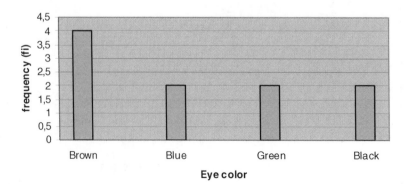

440

3.3. – MEASURES OF DISPERSION

1. In a certain Biology test the following results were obtained: 80, 80, 80, 80,

   a. Obtain the mean: m $= \underline{80}$
   b. Represent the results using a histogram:
   c. The standard deviation of a set of numbers is defined by:

   $$\sigma = \sqrt{\frac{\sum_i f_i (x_i - \mu)^2}{n}} = \sqrt{\frac{f_1 (x_1 - \mu)^2 + f_2 (x_2 - \mu)^2 + ...}{n}}$$

   In this case

   $$\sigma = \sqrt{\frac{1(80-80)^2 + 1(80-80)^2 + 1(80-80)^2 + 1(80-80)^2}{4}} = 0$$

   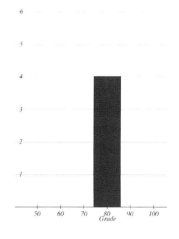

   d. How spread is this group of grades?   It is not spread at all, that means 0 standard deviation.

2. In a certain Physics test the following results were obtained: 70, 80, 80, 90

   a. Obtain the mean: m $= \underline{80}$
   b. Represent the results using a histogram:
   c. The standard deviation of a set of numbers is defined by:

   $$\sigma = \sqrt{\frac{\sum_i f_i (x_i - \mu)^2}{n}} = \sqrt{\frac{f_1 (x_1 - \mu)^2 + f_2 (x_2 - \mu)^2 + ...}{n}}$$

   In this case

   $$\sigma = \sqrt{\frac{1(70-80)^2 + 2(80-80)^2 + 1(90-80)^2}{4}} = \frac{\sqrt{200}}{2} \approx 7.07$$

   d. How spread is this group of grades? Is it more spread than the previous one? As can be seen both distributions have the same mean but the 2nd one is more spread, its S.D. is approximately 7.07.

3. The weights in kg of 6 different classes (A, B, C, D, E, F) was collected and represented in the following histograms:

The mean $\bar{x}$ and the S.D. σ are given in the table:

	1	2	3	4	5	6
$\bar{x}$	74.6	65.7	70	72.0	65.7	70.6
σ	14.5	15.6	20.6	12.7	12.1	10.3

a. Find the number of students in the sample: <u>27</u>
b. Which distribution has the highest SD: <u>E</u>
c. Which distribution has the lowest SD: <u>F</u>
d. Match between the histograms and the numerical results. Use the table:

$\bar{x}$ and σ	Class
1	C
2	D
3	E
4	B
5	A
6	F

4. In a certain math class the following grades were obtained:

68, 79, 75, 89, 54, 81, 88, 62, 67, 75, 64, 85, 97, 77, 79, 90, 75, 89, 76, 68
   a. State the number of elements in the set: <u>20</u>
   b. What kind of data is this? <u>Numerical discrete</u>
   c. Fill the table:

Grade	Mid – Grade (Mi)	Frequency (fi)	fi · Mi	$(Mi - m)^2$	$fi(Mi - m)^2$
51 – 60	55.5	1	55.5	$(55.5 - 76)^2$	$1(55.5 - 76)^2$
61 – 70	65.5	5	327.5	$(65.5 - 76)^2$	$5(65.5 - 76)^2$
71 – 80	75.5	7	528.5	$(75.5 - 76)^2$	$7(75.5 - 76)^2$
81 – 90	85.5	6	513	$(85.5 - 76)^2$	$6(85.5 - 76)^2$
91 – 100	95.5	1	95.5	$(95.5 - 76)^2$	$1(95.5 - 76)^2$
Total		20	1520		1895

d. Obtain the mean: m = <u>76</u>
e. The numbers in the 6th column give us an idea about the <u>contribution</u> of each <u>interval</u> to the spread of the data.
f. The sum of the numbers in the 6th column gives us an idea about the <u>total spread</u> of the data. In case this number is 0 it means that <u>the data is not spread at all (like in example 1)</u> for example:
g. The Variance: $Variance = \sigma^2 = \dfrac{\sum_i f_i(x_i - \mu)^2}{n} = \dfrac{1895}{20} = 94.75$

The Standard Deviation: $S.D. = \sigma = \sqrt{\dfrac{\sum_i f_i(x_i - \mu)^2}{n}} = \sqrt{\dfrac{1895}{20}} \approx 9.73$

442

h.   Write down the formula for the Variance of a population (s^2): <u>see part g.</u>

i.   Write down the formula for the SD of a population (s) : <u>see part g.</u>

5.   In a certain class the following heights (in m) of students were collected:
1.77, 1.60, 1.89, 1.54, 1.77, 1.65, 1.86, 1.51, 1.67, 1.94, 1.73, 1.70, 1.66

    a.   State the number of elements in the set: <u>13</u>

    b.   What kind of data is this? <u>Numerical continuous</u>

    c.   Fill the table:

Height	Mid – Height (Mi)	Frequency (fi)	Fi · Mi	$(Mi - m)^2$	$fi(Mi - m)^2$
[1.50 – 1.60)	1.55	2	3.1	$(1.55 - 1.72)^2$	$2(1.55 - 1.72)^2$
[1.60 – 1.70)	1.65	4	6.6	$(1.65 - 1.72)^2$	$4(1.65 - 1.72)^2$
[1.70– 1.80)	1.75	4	7	$(1.75 - 1.72)^2$	$4(1.75 - 1.72)^2$
[1.80 – 1.90)	1.85	2	3.7	$(1.85 - 1.72)^2$	$2(1.85 - 1.72)^2$
[1.90 – 2.00)	1.95	1	1.95	$(1.95 - 1.72)^2$	$1(1.95 - 1.72)^2$
Total			22.35		0.1677

    d.   Obtain the mean: $m = \dfrac{22.35}{13} \approx 1.72m$

    e.   The numbers in the 6th column give us an idea about the <u>contribution</u> of each <u>interval</u> to the spread of the data.

    f.   The sum of the numbers in the 6th column gives us an idea about the <u>total spread</u> of the data. In case this number is 0 it means that <u>the data is not spread at all (like in example 1)</u> for example:

    g.   Find the Variance (assuming population):

$$Variance = \sigma^2 = \frac{\sum_i f_i(x_i - \mu)^2}{n} = \frac{0.1677}{13} = 0.0129m^2$$

    h.   Find the Standard Deviation S.D. (assuming population):

$$S.D. = \sigma = \sqrt{\frac{\sum_i f_i(x_i - \mu)^2}{n}} = \sqrt{\frac{0.1677}{13}} \approx 0.114m$$

6.   In a certain class students eye color was collected: Brown, Black, Brown, Blue, Brown, Blue, Green, Brown, Black, Green

    a.   State the number of elements in the set: <u>10</u>

    b.   What kind of data is this? <u>Categorical</u>

    c.   Fill the table:

    d.   What can you say about the measures of spread in this case? <u>There is no meaning to spread in case of categorical data</u>

Eye Color	Mid – Color (Mi)	Frequency (fi)	Fi · Mi
Brown	N/A	4	N/A
Blue	N/A	2	N/A
Green	N/A	2	N/A
Black	N/A	2	N/A
Total	N/A	10	N/A

7. The sum of the grades of a group of 3 students is 240. Given that the grades for an arithmetic sequence and that its standard deviation is $\sqrt{128}$:

   a. The mean grade: $\mu = \dfrac{240}{3} = 80$ $I) x + x + d + x + 2d = 240; x + d = 80$

   b. The grades of the students:
   66.1, 80, 93.9

   $II) \sqrt{128} = \sqrt{\dfrac{(x-80)^2 + (x+d-80)^2 + (x+2d-80)^2}{3}}$

   $II) \sqrt{128} = \sqrt{\dfrac{2(x-80)^2}{3}}; x = 93.9; d = -13.9$

8. The time it takes a pool to be filled was measured by using a sample of 80 pools and the following results were obtained Find

   a. The mean: $\mu = \dfrac{326}{44} \approx 7.41h$

   b. The standard deviation: $\sigma \approx 1.39h$

   c. Later it was discovered that one more pool was tested. If the standard deviation has not changed by adding it to the sample, find out how much time it took to fill this pool.

Time (hours)	Number of pools
$3 \le t \le 4$	1
$4 < t \le 5$	2
$5 < t \le 6$	3
$6 < t \le 7$	9
$7 < t \le 8$	12
$8 < t \le 9$	13
$9 < t \le 10$	4
Total	

Before: $1.39 = \sqrt{\dfrac{\sum_i f_i (x_i - \mu)^2}{44}}; \sum_i f_i (x_i - \mu)^2 = 85.0124$

After: $1.39 = \sqrt{\dfrac{85.0124 + (x_{newPool} - 7.41)^2}{45}}; x_{newPool} = 8.8h \ or \ 6.02h$

9. A group of students obtained the following grades: 60, x, y, 50, 80. The mean of the sample is 68 and its variance is 136. Find x and y.

   $\mu = \dfrac{x + y + 190}{5} = 68; x + y = 150$

   $\sigma^2 = \dfrac{(x-68)^2 + (y-68)^2 + (60-68)^2 + (50-68)^2 + (80-68)^2}{5} = 136$

   $x = 70, y = 80 \quad or \quad x = 80, y = 70$

3.4. – PERMUTATIONS AND COMBINATIONS

1. Permutations represent a counting process <u>where</u> order must be taken into account. For example if we have the 2 elements A, B these 2 elements can be arranged in <u>2</u> ways: <u>AB, BA</u>

2. Sometimes the word <u>combination is</u> used instead of permutation.

Multiplication principles

3. n different, mutually exclusive and exhaustive events, k trials. Number of possible outcomes is n^k. For example if a die is rolled 2 times the number of possible results is $\underline{6^2}$

4. if n changes in every trial. Number of possible outcomes is $n_1 \times n_2 \times n_3 ....$ For example in case you roll a die twice and a coin 3 times the number of possible results is $\underline{6^2 2^3}$

5. The total number of ways in which n different objects can be arranged in order is $n! = n \times (n-1) \times (n-2)......3 \times 2 \times 1$. For example if we have 5 books we want to order on a shelf the number of possible orders is $5 \cdot 4 \cdot 3 \cdot 2 \cdot 1 = 5! = 120$

6. The total number of ways of <u>arranging</u> n objects, taking r at a time is given by For example if we have 5 books in a bag out of which we pick 3 and order those 3 on a shelf. How many possible orders exist?

$$^nP_r = \frac{5!}{(5-3)!} = 5 \cdot 4 \cdot 3 = 60$$

7. The number of permutations of n objects of which n_1 are identical, n_2 are identical…is
    For example if we want to order 5 books on a shelf out of which 2 are identical and the other 3 are identical. How many possible orders exist?

$$\frac{n!}{n_1 \times n_2 \times n_3 ....} = \frac{5!}{2!3!} = 10$$

8. The total number of ways of <u>selecting</u> n objects, taking r at a time is given by For example if we have 5 books in a bag out of which we want to select 3 (<u>without ordering them on the shelf</u>, just maybe putting them in a different bag so that order doesn't matter). How many possible orders exist?

$$^nC_r = \binom{5}{3} = \frac{5!}{(5-3)!2!} = 10$$

3.5. – PROBABILITY

Probability is the science of chance or likelihood of an event happening. If a random experiment is repeated <u>n</u> times in such a way that each of the trials is identical and independent, where n(A) is the <u>number of times</u> event A occurred, then:

$$\text{Relative frequency of event A} = P(A) = \frac{n(A)}{N} \qquad (N \to \infty)$$

Exercises

1. In an unbiased coin what is P(head) ?
   This probability is called <u>"theoretical probability"</u>
2. Explain the difference between theoretical probability and "regular" probability. <u>Theoretical probability is calculated, predicted. "regular" probability is measured in an experiment. The probability for head is theoretically 0.5, we would need to repeat an experiment an infinite number of times to make sure it is. In reality the coin has some small probability to lend on its thin side (more than 0) so it is not really 0.5 for head...</u>

3. Throw a drawing pin, fill the table: <u>This experiment should be done in class</u>
4. The definition of probability ("***Laplace law***")is:

$$P(A) = \frac{\text{Number of times A ocurred}}{\text{Total numberof times experiment repeated}}$$

Venn diagrams

Event	Set Language	Venn diagram	Probability result
Complementary event (A')	Not A		$P(A') = 1 - P(A)$
The <u>intersection</u> of A and B (A∩B)	Set of elements that belongs to A <u>and</u> B		$P(A \cup B) = P(A) + P(B) - P(A \cup B)$
The <u>union</u> of A and B (A∪B)	Set of elements that belongs to A <u>or</u> B <u>or</u> <u>both</u>		
If (A∩B) = ∅ A and B are said to be: mutually exclusive	The sets A and B are Mutually exclusive		$P(A \cup B) = P(A) + P(B)$ $P(A \cap B) = 0$

1. The events A and B are such $P(A) = 0.2$, $P(B) = 0.4$ and $P(A \cup B) = 0.5$. Find:

   a. $P(A \cup B) = P(A) + P(B) - P(A \cap B)$
      $0.5 = 0.2 + 0.4 - P(A \cap B)$; $P(A \cap B) = 0.1$
   b. $P(B') = 1 - P(B) = 0.6$
   c. Sketch the corresponding Venn diagram.
   d. $P(A' \cap B)$ is the size of the shaded area so 0.3

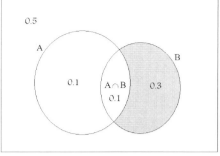

   e. $P(A' \cap B')$ is the size of the shaded area so 0.5
   f. Are the events A and B Independent? Explain.
      In case events are independent
      $P(A \cap B) = P(A) \, P(B)$, in this case
      $0.1 \neq (0.2)(0.4)$ therefore these events are not independent.

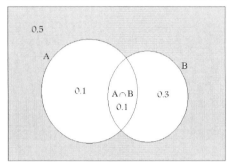

2. The events A and B are such $P(A) = 0.15$, $P(B) = 0.3$ and $P(A \cup B) = 0.4$, find:
   a. $P(A \cap B) = \qquad$; $P(A \cup B) = P(A) + P(B) - P(A \cap B)$
      $0.4 = 0.15 + 0.3 - P(A \cap B)$; $P(A \cap B) = 0.05$
   b. $P(B') = 1 - P(B) = 0.7$
   c. Sketch the corresponding Venn diagram.

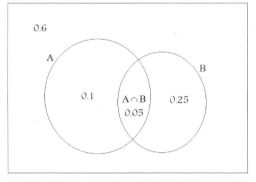

   d. $P(A' \cap B)$ is the size of the shaded area so 0.25

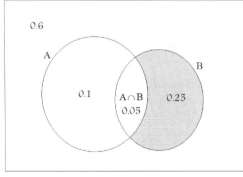

   e. $P(A' \cap B')$ is the size of the shaded area so 0.6
   f. Are the events A and B Independent? Explain.
      In case events are independent $P(A \cap B) = P(A) \, P(B)$, in this case
      $0.05 \neq (0.15)(0.3)$ therefore these events are not independent.

3. The events A and B are such $P(A) = 0.3$, $P(B) = 0.6$ and $P(A \cup B) = 0.9$, Find:

a. $P(A \cap B)$
$P(A \cup B) = P(A) + P(B) - P(A \cap B)$
$0.9 = 0.6 + 0.3 - P(A \cap B);$ $P(A \cap B) = 0$ That means no intersection
So events are mutually exclusive.

b. $P(B') = 1 - P(B) = 0.4$

c. Sketch the corresponding Venn diagram.

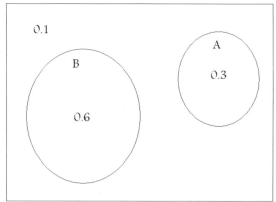

d. $P(A' \cap B) = P(B) = 0.6$ (the size of the shaded area)

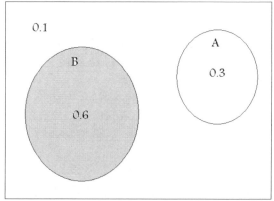

e. $P(A' \cap B') = 0.1$ (the size of the shaded area)

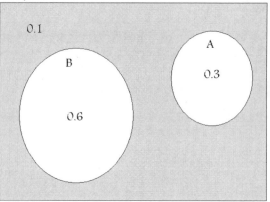

f. Are the events A and B Independent? Explain.
In case events are independent $P(A \cap B) = P(A)\ P(B)$, in this case
$0 \neq (0.3)(0.6)$ therefore these events are not independent.

4. The events A and B are such $P(A) = 0.2$, $P(B) = 0.9$ and $P(A \cap B) = 0.1$, Find:
   a. $P(A \cup B) = P(A) + P(B) - P(A \cap B)$
      $P(A \cup B) = 0.2 + 0.9 - 0.1$;　　$P(A \cup B) = 1$, that means there is no "outside" the events "fill" the entire rectangle.
   b. $P(B') = 1 - P(B) = 0.1$
   c. Sketch the corresponding Venn diagram.

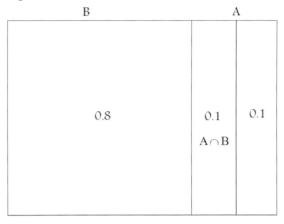

   d. $P(A' \cap B) = 0.8$ (the size of the shaded area)

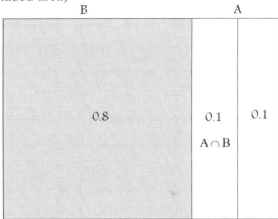

   e. $P(A' \cap B') = 0$
      There is no "outside"
   f. Are the events A and B Independent? Explain.
      In case events are independent $P(A \cap B) = P(A)\ P(B)$, in this case
      $0.1 \neq (0.2)(0.9)$ therefore these events are not independent.

5. 20% of certain city census consume alcohol regularly, 40% do sport regularly and 10% do both.
   a. Represent the information in a diagram.
      $P(A \cup S) = P(A) + P(S) - P(A \cap S)$
      $P(A \cup S) = 0.2 + 0.4 - 0.1$;
      　　　$P(A \cup S) = 0.5$

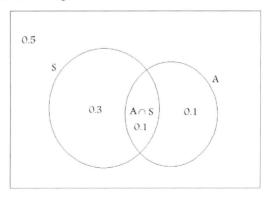

   b. Calculate the probability that someone chosen at random only drinks alcohol regularly.
      $P(A \text{ only}) = 0.1$ (see venn diagram)

c. Calculate the probability that someone chosen at random only drink alcohol regularly or only practices sport regularly (but not both).
P(A or S but not both) = 0.1 + 0.3 = 0.4 (see venn diagram)

d. Calculate the probability that someone picked at random does not drink alcohol nor practices sport regularly.
P(A' ∩ S') =0.5 (The "outside")

6. P(A) = 0.46, P(B) = 0.33, P(A∩B) = 0.15.
   a. Represent the information in a diagram.
   P(A ∪ B) = 0.46 + 0.33 –0.15 = 0.64

   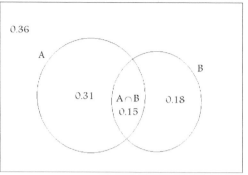

   b. Find the probability that an event is not A nor B.
   P(A' ∩ B') =1 – 0.64 = 0.36

7. Given the Venn diagram. Shade A ∩ B

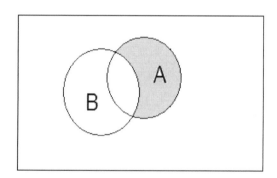

8. Given the Venn diagram. Shade A ∩ B'

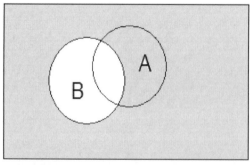

9. Given the Venn diagram. Shade B'

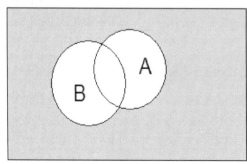

10. Given the Venn diagram. Shade A' ∩ B'

11. Given the Venn diagram. Shade A ∪ B

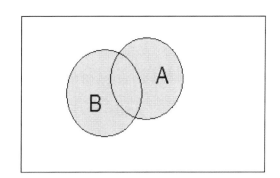

12. Given the Venn diagram. Shade A' ∪ B

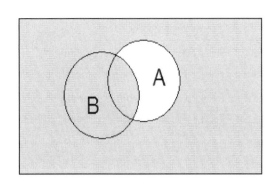

13. Given the Venn diagram. Shade A' ∪ B'

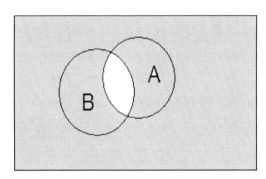

14. Given the Venn diagram. Shade A ∪ B

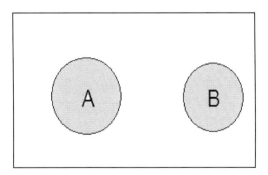

15. Given the Venn diagram. Shade A ∪ B'

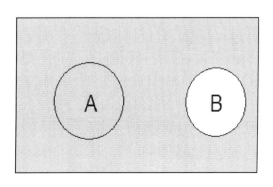

16. Given the Venn diagram. Shade A ∩ B'

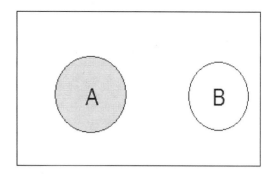

17. Given the Venn diagram. Shade A ∩ B(None - Empty)

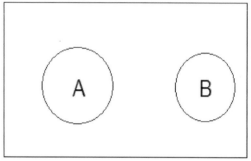

18. Given the Venn diagram. Shade A ∩ B ∩ C   (None - Empty)

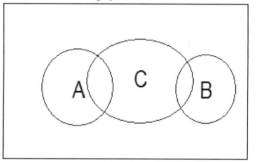

19. Given the Venn diagram. Shade (A ∪ B) ∩ C

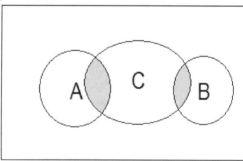

20. Given the Venn diagram. Shade (A' ∪ B) ∩ C

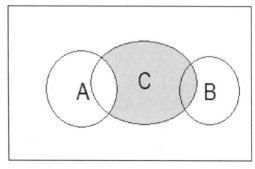

21. Given the Venn diagram. Shade $(A \cup B) \cap C'$

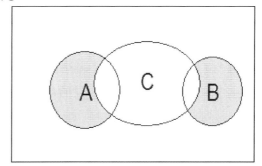

22. Given the Venn diagram. Shade $A \cap B \cap C$

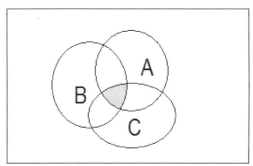

23. Given the Venn diagram. Shade $(A \cap B) \cap C'$

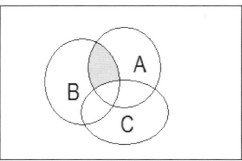

24. Given the Venn diagram. Shade $(A' \cap B) \cap C$

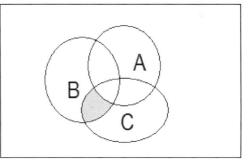

25. Given the Venn diagram. Shade $(A \cap B') \cap C$

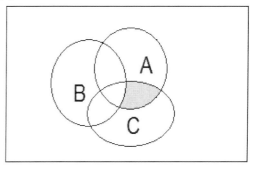

INDEPENDENT EVENTS

Exercises

1. What is the difference between independent events and mutually exclusive events?

   In case of independent events $P(A \cap B) = P(A)P(B)$

   In case of mutually exclusive events $P(A \cap B) = 0$

2. Give an example of independent events:

   - Tossing a coin, the probability of obtaining a head or tail is independent of previous times the coin was tossed.

   - Each time the ball of casino roulette is launched is an independent event of previous launches.

3. In a certain town the probability of a rainy day is 0.58 and the probability of strong wind is 0.76. If these are independent events, find the probability of:
   a. A rainy windy day.

      $P(R \cap W) = P(R)P(W) = (0.58)(0.76) = 0.4408$
   b. A dry windy day.

      $P(R' \cap W) = P(R')P(W) = (0.42)(0.76) = 0.3192$
   c. A dry and not windy day.

      $P(R' \cap W') = P(R')P(W') = (0.42)(0.24) = 0.1008$
   d. 2 consecutive rainy days.

      $P(R \cap R) = P(R)P(R) = (0.58)(0.58) = 0.3364$
   e. 2 consecutive windy rainy days.

      $P(R \cap W) \, P(R \cap W) = (0.4408)(0.4408) = 0.194$

CONDITIONAL PROBABILITY

4. Two dice numbered one to six are rolled onto a table.

   a. Sketch a corresponding diagram.

   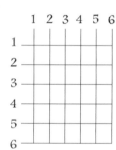

   b. Find the probability that the sum is 7.

      $$P(\text{Sum} = 7) = \frac{6}{36}$$

   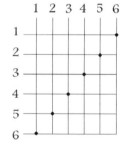

   c. Find the probability that the sum is more than 7.

      $$P(\text{Sum} > 7) = \frac{15}{36}$$

   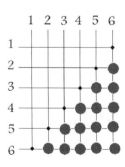

d. Find the probability that the sum is less than 4.

$$P(\text{Sum} < 4) = \frac{3}{36}$$

e. Find the probability that the sum is even.

$$P(\text{Sum} = \text{even}) = \frac{18}{36}$$

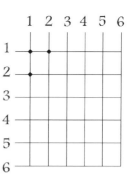

f. Find the probability of obtaining a sum of five <u>given</u> that the sum is seven or less.

Conditional probability: $P(A|B) = \dfrac{P(A \cap B)}{P(B)}$ in this case:

$$P(sum = 5 | sum \leq 7) = \frac{P(sum = 5 \cap sum \leq 7)}{P(sum \leq 7)} = \frac{\left(\dfrac{4}{36}\right)}{\left(\dfrac{21}{36}\right)} = \frac{4}{21}$$

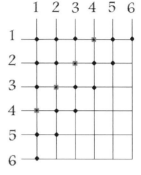

g. Find the probability of obtaining a sum of 4 <u>given</u> that the sum is even.

Conditional probability: $P(A|B) = \dfrac{P(A \cap B)}{P(B)}$ in this case:

$$P(sum = 4 | sum = even) = \frac{P(sum = 4 \cap sum = even)}{P(sum = even)} = \frac{\left(\dfrac{3}{36}\right)}{\left(\dfrac{18}{36}\right)} = \frac{3}{18}$$

5. A regular and special dice rolled on a table. The special is a 4 sided pyramid numbered with the numbers 1,3,5,7.

a. Sketch a corresponding diagram.

b. Find the probability that the sum of the dice will be odd.

$$P(sum = Odd) = \frac{12}{24} = \frac{1}{2}$$

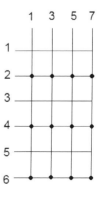

455

c. Find the probability that the sum of the dice will be 8.

$$P(sum = 8) = \frac{3}{24} = \frac{1}{8}$$

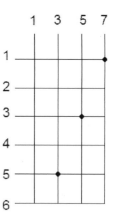

d. Find the probability that the sum of the dice will be less than 9.

$$P(sum < 9) = \frac{15}{24}$$

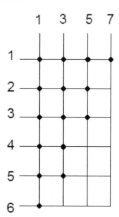

e. Find the probability of obtaining a sum of 10 knowing that the sum was more or equal to 6.

$$P(sum = 10 | sum \geq 6) = \frac{P(sum = 10 \cap sum \geq 6)}{P(sum \geq 6)} = \frac{\left(\frac{2}{24}\right)}{\left(\frac{18}{24}\right)} = \frac{2}{18} = \frac{1}{9}$$

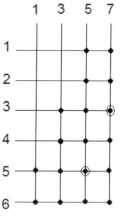

TOTAL PROBABILITY
Lattice diagrams

6. Two special dice numbered one to seven are rolled onto a table.

    a. Sketch a corresponding diagram.

    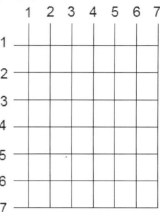

    b. Find the probability that the product is 6.

    $$P(product = 9) = \frac{4}{49}$$

    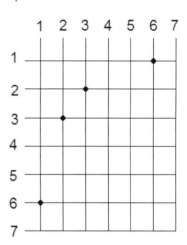

    c. Find the probability that the quotient is more than 3.

    $$P(quotient > 3) = \frac{5}{49}$$

    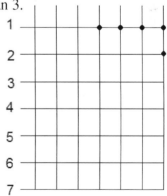

    d. Find the probability that the sum is a prime number.

    $$P(sum = prime) = \frac{19}{49}$$

    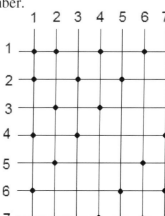

e. Find the probability that the sum is a perfect square given it is not a prime number.

$$P(sum = perfectSquare \mid sum \neq prime) =$$

$$= \frac{P(sum = perfectSquare \cap sum \neq prime)}{P(sum \neq prime)} =$$

$$\frac{\left(\dfrac{9}{24}\right)}{\left(\dfrac{30}{49}\right)} = \frac{9}{30} = \frac{3}{10}$$

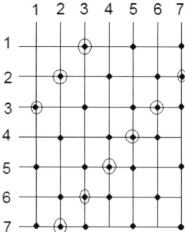

f. Find the probability of obtaining an even sum given that the sum is six or less.

$$P(sum = even \mid sum \leq 6) =$$

$$= \frac{P(sum = even \cap sum \leq 6)}{P(sum \leq 6)} =$$

$$\frac{\left(\dfrac{9}{49}\right)}{\left(\dfrac{15}{49}\right)} = \frac{9}{15} = \frac{3}{5}$$

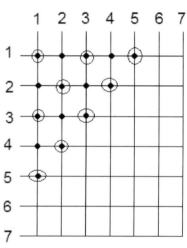

7. A die and coin are rolled on a table.

g. Sketch a corresponding diagram.

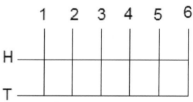

h. Find the probability of getting Tail and an even number.

$$P(Tail \cap even) = \frac{3}{12} = \frac{1}{4}$$

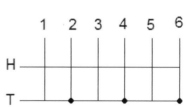

i. Find the probability of getting Tail and a 4.

$$P(Tail \cap 4) = \frac{1}{12}$$

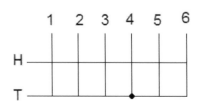

TREE DIAGRAMS

8. If the probability of tail is 0.53, find the probability of at least one tail in 2 throws.

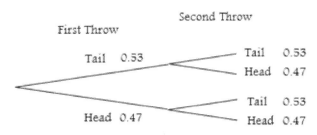

$$P(T \cap T) + P(T \cap H) + P(H \cap T) = (0.53)^2 + (0.53)(0.47) + (0.47)(0.53) = 0.7791$$

Can be done easier:

$$1 - P(H \cap H) = 1 - (0.47)^2 = 0.7791$$

9. An urn contains 8 cubes of which 5 are black and the rest are white.

a. What is the probability to draw a white cube? $P(W) = \dfrac{3}{8}$

b. Draw a tree diagram in case a 1st cube is drawn, it is **NOT replaced** and then another cube is drawn. Indicate all the probabilities on the tree diagram.

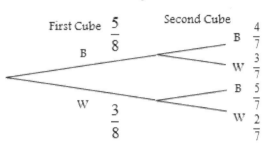

c. Calculate the probability to draw 2 consecutive black cubes.

$$P(B \cap B) = \frac{5}{8} \cdot \frac{4}{7} = \frac{20}{56}$$

d. Calculate the probability to draw **at least** 1 black cube.

$$P(B \cap B) + P(B \cap W) + P(W \cap B) = \frac{50}{56}$$

Can be done easier:

$$1 - P(W \cap W) = 1 - \frac{3}{8} \cdot \frac{2}{7} = 1 - \frac{6}{56} = \frac{50}{56}$$

e. <u>Given</u> that the first cube drawn was white, calculate the probability that the 2nd is black.

Conditional probability: $P(A|B) = \dfrac{P(A \cap B)}{P(B)}$ in this case:

$$P(2ndB|1stW) = \frac{P(2ndB \cap 1stW)}{P(1stW)} = \frac{\left(\dfrac{3}{8} \cdot \dfrac{5}{7}\right)}{\left(\dfrac{3}{8}\right)} = \frac{5}{7}$$

10. A bag contains 3 red balls, 4 blue balls and 5 green balls. A ball is chosen at random from the bag and is not replaced. A second ball is chosen. Find the probability of choosing one green ball and one blue ball in any order.

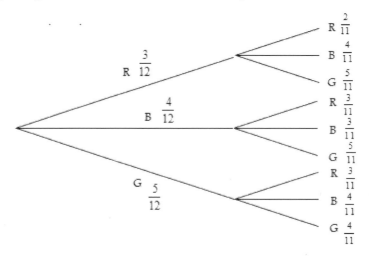

$$P(B \cap G) + P(G \cap B) = \frac{4}{12} \cdot \frac{5}{11} + \frac{5}{12} \cdot \frac{4}{11} = \frac{40}{132}$$

11. Given that events A and B are independent with $P(A \cap B) = 0.4$ and $P(A \cap B') = 0$. Find $P(A \cup B)$.
$P(A \cap B') = 0$ means that A is inside B (it has no intersection with the "outside" of B), the Venn diagram is:

In consequence:
$P(A \cup B) = P(B)$
$P(A \cap B) = P(A) = 0.4$

Since events are independent
$P(A \cap B) = P(A) \, P(B)$
$0.4 = (0.4)P(B)$
$P(B) = 1 = P(A \cup B)$.

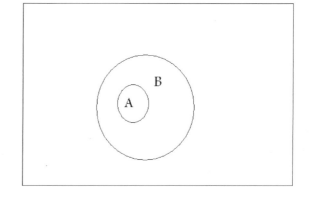

12. Given that $P(A) = 0.4$, $P(B) = 0.7$ and $P(A \cup B) = 0.8$. Find:

a. $P(A \cap B)$
$P(A \cup B) = P(A) + P(B) - P(A \cap B)$
$0.8 = 1.1 - P(A \cap B);$ $P(A \cap B) = 0.3$

b. $P(A | B)$
$$P(A|B) = \frac{P(A \cap B)}{P(B)} = \frac{0.3}{0.7} = \frac{3}{7}$$

c. Determine if A and B are independent events.
Check if $P(A \cap B) = P(A) \, P(B)$ is satisfied:
$0.3 \neq (0.4)(0.7)$ so events are not independent.

13. Given that $P(A) = 0.4$, $P(B) = 0.6$ and $P(A \cup B) = 0.76$.

    a. Find $P(A \cap B)$
       $P(A \cup B) = P(A) + P(B) - P(A \cap B)$
       $0.76 = 0.4 + 0.6 - P(A \cap B) ;$ $P(A \cap B) = 0.24$

    b. Are events A and B mutually exclusive? Explain.
       The events are not mutually exclusive since their intersection exists
       and it is bigger than 0.

    c. Are events A and B independent?
       Check if $P(A \cap B) = P(A)\,P(B)$ is satisfied:
       $0.24 = (0.4)(0.6)$ so events are independent.

14. The events A and B are independent, where A is the event "it will rain today"
    and B is the event "We will go out for pizza". It is known that

$$P(B) = 0.3, \quad P(A \mid B) = 0.6, \quad P(A \mid B') = 0.5.$$

    a. Complete the following tree diagram.

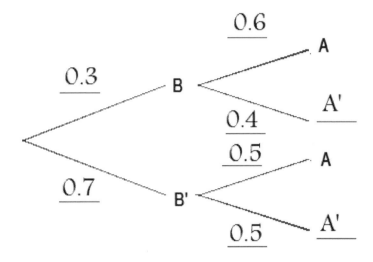

    b. Calculate the probability that it rains knowing we went out for
       pizza.

       $P(A \mid B) = 0.6$

USING PERMUTATIONS AND COMBINATION IN PROBABILITY

1. 2 oranges and 3 apples are put together in a row. Find the probability that:

   a. The oranges are next to each other. $\dfrac{4!}{5!} = \dfrac{1}{5}$

   b. The oranges are not next to each other. $1 - \dfrac{1}{5} = \dfrac{4}{5}$

   c. The apples are next to each other. $\dfrac{3!}{5!} = \dfrac{1}{20}$

   d. The apples are not next to each other. $1 - \dfrac{1}{20} = \dfrac{19}{20}$

   e. There are oranges on the sides (assuming on <u>both</u> sides). $\dfrac{2 \cdot 3!}{5!} = \dfrac{1}{10}$

   f. There are no oranges on the sides. $\dfrac{2 \cdot \binom{3}{2} 3!}{5!} = \dfrac{6}{20} = \dfrac{3}{10}$

   g. There are apples on the sides (assuming on <u>both</u> sides). $\dfrac{2 \cdot \binom{3}{2} 3!}{5!} = \dfrac{6}{20} = \dfrac{3}{10}$

   h. There are no apples on the sides. $\dfrac{2 \cdot 3!}{5!} = \dfrac{1}{10}$

   i. Oranges and apples alternate. $\dfrac{2! \cdot 3!}{5!} = \dfrac{1}{10}$

2. A committee of 4 is to be selected out from 7 men and 6 women. Find the probability that:

   a. There are 2 women on the committee. $\dfrac{\binom{6}{2} \cdot \binom{7}{2}}{\binom{13}{4}} = \dfrac{63}{143}$

   b. There are 3 women on the committee. $\dfrac{\binom{6}{3} \cdot \binom{7}{1}}{\binom{13}{4}} = \dfrac{28}{143}$

   c. There are 2 women and 2 men on the committee. $\dfrac{\binom{6}{2} \cdot \binom{7}{2}}{\binom{13}{4}} = \dfrac{63}{143}$

   d. There is at least one man on the committee. $1 - \dfrac{\binom{6}{4} \cdot \binom{7}{0}}{\binom{13}{4}} = \dfrac{3}{143}$

   e. There is at least one of each sex on the committee.

$$1 - \dfrac{\binom{6}{4} \cdot \binom{7}{0}}{\binom{13}{4}} - \dfrac{\binom{6}{0} \cdot \binom{7}{4}}{\binom{13}{4}} = 1 - \dfrac{3}{143} - \dfrac{7}{143} = \dfrac{133}{143}$$

3.6. – DISCRETE RANDOM VARIABLES

1. A <u>Discrete Random Variable</u> takes exactly n numerical values and each of these values corresponds to a single event in the sample space.
2. For example in rolling a die the possible values of X are: $\{1,2,3,4,5,6\}$
3. A discrete random variable is one in which we can produce a <u>countable</u> number of events.
4. If we roll 2 dice the possible values of X are: $\{2,3,4,5,6,7,8,9,10,11,12\}$
   a. Fill the following table:

x	2	3	4	5	6	7	8	9	10	11	12
P(X = x)	$\dfrac{1}{36}$	$\dfrac{2}{36}$	$\dfrac{3}{36}$	$\dfrac{4}{36}$	$\dfrac{5}{36}$	$\dfrac{6}{36}$	$\dfrac{5}{36}$	$\dfrac{4}{36}$	$\dfrac{3}{36}$	$\dfrac{2}{36}$	$\dfrac{1}{36}$

   b. Represent the information in the table graphically:

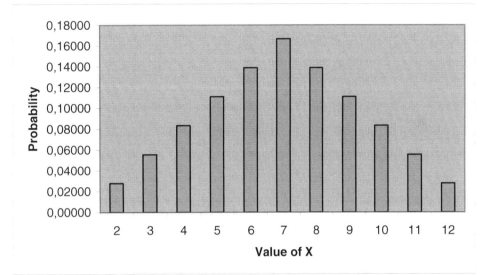

   c. $\displaystyle\sum_{i=1}^{i=n} P(X = x_i) = P(X = x_1) + P(X = x_2) + ... + P(X = x_n) = 1$

   d. Show that the last statement is satisfied in the problem mentioned:
   $$\frac{1}{36} + \frac{2}{36} + \frac{3}{36} + \frac{4}{36} + \frac{5}{36} + \frac{6}{36} + \frac{5}{36} + \frac{4}{36} + \frac{3}{36} + \frac{2}{36} + \frac{1}{36} = 1$$

Mean value or Expected of value

   e. Find the mean value of the distribution E(X) = m.
   $$E(x) = 2 \cdot \frac{1}{36} + 3 \cdot \frac{2}{36} + 4 \cdot \frac{3}{36} + 5 \cdot \frac{4}{36} + 6 \cdot \frac{5}{36} + 7 \cdot \frac{6}{36} + 8 \cdot \frac{5}{36} + 9 \cdot \frac{4}{36} + 10 \cdot \frac{3}{36} + 11 \cdot \frac{2}{36} + 12 \cdot \frac{1}{36} =$$
   $$\frac{252}{36} = 7$$

   f. Deduce the general expression for the mean E(X) discrete probability distribution:
   $$E(X) = \sum_{i=1}^{i=n} x_i \cdot P(X = x_i)$$

   g. This mean is usually called "the <u>expected value</u> of X".

h. This number, E(X) can be interpreted in 2 ways:
   A <u>Weighted</u> Average.
   A <u>long-term</u> Average.

5. The number of customers entering a shop during 1 hour follows the following table:

x	0	1	3	4	5
P(X = x)	$\dfrac{1}{6}$	$\dfrac{1}{12}$	$\dfrac{5}{12}$	$\dfrac{1}{6}$	$\dfrac{1}{6}$

   a. Fill the blank in the table.
   b. Represent the information in the table graphically:

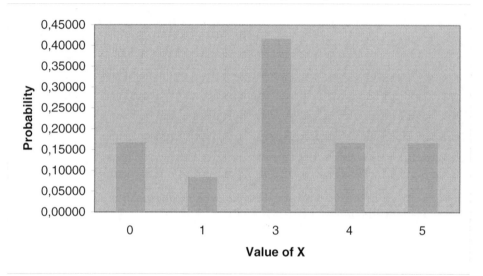

   c. $\displaystyle\sum_{i=1}^{i=n} P(X = x_i) = P(X = x_1) + P(X = x_2) + ... + P(X = x_n) = 1$
   d. Show that the last statement is satisfied in the problem mentioned:
   $$\frac{1}{6} + \frac{1}{12} + \frac{5}{12} + \frac{1}{6} + \frac{1}{6} = 1$$
   e. Find the mean value of the distribution E(X).
   $$E(X) = 0 \cdot \frac{1}{6} + 1 \cdot \frac{1}{12} + 3 \cdot \frac{5}{12} + 4 \cdot \frac{1}{6} + 5 \cdot \frac{1}{6} = 1$$

6. Fill the blanks:

   a. E(a) = <u>a</u> (a is a constant). Give an example:
   b. E(aX) = <u>aE(X)</u>
   c. $E(f(X)) = \displaystyle\sum_{i=i}^{i=n} f(x_i) \times P(X = x_i)$. An example would be:

   $$E(aX + b) = \sum_{i=i}^{i=n}(ax_i + b) \times P(X = x_i) = \sum_{i=i}^{i=n} ax_i \times P(X = x_i) + b \times P(X = x_i) =$$

   $$a\sum_{i=i}^{i=n} x_i \times P(X = x_i) + b\sum_{i=i}^{i=n} P(X = x_i) = aE(X) + b$$

7. Given the following probability distribution

x	2	3	5	6	10
P(X = x)	$\dfrac{1}{6}$	$\dfrac{1}{12}$	$\dfrac{5}{12}$	0	$\dfrac{4}{12}$

a. Fill the blank.

b. E(X) =
$$2\cdot\frac{1}{6}+3\cdot\frac{1}{12}+5\cdot\frac{5}{12}+6\cdot0+10\cdot\frac{4}{12}=\frac{72}{12}=6 \text{ (Expected value never occurs)}$$

c. E(2X) = $2E(X)=12$

d. E(4X) = $4E(X)=24$

e. 2E(X) = 12

f. 4E(X) = 24

g. $(E(X))^2 = 36$

h. E(X²) = $4\cdot\frac{1}{6}+9\cdot\frac{1}{12}+25\cdot\frac{5}{12}+36\cdot0+100\cdot\frac{4}{12}=\frac{542}{12}\approx45.2$

i. E(X³) = $8\cdot\frac{1}{6}+27\cdot\frac{1}{12}+125\cdot\frac{5}{12}+216\cdot0+1000\cdot\frac{4}{12}=\frac{4668}{12}=389$

j. $E(\sqrt{X})=\sqrt{2}\cdot\frac{1}{6}+\sqrt{3}\cdot\frac{1}{12}+\sqrt{5}\cdot\frac{5}{12}+\sqrt{6}\cdot0+\sqrt{10}\cdot\frac{4}{12}\approx2.37$

k. Repeat the process using your GDC.

l. In general is $(E(X))^2 = E(X^2)$? No Is it possible in a specific case? Yes

Variance and standard deviation

a. The Variance measures the spread of the distribution

b. Variance is defined as:
$$Var(X)=E((X-\mu)^2)=\sum_{i=i}^{i=n}(x-\mu)^2 P(X=x) \qquad \text{Or}$$
$$Var(X)=E(X^2)-(E(X))^2=E(X^2)-\mu^2$$

Use the data from exercise 7 to find:

Find Var(X) = $E(X^2)-\mu^2=45.2-36=9.2$

c. Standard deviation is defined as Sd(X) = $\sqrt{Var(X)}=\sqrt{E(X^2)-\mu^2}$

d. In this case Sd(X) = $\sqrt{45.2-36}=\sqrt{9.2}\approx3.03$. We use the Sd(X) and not the variance because Sd has the same units as the original distribution.

e. Calculate Var(2X) =
$$E((2X)^2)-(E(2x))^2=4E(X^2)-(E(2x))^2=4\cdot45.2-144=36.8$$
How is it related to Var(X)? Var(2X) = $2^2Var(X)=4\ Var(X)=4\cdot9.2=38.4$

f. Var(aX) = $a^2Var(X)$

g. Var(a) = 0 (a is a constant)

Given 2 distributions:

x	1	2	3	4
P(X = x)	$\dfrac{1}{6}$	$\dfrac{2}{6}$	$\dfrac{1}{6}$	$\dfrac{2}{6}$

x	7	8	9	10
P(X = x)	$\dfrac{1}{6}$	$\dfrac{2}{6}$	$\dfrac{1}{6}$	$\dfrac{2}{6}$

h. Represent them both on the same graph:

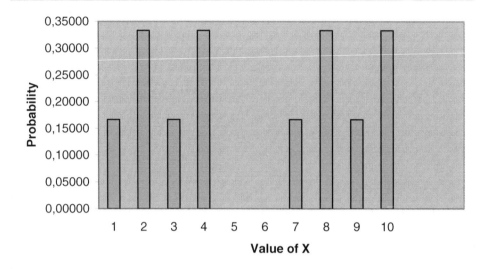

i. The 2nd distribution is <u>the same</u> as the 1st one only <u>shifted 6 to the right</u>

j. $E(X_{first}) = 1 \cdot \dfrac{1}{6} + 2 \cdot \dfrac{2}{6} + 3 \cdot \dfrac{1}{6} + 4 \cdot \dfrac{2}{6} = \dfrac{16}{6} = \dfrac{8}{3}$

k. $E(X_{second}) = 7 \cdot \dfrac{1}{6} + 8 \cdot \dfrac{2}{6} + 9 \cdot \dfrac{1}{6} + 10 \cdot \dfrac{2}{6} = \dfrac{52}{6} = \dfrac{26}{3} = \dfrac{8}{3} + 6$ (expected value suffered the same translation)

l. $E(X^2_{first}) = 1 \cdot \dfrac{1}{6} + 4 \cdot \dfrac{2}{6} + 9 \cdot \dfrac{1}{6} + 16 \cdot \dfrac{2}{6} = \dfrac{50}{6} = \dfrac{25}{3}$

m. $E(X^2_{second}) = 49 \cdot \dfrac{1}{6} + 64 \cdot \dfrac{2}{6} + 81 \cdot \dfrac{1}{6} + 100 \cdot \dfrac{2}{6} = \dfrac{458}{6} = \dfrac{229}{3}$

n. $Var(X_{first}) = E(X^2) - (E(X))^2 = \dfrac{25}{3} - \dfrac{64}{9} = \dfrac{11}{9}$

o. $Var(X_{second}) = E(X^2) - (E(X))^2 = \dfrac{229}{3} - \dfrac{676}{9} = \dfrac{11}{9}$

p. Your conclusions: As can be seen translating a distribution left or right does not change its spread and variance and SD therefore stay invariant.

q. $Var(X + b) = Var(X)$

r. $Var(a(X + b)) = Var(aX) = a^2 \, Var(X)$

3.7. – PROBABILITY DENSITY FUNCTIONS

1. In occasions, a random variable, does not take exactly n numerical values but an infinite number of values, for example the speed of an object is usually of this nature. This kind of variable is called <u>continuous random variable</u>.

2. For example The probability for a velocity of an object (in m/s) is given by P(x) as a function of its mass x can be given by:

$$P(x) = \begin{cases} \dfrac{4-x}{8} & 0 \le x \le 4 \\ 0 & otherwise \end{cases}$$

   a. Sketch this function.
   b. Calculate the area enclosed between the function and the axes. Explain its significance.

   $Area = 4 \cdot \dfrac{1}{2} \cdot \dfrac{1}{2} = 1$. It represents probability.

   c. Write down the most probable velocity of an object (the mode) <u>0 m/s</u>
   d. Write down P(3) = 0.125, probability for velocity 3 m/s.

   e. The expected value E(x) is given by: $\displaystyle\int_{-\infty}^{\infty} P(x)x\,dx$, find it.

   $$\int_0^4 \frac{4-x}{8} x\,dx = \left[\frac{x^2}{4} - \frac{x^3}{24} \right]_0^4 = \left[\frac{16}{4} - \frac{64}{24} \right] = \frac{4}{3}$$

   f. The median value M is given by: $\displaystyle\int_{x_i}^{M} P(x)\,dx = 0.5$, find it.

   $$\int_0^M \frac{4-x}{8}\,dx = \left[\frac{x}{2} - \frac{x^2}{16} \right]_0^M = \left[\frac{M}{2} - \frac{M^2}{16} \right] = \frac{1}{2}; M = 4 - \sqrt{8}$$

   g. Calculate $\displaystyle\int_0^1 P(x)\,dx$, explain its meaning.

   $$\int_0^1 \frac{4-x}{8}\,dx = \left[\frac{x}{4} - \frac{x^2}{16} \right]_0^1 = \left[\frac{1}{4} - \frac{1}{16} \right] = \frac{3}{16}$$ Probability for the velocity between 0 and 1.

3. The probability to have a car accident as a function of age is given by P(x):

$$P(x) = \begin{cases} \dfrac{a}{x-17} & 18 \le x \le 100 \\ 0 & otherwise \end{cases}$$

   a. Find the value of *a*, sketch the function.

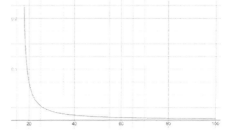

   $$\int_{18}^{100} \frac{a}{x-17}\,dx = a\left[ln(x-17) \right]_{18}^{100} = a\left[ln(83) \right] = 1; a = \frac{1}{ln(83)}$$

b. Write down the age with highest probability to have an accident. <u>18</u>

c. Write down P(3) = <u>out of domain (3 years old do not drive)</u>

d. Write down $P(47) = \dfrac{1}{30\ln(83)}$ Probability of having an accident when 47 years old.

e. The expected value E(x) is given by: $\displaystyle\int_{-\infty}^{\infty} P(x)x\,dx$, find it.

$$\int_{18}^{100} \frac{ax}{(x-17)}dx = a\left[x+17ln(x-17)\right]_{18}^{100} = a\left[82+17\ln(83)\right] = \frac{82+17\ln(83)}{\ln(83)} \approx 35.6$$

f. The median value M is given by: $\displaystyle\int_{x_i}^{M} P(x)\,dx = 0.5$, find it.

$$\int_{18}^{M} \frac{a}{(x-17)}dx = a\left[ln(x-17)\right]_{18}^{M} = \frac{1}{2}; M = 17+\sqrt{83} \approx 26.1$$

g. Calculate $\displaystyle\int_{20}^{30} P(x)\,dx$, Probability to have an accident between 20 and 30 years old.

$$\int_{20}^{30} \frac{a}{(x-17)}dx = a\left[ln(x-17)\right]_{20}^{30} = a\left[ln(\frac{13}{3})\right]_{20}^{30} = \frac{ln(\frac{13}{3})}{\ln(83)}$$

4. The probability to succeed in a game as a function of the age in which a young person starts to practice is given by:

$$P(x) = \begin{cases} -b(x^2 - 24x + 108) & 6 \le x \le 18 \\ 0 & otherwise \end{cases}$$

a. Find the value of b, sketch the function.

$$\int_{6}^{18} -b(x^2 - 24x + 108)dx = -b\left[\frac{x^3}{3} - 12x^2 + 108x\right]_{6}^{18} =$$

$$288b = 1; b = \frac{1}{288}$$

b. Find the age with highest probability to succeed: <u>12</u>

c. Write down P(12) = <u>0.125 probability to succeed if starts to practice at 12 years old</u>

d. Write down P(3) = <u>out of domain.</u>

e. The expected value E(x) is given by: $\displaystyle\int_{-\infty}^{\infty} P(x)x\,dx$, find it.

$$\int_{6}^{18} -bx(x^2 - 24x + 108)dx = -b\left[\frac{x^4}{4} - 8x^4 + 56x^2\right]_{6}^{18} = 12$$

f. The median value M is given by: $\int_{x_i}^{M} P(x)dx = 0.5$, find it.

$$\int_{6}^{M} -b(x^2 - 24x + 108)dx = -b\left[\frac{x^3}{3} - 12x^2 + 108x\right]_{6}^{M} = \frac{1}{2}; M = 12 \text{ (Symmetry)}$$

g. Calculate $\int_{4}^{10} P(x)dx$, explain its meaning.

$$\int_{4}^{10} -b(x^2 - 24x + 108)dx = -b\left[\frac{x^3}{3} - 12x^2 + 108x\right]_{4}^{10} = \frac{1}{6}$$

Probability to win if started practicing between 4 and 10 years old.

5. The probability density function of a certain continuous random variable is given by P(x).

$$P(x) = \begin{cases} ae^{-x} & 0 \le x \le 1 \\ 0 & otherwise \end{cases}$$

a. Find the probability that the random variable X has a value that lies between 0 and $\frac{1}{2}$? Give your answer in terms of e.

$$\int_{0}^{1} ae^x dx = a\left[e^x\right]_{0}^{1} = a[e-1] = 1; a = \frac{1}{e-1}$$

$$\int_{0}^{\frac{1}{2}} ae^x dx = a\left[e^x\right]_{0}^{\frac{1}{2}} = a\left[\sqrt{e} - 1\right] = \frac{\sqrt{e}-1}{e-1}$$

b. Find the expected value and the variance of the distribution. Give your answers exactly, in terms of e.

$$\int_{0}^{1} axe^x dx = a\left[(x-1)e^x\right]_{0}^{1} = a[0+1] = a = \frac{1}{e-1}$$

$$\int_{0}^{1} a(x-a)^2 e^x dx =$$

$$-\left(\frac{1}{e-1}\right)^3 - 2\left(\frac{1}{e-1}\right)^2 - 2\left(\frac{1}{e-1}\right) + e\left(\frac{1}{e-1}\right)^3 + e\left(\frac{1}{e-1}\right) \approx 0.0793$$

3.8. – THE BINOMIAL DISTRIBUTION

1. Dichotomous Experiment – An experiment with two possible results: heads or tail male or female, adult or child etc.
2. The probabilities of the results are P(A) and P(A') = 1 – P(A)
3. The variable X is discrete. It is called a Binomial Distribution to B(n, p). n is the number of times the experiment took place. p is the probability for "success" and q is 1 – p
4. The probability that X would have the value k is given by:

$$P(X = k) = \binom{n}{k} p^k q^{n-k}, k = 0, 1, 2 \ldots n$$

$$E(x) = \mu = np$$

$$Var(X) = \sigma^2 = npq$$

$$Sd(X) = \sigma = \sqrt{npq}$$

The mode of X is the value of x with the largest probability.

5. If $B(1, \frac{1}{2})$ find: (this experiment is similar to tossing a coin once)

   a. $P(X = 0) = \binom{1}{0}(\frac{1}{2})^0(\frac{1}{2})^1 = \frac{1}{2}$

   b. $P(X = 1) = \binom{1}{1}(\frac{1}{2})^1(\frac{1}{2})^0 = \frac{1}{2}$

   c. P(X = 2) = Not possible, if the experiment took place once, "success" cannot be obtained twice.

   d. Mode of X is 0, 1 both have the same probability

   e. $E(X) = np = 1 \cdot \frac{1}{2} = \frac{1}{2}$ $Var(X) = npq = 1 \cdot \frac{1}{2} \cdot \frac{1}{2} = \frac{1}{4}$ $Sd(X) = \sqrt{\frac{1}{4}} = \frac{1}{2}$

   f. Write down the probability of the expected value: 0 ($\frac{1}{2}$ will never be obtained)

6. If $B(3, \frac{1}{2})$ find:

   a. $P(X = 0) = \binom{3}{0}(\frac{1}{2})^0(\frac{1}{2})^3 = \frac{1}{8}$

   b. $P(X = 1) = \binom{3}{1}(\frac{1}{2})^1(\frac{1}{2})^2 = \frac{3}{8}$

   c. $P(X = 2) = \binom{3}{2}(\frac{1}{2})^2(\frac{1}{2})^1 = \frac{3}{8}$

   d. $P(X = 3) = \binom{3}{3}(\frac{1}{2})^3(\frac{1}{2})^0 = \frac{1}{8}$

e. $P(X = 2) = \dfrac{3}{8}$ means that <u>there is a probability of $\dfrac{3}{8}$ that success will occur twice if the experiment takes place 3 times (n = 3)</u>

f. Mode of X <u>is 1, 2, both have the same highest probability</u>

g. $P(X < 2) = \underline{P(X = 0) + P(X = 1)} = \dfrac{4}{8}$

h. $P(X \geq 2) = \underline{P(X = 2) + P(X = 3)} = \dfrac{4}{8}$

i. $E(X) = np = 3 \cdot \dfrac{1}{2} = \dfrac{3}{2}$ $Var(X) = npq = 3 \cdot \dfrac{1}{2} \cdot \dfrac{1}{2} = \dfrac{3}{4}$ $Sd(X) = \sqrt{\dfrac{3}{4}}$

j. Write down the probability of the expected value: 0 ($\dfrac{3}{2}$ will never be obtained)

7. If $B(3, \dfrac{1}{6})$ find:

a. $P(X = 0) = \begin{pmatrix} 3 \\ 0 \end{pmatrix} (\dfrac{1}{6})^0 (\dfrac{5}{6})^3 = \dfrac{125}{216}$

b. $P(X = 1) = \begin{pmatrix} 3 \\ 1 \end{pmatrix} (\dfrac{1}{6})^1 (\dfrac{5}{6})^2 = \dfrac{75}{216}$

c. $P(X = 2) = \begin{pmatrix} 3 \\ 2 \end{pmatrix} (\dfrac{1}{6})^2 (\dfrac{5}{6})^1 = \dfrac{15}{216}$

d. $P(X = 3) = \begin{pmatrix} 3 \\ 3 \end{pmatrix} (\dfrac{1}{6})^3 (\dfrac{5}{6})^0 = \dfrac{1}{216}$

e. $P(X = 2) = \dfrac{15}{216}$ means that <u>there is a probability of $\dfrac{15}{216}$ that success will occur twice if the experiment takes place 3 times (n = 3)</u>

f. Mode of X is <u>0, the value with highest probability</u>

g. $P(X < 2) = \underline{P(X = 0) + P(X = 1)} = \dfrac{200}{216}$

h. $P(X \geq 2) = \underline{P(X = 2) + P(X = 3)} = \dfrac{16}{216}$

i. $E(X) = np = 3 \cdot \dfrac{1}{6} = \dfrac{1}{2}$ $Var(X) = npq = 3 \cdot \dfrac{1}{6} \cdot \dfrac{5}{6} = \dfrac{15}{36}$ $Sd(X) = \sqrt{\dfrac{15}{36}}$

j. Write down the probability of the expected value: : 0 ($\dfrac{1}{2}$ will never be obtained)

8. If B(20, $\frac{1}{2}$) Using GDC binompdf(n,p,x), binompdf(n,p,(x₁,xₙ)),

   binomcdf(n,p,x) for P(X ≤ x)
   a. P(X = 5) = binompdf(20,0.5,5) = 0.148
   b. P(X = 10) = binompdf(20,0.5,10) = 0.176
   c. P(X = 18) = binompdf(20,0.5,18) = 0.000181
   d. P(X < 8) = binomcdf(20,0.5,7) = 0.132
   e. P(X ≤ 8) = binomcdf(20,0.5,8) = 0.252
   f. P(X ≥ 13) = 1 – binomcdf(20,0.5,12) = 0.132
   g. P(X > 13) = 1 – binomcdf(20,0.5,13) = 0.0577
   h. E(X) = $np = 20 \cdot \frac{1}{2} = 10$ Var(X) = $npq = 20 \cdot \frac{1}{2} \cdot \frac{1}{2} = 5$ Sd(X) = $\sqrt{5}$
   i. Write down the probability of the expected value: 0.176
9. If B(70, 0.2) Find:
   a. P(X = 17) = binompdf(70,0.2,17) = 0.0755
   b. P(X = 36) = binompdf(70,0.2,36) = $3.80 \cdot 10^{-9}$
   c. P(X = 28) = binompdf(70,0.2,28) = $6.39 \cdot 10^{-5}$
   d. P(X < 50) = binomcdf(70,0.2,49) ≈ 1 (limitations of GDC are seen)
   e. P(X ≤ 70) = 1
   f. P(X ≥ 38) = 1 – binomcdf(70,0.2,37) = $2.38 \cdot 10^{-10}$
   g. P(X > 10) = 1 – binomcdf(70,0.2,10) = 0.853
   h. E(X) = $np = 70 \cdot \frac{1}{5} = 14$ Var(X) = $npq = 70 \cdot \frac{1}{5} \cdot \frac{4}{5} = \frac{56}{5}$ Sd(X) = $\sqrt{\frac{56}{5}}$
   i. Write down the probability of the expected value: 0.118

10. A machine that makes products has a probability of 0.03 to build a
    defective product. The machine produces 500 products B(500, 0.03)
    a. The most probable number of defective products, its probability
       $E(X) = np = 500 \cdot 0.03 = 15$, binompdf(500,0.03,15) = 0.104
    b. Probability for 10 defective products: binompdf(500,0.03,10) = 0.0479
    c. Less than 12 defective products: binomcdf(500,0.03,11) = 0.181
    d. Probability for more than 18 defective products:
       1 – binomcdf(500,0.03,18) = 0.177

11. A die it thrown 50 times.

    a. B(50, $\frac{1}{6}$) Probability 5 "ones": binompdf(50,1/6,5) = 0.0745

    a. B(50, $\frac{1}{2}$) Probability 20 even: binompdf(50,1/2,20) = 0.0419

    b. B(50, $\frac{1}{6}$) Probability less than 12 "ones" binomcdf(50,1/6,11) = 0.883

    c. B(50, $\frac{1}{3}$) Probability more than 17 times a "six" or "five"

       1 – binomcdf(50,1/3,17) = 0.395

3.9. – THE POISSON DISTRIBUTION

1. Sometimes presented as "the distribution of the probability of the number of events that will happen in a certain time in a random process". Examples:
   - If we study the number of cars crossing a bridge in a given time, a possible event can be: "Number of red cars crossing the bridge in 2 hours".
   - If we study the number of rabbits in a given area a possible event can be: "number of rabbits in 1 km^2"
   - If we study the number of particles emitted by a radioactive source a possible event can be:
     "number of particles emitted by a radioactive in 3 years"
2. In case an event takes place in a given moment, place, volume etc. it is independent of when (or where) other events took place.
3. The longer the time or the bigger the area is etc. the higher the expected number of events is.

4. The distribution is given by $P(X = x) = \dfrac{e^{-\mu}\mu^x}{x!}, x = 0, 1, 2...$

   $x(t)$ is the number of events in a time t. λ is the rate of events per unit of time.

   $\mu = \lambda t \qquad E(x) = \mu \qquad Var(X) = \sigma^2 = \mu \qquad Sd(X) = \sigma = \sqrt{\mu}$

   GDC: poissonpdf(m ,x), poissoncdf(m ,x) = P(X > x)

5. Lets observe the Poisson distribution for $\mu = 1$
6. Lets observe the Poisson distribution for $\mu = 2$
7. Lets observe the Poisson distribution for $\mu = 3$
8. In a certain webpage the number of visitors is 200 per hour. Given that the number of visitors was observed during 2 hours, answer:

   a. Write down the probability distribution:
   $$\mu = \lambda t = 200 \cdot 2 = 400$$
   $$P(X = x) = \frac{e^{-400}400^x}{x!}, x = 0, 1, 2...$$

   b. Make a qualitative sketch of the distribution:

   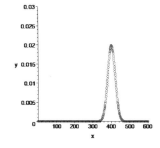

   c. μ = 200 True / **False**
   d. λ = 400 True / **False**
   e. P(X = 400) > P(X = 200) **True** / False
   f. P(X = 800) > P(X = 400) True / **False**
9. In a certain ski site the number of visitors is 300 per day. Given that the number of visitors was observed during 3 days, answer:

   a. Write down the probability distribution:
   $$\mu = \lambda t = 300 \cdot 3 = 900$$
   $$P(X = x) = \frac{e^{-900}900^x}{x!}, x = 0, 1, 2...$$

   b. Make a qualitative sketch of the distribution:
   c. μ = 900 **True** / False
   d. λ = 900 True / **False**
   e. P(X = 900) > P(X ≠ 900) **True** / False
   f. P(X = 820) > P(X = 821) True / **False**

   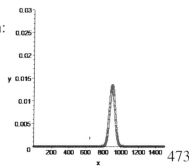

10. Find average number of visitors in a museum is x per hour given that the most probable value of visitors in 3 hours is 180.

$\mu = \lambda t = 180 = 3\lambda; \lambda = 60 \quad visitors / hour$

11. Given that an atom emits 1 particle in 2 hours, find the probability that in 3 hours the following events will happen.

   a. $\lambda = 0.5$ particles/h

   b. $\mu = 2 \cdot 0.5 = 1 \quad particles$

   c. x(t) is the number of particles emitted after t hours.

   d. $P(X = x) = \dfrac{e^{-1}}{x!}, x = 0, 1, 2...$

   e. $P(X = 0) = e^{-1}$

   f. $P(X = 1) = e^{-1}$

   g. $P(X = 2) = \dfrac{e^{-2}}{2}$

   h. $P(X = 3) = \dfrac{e^{-3}}{6}$

   i. $P(X < 2) = P(X = 0) + P(X = 1) = 2e^{-1}$

   j. $E(X) = \underline{1} \quad Var(X) = \underline{1} \quad Sd(X) = \underline{1}$

   k. $P(X \geq 2) = 1 - P(X < 2) = 1 - 2e^{-1}$

   l. $P(X \geq 3) = 1 - P(X < 3) = 1 - 2e^{-1} - \dfrac{e^{-2}}{2}$

   m. $P(X > 3) = 1 - P(X \leq 3) = 1 - 2e^{-1} - \dfrac{e^{-2}}{2} - \dfrac{e^{-3}}{6}$

12. Given that average number of customers in a store is 10 per hour. Find the probability that in 4 hours:

   a. $E(X) = 40 \quad Var(X) = 40 \quad Sd(X) = \sqrt{40}$

   b. $P(X = 40) = \dfrac{e^{-40} 40^{40}}{40!} \approx 0.0629$

   c. $P(X = 45) = \dfrac{e^{-40} 40^{45}}{45!} \approx 0.0440$.

   d. $P(X < 38) = P(X \leq 37) = poissoncdf(40, 37) \approx 0.355$

   e. $P(X > 43) = 1 - P(X \leq 43) = 1 - poissoncdf(40, 43) \approx 0.284$

13. Given that average number of defects in 5 meters of road is 2. Find the probability that in 1 km of road:

   a. $E(X) = \underline{2 \cdot 200 = 400} \quad Var(X) = \underline{400} \quad Sd(X) = \underline{20}$

   b. $P(X = 350) = \dfrac{e^{-400} 400^{350}}{350!} \approx 8.15 \cdot 10^{-4}$

   c. $P(X = 450) = \dfrac{e^{-400} 400^{450}}{450!} \approx 9.34 \cdot 10^{-4}$

   d. $P(X < 370) = P(X \leq 369) = poissoncdf(400, 369) \approx 0.0622$

   e. $P(X > 300) = 1 - P(X \leq 300) = 1 - poissoncdf(400, 300) \approx 0.999999899$

3.10. – NORMAL DISTRIBUTION

What do you observe? Can you guess how would a bigger sample look like? <u>It will become more and more similar to a "bell" shaped distribution, this distribution is called the "normal distribution".</u>

1. The normal distribution is characterized by two numbers: The <u>mean</u> μ and the <u>standard deviation</u> σ

2. Fill the missing data for the following distributions:

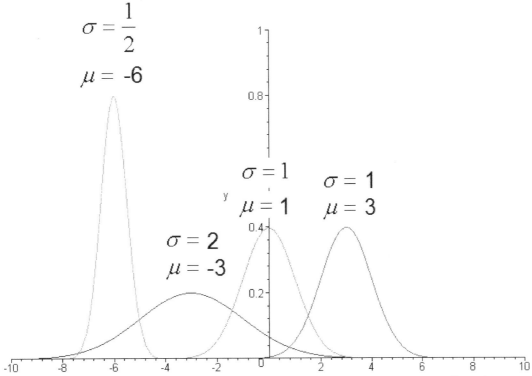

3. **The standard normal distribution** is the one with $\mu = 0$ y $\sigma = 1$ (Green)

4. The mean μ is located at the <u>centre</u> of the distribution.

5. The standard deviation σ represents the distance between the mean and the <u>inflection point</u>

Properties of the normal distribution

6. The <u>area</u> under the curve from negative infinity to plus infinity is <u>1</u>

7. The normal distribution is symmetrical that means that the area under the graph on each side of the mean is <u>0.5</u>.

8. The shape and position of a normal distribution depend on the parameters μ and σ therefore there is an <u>infinite</u> number of normal distributions. The distribution gets will narrower and taller as σ <u>gets smaller</u>

9. In general the area under the curve in the interval $\mu \pm 1\sigma$ is $\approx 68\%$

10. In general the area under the curve in the interval $\mu \pm 2\sigma$ is $\approx 95\%$

11. In general the area under the curve in the interval $\mu \pm 3\sigma$ is $\approx 99.7\%$

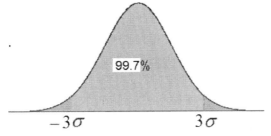

12. σ (the standard deviation) gives us an idea about the spread of the distribution
13. μ (the mean) indicates the centre of the distribution
14. Normally the normal distribution is written as N(μ, σ^2), that means that a distribution N(28, 4) will have a mean of 28 and a SD of 2

FINDING PROBABILIT OF a < Z < b
Shade and calculate use **GDC**: ShadeNorm(a, b) or ShadeNorm(a, b, μ, σ)
(Use large numbers for ∞ or $-\infty$)

15. **All Diagrams not to scale**

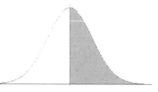

a. $P(Z \geq 0) = 0.5$
b. $P(Z = 1) = 0$ (the corresponding area is 0)
c. $P(Z < 1) = \underline{ShadeNorm(-1000, 1) = 0.841}$

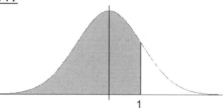

d. $P(Z \geq 2) = \underline{ShadeNorm(2,1000) = 0.0228}$

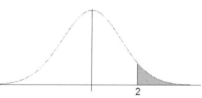

e. $P(Z \geq 2.23) = \underline{ShadeNorm(2.23,1000) = 0.0129}$

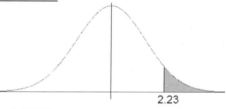

f. $P(Z \geq 1.57) = \underline{ShadeNorm(1.57,1000) = 0.0582}$

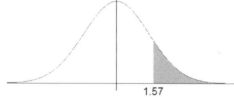

g. $P(Z \leq 1.86) = \underline{ShadeNorm(-1000, 1.86) = 0.967}$

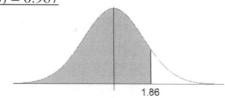

h. P(Z ≤ –2) = <u>ShadeNorm(–1000,2) = 0.0228</u>

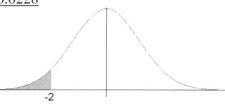

i. P(Z ≤ –2.1) = <u>ShadeNorm(–1000, –2.1) = 0.0179</u>

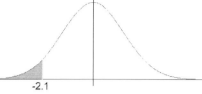

j. P(Z ≥ –3.11) = <u>ShadeNorm(–3.11, 1000) = 0.999</u>

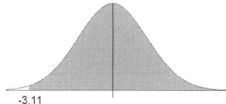

k. P(Z ≥ –2) = <u>ShadeNorm(–2,1000) = 0.977</u>

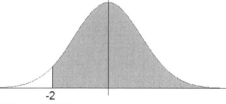

l. P(Z ≥ –0.58) = <u>ShadeNorm(–0.58,1000) = 0.719</u>

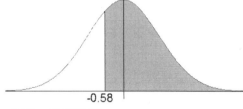

m. P(Z ≤ –2.7) = <u>ShadeNorm(–1000, –2.7) = 0.00347</u>

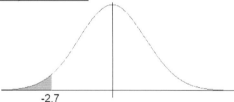

n. P(–∞ ≤ Z ≤ –2.7) = <u>ShadeNorm(–1000, –2.7) = 0.00347 (same as previous</u>
<u>example)</u>

o. P(3 ≤ Z ≤ –2.7) = Not possible, the number on the left is bigger than the
number on the right.

p. P(1 ≤ Z ≤ 2) = <u>ShadeNorm(1,2) = 0.136</u>

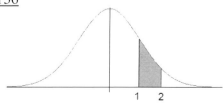

q. P(–1.25 ≤ Z ≤ 0) = <u>ShadeNorm(–1.25,0) = 0.394</u>

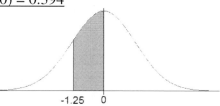

r. P(–2.12 ≤ Z ≤ 1.65) = <u>ShadeNorm(–2.12,1.65) = 0.934</u>

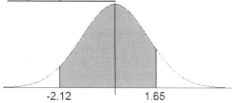

s. P(–1.02 ≤ Z ≤ –0.25) = <u>ShadeNorm(–1.02, –0.25) = 0.247</u>

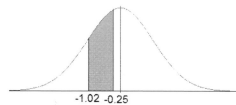

t. P(0.97 ≤ Z ≤ 1.76) = <u>ShadeNorm(0.97,1.76) = 0.127</u>

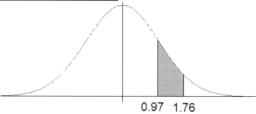

u. P(1.54 ≤ Z ≤ ∞) = <u>ShadeNorm(1.54,1000) = 0.0618</u>

v. P(1.31 ≤ Z ≤ 3.06) = <u>ShadeNorm(1.31,3.06) = 0.0940</u>

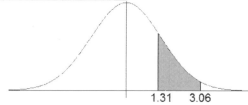

FINDING PROBABILITY FOR $a < X < b$

The amount of time to produce a product follows a normal distribution with mean of 40 minutes and S. D. of 8 minutes.

16. Find the probability that the product is produced between 35 and 50 minutes. Shade the corresponding area on the following diagram.
Use **GDC** to find your answer: normalcdf(35, 50, 40, 8) = 0.628

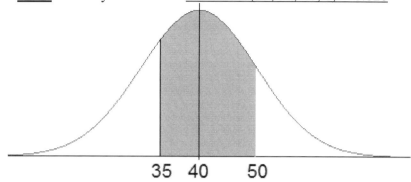

17. Find the probability that the product is produced in more than 38 minutes. Shade the corresponding area on the following diagram.
Use GDC to find your answer: normalcdf(38, 1000, 40, 8) = 0.599

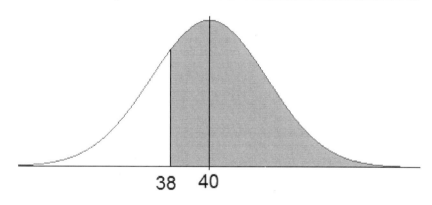

18. Find the probability that the product is produced in less than 34 minutes. Shade the corresponding area on the following diagram.
Use GDC to find your answer: normalcdf(–1000,34, 40, 8) 0 0.227

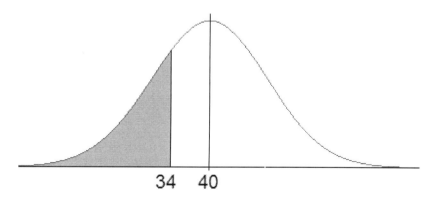

Exercises

19. In a normal distribution N(24, 6) Find and shade:

    a. P(X = 25) = 0 (No area)

    b. P(X ≥ 25) = normalcdf(25,1000, 24, 6) = 0.434

    c. P(X ≤ 25) = normalcdf(–1000, 25,24,6) = 0.566

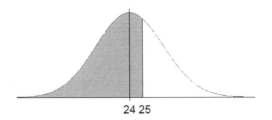

    d. P(X ≥ 15) = normalcdf(15,1000, 24, 6) = 0.933

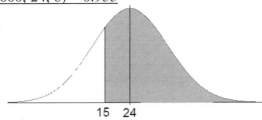

    e. P(14 ≤ X ≤ 20) = normalcdf(14,20, 24, 6) = 0.205

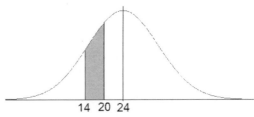

    f. (19 ≤ X ≤ 31) = normalcdf(19,31, 24, 6) = 0.676

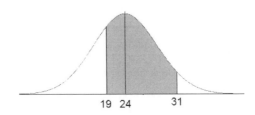

20. In a lake there are 3000 fish distributed according to a normal distribution with a mean of 26cm and a standard deviation of 7cm.

a. Find and shade on the graph the interval in which 68% of the fish lengths are. How many fish in this case? This exactly the percentage the corresponds 1 SD therefore the interval is (19, 33) cm, 68% of 3000 is 2040 Fish.

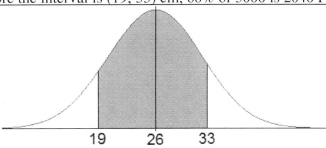

19   26   33

b. Find and shade on the graph the interval in which 95% of the fish lengths are. How many fish in this case? This exactly the percentage the corresponds 2 SD therefore the interval is (12, 40) cm, 95% of 3000 is 2850 Fish.

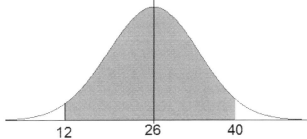

12   26   40

c. Find and shade on the graph the interval in which 99.7% of the fish lengths are. How many fish in this case? This exactly the percentage the corresponds 3 SD therefore the interval is (5, 47) cm, 99.7% of 3000 is 2991 Fish.

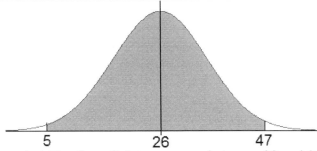

5   26   47

d. Find and the probability for a fish to measure between 23 and 28 cm. Shade on graph. How many fish in this would you expect in this case to be in this interval? normalcdf(23,28, 26, 7) = 0.278, $0.278 \times 3000 = 834$ fish

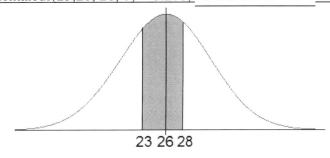

23 26 28

e. Find and the probability for a fish to measure between 12 and 24 cm. Shade on graph. How many fish in this would you expect in this case to be in this interval? normalcdf(12,24, 26, 7) = 0.365, <u>0.365×3000=1095</u> fish

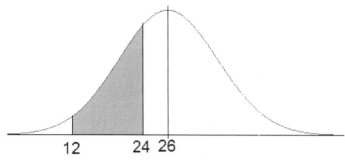

f. Find and the probability for a fish to measure between 27 and 28 cm. Shade on graph. How many fish in this would you expect in this case to be in this interval? normalcdf(27,28, 26, 7) = 0.0557, <u>0.0557×3000=167</u> fish

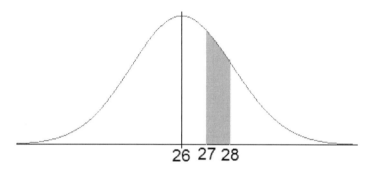

g. Find and shade on graph the probability for a fish to measure more than 26 cm. How many fish in this case? <u>normalcdf(26,1000, 26, 7) = 0.5, 1500 fish</u>

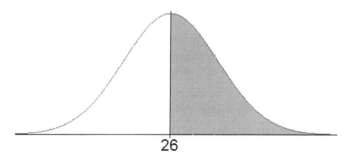

h. Find and shade on graph the probability for a fish to measure exactly 27 cm. <u>0, no corresponding area</u>
i. Find and shade on graph the probability for a fish to measure exactly 20 cm <u>0, no corresponding area</u>

STANDARDIZATION OF THE NORMAL DISTRIBUTION

21. As we already know there is an <u>infinite</u> number of normal distributions, depending on <u>mean</u> and <u>Standard Deviation</u>. The standard distribution is one of them, the distribution in which the <u>mean</u> is <u>0</u> and the SD is <u>1</u>.

22. Usually in a problem the distribution is not the standard therefore <u>the mean</u> is not <u>0</u> and <u>the Standard Deviation</u> is not <u>1</u>. The way to transform any normal distribution to the standard one is the following:

$$Z = \frac{X - \mu}{\sigma}$$

23. In reality what this expression means is rescaling the variable. And Z is the number of <u>Standard Deviations</u> away from the mean.

24. Given a distribution $N(22, 5)$, find the standard variable Z, shade and calculate:

   a. $P(X \geq 22) = P(Z \geq 0) = 0.5$

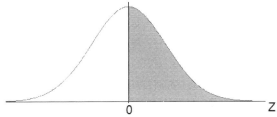

   b. $P(X = 27) = P(Z = 1) = 0$, no corresponding area.

   c. $P(X < 20) = P(Z < \frac{20-22}{5}) = P(Z < -0.2) = \underline{normalcdf(-1000, -0.2) = 0.421}$

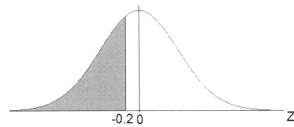

   d. $P(X \geq 25) = P(Z > \frac{25-22}{5}) = P(Z > 0.6) = \underline{normalcdf(0.6, 1000) = 0.274}$

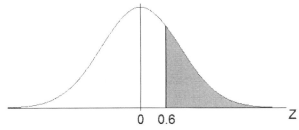

   e. $P(X \geq 15) = P(Z > \frac{15-22}{5}) = P(Z > -1.4) = \underline{normalcdf(-1.4, 1000) = 0.919}$

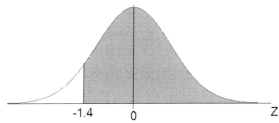

f. $P(X \geq 0) = P(Z > \dfrac{0-22}{5}) = P(Z > -4.4) = \underline{\text{normalcdf}(-4.4, 1000) \approx 1}$

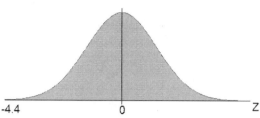

g. $P(X \leq 18) = P(Z < \dfrac{18-22}{5}) = P(Z < -0.8) = \underline{\text{normalcdf}(-1000, --0.8) = 0.219}$

h. $P(-\infty \leq X \leq 27) = P(Z < \dfrac{27-22}{5}) = P(Z < 1) = \underline{\text{normalcdf}(-1000, 1) = 0.841}$

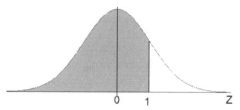

i. $P(20 \leq X \leq 25) = P(\dfrac{20-22}{5} < Z < \dfrac{25-22}{5}) = P(-0.2 < Z < 0.6) =$
    $\underline{\text{normalcdf}(-0.2, 0.6) = 0.305}$

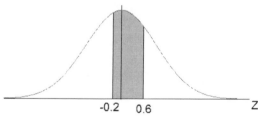

j. $P(12 \leq X \leq 18) = P(\dfrac{12-22}{5} < Z < \dfrac{18-22}{5}) = P(-2 < Z < -0.8) =$
    $\underline{\text{normalcdf}(-2, -0.8) = 0.189}$

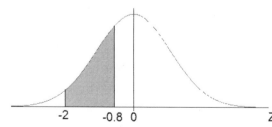

FINDING INVERSE NORMAL PROBABILITIES

25. The amount of time (X) to produce a product follows a normal distribution with mean of 40 minutes and S. D. of 8 minutes.

   a. Find the value of a, if 6% of the products are produced in less than a min. Shade the corresponding area on the following diagram. Use GDC to find your answer: invNorm(0.06, 40, 8) = 27.6min

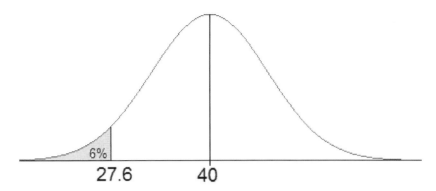

   b. Find the value of a, if 13% of the products are produced in more than a min. Shade the corresponding area on the following diagram. Use GDC to find your answer: invNorm(0.87, 40, 8) = 49.0

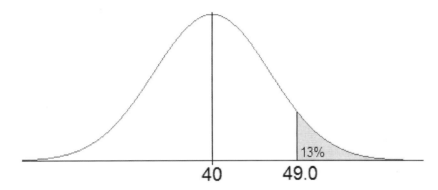

   c. Find the value of a and b if the middle 50% of the products are produced in between a and b min. Shade the corresponding area on the following diagram. Use GDC to find your answer: , invNorm(0.25, 40, 8) = 34.6 invNorm(0.75, 40, 8) = 45.4

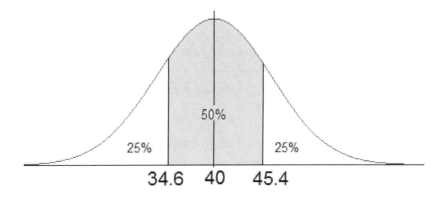

26. In a lake there are 2000 fish distributed according to a normal distribution with a mean of 26cm and a standard deviation of 7cm.

a. Find and shade the length interval for 80% of the fish. How many fish are expected to be in the interval in this case? invNorm(0.1, 26, 7) = 17.0
invNorm(0.9, 26, 7) = 35.0

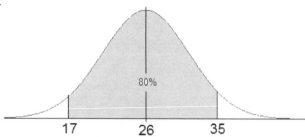

b. Find and shade the length interval for 90% of the fish. How many fish are expected to be in the interval in this case? invNorm(0.05, 26, 7) = 14.5
invNorm(0.95, 26, 7) = 37.5

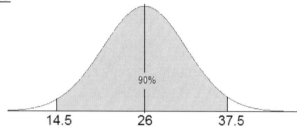

c. Find and shade the length interval for 75% of the fish. How many fish are expected to be in the interval in this case? invNorm(0.125, 26, 7) = 17.9
invNorm(0.875, 26, 7) = 34.1

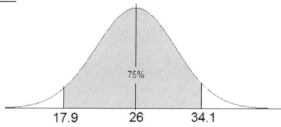

d. There is a probability of 0.2 that a fish's length is more than q, find q. How many fish are expected to be in the interval in this case?

q = invNorm(0.8, 26, 7) = 31.9, $0.2 \times 3000 = 600$ fish

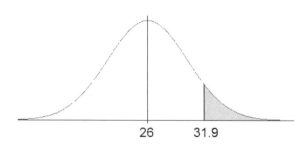

e. There is a probability of 0.32 that a fish's length is less than w, find w. How many fish are expected to be in the interval in this case?

w = invNorm(0.32, 26, 7) = 22.7,   0.32×3000=960 fish

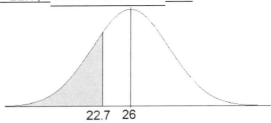

f. There is a probability of 0.4 that a fish's length is between a and b, find a and b. How many fish are expected to be in the interval in this case?

invNorm(0.3, 26, 7) = 22.3, invNorm(0.7, 26, 7) = 29.7

0.4×3000=1200 fish

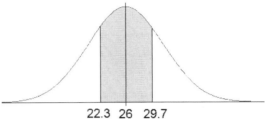

g. There is a probability of 0.6 that a fish's length is between a and b, find a and b. How many fish are expected to be in the interval in this case?

invNorm(0.2, 26, 7) = 20.1, invNorm(0.8, 26, 7) = 31.9

0.6×3000=1800 fish

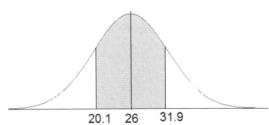

h. There is a probability of 0.1 that a fish's length is less than t, find t. How many fish are expected to be in the interval in this case?

t=invNorm(0.1, 26, 7) = 17.0,   0.1×3000=300 fish

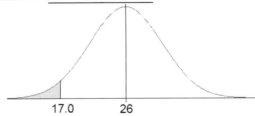

i. Find and shade the interval in which 65% of the fish measure. How many fish are expected to be in the interval in this case?

invNorm(0.175, 26, 7) = 19.5, invNorm(0.825, 26, 7) = 32.5

0.65×3000=1950 fish

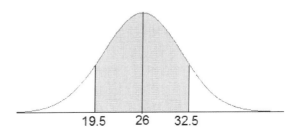

25. Calculate k if $P(X \leq k) = 0.6103$ and X is a normal distribution $N(15, 4)$

   $\underline{k = invNorm(0.6103, 15, 4) = 16.1}$

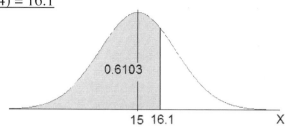

26. It is known that $P(X \leq 7) = 0.9147$ and $P(X \leq 6.5) = 0.7517$. Calculate

   a. μ and σ

   $\underline{invNorm(0.9147, 0, 1) = 1.37, \ invNorm(0.7517, 0, 1) = 0.680}$

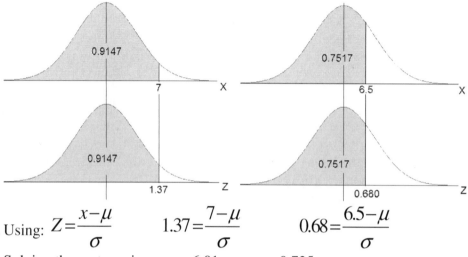

   Using: $Z = \dfrac{x - \mu}{\sigma}$ $1.37 = \dfrac{7 - \mu}{\sigma}$ $0.68 = \dfrac{6.5 - \mu}{\sigma}$

   Solving the system gives: $\mu = 6.01$ $\sigma = 0.725$

   b. k so that $P(X \geq k) = 0.3$

   $\underline{invNorm(0.7, 6.01, 0.725) = 6.39}$

27. 500 high school students' grades are distributed normally with a mean of 72 and a standard deviation of 6.

   a. Find the interval mean plus/minus 2 standard deviations: (60, 84)

   b. What percentage of scores are between scores 60 and 70? How many students in this group? $\underline{normalcdf(60, 70, 72, 6) = 0.345 = 34.5\%}$

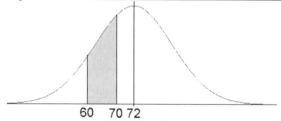

   c. What percentage of scores are more than 88? How many students in this group? $\underline{normalcdf(88, 1000, 72, 6) = 0.00383 = 0.383\%}$

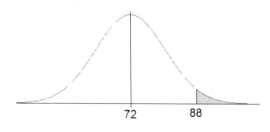

d. What percentage of scores are less than 60? How many students in this group? <u>normalcdf(–1000, 60, 72, 6) = 0.0228 = 2.28%</u>

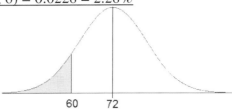

e. Can students' grades distribute normally? Explain. <u>Not really as this implies there is a certain probability (more than 0) of obtaining a grade of more than a 100% or less than 0. The same happens with height or weight. However, these probabilities may be so lo that the error is very small..</u>

28. The time it takes to complete a certain journey is normally distributed with a mean of 50 days and a standard deviation of 4 days.

   a. The probability that the length of the journey lies between 53 and 60 days is represented by the shaded area in the following diagram.

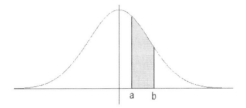

   Write down the values of a and b. <u>a = 53</u>   <u>b = 60</u>

   b. Find the probability that the length of the journey is more than 57 days. <u>normalcdf(57, 1000, 50, 4) = 0.401</u>

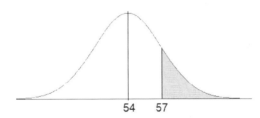

   c. Find the probability that the length of the journey is between 56 and 61 days. <u>normalcdf(56, 61, 50, 4) = 0.0638</u>

   d. 80% of the travellers complete the journey after x days. Find x. <u>x = invNorm(0.8, 50, 4) = 53.4 days</u>

29. The weight of a certain animal is normally distributed with mean of 150 kg and standard deviation of 12 kg. We classify the animals in the following way:
   a. Find the probability for each one the cases described.
       P(weight < 130) = <u>normalcdf(–1000, 130, 150, 12) = 0.0478</u>
       P(130 < weight < 170) = <u>normalcdf(130, 170, 150, 12) = 0.904</u>
       P(weight > 170) = <u>normalcdf(170, 1000, 150, 12) = 0.0478</u>
   b. There is a probability of 0.2 for an animal to have a weight bigger than q. Find q. P(weight > q) = 0.2   <u>q = invNorm(0.8, 150, 12) = 160 kg</u>
   c. In a jungle with 3000 animals how many are expected to have a weight bigger than q? <u>0.2×3000 = 600</u> animals

Made in the USA
San Bernardino, CA
28 January 2018